THE LEADERSHIP CHALLENGE ACTIVITIES BOOK

ABOUT THIS BOOK

WHY IS THIS TOPIC IMPORTANT?

The Leadership Challenge focuses on how to be a successful leader. The Five Practices of Exemplary Leadership® present five practices that individuals can put into action to bring out the best in themselves and those they lead. Authors Jim Kouzes and Barry Posner have also identified Ten Commitments of Leadership that correspond to The Five Practices. This book is important because it provides experiential learning activities that allow individuals to practice the skills related to The Five Practices and The Ten Commitments.

WHAT CAN YOU ACHIEVE WITH THIS BOOK?

The book offers you a selection of 107 creative activities that address The Five Practices. The key purpose of this book is to provide trainers, consultants, facilitators, instructors, coaches, and others working with The Five Practices of Exemplary Leadership® a grand selection of activities that can be used with your clients, participants, and students. Although the activities have been primarily designed for training sessions, they can easily be adapted for one-on-one coaching situations or for educational classroom settings. You can draw on the expertise of our seasoned contributors to enhance your next training sessions.

HOW IS THIS BOOK ORGANIZED?

The book includes ten chapters. The first chapter presents an overview of the elements of *The Leadership Challenge,* explains why this book is important, and reviews how to use the book and select activities. Chapter Two reminds the trainers of key aspects to ensure an excellent training. This chapter also provides tips for facilitating activities and ideas for forming small groups. The next five chapters present activities that address each of The Five Practices: Model the Way; Inspire a Shared Vision; Challenge the Process; Enable Others to Act; and Encourage the Heart. Some of the activities that were submitted addressed all of the practices, and you will find those overarching activities in Chapter Eight. Chapter Nine shares tools that are required of a leader, but are not a part of the Kouzes/Posner model. It also presents activities that can be used in scenarios other than a classroom or in unusual circumstances. Finally, Chapter Ten describes next steps for the reader and discusses other growth opportunities.

KOUZES
POSNER

THE
LEADERSHIP
CHALLENGE
ACTIVITIES
BOOK

JAMES M. KOUZES AND BARRY Z. POSNER

WITH ELAINE BIECH

Pfeiffer
A Wiley Imprint
www.pfeiffer.com

Copyright © 2010 by James M. Kouzes and Barry Z. Posner. All Rights Reserved.
Published by Pfeiffer
An Imprint of Wiley
989 Market Street, San Francisco, CA 94103-1741
www.pfeiffer.com

Library of Congress Cataloging-in-Publication Data

Kouzes, James M.
    The leadership challenge activities book / James M. Kouzes and Barry Z. Posner with Elaine Biech.
        p. cm.
    ISBN 978-0-470-47713-7 (pbk.)
      1. Leadership. I. Posner, Barry Z. II. Biech, Elaine. III. Title.
    HD57.7.K6814 2010
    658.4'092—dc22
                                                                                         2010005202

Acquiring Editor: Lisa Shannon/Marisa Kelley
Development Editor: Susan Rachmeler
Editor: Rebecca Taff
Design: Riezeboz Holzbaur Group

Director of Development: Kathleen Dolan Davies
Production Editor: Dawn Kilgore
Manufacturing Supervisor: Becky Morgan
Printed in the United States of America

Printing 10 9 8 7 6 5 4 3 2 1

CONTENTS

Contents

Contents

Contents

Contents

Contents

Contents

Contents

Contents

Other Times and Other Places

Contents

ABOUT THE WEBSITE

Reproducible materials from this book are available for free online.

URL: www.leadershipchallenge.com/go/tlcactivitybook
Username: tlcactivity
Password: leadership

The following activities and their handout materials can be found on the website:

Chapter Three: Model the Way

- Anatomy of Power by Teri-E Belf
- Leadership in Context by Mohandas Nair
- Ethics for the 21st Century by Charlotte S. Waisman and Linda Bedinger

Chapter Four: Inspire a Shared Vision

- Inspiration Becomes a Reality by Jean Barbazette
- Can You Picture This? by Timothy Ewest
- Another Leader's Dream by Donna Goss and Don Robertson
- The Spiritual Leader by Mohandas Nair
- Define Your Values Through a Vision Statement by Steve A. Rainey
- Claiming a Breakthrough by Sherene Zolno

Chapter Five: Challenge the Process

- Game of the Generals by Elisa May Arboleda-Cuevas and Audie Bautista Masigan
- Take Off the Blindfolds by Douglas Austrom
- Change: Feel the Pain, See the Gain by Daryl R. Conner
- Take a Risk! by Dennis E. Gilbert
- When Questions Are the Answer—Challenging the Process by Barbara Pate Glacel
- Change Project Summary by Edith Katz
- Constructing a Global Team Communications Device by John Lybarger
- Identify Perceived Causes of Resistance by Consuelo Meux
- In-Basket Exercise by Alan Richter
- Challenge the Process in Real Time by L.J. Rose
- You Be the Judge!™ by Karen Travis

Chapter Six: Enable Others to Act

- Enabling Cross-Functional Leadership by Christopher Chaves
- Building Resilience for Change by Daryl R. Conner
- Enabling with Style by Ann Hermann-Nehdi
- Team Competency Development Plan by Edith Katz
- Double Overlapping Strategic Cross by Sharon Landes
- What Makes You Trust Someone? by Sherri Dosher
- No Easy Way Out by Mona Lee Pearl
- Coaching Versus Telling by Lou Russell

Chapter Seven: Encourage the Heart

- Accelerating Change-Readiness by Herb Cohen and Bruce Fern
- Conundra by Brian Jackson
- Writing and Receiving Class Affirmations by Edith Katz

CHAPTER ONE: LEADERSHIP AND THE CHALLENGE TO MAKE IT WORK

In This Chapter

- An overview of *The Five Practices of Exemplary Leadership*®
- Why this book is important
- What's in this book
- The luminary contributors
- How to use this book
- How to select and use the activities

THE FIVE PRACTICES OF EXEMPLARY LEADERSHIP®

The Leadership Challenge focuses on how leaders struggle to get things done in organizations. It presents five practices that ordinary people can put into action to bring þzout the best in themselves and those that they lead. The Five Practices of Exemplary Leadership® include:

1. Model the Way
2. Inspire a Shared Vision
3. Challenge the Process
4. Enable Others to Act
5. Encourage the Heart

What does each of these mean?

- Model the Way is what leaders need to do to identify their values and transform those values into action.
- Inspire a Shared Vision addresses how a leader envisions a preferred future and involves others in the vision.
- Challenge the Process seeks out opportunities for improvement, generating small wins, and learning from mistakes.
- Enable Others to Act promotes collaboration by building trust and relationships.
- Encourage the Heart addresses how leaders reward and recognize individuals and create a sense of community.

The authors of *The Leadership Challenge*, Jim Kouzes and Barry Posner, have also identified Ten Commitments of Leadership that correspond to The Five Practices. The commitments, or behaviors, give a deeper understanding to The Five Practices. They specify what a leader does to demonstrate each of The Five Practices.

1. Model the Way
   - Clarify values by finding your voice and affirming shared ideals.
   - Set the example by aligning actions with shared values.

2. Inspire a Shared Vision
   - Envision the future by imagining exciting and enabling possibilities.
   - Enlist others in a common vision by appealing to shared aspirations.

3. Challenge the Process
   - Search for opportunities by seizing the initiative and by looking outward for innovative ways to improve.

- Experiment and take risks by constantly generating small wins and learning from experience.
4. Enable Others to Act
   - Foster collaboration by building trust and facilitating relationships.
   - Strengthen others by increasing self-determination and developing competence.
5. Encourage the Heart
   - Recognize contributions by showing appreciation for individual excellence.
   - Celebrate the values and victories by creating a spirit of community.

WHY THIS BOOK

The Leadership Challenge and its related materials have been around for more than twenty-five years. During that time, hundreds of trainers, facilitators, and consultants have adapted the materials to their own use. This also includes The Leadership Challenge Certified Masters, whose work you will find in this book.

This book compiles many of the good ideas that have been created over the years and begins to catalog them in one handy place for all of you who use the Kouzes/Posner concepts and materials.

WHAT'S IN THIS BOOK

This book is chock full of 106 leadership activities.

The chapter you are currently reading, Chapter One, provides you with an overview of the entire book.

Chapter Two presents you with tools, tips, and techniques to deliver a professional training session. It discusses the characteristics that make a good trainer and reviews adult learning principles—something all trainers should be reminded of regularly. It provides practical suggestions to make your job as a trainer successful, including ways to prepare, ideas for how to create a supportive environment, and practical ways for how to increase participation. Suggestions for facilitating activities, ideas for forming small groups, and practical tips for managing your time in a training session will increase your efficiency and effectiveness in your learning setting.

Chapters Three through Seven present each of The Five Practices, an overview, and the related activities. You should feel empowered to select any of The Five Practices in any order, since the framework is not a step-by-step process that proceeds from one practice to another. The same is true for the selection of activities. Select the one(s) that are most appropriate for your leader(s).

Chapter Eight and Nine continue to offer activities. Chapter Eight assembles fifteen overarching activities that incorporate all of The Five Practices. They can be used as introductory or review activities—or to meet other needs. Chapter Nine brings together eleven activities that relate to specific leadership skills, but that do not fit neatly into The Five Practices--networking or running a virtual meeting, for example. This chapter is also the vessel for four activities we call Other Times and Other Places because they do not fit into the typical training mold.

LUMINARY CONTRIBUTORS

Jim Kouzes and Barry Posner have a huge following. *The Leadership Challenge* has sold almost 1.5 million copies and has been translated into over a dozen languages. Over one million people have taken the highly acclaimed *Leadership Practices Inventory* (LPI) and more than four hundred doctoral dissertations and academic research projects have been based on The Five Practices of Exemplary Leadership Model.

It is no wonder then that when a call for submissions was placed for this book, many of the Kouzes/Posner "fan club" members were the first to respond. Several of these contributors are leaders in their own right. They include:

- Jean Barbazette, author, *Managing the Training Function for Bottom-Line Results*
- Geoff Bellman, author, *Getting Things Done When You Are Not in Charge*
- Herb Cohen and Bruce Fern, co-owners, Performance Connections International
- Daryl Conner, author, *Leading at the Edge of Chaos*
- Debra Dinnocenzo, author, *How to Lead from a Distance*
- Barbara Pate Glacel, author, *Light Bulbs for Leaders*
- Len Goodstein, author; former CEO, University Associates
- Ann Herrmann-Nehdi, CEO of Herrmann International
- Beverly Kaye, author, *Love 'em or Lose 'em*
- Toni Lucia, author, *The Art and Science of 360-Degree Feedback*
- Nanette Miner, The Training Doctor
- Lou Russell, CEO, consultant, speaker, and author
- Darryl Sink, three-time winner of ISPI's Outstanding Product of the Year award
- Joanne Sujansky, author, *Keeping the Millennials: Why Companies Are Losing Billions to This Generation*
- Lorraine Ukens, author and editor, *What Smart Trainers Know*

- Charlotte Waisman, author, *Her Story: A Timeline of the Women Who Changed America*
- Cal Wick and Andy Jefferson, authors, *The Six Disciplines of Breakthrough Learning*

Several contributors are Certified Masters of *The Leadership Challenge*. This label indicates the highest level of expertise in all applications of The Leadership Challenge® Model and is evidenced through the designee's high-level delivery and facilitation of workshops, LPI coaching competence, a wide range of organization development experiences, established client credibility, a global mindset, publishing, and a collaborative, curious spirit that leads to ongoing, innovative product development. This group includes:

Lily Cheng	Steve Houchin
Peter Cheng	Sharon Landes
Kim Chesky	L.J. Rose
Beth High	Valarie Willis

Several contributors are also designated as Certified Facilitators of *The Leadership Challenge*. The certified label indicates a level of understanding of the model that enables the participant to deliver workshops and services in a manner consistent with the level of excellence and integrity associated with the brand. This group includes:

Daren Blonski	Jean Lee
Angie Chaplin	John Lybarger
Ricky Foo	

Each of these contributors is an exemplary leader in the profession. Their activities can be found within the activity pages under each of The Five Practices. We thank them profusely for taking time from their busy schedules to share their expertise with all of us.

HOW TO USE THIS BOOK

There are several ways to get the most out of this book. We suggest that you turn to Chapter Two to brush up on your training delivery skills.

Decide which of The Five Practices you require ideas or activities for and turn to that chapter to be inspired. Peruse the activities based on the number of people you will have in your session or the amount of time you have. Read the objectives; they will help you to define exactly what you need.

Remember, as we said earlier, The Five Practices may be taught in any order. If you are focusing on one of The Five Practices, you may select two or more activities that have a different focus. Or you might wish to select activities from more than one of the practices.

If you are looking for inspiration for yourself, check out the last chapter. It will help you think about how to continue to learn and grow yourself.

HOW TO USE AND SELECT ACTIVITIES

Each of the chapters contains from twelve to eighteen activities.

You should find enough information on the first page of each activity to know whether it will work in your situation. You will find the title of the activity, the objectives, anything special about the audience (such as whether it needs to be an intact team), amount of time it will take, the materials and equipment the activity requires, and the room setup.

If you read the first page of the activity and all your criteria are met, turn the page and begin to read the step-by-step process. We tried to keep the directions for conducting the activity as concise as possible without eliminating any important steps.

Before you conduct an activity, be sure to allow enough time. If your group is at the high end of the number of participants, plan on the maximum amount of time. To be on the safe side, add an additional 10 percent the first time you conduct any activity. Manage your time during the activity by not letting time get away from you during group discussion or small group breakout activities.

Practice It

Bring a group of colleagues together to practice a new activity before you debut in front of the group. This is a great way for you to gain experience with the activity and an even better way for you to get feedback.

Follow the guidelines for introducing, conducting, and processing an activity in Chapter Two to ensure that the activity produces all the learning that you want it to.

Other Times and Places

Although the activities have been written for a training room scenario, most of the activities could be adapted for a number of other situations:

- Coaching a leader one-on-one
- Follow-up to the *Leadership Practice Inventory* (LPI)
- Self-study for a leader, especially some of the handouts that are content-rich
- Webinar material
- Refresher activities a month after the session
- The basis for a brown-bag discussion in your company
- The start of a conference presentation design
- Teaching a class at your local university
- An ASTD or other association presentation

Activities as Follow-Up to the LPI

Many of these activities can be used with individuals who have completed *The Leadership Practices Inventory* (LPI). You will most likely adjust the process to accommodate just one person. For example, if discussion with others in a classroom setting enriches the activity, you might have the individual identify a colleague with whom to discuss the activity.

Use the activities in Chapters Three through Seven to supplement other LPI material you might be using. Mix things up—insert new activities into the context of The Leadership Challenge® Workshop, Leadership Is Everyone's Business Workshop, or the new The Challenge Continues Workshop. This newest workshop is designed specifically to follow up and reinforce understanding of the model. What better way to do this than with experiential learning activities?

That's enough for this chapter. It is time for you to dig in to experience some of the fun we've had as we've edited the 106 activities in this book.

CHAPTER TWO: FOR A DYNAMIC DELIVERY

In This Chapter

- Characteristics of a successful trainer
- Adult learning principles
- Ways to prepare to deliver training
- How to create a supportive environment
- How to increase participation
- Tips for facilitating activities
- Ideas for forming small groups
- Ideas for managing time in a training session

What's your job as a trainer? Whether you conduct classroom training, coach individuals, provide support on the job, or lead virtual training through webinars or other electronic means, all of the characteristics presented in this chapter are important. Note that while we use the terms trainer or facilitator most often, we are not ignoring teachers, coaches, educators, counselors, or others.

This chapter will provide you with several techniques that will make you an even more effective trainer.

CHARACTERISTICS OF A SUCCESSFUL TRAINER

How do you rate yourself as a trainer? Training is one of those professions in which you must keep two dissimilar, even competing, characteristics in mind at all times. For example, a successful trainer must be

- Logical as well as creative
- An excellent presenter as well as listener
- Well organized as well as spontaneous
- Able to maintain an on-time agenda yet allow flexibility
- People- as well as process-oriented
- Knowledgeable of specifics, yet tolerant of ambiguity
- Detail-oriented while staying big-picture focused

Successful trainers are also assertive and influencing, trust builders, confident and poised, customer-focused, articulate, enthusiastic, excellent writers, impartial and objective, patient, warm and approachable, self-sufficient, results-oriented, and team players. It is useful for them to possess a good sense of humor and to have a strong business sense. They need to understand the businesses their organizations are in and be able to work with people at all levels in an organization. Given all these characteristics, it is no wonder that successful trainers must also be life-long learners. The last chapter in this book will address what it takes to be a life-long learner.

ADULTS LEARN BEST WHEN

Adults learn because they *want* to or *need* to learn. Think about all the things you have learned in the past couple of months. Write them on a piece of paper. Before going on to the next paragraph, think about why you learned each and note that next to what you learned.

Perhaps you *wanted* to learn how to use Twitter to stay in touch with a colleague who was attending a conference with you. Maybe you *wanted* to learn conversational French because you are going to go to Paris next year. Maybe you *wanted* to learn how to prune roses so they would have more blossoms next year. Or you ***wanted*** to learn to golf to get exercise while enjoying time with your customers. Chances are, however, that you did not necessarily ***want*** to learn how to cancel your credit card. You probably lost the credit card and ***needed*** to learn how to cancel it.

Whatever the reason, whether you learned because you wanted to or needed to, it is important to understand why you and all adults invest time learning. It helps you appreciate what motivates the adults you train. Keep this in mind later when you begin to select activities from the upcoming chapters.

Malcolm Knowles (1973), author of *The Adult Learner: A Neglected Species*, is considered the father of adult learning theory. He is known for taking the topic of adult learning from the theoretical to the practical with his adult learning principles:

- Adults have a need to know why they should learn something before investing time in a learning event.
- Adults enter any learning situation with an image of themselves as self-directing, responsible grown-ups.
- Adults come to a learning opportunity with a wealth of experience and a great deal to contribute.
- Adults have a strong readiness to learn those things that will help them cope with daily life effectively.
- Adults are willing to devote energy to learning those things that they believe will help them perform a task or solve a problem.
- Adults are more responsive to internal motivators such as increased self-esteem than external motivators such as higher salaries.

Knowles' work is admired by many and ridiculed by some as too simplistic and duplicative. Many point out (and rightly so) that these same concepts are also important to children. Whatever anyone thinks about his work, we can all admire that fact that

Knowles brought a basic, but incredibly important concept to the fore-front of the field of learning.

Theory is fine. Practicality is better. How can you ensure that you are building in these concepts when you conduct training? Here are a few to consider when you are designing and delivering training.

DESIGN AND DELIVERY THAT DRAW FROM ADULT LEARNING THEORY

Integrating adult learning theory into your design and delivery addresses your participants' concerns. You certainly don't tell them that's what you are doing. Instead, you show them with your actions. Before designing or delivering your next training session, consider answering the six questions that correspond to Knowles' assumptions. Imagine that your participants have asked these questions.

1. Why should I invest time here?

Design

- Design time in at the beginning of your course to address the purpose.
- Build in time to respond to questions.
- Create time to ask participants for their expectations.
- Propose clear learning objectives.

Delivery

- Post the purpose on a wall chart.
- List participants' expectations on a flip chart and hang them on the wall.
- Prepare to respond to "my boss should be here!"
- As you present, link the content to specific examples from the participants.

2. Will I be treated as a self-directing, responsible adult?

Design

- Build in time for self-reflection about content.
- Design self-assessments that allow participants to plan for their future.
- Create time for participants to share their knowledge and expertise.

Delivery

- Give participants permission to move, stand, get coffee, whatever makes them comfortable.
- Ensure participants that all questions are welcomed.
- Give participants the opportunity to establish their own ground rules.

3. Will my experience and expertise be recognized?

Design

- Design time for participants to share their knowledge with other participants.
- Learn about participants' expertise and experience before the session.
- Schedule time for discussion.
- Design an icebreaker that allows participants to learn about others' competencies.

Delivery

- Use teach-backs (participants teaching other participants).

- Invite participants to add to the objectives.
- Designate a place where participants can share their experiences, resources, and ideas by writing them on Post-its and posting them on a flip-chart page.
- Adjust your agenda to meet the needs of participants.

4. How will this workshop help me with daily life and to do my job better?

Design

- Develop case studies, critical incidents, and role plays that address participants' daily situations.
- Interview participants to find specific examples of what they need to do their jobs better.

Delivery

- Invite discussion about situations that participants experience on the job.
- Create a discussion about their daily needs.
- Be available at breaks and before or after the session for individual discussions.

5. How will this content help me solve problems?

Design

- Design a problem-solving clinic into the session.
- Develop experiential learning activities (ELAs) to link the content to specific problems.
- Build in time for self-reflection so participants can relate the content to their specific situations.

Delivery

- Post a "parking lot" to encourage participants to list their questions.
- Share problem situations and lessons learned throughout the session.

6. How will this session build my self-esteem?

Design

- Ensure that your design shows participants how they (and what they are learning) fit into the bigger picture and support the organization.
- Design opportunities for participants to explore their personal growth and development needs.

Delivery

- Encourage journaling or personal reflection during the session that allows participants to explore their own motivation.
- Create a safe learning climate that allows participants to be themselves.
- Get to know participants and what they take pride in; showcase these things if possible.
- Recognize input and ideas from participants.

These may seem like small things, but when added up they make a big difference to participants.

Next time you design or deliver a training session, remember these key assumptions of adult learning and determine how you can put them to use to improve the experience for your participants.

PREPARE TO SUCCEED

Bob Pike is fond of saying, "Proper preparation and practice prevent poor performance!" Pike's Six Ps for effective training have been the bedrock of many trainers' work.

If trainers are lax about anything, it is generally the amount of preparation and practice they put into each training session. As trainers you are completely in control of the amount of time you put into preparing for a training session. Everyone is overworked these days, and few professionals work fewer than fifty hours each week. This means that you will need to cut into some of your personal time to complete the kind of preparation that "prevents poor performance!"

Preparation must be done on three fronts: the training setting, the participants, and yourself.

Prepare the Training Setting

Everything you do will make a difference as to whether your participants have a satisfactory experience or not. Everything you do should be done with a purpose—your room setup, for example. Are you trying to develop small teams within the group? Set up in rounds of five to six. Are you trying to open discussion among all participants? Try a U-shaped setup.

Ensure that everything is in place for a pleasant learning experience. Don't let anything prevent that from occurring. Select a room that is the right size—too big can be just as bad as too small. Ensure the room is accessible to everyone, including those who have limited mobility. Select a room that is conveniently located to restrooms, snacks, lunch accommodations, parking, and public transportation. Choose a room that is free of distractions and noise as well as obstructions.

Furniture is equally important. Are the chairs comfortable and adjustable? Can everyone in every seat see the front of the room? For you as the facilitator, set a table in the front of the room so you can organize materials you need for activities, your notes, visuals, props, and other tools of the trade. Avoid speaking from a lectern; it will only create a barrier between you and your participants.

Lighting should be as bright as possible. Ideally, you will have natural lighting, but when you don't, turn the lights on as bright as possible. All projectors have enough lumens of light to project clearly and brightly in a well-lit room. Those who turn the lights down are remembering the days in the 1970s when one had to dim the lights to show a reel to reel movie! The only time you might want to consider less light is if an early morning sunrise or late afternoon sunset interferes with learning.

Identify all the controls in the room: climate control, window shades or blinds, lighting, microphones, telephone (so you can turn the ringer off), projection equipment, and so on.

If anything is going to go wrong, it will be with your audiovisuals. Know everything you can about the equipment and use your own equipment when possible. Preview your PowerPoint slides or DVDs at least one week before the event. Don't just pretend! Use the same equipment and the slides you will use for your presentation. Set your equipment up the day or evening before. Be certain the equipment works, you have all the cords, it's in focus, and you know how to adjust volume control. Be sure you have the right size screen for the size of the group that you have.

Be prepared for an emergency. Learn a few troubleshooting tricks for the equipment you use most often and pack an extension cord and even a roll of duct tape just in case. Assume that the electricity will go out or that the projector will blow up. Have a plan—even if that plan is a flip chart and a few colorful markers.

Prepare the Participants

The first things you think of for preparing participants may not be the things that work best. For example, sending pre-reading is what usually comes to mind. Unfortunately, it generally does not accomplish what you want it to. If you are trying to save time or provide background, you will be disappointed. Generally, 30 percent of your participants will read it; 30 percent will ignore it; and 40 percent will say they never received it. The 30 percent who read the materials will be upset that you need to go over it in class and "waste their time." However, if you do not, the other 70 percent will be at a disadvantage. If the success of the session is dependent on everyone completing the pre-work, don't assign it.

What can you do instead? Connect with people before the session. Get them thinking about the topic, ask what they need to learn, determine their level of skill and knowledge, and tell them what's in it for them (Bob Pike's radio station, WII-FM). You could send an agenda, a welcome letter, or an email. You might send a puzzle or brain teaser that arouses their curiosity. Sometimes it is valuable to send the roster of all participants. You should also connect with your participants' managers to identify what they hope their employees will gain at the training session. Consider involving participants early by sending them a questionnaire and using their responses to customize the agenda. And don't forget to send them all the logistics so they know where the room is, the start and end times, lunch arrangements, how they can obtain messages, whether they will be able to check their email, whether public transportation is available, and where to park if they drive to the site.

Prepare Yourself

You represent the training. Participants may remember you more than they remember the training. Therefore you want them to remember only the best. Begin by getting organized long before the session begins. Create your own generic packing list that you can customize for each session. Some things that might be on your list include masking tape, index cards, Post-its, wireless remote, training notes, markers, table tents, etc.

Practice enough to ensure that the materials are a part of who you are. Create notes that work for you and practice with them. Practice the theatrics if you are telling a story or a joke. Practice with the pauses. Practice the mechanics of rolling your flip chart, of using a prop, showing a picture, or using the revealing technique with your PowerPoint. Practice some of the activities with a small group of your peers. Practice in the room where you will present whenever possible. Film yourself during one of your practice sessions. You are your own best critic. What do you need to do to improve? Anticipate the questions that might be asked. Think about the questions you want to ask. Where will you plant them throughout your presentation?

Learn about your participants. Who will attend? What are their positions and jobs in the organization? How much responsibility or authority do they have? What is their level of understanding of the subject matter? What is the reason they are attending this training session: Poor performance? Reward? New employees? Is attendance voluntary or mandatory? What are their opinions about the topic?

What baggage might they bring into the session? Answers to these questions will help you plan your approach to the group.

CREATING A SUPPORTIVE ENVIRONMENT

One of the most important things you can do for your participants is to create a supportive environment, one in which they feel comfortable enough to ask questions; are confident enough to try something new—even at the risk of failure—and are content enough to want to return for more.

Creating a supportive environment begins the first minute you walk into the training room. How can you make this the most inviting room possible? Is the room appealing? Does it have adequate lighting? Are the chairs comfortable? Is there a place to serve coffee? Is the room attractive? Are the tables clean? Do the shades work? Is it clear of clutter? Is the room engaging? Does it encourage conversation? Is there room to stand to form small groups during the session? Does the room promote conversation during breaks?

You should be completely prepared one hour before starting so that you can greet participants and put them at ease about the session. Once the session starts, involve everyone quickly. Start with a bang. Don't present all the housekeeping stuff first—boring! Begin with something that grabs your learners' attention and then move them quickly into an engaging icebreaker.

Remember and use participants' names. Let them know who you are, too. Many people will trust you more if they feel they know you better. Build professional credibility with them, but let them in on you the person, too. Make yourself available during breaks to continue to build rapport.

Create opportunities for participants to meet and work with each other. Everyone in the session should be seen as a part of the support network. Encourage participants to share contact information so they can connect after the session has ended.

INCREASE PARTICIPATION

Why increase participation? There are many reasons: to create an enjoyable experience, to build the team, to ensure participants are following you, and the most important reason, to ensure that they are reinforcing and cementing what they are learning.

At the beginning of this chapter you identified things that you learned in the past couple of months. Let's imagine that one of those was golf. How can you learn to golf? You could talk to someone to learn how to keep score or to determine the best clubs to purchase. You could read a book to learn the history and the rules of the game. You could observe several tournaments to learn what the greens look like or how the players interact. You could have someone show you how to hold the club or how to tee off. You could practice on a putting green to learn how to improve your short strokes or you could practice on a driving range to learn how to direct the ball. You could do all of these things and learn a great deal. However, to truly learn the game of golf you need to ***participate***. You need to participate with other players on the greens. You need to participate in a game of eighteen holes to truly ***learn*** the game of golf.

Learners in your training sessions need the same experiences as you require when learning golf or rose bush pruning or twittering. They need to participate. They need to get in the game.

You may come upon obstacles that prevent you from encouraging as much participation as you would like. Time constraints, organizational culture, group size, or facility limitations might all prevent ideal participation circumstances. You will, of course, do all that you can to work around these obstacles.

What about those times when you have overcome the listed obstacles and you have chosen an activity to increase participation, but your learners are just not buying it? Check your training skills first. Here are seven things you can consider to ensure that you are doing everything you can to increase participation.

Communication Skills

The most basic skill is, of course, your communication skills. Are you an excellent listener, avoiding hasty judgments? Do you accept input and balance that with assertiveness? You need to be accepting, but not allow anyone to leave the training session with incorrect information. You also need your assertiveness skills to ensure that disruptive or overly zealous participants do not interfere with other learners' ability to participate. Asking questions is one of the best ways to encourage participation. Be sure to allow enough time for participants to respond. Encourage questions from your learners. Certainly it is okay to ask participants to hold a question or to post it on a parking lot. However, if you do it too often, participation will wane. Review the design; perhaps there is something out of sequence or you are not moving through the information quickly enough.

Interpretive Skills

You don't need to be a mind reader, but to increase participation the best trainers pay attention to non-verbal cues. If you sense something is amiss, it probably is. If it is one person, probe during a break. You may find it has nothing to do with the training session. If, on the other hand, the entire group is staring into space, have their arms crossed, and are not readily participating, you need to check it out.

Be aware of hot buttons—those issues that can set your participants off—and know how to handle them if they are inadvertently brought up during your session. You will build trust with the group and increase participation if you can translate correctly what others are saying and if you can personally relate to all situations participants suggest.

Personal Traits

Several basic characteristics ensure more participation. Do you have a good sense of humor? Are you open to all ideas? Do you have patience with those who need more time to learn or practice? Are you trustworthy, doing what you say you will do and not betray confidences? Do you come across as sincere? You must *be* sincere, as well as *look* sincere. Sometimes a silly grin or an inadvertent frown prevents you from looking sincere. These personal traits must be evident; their absence will discourage participation.

Interpersonal Skills

You've probably completed an instrument that identifies your interpersonal style, its strengths and weaknesses. Do you know yours? Start with your strengths, but work hard on overcoming your weaknesses. Super-organized? Be sure you are also people-oriented and approachable. Analytical genius? Be sure you also attend to having fun. Deliberate and detail-oriented? Be certain that you also see the big picture and can make decisions fast when necessary. Life of the party? Know when to get down to business, too. You need to balance what comes naturally to you with what comes naturally to others. Flexibility is key to increasing participation.

Learning Techniques

Effective training techniques are important to increase participation, so go back to Training 101. Provide clear directions and coach your learners when necessary. A successful learner is a happy learner. And we all know that happy learners participate more than disgruntled learners. Allow the learning process to occur naturally, even if it means that some individuals must struggle a bit. Support the learning with coaching and feedback. Finally, remember reinforcement: catch 'em being good. Reinforce for both correct content as well as behaviors that encourage participation, such as volunteering, contributing, and encouraging others to contribute.

Attending Skills

Although these skills are sometimes lumped with communication, they have their own unique attributes. Attending skills go beyond communication. Attending means that you send messages that you care about the participants and want them to succeed. Ensure that your eye contact is consistent and balanced. Scan the group regularly to gather information, but also provide good eye contact to individuals. Trainers tend to focus the majority of their eye contact on the 75 percent of the group to their non-dominant side. Ensure you are looking at everyone. Move into the group when presenting to build rapport and encourage responses instead of staying welded to the floor behind your presentation table. Provide affirmative non-verbals, such as nods and smiles, to keep comments flowing. Stay engaged whether participants are having a large group discussion or working in small groups. Small group activities do not give you permission to check your BlackBerry. Move among participants, listening in on discussions and offering assistance when appropriate.

Process Factors

Balancing participation will be dependent upon the process you use. Begin to build participation slowly. Start with just a show of hands. Then move to requesting volunteers. Move to using a round robin and calling on specific individuals. Participants can be a part of a small group and finally the leaders or reporters for groups. By starting slowly and building to more independent and riskier roles, you will obtain more participation. During this process, balance participation, encouraging more quiet learners, but not curtailing discussion from those who are more vocal. You will also want to reinforce correct responses, but not negate incorrect ones. Stay on track while still allowing participants to raise their own concerns. Finally, create an inclusive environment by demonstrating that you value everyone's input. Help participants feel that it is safe to participate.

TIPS FOR FACILITATING ACTIVITIES

For the activities in this book to be effective, you will need to set them up *concisely, conduct* them carefully, and process them *completely*— the three Cs required to effectively facilitate activities.

Introducing Activities

Give enough information, but not so much that participants do not have an ah-ha moment. Provide brief instructions, including any materials they need. Establish a clear objective, unless the point of the activity is for them to identify their own learning objectives. Form small groups before you tell them what to do—otherwise they will forget by the time they get to their groups and greet everyone. Clarify how much involvement is expected during the activity, as well as what will occur after the activity. Are they expected to report out? Will there be a discussion? Are they in competition for the highest score? Announce how much time they will have to complete the activity. Before they begin, ensure that they have the right materials, are on the right page, and do not have any questions.

Conducting Activities

Provide support throughout the activity. Assist with the timekeeping using cues such as "time is half up" or "five minutes left" or "you should be on the last two questions." Remind participants of the rules if necessary. If you need to make suggestions to ensure a successful learning experience, don't give the answer. Ask questions instead of directing. Walk among the participants to identify any problems, confusion, or questions. Adjust the time if necessary and announce it to the entire group.

Processing Activities

Debrief the activity at its conclusion. Use a good experiential learning model for your questions following these steps:

- What: What happened?
- Why: Why did it happen?
- So what: What did you learn?
- Now what: What will you do differently?

Share pertinent observations, but avoid teaching, preaching, or lecturing. You are working with adults who have lots to share with each other. Use representatives from each group to conduct the debriefing portion. Correct only when they have come to an incorrect solution, and then use a question or try to draw the right answer out of the group.

SMALL GROUPS

In many activities you are asked to form small groups. In most cases the activity's designer states the best number of people to achieve the purpose. Small groups are important for a number of reasons:

- Learning is more dynamic in small groups.
- Each person in a small group gets more time to speak.
- Small groups allow for more questions.
- Small groups are better for "discovery."
- Learners receive feedback more quickly and personally in a small group.
- Participants learn from each other in small groups.
- Small groups are better for forming teams, building relationships, and improving communication.
- Small groups allow more people to practice the same skills at the same time.

Use creative ways to form small groups. You can always rely on the normal "count off by 4s," but why not make even group formation exciting with different techniques each time? For example, have participants count off by 4s in a foreign language (you'll need to teach them first, of course). Use personal information such as birthdays that are in the four quarters of the year; birth order (first, middle, youngest, only child); last digit in their phone numbers; or the color of shoes they are wearing. You could code the materials, for example, everyone with a red folder or all who have yellow dots on the back of their books or the color of marker used to create their table tents.

What if you don't have the exact number of people required for a group? One person could be an observer. If there are too few participants, you could fill in. In some instances, participants from one group could rotate to another group.

Small groups are a part of every training session. Be practical in their purpose. Plan ahead. Be creative in their formation.

WATCH YOUR TIME

Any time you interject participation and learning activities, you will naturally increase the amount of time it takes to complete a segment of learning. Of course, it also means that participants will grasp the concepts more readily and maintain them longer. This matters little when you only have a seven-hour training day. Don't squander precious minutes in your session. Conduct the activities, but use these ideas to save time.

Use More Than One Objective

Plan to use one activity to teach more than one skill. You can easily use one of the activities from the Challenge the Process section to also discuss the level of teamwork or what aspect of communication could be improved. Work your activities.

Nudge Them Along

Use a variety of "nudges" to keep participants focused on the task. It is easy for them to go astray. Comments such as "You should be halfway through the activity" or "Start to wrap up" or "You have five minutes left" keep things moving along. Nudges save time by preventing the activities from going overtime.

Share the Load

Everyone in the session does not have to do all the activities. For example, you could assign different groups to complete different parts of a worksheet or activity and have them share the results with each other. If you have a list of items to discuss, you could have one-half of the group start at the top and work down and the other half start at the bottom and work up.

Use Timekeepers

You don't always need to be the timekeeper. You can assign others to this task for everything from activities to ensuring everyone returns on time from breaks. By the way, don't allow breaks to eat into your precious training time. If you have planned for a 15-minute break, don't let it slip into 25 minutes.

Watch Time Yourself

Start on time. Don't let large group discussions get out of hand. You don't need to hear from every person about every topic. Use phrases such as, "Martin, we've heard your thoughts about note 1; let's hear from someone else." This is one of those times when you may need to exercise assertiveness to maintain control of time. Be prepared and organized. Don't waste time looking for supplies or counting out materials. These things can be prepared before your session begins.

Select the Right Number of Groups

Save time during small group exercises by forming more groups with fewer people. Smaller groups complete a task faster. If you need to save time during the reporting stage, form fewer groups. All groups do not need to report on everything. You could ask for just one idea or the best idea or the most creative idea from each group. Ask groups to summarize their thoughts on flip-chart pages. You could conduct a gallery walk where everyone views the charts. Or they could be posted and viewed as participants leave for a break.

Many skills are required to be an excellent trainer. This book provides you with content in the form of energizing and practical activities. It still requires that you practice all the basics of good training: implementing adult learning principles; being well prepared; creating a supportive environment; building in increased participation; and finding ways to invest your time wisely in your training session.

We've provided a series of the best activities for The Five Practices of Exemplary Leadership®. Now it's up to you to provide the best trainer skills for implementing them.

Reference

Knowles, M. (1973). *The adult learner: A neglected species*. Houston, TX: Gulf.

CHAPTER THREE: MODEL THE WAY

In This Chapter

- Provide an overview of Model the Way.
- Discuss the corresponding commitments of leadership.
- Consider the importance of this practice.
- Introduce the activities for this practice.
- Present the activities for this practice.

The Leadership Challenge focuses on how leaders mobilize others to struggle to get things done in organizations. It begins with Model the Way, the first step in transforming values into action. This practice clarifies personal values and allows a leader to set an example.

Values must go beyond catchy slogans; they must represent a leader's deeply held belief system. But to truly be beneficial, values must become a part of the fabric of the organization. They must be woven together by everyone on the team or in the organization. This occurs when everyone endorses the values.

HOW DOES A LEADER IMPLEMENT MODEL THE WAY?

How do leaders achieve the kind of endorsement of values that make a difference? Leaders must provide opportunities for people to hear, observe, and understand their values.

The first two commitments of leadership support how to Model the Way.

- Clarify values by finding your voice and affirming shared ideals.
- Set the example by aligning actions with shared values.

Clarify Values

Think of a leader who has had an impact on you. You can probably readily list the leader's principles, the moral tenants that guide that individual's decisions and actions. Several things have occurred so that you are able to identify leaders with their principles.

First, leaders have taken time to identify their values. Second, leaders have prioritized their values. Third, leaders have expanded their value bases by involving others to create shared ideals. And finally, leaders have put the resulting values into formats that are readily understood and easily modeled. These steps are critical for a leader to find his or her "voice." What exactly are the leader's values? Can the leader be succinctly passionate about what he or she believes?

Exemplary leaders know what principles they embrace and what their values embody. They speak openly and fervently about their values to ensure others know what they represent.

Set the Example

Leaders go beyond speaking about their values. To Model the Way, leaders must take values to the next level. You can identify the principles leaders uphold because they exhibit a burning desire to live their values. They weave their values into everything they do in the organization and in their lives in general.

Excellent leaders have a driving desire within to live their values in a way that makes others want to go beyond being followers and to be leaders of those same values. What do you see when leaders are setting the example? They go beyond communication and ask others to communicate. They go beyond modeling and encourage others to model. They reflect on all they learn and take action.

Leaders communicate their values in a two-way dialogue. They ask questions and answer questions candidly regarding the values. They practice open communication and accept and provide feedback freely. They engage others in communicating about the values to ensure clear understanding.

Leaders do what they say they will do. They also help others to model the values by sharing stories and examples that illustrate values in action. Leaders reinforce those who are modeling the values and confront situations that oppose the values. Each of these leadership actions increases the number of people who are setting the example.

Leaders seek input and reflect on all that they learn so that they can refine both their values and how they model them.

WHY IS MODELING THE WAY IMPORTANT?

Espousing and modeling clear values is critical to forming a baseline of expectations and beginning to establish credibility as a leader. A clear set of values creates a solid foundation on which to build a vision for the future. A clear set of values allow others to challenge the process and to take charge. A clear set of values creates the underpinning of everything else the leader will do. People may not remember everything a leader has accomplished, but they do remember what he or she represents.

ACTIVITY INTRODUCTION

The activities in this section represent a broad variety of approaches to address the value-clarifying practice, Model the Way.

The activities vary in time from 10 minutes to 3 hours, and many can be adjusted for any size group. The activities explore a leader's source of power, clarify the meaning and alignment of values, and explore the relationship of culture to values.

Activities broach the negative side as well, including a demonstration of what happens when a stated mission is not modeled and modeling the limitations of only setting an example.

The activities also drill down to the commitments of leadership, addressing both clarifying values and setting an example.

Activity List

- Anatomy of Power by Teri-E Belf
- Values from the Movie *Gandhi* by Lily Cheng
- Shared Values: Drive-By Conversations by Kim Chesky
- Toothpick Activity by Mary Cooper and Debbie Zmorenski
- One Step Forward, Two Steps Back by Cher Holton
- A Leadership Point of View by Edith Katz
- It's All in a Name by Jan Miller and Denise Knight
- Leadership in Context by Mohandas Nair
- Cultural Artifacts by Anne Reilly and Homer Johnson
- Setting an Example to Mirror Is Not Enough by Cheryl L. Rude
- Ethics for the 21st Century by Charlotte S. Waisman and Linda Bedinger
- Model Behavior by Devora Zack

ANATOMY OF POWER

Submitted by Teri-E Belf

Objectives

- To explore the various aspects and sources of power.
- To explore the relationship of values to power.
- To have a keener sense of your own power and implications as a leader.
- To learn others' perceptions of your power.

Audience

Ten to fifty participants.

Time Required

1 ½ to 2 hours.

Materials and Equipment

- Flip-chart paper with three to five colored markers for each group of five to eight participants.
- One flip-chart stand.
- One Anatomy of Power handout for each participant.
- Twelve pieces of paper or note cards about 3 by 5 or 4 by 6 for each participant.

Area Setup

Movable chairs in two U-shaped groups.

Process

1. Ask participants to form groups of five to eight (preferably with people they do not know or do not know well) to explore what leadership power means to them. Tell them to free-associate what comes to mind when they hear the words "leadership power." What do they feel and think? Ask them, as a group, to create something using pictures, symbols, words, mime, or a physical demonstration or an activity to represent their associations. They may use a combination of modalities. This demonstration may be serious or humorous, and they should ensure that everyone's contribution is honored. Say, "Be your powerful self in this experience." Tell them they have 15 minutes.

2. Give each group 3 minutes to show and explain the group's interpretation of power to the whole group. At the end of each demonstration, ask a recorder to capture on a flip-chart page words used to explain each interpretation.

3. Conduct a mini-summary using some of these questions:
   - What is the power of a leader? Did anything stand out?
   - What are the sources of power? How do we acquire it?
   - Is power good or bad or both or neither?
   - Think for a moment about who is/are the most powerful person/people you know professionally and why.
   - What characteristics make those people powerful?
     Add characteristics to the flip chart as they are mentioned. Some characteristics that might be discussed include:
   - Ascribed power, put on a pedestal, like parent, teacher, mentor, boss, responsible for resource allocation.
   - Comes from values within.

- Creates a safe space for trust and rapport.
- Ability to recognize a learning moment.
- Detachment, neutrality, objectivity.
- Trust managers' and employees' abilities to get the job done.
- Inspirational and optimistic.

4. Provide the Anatomy of Power handout to participants and lead a brief discussion, stating that we have two key power struggles.
   - We are attached to our own identity or self-esteem, that is, I need to look good so I take control over meetings or decisions to ensure that there will be value (as I perceive it) for the organization.
   Or I need approval and I want my managers/staff to like me.
   Or I want my managers/staff to recognize that I am competent.
   - We must be right. For example, My way is the only way or My words are the right words.

5. State that there are three qualities we must have to receive someone's power: curiosity, interest, and appreciation.

6. State that there is a power larger than the two people in a relationship. It is the power of the relationship. Ask participants to describe it. What is it like? How do they know it? If you wish, post one of these quotes on the flip chart to continue the discussion:

"Not the power to conquer others, but the power to become ONE with others, is the ultimate power."

Sri Chinmoy, spiritual master

"Our scientific power has outrun our spiritual power. We have guided missiles and misguided men."

Martin Luther King, Jr.

7. Continue the discussion, making and soliciting comments such as these:
   - Power is intentional use of one's energy (influence) over behavior, self and others.
   - Power is understanding one's value base.
   - Power is the speed it takes to turn possibility into reality.
   - Power is the ability to choose to make things happen or block things from happening.
   - Power is energy in use; therefore, energy is needed to be powerful.

8. State that there are four facets of power in humans: mental, emotional, physical, and spiritual. Ask participants to read the portion of the handout containing the points about these facets of power and the challenges of each. Allow about 5 minutes. Ask what questions participants have about this content. While participants are reading, you may wish to post this quote on the flip chart.

   "It is for us to pray not for tasks equal to our powers, but for powers equal to our tasks."

   Helen Keller

9. State that we often have first-hand perceptions about someone's power with little information. If leaders Model the Way, they need to be comfortable receiving feedback from people about perceptions of their power. Provide each person with twelve pieces of paper or note cards. Ask them to select partners they do not know or don't know well. Tell them to spend a minute with this person in any way they choose. Tell them they may speak or be silent.

After the minute, they are to write down a word, words, or phrase that describes the other person's power, completing this sentence: "From my perspective, what I see and hear in you that makes you powerful is _____."

10. State that they should tell their partners what they wrote and give them the papers on which they completed the sentence.

11. Have participants switch roles by moving to other partners. Advise them that they will have 10 to 15 minutes for this exercise. Tell them to try to meet as many people as they can. Aim for at least eight different people's perceptions. Remind them not to linger and get into longer conversations and to remember that they are not just learning about themselves but are also obtaining information about their colleagues. If you wish, you may post this quote on the flip chart during this step.

"Let not thy will roar, when thy power can whisper."

Dr. Thomas Fuller, 1732

12. Use the following questions to process the exercise:
    • What did you learn about yourself? What themes or patterns emerged?
    • How was this different from your perception prior to the exercise?
    • What are the implications for you as a leader?
    • What is the relationship of values to power?
    • How has this exercise affected your shared values?
    • What might you do differently as a leader?
    • What advice do you have for leaders regarding power as it relates to setting an example of one's values?

Teri-E Belf, M.A., C.A.G.S., and the first M.C.C., is a purposeful coach trainer, author, and coach. In 1987 she founded Success Unlimited Network®, which is both an international network of coaches and has an ICF-accredited Coach Training and Certification Program rooted in life purpose and spiritual perspectives. Her current passion is creating DVDs demonstrating competent coaching. Her coaching books include *Coaching with Spirit, Simply Live It UP,* and *Facilitating Life Purpose.*

Teri-E Belf, M.A., C.A.G.S.
Success Unlimited Network®, LLC
2016 Lakebreeze Way
Reston, VA 20191-4021
   Phone: (703) 716-8374
   Email: coach@belf.org
   Website: www.successunlimitednet.com

ANATOMY OF POWER HANDOUT

My Power •• **The Power of the Relationship** •• **Someone Else's Power**

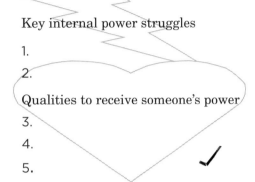

Key internal power struggles

1.
2.

Qualities to receive someone's power

3.
4.
5.

How do we use our power?*

	Challenges
1. **Mental Power** includes intuition, thoughts, beliefs, fantasy, knowledge, language too many goals • To make decisions • To make distinctions • To set direction, goals, results • To identify values for living	Lack of focus Self-esteem dips Limiting beliefs Cultural prescriptions
2. **Emotional Power** includes heart, love, charisma, resistance, fear, anger to determine how forcefully, persistently and passionately we will carry out our decisions and move towards our goals. The stronger the emotion the more energy available to move.	Taught not to show emotion Stifle emotion Fear of exposure
3. **Physical Power** includes strength, passivism • To implement our decisions and actions`	Negative beliefs regarding physical ability How we use our bodies
4. **Spiritual Power** includes infinite energy, macro perspective, power for the whole fear around misuse • To access wisdom • To return to a state of centered peacefulness	Lack of trust Religious teachings

*Adapted from an article about Power and Empowerment by Michael F. Broom and Donald C. Klein

Model the Way

"Knowing others is intelligence; knowing yourself is true wisdom. Mastering others is strength, mastering yourself is true power."

Lao Tzu

My power comes from:

My power manifests itself in my values by:

What I learned about my power:

VALUES FROM THE MOVIE *GANDHI*

Submitted by Lily Cheng

Objectives

- To understand the meaning of values.
- To be able to see how one's values are espoused.
- To understand and appreciate the alignment between one's personal and professional values.

Audience

Suitable for any group size.

Time Required

20 to 40 minutes.

Materials and Equipment

- CD, DVD, or video player.
- Movie *Gandhi* – segment from 20.52 to 20.56 (*Note:* The Federal Copyright Act requires a performance license for showing films. Information about licensing can be obtained from the Motion Picture Association of America on their Internet website at www .mpaa.org/Public_Performance.asp.)

Area Setup

Nothing in particular.

Process

1. Provide a brief background of Gandhi and prepare learners to watch for how this movie clip relates to values.

2. Show the 10-minute video segment.
3. Debrief what learners saw using the following questions:
   - What are values?
   - How do personal and professional values differ?
   - How are personal and professional values the same?
   - What are the consequences of a lack of alignment of one's values and actions?
   - How can you ensure alignment for yourself?
   - What is your responsibility as a leader regarding values and alignment?
   - What are your next steps with regard to your values?

Lily Cheng, led by her deep passion and vision in people development and performance, has twenty-eight years of work experience in the fields of education, counseling, executive coaching, general management, human resource management and human resource development. She has chosen to anchor her career in the organization development field for the last thirteen years. Lily established PACE in 1988 with co-founder Peter Cheng. She is a Certified Master Coach with the Behavioral Coaching Institute (BCI) and one of the first two Leadership Challenge® Certified Master Facilitators in Asia. Lily holds a master of arts in education and human development from The George Washington University.

Lily Cheng
PACE Organization Dynamics Pte Ltd
Blk 162 Bukit Merah Central
#06-3555, Singapore 150162
   Phone: +65 6278 8289
   Email: lilycheng@pace-od.com
   Website: http://www.pace-od.com

SHARED VALUES: DRIVE-BY CONVERSATIONS

Submitted by Kim Chesky

Objectives

- To engage in conversations about shared values.
- To identify the organization's values that matter most to participants personally and why that is.
- To dialogue about the meaning of individual organizational values.
- To strengthen relationships with others.

Audience

Participants from the same organization for each small group.

Time Required

30 to 50 minutes, depending on group size.

Materials and Equipment

- List of the organization's core values displayed on a flip chart or PowerPoint slide (one for each organization if participants are from more than one).
- Question: "What value resonates the most for you today and why?" posted on a flip chart or shown on a screen.

Area Setup

An open area for people to meet and greet each other. Round tables for four to five to share their experiences with others.

Process

1. Introduce this exercise by saying, "In a minute we will be asking you to share an organizational value that is important to you. Who remembers what those values are? After a few responses, state that you have them listed for participants. Display the values on either a PowerPoint slide or a flip chart.

2. Ask each participant to choose a value that is most important to him or her today and to think about why it is important.

3. Explain that they will meet one-one-one with as many people as possible to share the values they selected and the reasons why. State that their goal is to get to as many other people as possible. Once they finish with the first person, they are to move on to the next person until time is up or until they have met and shared with most of the other participants. Say, "On your mark, get set, go" and play some upbeat music to set the tone. Allow 10 to 15 minutes, depending on the number of people. It takes about 1 minute for each dyad to share their values.

4. When time is coming to an end, let participants take a moment to finish the conversations they are in.

5. Debrief the exercise using these questions:
   - What are some of the things you observed while sharing your values (energy, commitment, engaged, sense of shared meaning)?
   - What were some of the common themes?
   - What did you find most interesting?
   - What are some of the things you observed about values from this exercise?
   - Think about people who chose the same value as you did. Did they choose it for the same reason as you did? If not, what was different?

- What are some of the challenges associated with shared values (common meaning, espoused values vs. values in use)?
- Would you have selected the same value three months ago? If not, why not? What changed?
- Why are shared values important to a leader and to an organization?
- What is a leader's responsibility to build commitment to an organization's espoused values?
- What can you do to build commitment to your organization's values?

Kim Chesky is president of LeadingWise, a consulting company dedicated to enhancing individual, team, and organizational effectiveness. For over twenty years his passion and work have focused on leadership development, leadership coaching, team development, organizational change, associate engagement, and business strategy. Kim is a Leadership Challenge® Master Facilitator and a registered corporate leadership coach. He earned his BA and MBA degrees from the University of Wisconsin-Madison. He has helped organizations of all sizes, from Fortune 50 clients to small businesses and non-profits, achieve extraordinary results.

Kim Chesky
LeadingWise
8622 Sargent Creek Lane
Indianapolis, IN 46256
  Phone: (317) 752-1101
  Email: kimchesky@netscape.net
  Website: leadingwise.com

TOOTHPICK ACTIVITY

Submitted by Mary Cooper and Debbie Zmorenski

Objectives

- To illustrate an understanding of clarity.
- To realize the impact of a visual in setting the example to follow.
- To identify behaviors a leader must complete to clearly Model the Way.

Audience

Any.

Time Required

10 to 20 minutes.

Materials and Equipment

- Fourteen toothpicks per participant.
- Straight-line pattern, such as a star or a house, that could be re-created using toothpicks.

Area Setup

Participants will need table space to create the patterns.

Process

1. Introduce the activity by reviewing the objectives and why they are important. State the objectives and add other thoughts such as these:

- To illustrate the understanding of clarity is critical. It could be the clarity of values, principles and standards, or shared ideals. It could also be the two-way dialogue of asking for and receiving feedback and building consensus on a team.
- To realize the impact of a visual in setting the example to follow. This visual is the leader, setting the example by following through on commitments, acting on the feedback she or he has received, and being a behavioral example of "credible" leadership.

2. Ask each participant to take fourteen toothpicks. Ask for a volunteer.

3. As the participants are taking their toothpicks, explain to the volunteer that she or he will be giving instructions to the participants to assemble the toothpicks in a specific pattern. Provide the volunteer with the pattern and have him or her turn away from the audience so the volunteer cannot see the participants.

4. Explain to the entire group that the volunteer will be giving them instructions to create a specific pattern with their toothpicks and the following rules must be followed:
- No questions can be asked of the volunteer.
- She/he can only give verbal instructions.
- She/he cannot state the name of the patterned being created.
- She/he may not repeat any instruction given.
- They have 3 minutes.

5. Allow the volunteer to give verbal instructions for creating the pattern, and ensure the rules are followed.

6. At the conclusion of 3 minutes, stop any instructions and have the participants compare executed patterns with each other first, and then with the volunteer's pattern.

7. Debrief the activity and learning. Possible questions might be:
   - How did we all do?
   - Are there differences among your patterns? Why are they so different when the instructions were the same?
   - Compare your creations with the actual pattern. Do they match? Why or why not?
   - What would have helped you to replicate the pattern successfully (opportunity to ask questions, having a visual)?
   - How does this exercise relate to the first practice of Model the Way and the two commitments (the necessity for clarity, two-way communication to ensure shared ideal, and the benefit of an example visual)?
   - What specific behaviors must a leader complete to ensure values are clear to all?
   - What are you doing at work right now where you could practice this skill?

Variation

- This activity could also be used with Inspiring a Shared Vision.

Mary Cooper and **Debbie Zmorenski** are authors of *The Voice of Leadership*. Formerly with the Disney Institute, they are the current principles of LSA Partners, a management consulting and training firm. Aligned values and a passion for assisting leaders with the implementation of ideas and solutions inspired them to leave Disney and use their forty-six years of combined Cast Member experience, knowledge, and skills in helping leaders and organizations achieve sustainable results. Both have owned small businesses and are graduates of the Dale Carnegie course. Mary received her MBA from

the Crummer Graduate School at Rollins College and Debbie received
her MBA from the University of Phoenix.

Mary Cooper
LSA Partners
9845 Portofino Drive
Orlando, FL 32832
   Phone: (407) 497-0468
   Email: maryc@LSAPartners.com
   Website: www.LSAPartners.com

Debbie Zmorenski
LSA Partners
9845 Portofino Drive
Orlando, FL 32832
   Phone: (407) 497-0468
   Email: debbiez@LSAPartners.com

ONE STEP FORWARD, TWO STEPS BACK
Submitted by Cher Holton

Objectives

- To demonstrate the dissonance created when a stated mission is not modeled.
- To create a list of specific examples of a mission in action.

Audience

Ten to fifty participants.

Time Required

45 to 60 minutes.

Materials and Equipment

- One copy of the company's/team's mission for each subgroup.
- Flip-chart paper and markers for each subgroup.

Area Setup

Tables for ease in creating groups, including space around the tables to facilitate the first part of activity.

Process

1. Inform the group that you are going to give them an opportunity to demonstrate how well they can follow your instructions. They will be moving according to your signal, as follows:
   - When you point up toward the ceiling that is an indication for them to move one step forward while saying the word FORWARD.

- When you point to the floor, that is an indication for them to move one step backward while saying the word BACK.
- When you point to their right, that is an indication for them to move one step to the right, while saying the word RIGHT.
- When you point to their left, that is an indication for them to move one step to the left, while saying the word LEFT.
  Ask everyone to stand, and go through a round of movements to be sure everyone understands.

2. After a few movements, mention that no one seems too excited about this, and maybe it is too simple, so let's make it difficult. Say, "For the next round, I will give you the same directions, and I'd like you to move the way my directions indicate, but SAY the opposite. For example, if I point to the ceiling, you will move FORWARD, while saying BACK."

3. Test this out to be sure they understand; then begin the round giving any variety of directions you want. It won't take long for people to be confused and running into one another! At this point, stop the activity and say that obviously it is too confusing to say one thing while seeing movement to the contrary. So let's make a change.

4. Tell them that this time, they will say the same direction as you are giving them, but MOVE in the opposite direction! For example, if you point to the ceiling, they will say FORWARD while moving one step back! "Ready? Let's go!"

5. Do a few directions, and again, it won't be long before people are confused and running into each other. At this point, stop and say, "Okay! This isn't working either! Let's go back to the original. I'd like you to DO and SAY exactly what my directions tell you, but let's do it with gusto, as a team, with lots of energy and enthusiasm! Ready? Begin."

6. Go through four or five movements, with the group shouting out the movements and moving in unison. Then bring it to a close with cheers all around.

7. Debrief this segment using questions such as:
   - What are the core messages you get from this activity (importance of modeling what you say; confusion that comes when you try to say one thing and do another; ineffectiveness of teams that have no shared mission)?
   - How did you feel trying to do one thing and say the opposite? Why was it confusing?
   - How does this relate to the mission we have as a company (it is important to send a message through behavior that always aligns with the mission and values that are stated)?

8. Divide participants into small subgroups of five to seven people per group. Give each group a copy of the company or team's mission and values, and chart paper with markers.

9. Ask each group to identify five specific real-life examples of how they have actually seen the mission or values in action. The more specific and detailed the examples, the better. Allow about 15 minutes.

10. Ask each group to share examples in a round-robin fashion. Prepare to share with the entire group one specific example that shows people what Model the Way looks like.

Variations

- As a post-activity, all the examples can be gathered together and published as a booklet of "Living the Mission Examples," which could be given to every new employee.

- Encourage as a follow-up that every team meeting include an agenda item entitled Modeling Our Values, where employees are encouraged to share actual examples with one another.

Cher Holton, Ph.D., combines the skills of speaker, trainer, consultant, and group facilitator in one dynamic bundle of energy. Most often requested for her Retreat Forward™ Team Building programs, her unique interactive keynotes, and her Presenting with Pizzazz workshops, Cher is a prolific author and is one of a small number of professionals world-wide who has attained both the Certified Speaking Professional and Certified Management Consultant designations.

Cher Holton, Ph.D.
The Holton Consulting Group, Inc.
1405 Autumn Ridge Drive
Durham, NC 27712
   Phone: (919) 767-9620
   Email: cher@holtonconsulting.com
   Website: www.holtonconsulting.com *and*
   www.presentingwithpizzazz.com

A LEADERSHIP POINT OF VIEW

Submitted by Edith Katz

Objectives

- To hear/see/experience a key leader share his or her leadership beliefs and vision.
- To relate the experience to the future leader's needs.

Audience

Ten to twenty-five participants.

Time Required

45 to 60 minutes.

Materials and Equipment

- None.

Area Setup

Ideally, participants will be sitting at a conference table or in a U-shaped configuration with the leader sitting at the table with them.

Process

1. Invite a key leader to address your group and to share his or her leadership point of view. Tell the leader that he or she should plan to speak for 10 minutes and be prepared to answer questions from the group following his or her presentation. Provide some questions for him/her to consider in preparation.

2. These questions could include:
   - Who were the most influential leaders in your life?
   - What did you learn from each of them about leadership?
   - How did they shape your point of view? How did they influence your values?
   - What do you want to accomplish at this organization?
   - What's your vision? Can you describe what you would see happening once your vision has been accomplished?
   - If we filmed your vision, what would the movie be about?
   - What are your core values?
   - How do your core values influence your vision?
   - What are some ways you'd like to see your values applied in our work setting?
   - What advice would you give to all potential leaders?

3. Introduce the leader to your group. Take notes while he or she is speaking so that you can synthesize and provide a summary to the participants as a guide for future discussions.

4. Open the floor for questions and discussion after the leader finishes.

5. After the leader leaves the room, you may wish to help participants relate the experience to themselves:
   - What message most resonated with you?
   - What did you learn about values and vision?
   - How did the leader's words affect your thinking?
   - What do you need to do to prepare yourself as a future leader?

Edith Katz is the manager of employee development at Brooks Health System, where she facilitates an eleven-part Leadership Challenge series. The series includes a lab session the week after each practice has been introduced. In the lab session, each participant presents his or her application assignment to the class and a discussion is opened to provide feedback, ideas, and suggestions. This active learning component helps participants to apply the knowledge to their real-life work challenges and allows participants to learn from others as well.

Edith Katz
Brooks Health System
3901 University Boulevard South, Suite 103
Jacksonville, FL 32216
    Phone: (904) 858-7334
    Email: edith.katz@brookshealth.org

IT'S ALL IN A NAME

Submitted by Jan Miller and Denise Knight

Objective

- To clarify personal values by sharing descriptive words and beliefs.

Audience

Five to fifty participants.

Time Required

20 to 30 minutes (could be longer with a very large group).

Materials and Equipment

- A sheet of flip-chart paper for each participant.
- A marker for each participant.

Area Setup

Any arrangement as long as everyone involved can see each participant's poster (it works best if participants are sitting in a circle).

Process

1. Ask participants to create a "name acronym." Have each person write his or her name down the left side of the chart paper.

2. Have each participant write a word or adjective that begins with each letter in his or her name to describe his or her personal beliefs. For example, John may look something like:

    J—Jolly
    O—Over-achiever

H—Hard working

N—Never ending

3. Ask each participant to share his or her name acronym.

4. Summarize with these questions:

- What does each name acronym say about individual's shared beliefs and values?
- How helpful was this exercise to you in beginning to clarify your values?

Jan Miller, Ed.D., currently serves as an assistant professor at the University of West Alabama in the College of Education–Instructional Leadership Department. She has twenty-two years of public school experience in the state of Mississippi. During those years, Jan has taught numerous grade levels, served as a lead teacher, and supervised two schools as principal. She earned a B.S. degree in elementary education from Livingston University, an M.Ed. in elementary education from Livingston University, an Ed.S. in elementary education from Mississippi State University, and an Ed.D. in educational leadership from NOVA Southeastern University.

Denise Knight, Ed.D., currently serves as an assistant professor at the University of West Alabama in the College of Education. She has twenty-three years of public school experience in the state of Mississippi. Denise has taught numerous grade levels, taught talented and gifted, served as a district-wide director of federal programs and elementary curriculum, and served as an elementary principal. She earned a B.S. degree in elementary education from Mississippi State University, an M.Ed. in elementary education from Livingston University, an M.Ed. in school administration from the University of West Alabama, an Ed.S. in curriculum and instruction from Mississippi State University, and an Ed.D. in educational leadership from NOVA Southeastern University.

Jan Miller, Ed.D.
University of West Alabama
Station #34
Livingston, Alabama 35470
   Phone: (205) 652-3445
   Email: jmiller@uwa.edu

Denise Knight, Ed.D.
University of West Alabama
Station #34
Livingston, Alabama 35470
   Phone: (205) 652-3801
   Email: dknight@uwa.edu

LEADERSHIP IN CONTEXT

Submitted by Mohandas Nair

Objectives

- To understand that different situations call for different strategies to exercise leadership.
- To obtain different perceptions on what contextual leadership means to different people and groups.
- To contemplate one's own leadership behavior when called upon to act in particular situations.

Audience

A maximum of five groups with three to four participants each. Participants must be in leadership positions or in line for a leadership position.

Time Required

About 3 hours for a group with four or five teams.

Material and Equipment

- A copy of the Leadership in Context lecturette for the facilitator.
- A Situation Sheet, cut apart so that each situation is on a separate slip of paper.
- Flip chart or whiteboard with markers.
- Note pads and pencils.
- Flip-chart paper for each group.
- Masking tape.

Area Setup

Large room with plenty of light and space for a maximum of five discussion teams and the ability to hang charts on the wall.

Process

1. Arrange participants into groups of three or four participants each.

2. Use the lecturette, Leadership in Context, to lead a discussion on the impact of the context on leadership behavior in groups.

3. Lead a discussion on the fundamental concepts underlying the Five Practices of Exemplary Leadership® as propounded by Jim Kouzes and Barry Posner. Emphasize that Model the Way is critical. A leader must consistently align his or her values with actions.

4. Provide a different situation from the cut up Situation Sheet to each group. Ask each group to prepare a brief story line around the situation. Ask each group to identify value concerns that are important to consider in its situation. Have each group list the details of its situation on a flip-chart page and hang it on the wall. Allow 10 to 15 minutes.

5. Have the first group present its situation to the remaining groups. Take questions as needed.

6. Have the entire group discuss and prepare a leadership strategy for handling the specific situation. Ask the group to identify the impact the leader's values would have on the situation. Allow about 15 minutes.

7. Move to the next group's situation. Continue to repeat the process with each situation.

8. Lead a general discussion on what was learned regarding leading in a specific context. Use these questions to summarize:
   - How do a leader's values impact decision making?
   - Does having a clear set of values make a leader's job easier or harder? Why?
   - What are you taking back to the workplace to implement?

Variation

- Instead of providing situations, request that participants use actual examples from their own lives to obtain useful feedback to take back to the workplace.

Mohandas Nair is a management educator, teacher, trainer, writer, and a facilitator of learning. He earned a B.Tech. (Mech.) from IIT Kharagpur, India. He has a diploma in training and development and has over thirty years of experience in industry and consultancy in the fields of industrial engineering and human resource development. He has published two books, written numerous articles, and facilitated many management development programs.

Mohandas Nair
A2 Kamdar Building
607, Gokhale Road (South)
Dadar, Mumbai 400 028
India
   Phone: 91 22 24226307; 09820935427
   Email: nair_mohandas@hotmail.com; mknair@vsnl.net

LEADERSHIP IN CONTEXT LECTURETTE

Leadership is a moving target. It varies with the individual being led and the situation. Many other factors impact it, too. The most important element, of course, is the follower. Even though leadership often involves a group of people, each individual in the group has specific expectations from the leader and will give the effort commensurate with the perception of the support provided by the leader.

The next most important element is the context in which the leadership process works. Different situations may call for different strategies. A leader who has worked in a specific situation may have a better chance to be effective in employing the strategy. The leader will have to understand the context first and use the support of his or her followers and associates to dig deep into the situation. Once the situation is understood, a leader and followers can work together to look for solutions.

Underlying all of this, no matter who the follower or what the situation, a leader must set the example by aligning actions with his or her values.

The Leadership Challenge Activities Book
Copyright © 2010 by James M. Kouzes and Barry Z. Posner.
Reproduced by permission of Pfeiffer, an Imprint of Wiley. www.pfeiffer.com.

SITUATION SHEET

1. A major order is cancelled overseas, either before the goods are shipped or after they were received by the customer (take your choice).

2. Plan for setting up a new greenfield project in a remote location.

3. A smaller company has been taken over. There is a need to install someone to run the new organization. The company is operating within your country or overseas (take your choice).

4. A major recession has hit. The company's products are not being purchased today; however, there are good prospects for the product in the future.

5. The organization is working on a cutting-edge technology to wipe out the current competitors' products in the market.

6. Merger with another company of the same size.

CULTURAL ARTIFACTS

Submitted by Anne Reilly and Homer Johnson

Objectives

- To understand the concept of culture, both organizational and national, and why it is important.
- To discuss the aspects of culture, such as values, beliefs, and ideas, that are intangible but may be reflected in tangible objects.
- To recognize personal underlying values and assumptions and how they are reflected in daily life.

Audience

Any.

Time Required

30 to 60 minutes, depending on how many participants and the activity format chosen.

Materials and Equipment

- Paper and pens.
- Board or flip chart with writing materials.
- Access to photocopier if matching list option is chosen.

Area Setup

Workplace with tables and room for small group work.

Process

1. Begin the session by talking about the concept of culture as the underlying values, norms, beliefs, and ideas that hold an

organization, a company, or a country together. Explain that some people call organizational culture the "personality" of the organization. Like an individual's personality, culture is hard to change, and it is also hard to define or describe. Indeed, many organizational change scholars argue that because organizational culture is so elusive and intangible, it is especially difficult to describe, manage, and change. Spend some time listing values of a particular country or organization, such as individualist versus collectivist; competitive versus cooperative; bureaucratic versus flexible; risk-taking versus risk-avoiding. How are these values reflected in behavior within firms or nations?

2. State that people learn about a culture through stories, language, and rituals, ranging from fairy tales to business jargon to company conventions. On another level, people may also learn about a culture through its symbols. A common metaphor used to describe culture is the "iceberg," in that key dimensions of the culture are found both above the surface (visible) and below the surface (invisible, yet still very important). Thus, some of the culture's values and beliefs may be easily observable, for example, a written, conservative dress code, but other cultural values and beliefs found below the surface must be interpreted based on other signals, for example, the presence or absence of personal photographs on office desks. (You could draw a simple iceberg on the board or flip chart and ask participants to identify some reflections of culture that are easily visible, *above the surface*, and others that must be sought more carefully, thus *below the surface*).

3. One way to describe the culture of the organization—in particular, the elements that may be found below the surface—is to use

concrete and tangible objects and to explain how these objects represent that culture. These objects are called "cultural artifacts," a concept that comes from anthropology. Such artifacts are visible, but they need interpretation to figure out what values, beliefs, or ideas they represent. In some ways, this process is similar to detective work, in which the meaning of tangible clues must be deciphered and linked to other relevant information. Provide some examples of cultural artifacts for organizations, professions, or countries, such as a company's logo, a doctor's stethoscope, or a nation's flag, and discuss them. What do these artifacts represent? (The artifacts may be considered visible clues about the invisible culture of the firm, the profession, or the nation). Here are some sample cultural artifacts drawn from prior experience with this activity:

- My father's pocket watch
- The company's ID card
- The cross on a steeple
- My first design patent
- My grandmother's ring
- An honorary U.S. flag
- A telescope
- Two small gray stones

4. Turn the activity over to the participants with the following directions: "Think about your personal life or your professional life, and choose one tangible object—a *cultural artifact*—that is symbolic of yourself or of your organization. Be very specific and try to convey your unique personality or your organization's culture, through this cultural artifact. This object is something that should reflect characteristics, interests, values, or beliefs that are

really important to you or your company." Emphasize that "We'll assume we all could use photos of our families to reflect how important they are to us. This assignment asks for a tangible object or item other than a family photo." Many participants will be able to come up with multiple cultural artifacts; tell them they must limit the discussion to one per participant.

5. Give the participants 5 to 10 minutes to think of artifacts and to write down a few sentences describing the artifacts and what they represent. They should be able to explain why their chosen artifacts are important to them and why they believe the visible object above the surface reflects the invisible personal or cultural dimensions below the iceberg. Ask:

- Why do these objects represent you and/or your organization's culture?
- What specific values do the artifacts convey?
  Here are two examples of participant descriptions from prior sessions. You may share one of these or use an example of your own.
- A blank sheet of paper. This artifact represents two things that are very important: a passion for writing and a desire to constantly learn new things. A blank sheet of paper can become anything: a poem, a love letter, the first few paragraphs of a Pulitzer Prize–winning article, a doodle, notes for an exam or a grocery list—each one a very important item to the person who creates it. A blank sheet of paper is an essential tool for teaching, learning, and communicating.
- My personal artifact is a model of a 1960s-era GMC bus used by Metro Transit. It sits on a bookshelf next to my desk at home. It is a fitting symbol of both my personal and

professional life, as my family's business has been a bus-part manufacturer and supplier for forty-eight years. The bus represents the era in which my grandfather started the business and it also reminds me of the passion for the industry my father had, while suggesting the changes we'll have to make to remain in business for another forty-eight years.

6. Depending on the time available, the number of participants, and the session format, the debriefing process can be implemented in one of several ways:
   - You may collect the participants' descriptions and share them anonymously for discussion. Comparisons can be made as to artifacts chosen, values represented, and personal versus professional objects chosen.
   - You may have participants form small teams to share their artifacts. Allow 2 to 3 minutes for each to share his or her artifacts.

7. Debrief using these questions:
   - What values were brought forward most often?
   - Were there more personal artifacts or more professional artifacts selected?
   - Why are personal values important?
   - How do espoused values (what the organization says it does) differ from values in use (what the organization actually does)?

8. Close the activity by linking the insights developed from the activity to the concept of culture and its role in organizations and nations. The following discussion questions may be helpful:
   - Now that you know what to look for, how will you use this activity to help you decipher and assess the invisible dimensions of the cultures in which you live and work?

(Possible responses: understand how values below the surface may be as important as those visible above; be more aware of the importance of symbols.)

- People may draw different conclusions from the same cultural artifact. What other sources of information can you use to better understand the hidden dimensions of a firm or country's culture? (Possible responses: look for other symbols, compare artifacts across firms, industries.)
- (Particularly relevant if participants are from the same culture): Why do people interpret culture differently?
- What happens if values are in conflict or if personal values conflict with organizational values? (Possible responses: individual differences in perception and interpretation lead to differences in shared meaning; values conflict may be manageable in the short-run but must be addressed for long-term cultural stability; groups may "secede" from the main culture and form subcultures in the event of serious values conflict.)
- Why is culture important?
- Many people argue that culture drives commitment to a firm or a country. What examples can you provide that would support that idea? (Possible responses: culture linked to shared commitment; a strong culture can reinforce values; culture helps predict how people within the culture will act.)

Variations

- If a continuing activity is possible, and if the participants are willing to "go public" with their artifacts, ask the participants to bring in the artifacts, to share the actual tangible objects. Photographs of the objects may also be used. This version of the activity can be very interesting with international participants. For example, a Japanese student brought in a sample of "furoshiki," which is Japanese wrapping cloth. She explained how the use of the cloth has changed as Japan has become more Westernized, yet she still uses it for packing her suitcase, as well as a reminder of home. This one example provided the opportunity to talk about many types of values found below the surface, using a simple piece of cloth.

- The activity can also be extended by having the facilitator collect the papers, then prepare a sheet that lists (separately) the artifacts and the participants in the session (see example). Then allow people time to match participants with the artifacts. This extension works best if the participants know something about each other beforehand and, as above, the participants must be comfortable sharing their individual artifacts and the underlying meanings with the whole group or in smaller groups.

Example: Match the Participant with the Cultural Artifact

Cultural Artifact	**Participants**
Bird—Bald Eagle	Amy A.
Book about adoption	Bob B.
Camera	Claudine C.
Company logo	Dan D.

Anne Reilly, Ph.D., is a professor of management in the Graduate School of Business at Loyola University Chicago. Her research interests are organizational change, gender and career issues, and teaching development; she has published extensively on these topics for both academic and managerial journals.

Homer Johnson, Ph.D., is a professor in the Department of Management, School of Business Administration, at Loyola University

Chicago, where he teaches courses on values-based leadership, often using the Leadership Challenge materials. He is a frequent contributor to the Pfeiffer *Annuals* and is the co-author (with Linda Stroh) of the recent best-selling book on consulting skills titled *Basic Principles of Effective Consulting* (Lawrence Erlbaum Associates, 2005).

Anne H. Reilly, Ph.D.
Department of Management
Loyola University Chicago
820 North Michigan Avenue
Chicago, IL 60611
   Email: areilly@luc.edu.

Homer H. Johnson, Ph.D.
Department of Management
Loyola University Chicago
820 North Michigan Avenue
Chicago, IL 60611
   Email: hjohnso@luc.edu

SETTING AN EXAMPLE TO MIRROR IS NOT ENOUGH

Submitted by Cheryl L. Rude

Objective

- To help learners appreciate the limitations of only setting an example.

Audience

Two people could do this as well as large groups. You are only limited by the number of mirrors.

Time Required

30 to 40 minutes.

Materials and Equipment

- Long framed mirrors—inexpensive ones sold at discount stores for dorm rooms, backs of closet doors (one per six people).
- Simple coloring book images (one page per person).
- Blue ink pens (one per two people).
- Poster board or card stock cut to 8 ½ by 11–inch size (one per two people).

Area Setup

Learners in small group settings of six around a table with chairs.

Process

1. State that this experience challenges the notion that is unconsciously held by many that, if a leader sets the example

for followers, that is all that is needed for a leadership relationship that results in positive change. Ask how many think this is untrue. Then say, "Let's demonstrate the limitations of simply setting an example."

2. Place participants in groups of six and give each group a mirror. Have three people hold a mirror so the longest side is horizontal on a table with the mirror facing the other three individuals who are seated in front of it. The three people holding the mirror should be behind it.
3. Give the three seated people a coloring book page. Have them place it on the table in front of them. Give them a pen.
4. The individuals who are seated should be able to see the paper by looking directly down and also by looking at it in the mirror.
5. Have the individuals holding the mirror also hold a poster board between the seated individuals' eyes and the paper on the table. The poster board obstructs vision down; thus, the only way for the seated individuals to see the coloring book image now is in the mirror. Tell the drawers to trace the image by looking at it in the mirror. Allow them to trace the image for 5 or 10 minutes.
6. Ask the mirror holders and the drawers to trade places and repeat the process giving the new drawers a clean image. Allow about 10 minutes.
7. Debrief the activity using these questions:
   - Why might a leader believe that simply being a good model is all that's needed?
   - How hard is it to copy a reflection of something? What was difficult about it?
   - When leaders are only setting the example of behavior for followers to mirror, they are asking followers to copy a behavior

Model the Way

without the underlying rationale for that behavior. What are the limitations for leaders who use setting the example as their primary or possibly solitary leadership behavior?

- When have you experienced something similar?
- What does a leader need to do in addition to setting an example?
- What will you do specifically beyond setting an example?

Cheryl L. Rude, Ph.D., an associate professor of leadership studies at Southwestern College, a private four-year liberal arts college in Kansas, has designed an undergraduate-level and master's-level degree program in leadership studies. Both programs provide opportunities for students to deepen their content expertise while at the same time shape their practice of leadership. Developed in collaboration with her students, Cheryl is the primary author of the *Roots to Branches: Children, Youth & Young Adult Leadership Development* curriculum edited by L.W. Morgan.

Cheryl L. Rude, Ph.D.
Southwestern College
100 College Street
Winfield, KS 67156-2499
   Phone: (620) 229-6381
   Email: cheryl.rude@sckans.edu
   Website: www.sckans.edu/leadership

79

ETHICS FOR THE 21ST CENTURY

Submitted by Charlotte S. Waisman and
Linda Bedinger

Objectives

- To acknowledge that ethics grow from your values.
- To affirm that effective leaders Model the Way with their ethics and values.
- To apply a decision-making model for working through ethical issues in a deliberate and thoughtful way so as to prepare participants for real-time ethical dilemmas.
- To understand that ethics are clear-cut standards that are the basis for actions.

Audience

Ten to twenty participants.

Time Required

2 hours.

Materials and Equipment

- Pens and paper.
- Flip charts (pads and easels), one for each small group.
- Markers.
- Masking tape to hang flip-chart pages.
- One copy of the Ethics Discussion Questions for each participant.
- One copy of the Ethics Scenarios for each participant.
- One copy of the Ethics Decision Worksheet for each participant.

- *(Optional)* One copy of the Ethics Pre-Work Assignment to complete before the session.

Area Setup

Movable tables and chairs to accommodate three to five participants at each table. One flip-chart easel, pad, and markers for each table. Wall space is required for posting flip-chart sheets.

Process

1. Ask an opening question. "How many in this room are ethical people?" (The expected response is that everyone raises his or her hand.)

2. Make the following comments and ask these rhetorical questions:
   - So at the grocery store, how do you answer "paper or plastic?" Or do you bring re-usable bags? Do you see this as an "ethical" decision? Why or why not?
   - Are all stop signs merely suggestions? Have you sometimes driven faster than the posted speed limit when you knew no police officer would be present? Is this an ethical decision? Why or why not? Is this a decision based on your values? Why or why not? How is your leadership affected, if in any way, by decisions made when no one is watching?
   - What messages do we send our children when we root for the football team who should have a penalty to quickly get off the next play so that we can win? What is ethical about this behavior?
   - What was considered ethical ten or fifteen years ago that we no longer worry about?
   Allow for discussion or comments if they arise.

3. Divide participants into small groups of three to five and distribute the Ethical Discussion Questions handout. Allow 25 minutes for small group discussions. Bring the participants back together as a whole and allow each small group up to 3 minutes to share their biggest "aha" from their small group discussion.

4. Discuss the moral dilemma of a society that condones, and in fact encourages, ideas and work that may not be truthful. Refer back to the opening discussion and use for an example a sports call by a referee that is vigorously denied by the offending player, despite instant replay. Another example might be pleading down a speeding ticket. (Add examples from your own life experiences.)

5. Continue relating the discussion back to the ethics definitions that have surfaced as a result of the discussion in Step 3. Then raise the issue—How it is that seemingly reasonable people find themselves in a work environment in which decisions are made that are so far from reality and do danger to our society? (Examples: Enron, Qwest and Joe Nacchio, Bernie Madoff, the current mortgage crisis, or any issue that is timely.) Ask how is it that people process and rationalize what they do or do not do and where they draw the line? What are their values? How are they modeling the way as leaders?

   Possible answers:
   • Ethics Creep—How we reconcile what is considered moral and ethical today versus five, ten, or twenty years ago.
   • Activity is within bounds and not really "illegal."
   • Self-interest versus corporate interest.
   • Safe because no one will ever know.
   • Group think.

- Because the outcome is good, the company will condone and protect.
- Lure of the stock price.
- Arrogance.

6. How do you prevent this kind of thing from happening? What is the antidote? Possible answers include:
   - How taking deliberate action can help.
   - Why avoiding group think is important.
   - Talking about various dilemmas and situations with others in order to fully consider alternatives and perspectives.
   - How using one's values can help one to focus on ethical decisions.
   - How important it is as a leader to step in and step up to point out when ethical dilemmas are ignored, when no one has the courage to ask the question (Model the Way by pointing out the issue).

7. Divide the participants into three subgroups and give each the Ethics Scenarios (there are four scenarios—you may use all of them or those that seem particularly relevant for your group) for discussion. Allow 10 minutes for small group discussion and 10 minutes for the total summary discussion.

8. *Note:* If no pre-work has been completed before the session, adjust your instructions to accommodate this. Review the Ethics Decision Worksheet. Ask each person to work privately on an ethical dilemma/issue he or she brought from work (see Ethics Pre-Work) using the Decision Worksheet. After 10 minutes of individual work, ask participants to find someone in the room they have not worked with during the session. Tell them to share both of their ethical dilemmas and discuss possible solutions.

The focus should include how their decisions would show them how to Model the Way as leaders. Allow about 10 minutes to work individually and 15 to 20 minutes to work in pairs.

9. Close the activity by asking:
   - How valuable were your discussions?
   - What have you learned today about the three concepts we have been dealing with: values, ethics, and modeling the way?
   - How are you, as a leader, going to change your current behavior as a result of our discussion?

Variation

- This activity could also be used in the Enable Others to Act section as a way to strengthen people's understanding of themselves and of their colleagues.

Charlotte S. Waisman, Ph.D., is a hands-on trainer/coach/leader and team motivator. Her extensive work history includes both training and human resource positions. She is currently a principal with the AthenA Group LLC, a consulting firm that leads large scale organizational, leadership, and cultural changes. Charlotte has a doctorate from the School of Communications at Northwestern University in Evanston, Illinois. She has published three books, including *Her Story: A Timeline of the Women Who Changed America* (HarperCollins, 2008). Her background also includes fourteen years as a tenured professor.

Linda Bedinger is the owner of Bedinger and Associates, a coaching, consulting, and training organization. She is chair of the Women's Vision Foundation Leadership Institute and also on the board. Emotional intelligence, leadership and diversity management, creativity and innovation are among the topics she trains. Linda served as the president and CEO of several banks: Wells Fargo, Norwest, and United Banks. Involved in acquisitions and mergers, she helped those acquired adapt to the newly formed organization culture.

Charlotte S. Waisman, Ph.D.
The AthenA Group, LLC
Women's Vision Leadership Institute
30334 Inverness Lane
Evergreen, CO 80439
　Phone: (303) 674-2345
　Email: charlotte@herstoryatimelline.com

Linda Bedinger
Bedinger and Associates
9296 East Evans Place
Denver, CO 80231
　Phone: (303) 745-7520
　Email: bedingerassoc@comcast.net
　Website: www.womensvision.org

ETHICS DISCUSSION QUESTIONS

1. What are ethics? Where do ethics come from?

2. What is the relationship between ethics and values?

3. What is ethical behavior? Provide at least one example.

4. Can ethics ever be dealt with using the phrase "good enough"? Why or why not?

5. How do your ethics and values influence how you Model the Way?

6. Are ethics and morals the same things? Which word is more emotionally charged? Why?

7. Why do leaders need to understand ethics and values? How do these affect a leader's behavior?

8. What place does "ethical or moral relativism" have in a corporation (relativism: meaningful only in relationship, relative rather than absolute)?

9. Does "whistle blowing" violate company loyalty? Why or why not?

10. Can an individual's personal virtue survive corporate pressures? Explain.

11. Should corporations adopt policies of corporate social responsibility?

ETHICS SCENARIOS

A

James, a young African-American male who recently graduated from college with honors, has joined a prominent consulting firm within the last month. He is an entry-level associate who is enthusiastic and highly motivated.

The buzz around the office is that an exciting new client is to be pitched; the opportunity for a large piece of business is possible. This project could mean significant revenues for several years; careers can be made from success with this venture.

James takes a call from one of the partners of the firm. The partner invites James to be on the team who will be making the presentation to the client in three weeks. This is a plum assignment. James is told that if the bid is accepted he will have a significant client-facing role in this project. James is surprised because he has not been involved in any work for this client. He speaks to his mentor, a partner in a different division, who explains to James that the CIO in the prospective company is an African-American man.

How do you proceed if you are James?

B

A young female professor with her Ph.D. securely in tow joins the teaching staff of one of the more prestigious colleges in her part of the country. She is enjoying her role and her students and is settling in nicely to the routine of a college professor. She has been invited back to teach for a second year and told that she is working her way toward tenure and the college is pleased with her contribution.

As the first year of teaching draws to a close, she is invited by the college president to address the graduating class, a distinctive honor. She is a little uncomfortable, as this is not something that is normally done; it is rare to have an untenured professor in this role at graduation.

As she mulls things over, she becomes suspicious that the reason she is being asked has to do with her gender; everyone else making an address at graduation is male. She decides to ask the president about his choice and, after hemming and hawing, he admits that he really wants a woman in this role. She asks whether she may address the issue in her remarks at graduation and the president declines; she can either make the address or not, but she may not bring up the issue of how or why she was chosen.

How would you go about making the decision to speak or not and why?

C

You are an experienced pharmaceutical sales representative for a major firm. You have been very successful in selling a major new drug that was released within the last year for the treatment of depression. Lately others in your company have been hinting that this drug is very effective in the treatment of weight loss, which is an unapproved use.

You note that sales of this particular drug are starting to be a very significant percentage of your overall sales. You are aware that the law forbids use or promotion of the drug for unapproved uses. You are also aware that the sales for this product are being used to treat unapproved uses.

You mention this to one of your fellow sales reps, who responds that his sales are of a similar makeup and he is really doing well. You and your fellow sales rep have just received special recognition and bonuses for your sales of the company's new drug.

You decide to better understand what the side-effects are for unapproved uses and you find them to be riskier and more prevalent than the public knows.

How do you proceed and why?

D

You are involved in a cross-functional team providing information to a due diligence team; your company is being acquired.

It comes to your attention that some numbers that have been put forth about the financial condition of your company to the acquirer are incorrect. An honest mistake has been made and you are currently the only person who knows of the error. As you investigate further you find out that, while the mistake is an honest one, the difference to the acquirer is substantial.

The due diligence effort has been completed and plans have been made for the closing and the celebrations, set for four weeks from now. The integration team members are meeting in earnest.

How do you proceed and why?

ETHICS DECISION WORKSHEET

1. Clearly state the ethical dilemma.

2. Detail the desired outcome.

3. Outline your intentions.

4. Weigh the importance of the decision. What purpose(s) will be achieved (absolutely needed, very important, important, desirable, worthwhile, etc.)?

5. Connect the outcome of this decision to your values. Explain how this decision involves: Principle? Shared value? Personal value?

6. Connect the outcome of this decision to leadership; how will you Model the Way?

7. Measure the risks of making this decision. What are the costs? What are the benefits? Be as specific as possible.

8. Describe who will be affected and how they will be affected.

9. Identify any allies who can be approached to discuss the decision and its implications.

10. What are your alternatives to this action?

11. What are your contingency plans? Briefly evaluate their usefulness in this instance.

ETHICS PRE-WORK ASSIGNMENT

Instructions: Write your answers to the questions below and be prepared to discuss and use your ideas in the session.

- Identify three to five personal ethical standards you live by.

- Revisit your values to help you make your ethical standards list.

- Identify any written or unwritten standards your company lives by.

- Identify a time at work when you felt that your ethical standard or ethical position was either threatened or required compromise.

- Reflect on and be prepared to discuss what you are reading about ethics in the news.

- Reflect on and be prepared to discuss the role ethics plays in leadership.

MODEL BEHAVIOR

Submitted by Devora Zack

Objectives

- For leaders to determine key elements of Model the Way.
- To consider vital leadership components from a new perspective.

Audience

Four to one hundred (on teams with two to ten participants each).

Time Required

45 to 60 minutes (more time may be required for larger groups)

Materials and Equipment

- Diverse sets of Lego® pieces (enough for each team to build a structure) covered by a sheet or cloth on each table.
- An easel with large flip-chart paper and markers for each team.

Area Setup

One table per team, each equipped with a large pile of Lego pieces initially hidden from view. The activity works best when a variety of diverse pieces are scattered among the traditional Lego blocks (windows, doors, trees, people, wheels, and others).

Process

1. Introduce the activity by stating the objectives. Ask participants to avoid touching the materials on the table or peeking under the covering. Ask each team to discuss how to best Model the Way for

94

others for 5 to 10 minutes. Ask them to summarize their ideas on an easel close to their table.

2. Invite the teams to lift up the sheets in the middle of their tables, revealing the large pile of Lego pieces. With everyone's involvement, ask teams to build a model of leadership using the Legos provided. Teams may ask whether they can share or trade Legos with other teams. The answer is yes; however, do not offer this information without being asked. Allow about 10 minutes.

3. Ask the teams to display their models to the whole group, pointing out elements that exemplify their leadership values. For example, groups may build symbolic structures such as bridges (connecting departments), rainbows (diversity), windows (open to new ideas), stairways (striving to excel), books (continual learning), one figure leading another (modeling the way), and so forth. Encourage groups to notice common and unique elements among the different models.

4. Have participants return to team discussions. Ask each team to make a list of three key methods to best Model the Way referring to their symbolic Lego model. Allow 10 minutes.

5. Ask the teams to share with the entire group one key aspect of their discussion. Discuss lessons learned and how these can be applied at the workplace. You may also lead a discussion about the process of this activity, including any observations such as whether groups coveted and/or shared pieces with other tables, if there was discussion of "fairness" (since resources vary from table to table) and how this was handled, and the benefit of moving from the symbolic to the literal rather than the other way around.

Devora Zack, president of Only Connect Consulting (OOC), provides leadership development, coaching, team training, and assessments to more than seventy-five clients, including Deloitte, America Online, the U.S. Patent & Trademark office, OPM, Enterprise, and the U.S. Treasury. Devora has been faculty for Cornell's leadership program for thirteen years. Devora holds an M.B.A. from Cornell University and a B.A. from the University of Pennsylvania. Her certifications include MBTI and Neuro-Linguistic Programming. She is a member of Phi Beta Kappa, Mensa, and ASTD. Her designs are featured in five publications. OCC is the recipient of USDA's Woman-Owned Business of the Year.

Devora Zack
Only Connect Consulting, Inc.
7806 Ivymount Terrace
Potomac, MD 20854
  Phone: (301) 765-6262
  Email: dzack@onlyconnectconsulting.com
  Website: www.onlyconnectconsulting.com

CHAPTER FOUR: INSPIRE A SHARED VISION

In This Chapter

- Give an overview of Inspire a Shared Vision.
- Discuss the corresponding Commitments of Leadership.
- Consider the importance of this practice.
- Introduce the activities for this practice.
- Present the activities for this practice.

The Leadership Challenge explains how leaders build on the foundation of values to create an exciting, worthwhile, and shared image of the future.

A vision paints the picture of the preferred future. It creates urgency and draws people in. Only if you have a vision of the future can you create that future. Employees who have a vision guiding them have a reason to take action.

Visions live in people, not on the paper on which they are written. They appeal to the heart as well as the brain. A good vision must offer employees something better than they currently have.

HOW DOES A LEADER INSPIRE A SHARED VISION?

How do leaders create a vision and how do they inspire others to sign up for it? By now Stephen Covey's concept of "starting with the end in mind" is accepted as common sense. Yet that common sense isn't all so common to all leaders. Exemplary leaders, on the other hand, are aware of this important role.

Consider the related Commitments of Leadership, the behaviors that lead to a shared vision:

- Envision the future by imagining exciting and ennobling possibilities.
- Enlist others in a common vision by appealing to shared aspirations.

Envision the Future

Look to the past and the present before you create the future. There are lessons to learn that enable you to create the right vision. Ensure that it is flexible enough to adapt to the changing environment.

When creating a vision, a leader should look for hot, passionate words, words that inspire, motivate, and encourage hope for a better future. A leader's vision should stir people to become involved; that occurs when the leader identifies a common purpose. A common purpose provides a rationale that makes sense for everyone, not just the leader. A leader's vision should arouse people to act; that occurs when the leader determines what is meaningful to others.

Enlist Others

A leader may have the utmost compelling vision, but if it doesn't become everyone's compelling vision, it will languish and not accomplish its intended goal. A vision is much more than impressive words on paper; a vision gives people a higher state to aspire to.

Leaders need to involve people right from the start. The more people who are involved in the creation, the more support you will have.

Ensure that the vision is easy to communicate. A picture is worth a thousand words so why not paint a picture or create a graphic that clarifies the vision. A leader can paint the vision in other ways as well by talking about it with the help of examples or analogies. Whatever the vision, making it easy to communicate makes it easier to enlist others.

Communicate the vision in various ways. Repetition is important. People will not get tired of hearing a compelling vision—especially if they feel a part of it. A leader should make the communication two-way. Just as leaders encourage feedback, listen to input, and reflect on what they learn about values, they must do the same with a vision.

A good vision comes from the head and the heart. Of course, a leader's vision needs to be something that accomplishes the common good. It also needs to be passionately authentic; it needs to come from the heart. The authors of *The Leadership Challenge* extol leaders to "breathe life into your vision," stating that a memorable vision must be evocative, even provocative.

WHY IT IS IMPORTANT TO INSPIRE A SHARED VISION

Inspiring a shared vision produces a number of secondary actions. You will find that when everyone is working toward a shared vision, productivity increases. A shared vision enhances communication and builds relationships across departments. A shared vision helps organizations reach goals faster with less frustration.

ACTIVITY INTRODUCTION

The sixteen activities in this section are a testimony to how important those embracing the Kouzes/Posner framework believe it is to Inspire a Shared Vision. This section had the most submissions from which to choose of all the sections. In addition, this practice seems to be the best understood and most clearly defined, as compared to the other four. However, in actual practice, Inspiring a Shared Vision—in the normative Leadership Practices diversity database—ranks as the least frequently used of The Five Practices.

The activities address establishing a vision and encouraging commitment from several angles. Some contributors wrote from the pure sense of establishing an overarching, organizational vision. Others approached the task from a change management perspective.

Some of the contributions provide practical advice to show how ideals can help transform a vision into a reality, to practice the mechanics of sharing a vision, and to practice developing a shared vision.

Several of the contributions address helping leaders envision the future and projecting success from a personal, team, and organizational perspective. Many of the activities can be used in a variety of ways and with various groups.

Activity List

- Inspiration Becomes a Reality by Jean Barbazette
- Inspiring a Shared Vision Mingle by Daren Blonski
- Show Me the Mission by Angie Chaplin
- Ensuring Sponsor Commitment to Change by Daryl R. Conner
- Can You Picture This? by Timothy Ewest
- Extra! Extra! Read All About It! by Leonard D. Goodstein
- Another Leader's Dream by Donna Goss and Don Robertson
- What Does Success Look Like? by Amanda Crowell Itliong
- Blindfold Square by Jean Lee
- The Perfect Place—Heaven on Earth by Jan Miller and Denise Knight
- Modeling the Future by Linda S. Eck Mills
- Defining a Vision That Others Will Follow by Nanette Miner and Lynn Little
- The Spiritual Leader by Mohandas Nair
- Define Your Values Through a Vision Statement by Steve A. Rainey
- Lights, Camera, Action! by Devora Zack
- Claiming a Breakthrough by Sherene Zolno

INSPIRATION BECOMES A REALITY

Submitted by Jean Barbazette

Objectives

- To identify how a common purpose helps achieve a positive outcome.
- To identify how common ideals can help transform a vision into a reality.

Audience

Small groups of four or five leaders.

Time Required

45 to 60 minutes.

Materials and Equipment

- Inspire a Shared Vision handout for each participant.
- Flip-chart paper and markers.
- Facilitator notes for facilitator.
- Pens or pencils.

Area Setup

Round tables of four or five people for each small group.

Process

1. Provide the Inspire a Shared Vision handout and pens or pencils to all participants. Tell them to take 10 minutes to read it individually and make notes.

2. Assign participants to work in small groups of four or five. Tell them to take 15 minutes to discuss their responses and to identify what they might do.

3. Ask each group to select a spokesperson to report the group's answers. After participants have had an opportunity to share their responses, wrap up with the following questions:
   - What factors ought to be in place for a leader to find a common purpose and share common ideals?
   - How do you work with your team to inspire a shared vision?
   - How do common ideals help transform a vision into a reality?
   - How can you develop better methods to find a common purpose and appeal to common ideals?
   - How can you animate the vision?
   - How will you develop your team so they can decide when inspiring a shared vision would make sense?

Jean Barbazette, M.A., is president of The Training Clinic, a training consulting firm she founded in 1977; she specializes in train-the-trainer, new employee orientation, and enhancing the quality of training and instruction for major national and international clients. She holds a master's degree in education from Stanford University. Published works include *Successful New Employee Orientation* (3rd ed.) (Pfeiffer, 2007) and *The Trainer's Support Handbook* (McGraw-Hill, 2001). Other books published by Pfeiffer include: *Instant Case Studies* (2003), *The Trainer's Journey to Competence: Tools, Assessments, and Models* (2005), *Training Needs Assessment* (2006), *The Art of Great Training Delivery* (2006), and *Managing the Training Function for Bottom-Line Results* (2008).

Jean Barbazette, M.A.
The Training Clinic
645 Seabreeze Drive
Seal Beach, CA 90740
Phone: (562) 430-2484
  Email: jean@thetrainingclinic.com
  Website: www.thetrainingclinic.com

INSPIRE A SHARED VISION

Your store has been asked by the owner of the chain of stores to develop and evaluate a new computer inventory system on a pilot basis. This would mean that the new system would be worked in a redundant (parallel) manner with the present system. To do this will make your employees' work demanding for at least the next two months. One of the key reasons your store has been approached to accomplish this job is because of your high level of confidence in them, which you have often expressed to the owner.

If your store succeeds, there will probably be significant rewards for your efforts. There is also a fairly high risk of failure, which, while not leading to any penalties, would mean far less in rewards. You and your employees have enjoyed an excellent relationship with mutual trust and respect existing among you. You suspect that this might be tested somewhat because of the demands of running two systems in parallel. However, you strongly feel that the possible benefits outweigh the risks and you want to develop the new system. Your answer is due to the owner by the end of the month.

Instructions: If you were this store manager, think about how you would appropriately lead these employees.

- What are the possible positive outcomes?

- How could you and the employees find a common purpose?

- What are the common ideals you share with these employees?

- How will you animate the vision to make it a reality?

FACILITATOR NOTES

Possible Case Answers

What are the possible positive outcomes?

- The employees and their store will be seen as visionary leaders in the chain.
- A share in the tangible rewards for being the proving ground for the new inventory system.
- An increase in trust and confidence among the employees and the leader.

How could you and the employees find a common purpose?

- Discuss the objectives of the inventory pilot with your employees.
- Discuss the benefits and risks of participating in the pilot.

What are the common ideals you share with these employees?

- Teamwork brings benefits.
- Success depends on the entire team.

How will you animate the vision to make it a reality?

- Discuss how the challenges presented by the pilot may hurt the group and ask the employees for their ideas to meet the challenges.

INSPIRING A SHARED VISION MINGLE

Submitted by Daren Blonski

Objectives

- To help participants practice the mechanics of sharing their visions.
- To give participants a realistic opportunity to receive feedback on their visions.
- To help participants distill their visions to their essence.

Audience

Eighteen to twenty-six participants.

Time Required

50 minutes.

Materials and Equipment

- Each participant's vision.
- Microphone (*optional*).
- Posted flip chart with the following text:
  - Participant A: 60 seconds to share vision.
  - Participant B: 30 seconds to give feedback.
  - Participant B: 60 seconds to share vision.
  - Participant A: 30 seconds to give feedback.
    (seven rotations.)

Area Setup

There should be enough room for participants to move around each other comfortably in the area you will be using. Participants will be standing, so there is no need for any specific setup.

Optional: This is an opportunity to take participants outside.

Process

1. State that in the next few minutes participants are going to share their visions with others in the room. This is an opportunity for them to practice what it feels like to share their visions with others. Say, "Remember, great leadership is created in the moment. Leaders need to be able to share their visions on demand, in the moment, and to have them resonate with those they are sharing them with. Just as Martin Luther King, Jr., had to refine and practice his I Have a Dream speech, you need to refine and practice sharing your vision. Like King's speech, some visions need to be more lengthy and detailed, but in the fast-paced world we live in, 99.9 percent of your interactions as a leader are in the moment; thus, it is important to learn to share your vision in the moment."

2. Say, "You will have a chance to share your vision with seven people. When I tell you, you will pair up with another person in the room. When you meet, each of you will share you vision, taking no longer than 60 seconds each." Show the flip-chart page and review that each participant will receive 30 seconds of feedback after sharing his or her vision. Say, "If you can't share the essence of your vision in 60 seconds, it's likely few people in your organization will remember it. You may use the paper with your notes as a reference, but remember, this is supposed to

convey your passion and conviction around an idea for the future. How compelling is it if you are reading from a page? Look at the person you are speaking with. Use your paper as a safety net only. Your vision needs to come from your heart, and needs to be authentic."

3. Have participants stand and find other participants in the room. Make sure everyone has a partner before you start. (*Note:* It is helpful to have a microphone during this activity because it is hard to get people's attention once they have started talking.) As the participants begin sharing their visions, watch and listen. If you notice participants reading from their papers, urge them to start speaking about their visions from their hearts.

4. Remind participants to give each other feedback on sharing of their visions. How did they feel when they heard the other participant's vision? Was the participant effective in communicating his or her vision? What feedback can you give that would be helpful?

5. After 3 minutes, call time and have them find the next person. Complete seven rounds. Keep people moving, even if they haven't quite finished.

6. Debrief the activity by asking the participants the following questions:
   • What did you learn by sharing your vision?
   • Did any particular vision stand out for you? Why?
   • What did the person do that would inspire others?
   • What skills were used to effectively communicate some of the visions?
   • How does effective communication help inspire?

- What have you learned about inspiring a shared vision that you will use in the future?

Variation

- It is likely that participants may want to refine their visions after sharing with seven people so that others can easily grasp them. Give participants 10 minutes to revisit their visions after the exercise so they can distill and clarify them.

Daren Blonski works with public and private organizations to design and deliver organization development solutions. He is an expert in helping his clients leverage leadership assessment tools to help them increase their leadership effectiveness. He is a facilitator and speaker on leadership development, generational diversity leadership, program design, blended learning solutions, and designing strategic organizational training initiatives. Daren is an active member in numerous professional associations and speaks regularly at conferences for his clients. He is a graduate of the University of California, Davis, where he majored in organizational studies and leadership, and he is also a graduate of the Sacramento Entrepreneurship Academy. He is currently completing his master's degree in organizational psychology at Sonoma State University.

Daren Blonski
Sonoma Leadership Systems
835 Broadway
Sonoma, CA 94576
   Phone: (530) 219-2981
   Email: daren@sonomaleadership.com
   Website: www.sonomaleadership.com

SHOW ME THE MISSION*

Submitted by Angie Chaplin

Objectives

- To inspire a shared vision by selling an organization's mission, vision, values, and services.
- To identify ways to improve the process of Inspiring a Shared Vision.

Audience

Fifteen to twenty-four participants.

Time Required

60 to 75 minutes. (*Note:* more teams will require more time.)

Materials and Equipment

- Flip charts and markers.
- Other materials *(optional)*.

Area Setup

A room large enough to accommodate a table and chairs for each team.

Process

1. Divide participants into three or four teams of five to eight people each. Tell participants they have the chance to create a new nonprofit organization, the start-up funding for which will come

---

*Adapted from "Phictional Philanthropy" in *The Big Book of Leadership Games* by Vasudha K. Deming.

from an anonymous benefactor who has appointed Jim Kouzes and Barry Posner as the trustees.

2. Because Jim and Barry can choose only one organization to fund, the competition is fierce. The benefactors have asked the finalists to prepare 5-minute presentations to pitch their proposed organizations to Jim and Barry, who will base their decision on how well the mission, vision, values, and services align with and demonstrate The Five Practices.

3. Working in teams of five to eight, participants have 30 minutes to prepare 5-minute oral presentations to "pitch" their organization to Jim and Barry and their Trustee Advisory Council. Presentations must include the following:
   - Name of the organization
   - Mission
   - Core values
   - Logo
   - Segment of the population who will benefit (for example, at-risk youth, homeless women, children in foster care, adjudicated delinquents)
   - Specific services delivered by the organization
   - Names of nine well-known leaders or celebrities who will serve as the inaugural board of directors, and why their involvement lends credibility

4. Teams may use flip charts, markers, and additional materials (if supplied) to enhance their presentations.

5. After 30 minutes, ask each team to give a 5-minute presentation. When not presenting, other participants serve as Jim and Barry's advisory council members.

6. At the conclusion of all the presentations, ask for a vote by secret ballot (one may not vote for his or her own group) of which organization should be awarded the funds.

7. Summarize by asking these questions or others:
   • What did some of the teams do that "inspired" you?
   • What have you learned from this exercise?
   • What ideas do you have for changes you might make in how you inspire a shared vision?

Angie Chaplin, M.A., C.P.B.A., is a nationally respected leadership presenter, practitioner, and professor who helps leaders bring out their personal bests. A Leadership Challenge® Certified Master Facilitator, Angie delivers capacity-building programs for nonprofit agencies through Lutheran Services in Iowa's Center for Learning and Leading and educates learning leaders at Seton Hall University's master of arts in strategic communication and leadership program.

Angie Chaplin, M.A., C.P.B.A.
Director, Center for Learning & Leading
Lutheran Services in Iowa
P.O. Box 848
106 16th Street Southwest
Waverly, IA 50677
  Phone: (319) 859-3517
  Cell: (319) 239-0750
  Fax: (319) 352-0773
  Email: angie.chaplin@lsiowa.org
  Website: www.lsiowa.org

ENSURING SPONSOR COMMITMENT TO CHANGE

Submitted by Daryl R. Conner

Objectives

- To determine the level of commitment in a group to a major shift or change.
- To provide a forum for a leader to request what commitment is needed for a successful change to occur.

Audience

Intended for a sponsor of a major, highly disruptive organizational change and his or her direct reports. To ensure an engaged discussion, keep the size of the group between eight and sixteen people. Because the sponsor will ask his or her direct reports for a commitment to the change, it is important that the direct reports have already had the opportunity to understand and emotionally process the nature of the change and its implications.

Time Required

60 to 90 minutes, depending on the size of the group.

Materials and Equipment

- Pens and pads of paper on which participants can write their thoughts.
- This activity is typically a closing exercise at the end of a day or a workshop, so much of the raw material that participants have used throughout the day might be helpful.

Area Setup

Tables and chairs so participants have a surface on which to write. Sufficient space so participants can work in pairs.

Facilitator Notes

- A sponsor is the individual (or group) who has the power to authorize or legitimize the change. Sponsors sanction initiatives through the use of influential communication and meaningful consequences (that is, rewards and punishments).
- If you ask a group outright, "Are you committed?" the answer will often be "yes," but it might be a hollow "yes." By exploring what they need to be committed, you legitimize having some reservation, while at the same time understanding the root of what is needed. In this activity, leaders are explicit about what is needed for individuals to commit to the desired future state. It provides a forum for requesting those needs openly, for receiving direct answers from the *sponsor,* and for asking individuals to commit to the change. It is worth noting that this exercise seems very basic, but it is not a feel-good exercise; it is more cathartic in nature.
- This exercise can be very effective in bringing closure to a significant workshop, design session, or announcement of a major change. It is more effective as a closure exercise to a larger session (or series of working sessions) than as a stand-alone activity.

Process

1. Prior to the activity, prepare the sponsor to play a facilitative role, stressing the importance of direct and explicit dialogue with participants; you will be responsible for recording the actions committed to by the sponsor and the participants.

2. To begin the activity, the sponsor should say to the group, "What do you need in order to be fully committed to this change?"

3. Ask individuals to make lists of primary things they need to commit to the change; for example, an individual might say that he or she needs two more people, needs to be able to delay implementing a particular system, or needs to first implement structural changes in the organization.

4. Pair the participants, asking them to share their lists with partners; this element of the activity provides an opportunity for validation of each individual's needs before sharing with the whole group.

5. In the large group, have each participant address the sponsor by saying: "I can commit to the change if you can meet this request," and then each participant should list his or her requests for the sponsor. They may, of course, commit without additional requests. To each request, the sponsor responds with one of the following three answers:
   - "Yes, I can give you that."
   - "Maybe, but I need to look into it more." (In this case the sponsor should be specific about what needs further consideration or analysis, and when it can be done.)
   - "No, I can't give you that; can you still commit?"

6. If a participant says that he or she doesn't need anything to commit to the change (or as a follow-up question to each of the sponsor's responses above), the sponsor should probe for action by asking, "What is the first thing you will do in support of the change?" The sponsor should not leave any request by a participant on the table. If a participant has requested something, the sponsor must agree to provide it, to research it further, or declare that he or

she is unable to satisfy the request. Regardless of the answer, there is always a call to action. The sponsor has given a definitive answer or agree to research further, and the participant has declared the first thing that he or she will do.

7. In closing the session, look at the needs that have surfaced and see whether any recognizable patterns have emerged. If so, acknowledge the patterns, such as "We appear to have a pattern of resource constraints to deal with." At a minimum, the sponsor should commit to closing the loop on unanswered questions, and close with a call to execute actions to which the sponsor and participants have agreed.

Daryl Conner is an internationally recognized leader in organizational change, a dynamic public speaker, and an advisor to senior executives. In more than thirty-five years of practice, Daryl has worked with successful organizations around the world to help them achieve the full intent of their most critically important initiatives. Daryl has authored two books: *Managing at the Speed of Change* (Random House, 1993) and *Leading at the Edge of Chaos* (John Wiley & Sons, 1998).

Daryl R. Conner
Chairman
Conner Partners
Suite 1000
1230 Peachtree Street, NE
Atlanta, GA 30309
   Phone: (404) 564-4800
   Email: daryl.conner@connerpartners.com
   Website: www.connerpartners.com

CAN YOU PICTURE THIS?

Submitted by Timothy Ewest

Objectives

- To understand how each person's unique perspective can contribute to an overall picture of the future.
- To practice the skill of building a collaborative vision.
- To prepare leaders for a discussion about or introduction to Inspire a Shared Vision.

Audience

This activity can be used with any size group; however, follow-up discussion is difficult with groups over fifty. Larger groups also pose challenges with everyone being able to view the media clip.

Time Required

35 minutes.

Materials and Equipment

- A DVD player, projector or T.V.
- A DVD or online video clip. Select a 5-minute movie clip that has a lot of action. The clip should have scenery, multiple characters, a noticeable plot, and products in the clip. (*Note:* The Federal Copyright Act requires a performance license for showing films. Information about licensing can be obtained from the Motion Picture Association of America on their Internet website at www.mpaa.org/Public_Performance.asp.)
- For each leader, paper and a pen.

118

- For each team, a set of the five handouts at the end of this activity, each copied onto a different colored sheet of paper.

Area Setup

This exercise requires groups of six who can be seated together. Also, all group members must be able to view the movie clip.

Process

1. Break the group into teams of six individuals. Have each group count off by six, assigning one number to each person. State that person number 6 will be the leader. Make sure everyone remembers his or her number because each will be assigned another task. Have the leaders (number 6) come to the front of the room and explain to them that they will watch a movie clip and that they are responsible to communicate what they see to the other team members. (The remaining team members should also be able to view the clip.)

2. Show the video clip and instruct the leaders to take notes on what they see. Make sure you don't put too much pressure on the leaders or the leaders can end up feeling as if the exercise is solely about their observational skills.

3. When the clip ends, instruct team leaders to return to their groups and tell the group members what they saw. Make it clear that *only the leader can explain the clip*; everyone else must simply listen—no conversations, no questions, no suggestions, no additions, just listen. Give them about 3 minutes. When the 3 minutes are up, press the leaders for details within the clip. (This will involve you pre-watching the clip a few times.) Continue until they begin to realize that they didn't catch all the facts.

4. Hand out to each table the five sheets of paper to the remaining five team members, matching their numbers to the numbers on the sheets. Tell these team members that they cannot reveal to any other team members what is on their sheets of paper. The team leader does not receive a piece of paper. Each sheet of paper should be a different color and be folded in half so only the person who receives the paper will read it. The five sheets of paper have the various topics written on them: Plot, Narrative, Characters, Clothing, Setting and Weather Conditions. The topics should represent what you believe the average person (leader) will not be able to observe from the first viewing of the clip. The instructions on the sheets of paper indicate that the participants are going to watch the clip again and should only pay attention to the topics on their sheets. Tell them that they are responsible to write down as much as possible about their topics. Encourage them to be very detailed.

5. Play the clip a second time. Ask the leaders whether they noticed anything different. After the leaders' responses, ask each of the other five viewers to describe for the leader what they saw. Tell the leaders to write down anything that is new or additional information about the clip.

6. After each person takes a turn, have the entire group assess which viewing of the clip was more holistic and representative of what really happened in the clip. Obviously, the combinations of perspectives are much more accurate and holistic.

7. Ask the group to reflect on the following questions:
   • When the leader first recounted the clip, did you see things that he or she didn't? If so, what?

- When you were assigned a role within your group (which is like being assigned a role within an organization), how did you feel about your responsibility?
- What effect did everyone's contribution detailing the clip have on the group? Did you feel any group interdependency? If so, why do you think that was?
- How do you think this exercise is representative of what can happen to leaders within organizations? What are the positives and negatives?
- What implications do the results of this activity have on being able to Inspire a Shared Vision?

8. Introduce Inspire a Shared Vision. Discuss how this activity is related.

Timothy Ewest is an assistant professor of business administration at Wartburg College. He has over nine years of experience in teaching, economic/community development, and organizational consulting. He has served as an instructor of economics and organizational behavior at the University of Alaska and currently at Wartburg College. Ewest holds a master's degree from Wheaton College, a master's degree from Regent University, an M.B.A. from George Fox University, is an ordained minister, and is completing his Ph.D. in management and education at Fox University.

Timothy Ewest
Wartburg College
100 Wartburg Boulevard
Waverly, IA 50677
   Phone: (319) 352-8416
   Email: timothy.ewest@wartburg.edu
   Website: www.wartburg.edu

Title of Film _____

Topic 1. Plot

The film clip will be played a second time. Your task is to observe the clip and pay close attention to the plot. List as many details as possible related to your assigned topic.

Do not tell anyone what your topic is.

Title of Film_____

Topic 2. Narrative

The film clip will be played a second time. Your task is to observe the clip and pay close attention to the narrative story. List as many details as possible related to your assigned topic.

Do not tell anyone what your topic is.

Title of Film _____

Topic 3. Characters

The film clip will be played a second time. Your task is to observe the clip and pay close attention to the characters. List as many details as possible related to your assigned topic.

Do not tell anyone what your topic is.

Title of Film_____

Topic 4. Clothing

The film clip will be played a second time. Your task is to observe the clip and pay close attention to the clothing. List as many details as possible related to your assigned topic.

Do not tell anyone what your topic is.

Title of Film_____

Topic 5. Setting and Weather Conditions

The film clip will be played a second time. Your task is to observe the clip and pay close attention to the setting and weather conditions. List as many details as possible related to your assigned topic.

Do not tell anyone what your topic is.

EXTRA! EXTRA! READ ALL ABOUT IT!

Submitted by Leonard D. Goodstein

Objectives

- To assist the leadership team to develop a shared vision of the future.
- To surface different views of the future within the leadership team.

Audience

The leadership team of the organization.

Time Required

60 to 90 minutes.

Materials and Equipment

- Writing paper and a pen or pencil for each member of the leadership team.
- Flip chart, paper, and felt-tipped markers.
- Masking tape to post chart paper.

Area Setup

A room with a chair and a writing surface for each member of the leadership team. Team members should be seated so that they can see each other, the facilitator, and the flip chart.

Process

1. Before beginning the activity, meet with the team leader to identify a trade paper, local newspaper, or some other print outlet

that would be likely to print a newsworthy article about the organization.

2. When the leadership group is assembled, announce that the purpose of this activity is to surface different views of how the organization will grow and change over the next ten years. Tell the leadership group to imagine that they are now ten years in the future. Write that date on the flip chart.

3. Ask each member of the leadership team to write the headline and the first few paragraphs of an article that has appeared in the print media outlet chosen in Step 1 above. Write the name of this paper on the flip chart, emphasizing that this is an article that has appeared in the _____ paper on this date, ten years in the future. The article describes the several accomplishments that the organization has achieved during the past ten years and where it seems to be currently headed. Allow 15 to 20 minutes for this part of the activity. Remain available to answer any questions and to urge early completers to flesh out their story.

4. Once it appears that all participants have completed their stories, ask for a volunteer to read aloud his or her story, followed by another volunteer, until everyone has had an opportunity to read aloud his or her story. No questions or comments should be allowed during the serial reading of the stories.

5. Record the major theme(s) of each story on the flip chart, checking with the participant whether the essence of his or her story has been captured in writing.

6. Ask the leadership group to review the flip charts to determine the common views of the future that have been captured and which ones are disparate. Capture the common themes on a fresh

sheet of chart paper and help the team reach consensus about how to rank order these common themes. The group needs to decide what to do with the disparate themes, to include them or not.

7. Ask a volunteer subgroup of the leadership team to be responsible for drafting a single, coherent statement about what has emerged from this activity about the desired future state of the organization and the policies and actions necessary to achieve that future state.

8. After the subgroup has had sufficient time to complete its work, it should share its product with the entire leadership team via email, and this product should serve as the focus of the next meeting of the leadership team as it strives to develop a shared view of the desired future of the organization—one to which they are willing to commit the necessary time and energy to achieve.

Leonard D. Goodstein, Ph.D., is a consulting psychologist based in Washington, D.C., who specializes in facilitating strategic planning and the implementation of strategic plans. After over thirty years as an academic, he became CEO of University Associates, now Pfeiffer, and then CEO and executive vice president of the American Psychological Association. He is a frequent contributor to the professional literature. His latest book (with E. P. Prien, J. Goodstein, & L. Gamble) is *A Practical Guide to Job Analysis* (Pfeiffer, 2009).

Leonard D. Goodstein, Ph.D.
4815 Foxhall Crescent, NW
Washington, DC 20007-1052
　　Phone: (202) 333-3134
　　Email: LenDG@aol.com

ANOTHER LEADER'S DREAM

Submitted by Donna Goss and Don Robertson

Objectives

- To identify how a leader can use language in a speech to share a vision.
- To demonstrate the value of descriptive and emotionally engaging language.

Audience

Small groups of four or five participants.

Time Required

30 to 45 minutes.

Materials and Equipment

- A copy of U.S. President Barack Obama's inauguration speech for each group.
- Flip charts—one for each small group.
- Markers.

Area Setup

Enough space to allow for small group discussion.

Process

1. Introduce the objectives. Ask the group, "How can a speech establish and set the tone for a vision?"

2. Ask what is important with regard to the past, the present, and the future when establishing a visionary speech. Anticipate these points:

   • Leaders speak respectfully of the past. There is nothing that can be done to change the past. It is because of the past that the leader now stands in front of the group, so leaders are careful to look to the past to learn from it but not to punish or berate people because of it. Leaders are respectful.

   • Leaders speak realistically of the present. They do not sugarcoat the present, nor do they dismiss it. They do not cheerlead their way through the challenges of the day, but they speak realistically of them.

   • Leaders speak optimistically of the future. The future has not yet been created, so how can it be anything less than optimistic? Leaders look to the future and share their vision of what could be in an uplifting and ennobling manner.

   • Leaders paint pictures with words. They use their voices to pull people forward. Leaders help people see what they see and feel what they feel.

3. Break the larger group into small groups of four or five. Give each group a copy of President Barack Obama's speech. Have the group examine the written words and discuss the techniques used.

4. Have the small groups discuss where, in the speech, they see "respect for the past," "the realities of the present," and "optimism for the future." Have each group note these on its flip chart.

5. Have each group share its observations, addressing the past, present, and future.

6. Summarize with these questions:

   • What descriptive language did you find?

- What emotional language did you read? What emotions does it evoke in you?
- What are the lessons in this speech for all leaders?
- Besides a speech, when can you emulate these concepts when inspiring a shared vision?
- What will you do to Inspire a Shared Vision as a result of this discussion?

Variations

- You may use this activity in conjunction with Martin Luther King, Jr.'s "I Have a Dream" speech. You may compare the techniques used by Dr. King to make his points with Barack Obama's techniques.
- If you are short on time, split the speech up and give one or two pages to each group.

Donna Goss and **Don Robertson** are the co-directors of the Leadership Development Institute, a consulting group in Bethlehem, Pennsylvania, which was built in partnership with the Center for Business and Industry. Both Don and Donna have extensive backgrounds in leadership and organization development, which they have been able to use to support the work of their clients.

Donna Goss
Leadership Development Institute
511 East Third Street
Bethlehem, PA 18015
   Phone: (610) 866-5590
   Email: dbgoss@northampton.edu

Don Robertson
Leadership Development Institute
511 East Third Street
Bethlehem, PA 18015
 Phone: (610) 866-5590
 Email: drobertson@northampton.edu

BARACK OBAMA'S INAUGURAL SPEECH

My fellow citizens:

I stand here today humbled by the task before us, grateful for the trust you have bestowed, mindful of the sacrifices borne by our ancestors. I thank President Bush for his service to our nation, as well as the generosity and cooperation he has shown throughout this transition.

Forty-four Americans have now taken the presidential oath. The words have been spoken during rising tides of prosperity and the still waters of peace. Yet, every so often, the oath is taken amidst gathering clouds and raging storms. At these moments, America has carried on not simply because of the skill or vision of those in high office, but because We the People have remained faithful to the ideals of our forebears, and true to our founding documents.

So it has been. So it must be with this generation of Americans.

That we are in the midst of crisis is now well understood. Our nation is at war, against a far-reaching network of violence and hatred. Our economy is badly weakened, a consequence of greed and irresponsibility on the part of some, but also our collective failure to make hard choices and prepare the nation for a new age. Homes have been lost; jobs shed; businesses shuttered. Our health care is too costly; our schools fail too many; and each day brings further evidence that the ways we use energy strengthen our adversaries and threaten our planet.

Barack Obama was sworn in as the 44th president of the United States and the nation's first African-American president on January 21, 2009. This is a transcript of his prepared speech.

These are the indicators of crisis, subject to data and statistics. Less measurable but no less profound is a sapping of confidence across our land—a nagging fear that America's decline is inevitable, and that the next generation must lower its sights.

Today I say to you that the challenges we face are real. They are serious and they are many. They will not be met easily or in a short span of time. But know this, America: They will be met.

On this day, we gather because we have chosen hope over fear, unity of purpose over conflict and discord.

On this day, we come to proclaim an end to the petty grievances and false promises, the recriminations and worn-out dogmas, that for far too long have strangled our politics.

We remain a young nation, but in the words of Scripture, the time has come to set aside childish things. The time has come to reaffirm our enduring spirit; to choose our better history; to carry forward that precious gift, that noble idea, passed on from generation to generation: the God-given promise that all are equal, all are free, and all deserve a chance to pursue their full measure of happiness.

In reaffirming the greatness of our nation, we understand that greatness is never a given. It must be earned. Our journey has never been one of shortcuts or settling for less. It has not been the path for the fainthearted—for those who prefer leisure over work, or seek only the pleasures of riches and fame. Rather, it has been the risk-takers, the doers, the makers of things—some celebrated, but more often men and women obscure in their labor—who have carried us up the long, rugged path toward prosperity and freedom.

For us, they packed up their few worldly possessions and traveled across oceans in search of a new life.

For us, they toiled in sweatshops and settled the West; endured the lash of the whip and plowed the hard earth.

For us, they fought and died, in places like Concord and Gettysburg; Normandy and Khe Sahn.

Time and again, these men and women struggled and sacrificed and worked till their hands were raw so that we might live a better life. They saw America as bigger than the sum of our individual ambitions; greater than all the differences of birth or wealth or faction.

This is the journey we continue today. We remain the most prosperous, powerful nation on Earth. Our workers are no less productive than when this crisis began. Our minds are no less inventive, our goods and services no less needed than they were last week or last month or last year. Our capacity remains undiminished. But our time of standing pat, of protecting narrow interests and putting off unpleasant decisions—that time has surely passed. Starting today, we must pick ourselves up, dust ourselves off, and begin again the work of remaking America.

For everywhere we look, there is work to be done. The state of the economy calls for action, bold and swift, and we will act—not only to create new jobs, but to lay a new foundation for growth. We will build the roads and bridges, the electric grids and digital lines that feed our commerce and bind us together. We will restore science to its rightful place, and wield technology's wonders to raise health care's quality and lower its cost. We will harness the sun and the winds and the soil to fuel our cars and run our factories. And we will transform our schools and colleges and universities to meet the demands of a new age. All this we can do. And all this we will do.

Now, there are some who question the scale of our ambitions—who suggest that our system cannot tolerate too many big plans. Their memories are short. For they have forgotten what this country has already done; what free men and women can achieve when imagination is joined to common purpose, and necessity to courage.

What the cynics fail to understand is that the ground has shifted beneath them—that the stale political arguments that have consumed us for so long no longer apply. The question we ask today is not whether our government is too big or too small, but whether it works—whether it helps families find jobs at a decent wage, care they can afford, a retirement that is dignified. Where the answer is yes, we intend to move forward. Where the answer is no, programs will end. And those of us who manage the public's dollars will be held to account—to spend wisely, reform bad habits, and do our business in the light of day—because only then can we restore the vital trust between a people and their government.

Nor is the question before us whether the market is a force for good or ill. Its power to generate wealth and expand freedom is unmatched, but this crisis has reminded us that without a watchful eye, the market can spin out of control—and that a nation cannot prosper long when it favors only the prosperous. The success of our economy has always depended not just on the size of our gross domestic product, but on the reach of our prosperity; on our ability to extend opportunity to every willing heart—not out of charity, but because it is the surest route to our common good.

As for our common defense, we reject as false the choice between our safety and our ideals. Our Founding Fathers, faced with perils we can scarcely imagine, drafted a charter to assure the rule of law and the rights of man, a charter expanded by the blood of generations. Those ideals still light the world, and we will not give them up for expedience's sake. And so to all other peoples and governments who are watching today, from the grandest capitals to the small village where my father was born: Know that America is a friend of each nation and every man, woman and child who seeks a future of peace and dignity, and that we are ready to lead once more.

Recall that earlier generations faced down fascism and communism not just with missiles and tanks, but with sturdy alliances and enduring convictions. They understood that our power alone cannot protect us, nor does it entitle us to do as we please. Instead, they knew that our power grows through its prudent use; our security emanates from the justness of our cause, the force of our example, the tempering qualities of humility and restraint.

We are the keepers of this legacy. Guided by these principles once more, we can meet those new threats that demand even greater effort—even greater cooperation and understanding between nations. We will begin to responsibly leave Iraq to its people, and forge a hard-earned peace in Afghanistan. With old friends and former foes, we will work tirelessly to lessen the nuclear threat, and roll back the specter of a warming planet. We will not apologize for our way of life, nor will we waver in its defense, and for those who seek to advance their aims by inducing terror and slaughtering innocents, we say to you now that our spirit is stronger and cannot be broken; you cannot outlast us, and we will defeat you.

For we know that our patchwork heritage is a strength, not a weakness. We are a nation of Christians and Muslims, Jews and Hindus—and nonbelievers. We are shaped by every language and culture, drawn from every end of this Earth; and because we have tasted the bitter swill of civil war and segregation, and emerged from that dark chapter stronger and more united, we cannot help but believe that the old hatreds shall someday pass; that the lines of tribe shall soon dissolve; that as the world grows smaller, our common humanity shall reveal itself; and that America must play its role in ushering in a new era of peace.

To the Muslim world, we seek a new way forward, based on mutual interest and mutual respect. To those leaders around the globe who seek to sow conflict, or blame their society's ills on the West: Know that your people will judge you on what you can build, not what you destroy. To those who cling to power through corruption and deceit and the silencing of dissent, know that you are on the wrong side of history; but that we will extend a hand if you are willing to unclench your fist.

To the people of poor nations, we pledge to work alongside you to make your farms flourish and let clean waters flow; to nourish starved bodies and feed hungry minds. And to those nations like ours that enjoy relative plenty, we say we can no longer afford indifference to suffering outside our borders; nor can we consume the world's resources without regard to effect. For the world has changed, and we must change with it.

As we consider the road that unfolds before us, we remember with humble gratitude those brave Americans who, at this very hour, patrol far-off deserts and distant mountains. They have something to tell us today, just as the fallen heroes who lie in Arlington whisper through the ages. We honor them not only because they are guardians of our liberty, but because they embody the spirit of service; a willingness to find meaning in something greater than themselves. And yet, at this moment—a moment that will define a generation—it is precisely this spirit that must inhabit us all.

For as much as government can do and must do, it is ultimately the faith and determination of the American people upon which this nation relies. It is the kindness to take in a stranger when the levees break, the selflessness of workers who would rather cut their hours than see a friend lose their job which sees us through our darkest hours. It is the firefighter's courage to storm a stairway filled with smoke, but also a parent's willingness to nurture a child, that finally decides our fate.

Our challenges may be new. The instruments with which we meet them may be new. But those values upon which our success depends—hard work and honesty, courage and fair play, tolerance and curiosity, loyalty and patriotism—these things are old. These things are true. They have been the quiet force of progress throughout our history. What is demanded then is a return to these truths. What is required of us now is a new era of responsibility—a recognition, on the part of every American, that we have duties to ourselves, our nation and the world; duties that we do not grudgingly accept but rather seize gladly, firm in the knowledge that there is nothing so satisfying to the spirit, so defining of our character, than giving our all to a difficult task.

This is the price and the promise of citizenship.

The Leadership Challenge Activities Book
Copyright © 2010 by James M. Kouzes and Barry Z. Posner.
Reproduced by permission of Pfeiffer, an Imprint of Wiley. www.pfeiffer.com.

This is the source of our confidence—the knowledge that God calls on us to shape an uncertain destiny.

This is the meaning of our liberty and our creed—why men and women and children of every race and every faith can join in celebration across this magnificent mall, and why a man whose father less than sixty years ago might not have been served at a local restaurant can now stand before you to take a most sacred oath.

So let us mark this day with remembrance, of who we are and how far we have traveled. In the year of America's birth, in the coldest of months, a small band of patriots huddled by dying campfires on the shores of an icy river. The capital was abandoned. The enemy was advancing. The snow was stained with blood. At a moment when the outcome of our revolution was most in doubt, the father of our nation ordered these words be read to the people:

> "Let it be told to the future world . . . that in the depth of winter, when nothing but hope and virtue could survive . . . that the city and the country, alarmed at one common danger, came forth to meet [it]."

America. In the face of our common dangers, in this winter of our hardship, let us remember these timeless words. With hope and virtue, let us brave once more the icy currents, and endure what storms may come. Let it be said by our children's children that when we were tested, we refused to let this journey end, that we did not turn back, nor did we falter; and with eyes fixed on the horizon and God's grace upon us, we carried forth that great gift of freedom and delivered it safely to future generations.

WHAT DOES SUCCESS LOOK LIKE?

Submitted by Amanda Crowell Itliong

Objectives

- To help leaders envision the future and turn their visions into inspiring stories that they can more easily share with others. To help leaders imagine project success not just in terms of numbers and outputs but also in terms of how people are affected by the success.
- To provide leaders feedback on how others understand their vision.

Audience

Five to twenty-five leaders.

Time Required

35 to 45 minutes.

Materials and Equipment

- One blank white sheet of paper per person.
- Two blank sheets of lined paper per person.
- Colored markers.
- Pen or pencil for each participant.
- Tape or sticky tack to hang all the participants' paper drawings on the walls.
- Five sticky notes for each participant.

Area Setup

Participants should sit at tables where they can write and draw. Wall space to hang participants' drawings and captions.

Process

1. Give each leader one blank sheet of paper, several colored markers, and two blank sheets of lined paper. Remind participants to write neatly during this activity so that others can read their handwriting.

2. Ask leaders to imagine a project that they just started working on or are about to start. Give them 3 minutes to write on one sheet of lined paper what success looks like for this project. What will have been done when the project is finished and declared a success? Each participant should keep these notes for him- or herself.

3. Have each leader imagine he or she was to use a camera to take a snapshot of the most successful moment of the project. Tell leaders to think about what and who is in the picture; include at least one person in the picture. What are the people doing, saying, or feeling? When and where is this event happening?

4. Give leaders 10 minutes to draw pictures of the snapshots they imagined on the blank sheets of paper. Remind everyone that the quality of drawing doesn't matter at all; this is just a different approach to help them explore their visions.

5. Have leaders take the second blank sheets of lined paper and write short captions for the pictures. Tell them to briefly answer who, what, when, where, and why in their captions.

6. Designate the location of the "vision gallery" and ask participants to hang their vision pictures around the room with the captions beneath.

7. Invite all participants to visit the "vision gallery." Ask: "What did others include in their visions that you might want to add to yours?" Ask each participant to leave a comment written on a

sticky note for each of the other five pictures. Suggest that the comment relate to something unique or practical about the vision. Have them post their notes on the lined caption page that is below each picture.

8. Leave the gallery up as long as you like. Sometimes participants like to explore the gallery on another break. At the end of the session, have each artist take his or her original vision, caption, and all the sticky note comments.

9. Suggest that participants may want to review the sticky note comments and add to or edit their visions based on the comments they received and/or what they noticed from looking at the other visions.

10. Encourage leaders to later return to their project teams and take the opportunity to describe what success looks like on the project using the pictures they drew, the captions, and the comments as a guide. Tell them that they do not need to actually show anyone the pictures, but they should go beyond describing just the numbers and logistical details of a successful project. It should include how people are involved and what they are saying and feeling. This can help all members of their teams feel more connected to their visions and more likely to work to achieve them.

Amanda Crowell Itliong is the student development and leadership Programs director at Stanford University's Haas Center for Public Service, where she teaches and advises emerging leaders in public service. She has spent the last ten years training and creating curriculum for students, faculty, community volunteers, and nonprofit leaders on topics related to service-learning, social justice, and leadership. She holds a B.A. in human services from The George

Washington University, an Ed.M. from Harvard's Graduate School of Education, and a certificate in dialogue, deliberation, and public engagement from Fielding Graduate University.

Amanda Crowell Itliong
Haas Center for Public Service
Student Development and Leadership Programs Director
Stanford University 562 Salvatierra Walk
Stanford, CA 94305
  Phone: (650) 724-9233
  Email: akc@stanford.edu
  Website: www.haas.stanford.edu

BLINDFOLD SQUARE*

Submitted by Jean Lee

Objectives

- To facilitate learners' understanding of the importance of vision clarity in achieving team goals.
- To help learners to identify the key factors that are critical in helping leaders to Inspire a Shared Vision.

Audience

Fifteen to thirty participants per group.

Time Required

Approximately 45 minutes.

Materials and Equipment

- One soft rope approximately 10 meters in length.
- One blindfold per participant, such as a large handkerchief.

Area Setup

A classroom appropriate for the group size. Furniture moved aside to make room for the activity as well as for safety considerations. Props are set up once planning stage is over and all participants are blindfolded.

---

*A variation of this activity appears in *The Leadership Challenge Workshop* (3rd ed., revised).

Process

1. Have the group elect a leader who will lead them through the activity. Ask the leader to step out of the room where you can brief him or her on the following:
   - *Team Task:* To form a square while holding onto a rope. The square should be formed with the members lining up in order of their birth-dates.
   - *Situation:* All members of team (including the team leader) will be blindfolded as they work through this challenge. Once the team enters into the execution stage, no verbal communication is allowed.
   - *Planning:* Team will be given 15 minutes of planning time before the activity begins.
   - *Execution:* Team is given 20 minutes to complete the task.
   - *Safety Consideration:* As all members will be blindfolded, team members should be taught to move around in a safe manner (for example, left arms across chest to protect the body from bumping against any obstacles and right arms extended to feel around so that they won't bump into obstacles)
   - *Environment:* The facilitator, who plays the role of the "environment," will introduce changes that the group may not foresee in the course of planning.

2. Send the leader back to the group to brief the team as well as to begin the planning process.

3. Once the 15-minute planning period is over, have team members put their blindfolds on and wait for instruction from you to indicate the beginning of the 20-minute execution phase. Before

giving the signal to start, separate the members by moving them away from their planned starting point, disengaging them from the team (one of the changes introduced by the "environment"). When you are satisfied with the amount of change, signal to indicate the start of the activity.

4. Once the learners enter into the execution stage, you can make other changes, such as:
   - Placing the rope in a location that is not easily found by learners.
   - Securing the rope with loose knots so that it is not easily removed.

5. During the course of the activity, you may want to introduce other changes, such as:
   - Bringing away one member and asking him or her to sit quietly at one corner.
   - Introducing interference into their planned communication process (not too often though!).

6. After 20 minutes or after the team has formed a square, have participants remove their blindfolds and sit down. Debrief using these questions:
   - What happened?
   - What could have prevented any problems?
   - As the "environment," I introduced change that you didn't anticipate. How is that similar to what happens in the workplace?
   - What might you have done differently?
   - How has this activity helped you to understand what it takes to Inspire a Shared Vision?
   - How has this prepared you to be a better leader?
   - What will you do differently as a result in the future?

Jean Lee is an honors graduate from Nanyang Technological University, Jean has achieved a rich portfolio of organization development qualifications, including being a certified administrator of the Myers-Briggs Type Indicator, a master trainer in The Leadership Profile™, and a Leadership Challenge® Certified Facilitator. Jean believes that, with a dynamic mix of right resources, there will always be unlimited opportunities and room for growth for both organizations and human resources. Her own learning journey continues as she currently pursues a master of arts in education and human development from The George Washington University.

Jean Lee
PACE Organization Dynamics Pte Ltd
Blk 162 #06-3555
Bukit Merah Central
Singapore 150162
  Phone: +65 6278 8289
  Email: jeanlee@pace-od.com
  Website: www.pace-od.com

THE PERFECT PLACE—HEAVEN ON EARTH

Submitted by Jan Miller and Denise Knight

Objectives

- To envision the perfect organization by imagining exciting and ennobling possibilities.
- To enlist the help of others while creating a common vision.

Audience

Fifteen to twenty participants, in small groups of four or five.

Time Required

30 to 45 minutes.

Materials and Equipment

- Chart paper.
- Markers.
- Paper and pencils for each participant.

Area Setup

Tables so that groups of four or five can work together.

Process

1. Ask participants to individually envision the perfect working organization. Ask them to list the characteristics of the perfect organization on sheets of paper.

2. Have the participants form subgroups of four or five members. Within subgroups, ask each participant to share his or her description of the perfect organization.

3. Ask each subgroup to decide what the perfect organization would look like. Ask them to illustrate their perfect organizations on the chart paper. They may also add descriptive words. Encourage them to think outside the box and be creative.

4. Ask each subgroup to present its perfect organization to the whole group.

5. Summarize with these questions:
   - What similarities did you see among groups?
   - What was different?
   - How would envisioning the perfect organization help a leader to create a vision?
   - How could you use something similar to this exercise to inspire a shared vision in your organization?

Jan Miller, Ed.D., currently serves as an assistant professor at the University of West Alabama in the College of Education–Instructional Leadership Department. She has twenty-two years of public school experience in the state of Mississippi. During those years, Jan has taught numerous grade levels, served as a lead teacher, and supervised two schools as principal. She earned a B.S. degree in elementary education from Livingston University, an M.Ed. in elementary education from Livingston University, an Ed.S. in elementary education from Mississippi State University, and an Ed.D. in educational leadership from NOVA Southeastern University.

Denise Knight, Ed.D., currently serves as an assistant professor at the University of West Alabama in the College of Education. She has twenty-three years of public school experience in the state of Mississippi. Denise has taught numerous grade levels, taught talented and gifted, served as a district-wide director of federal programs and elementary curriculum, and served as an elementary principal. She earned a B.S. degree in elementary education from Mississippi State University, an M.Ed. in elementary education from Livingston University, an M.Ed. in school administration from the University of West Alabama, an Ed.S. in curriculum and instruction from Mississippi State University, and an Ed.D. in educational leadership from NOVA Southeastern University.

Jan Miller, Ed.D.
University of West Alabama
Station #34
Livingston, AL 35470
   Phone: (205) 652-3445 or (205) 652-3801
   Email: jmiller@uwa.edu

Denise Knight, Ed.D.
University of West Alabama
Station #34
Livingston, AL 35470
   Phone: (205) 652-3445 or (205) 652-3801
   Email: dknight@uwa.edu

MODELING THE FUTURE

Submitted by Linda S. Eck Mills

Objective

- To use a model to initiate discussions of visions of the future.

Audience

Ten to twenty-five people in small groups of seven to ten.

Time Required

20 to 45 minutes, depending on number of groups.

Materials and Equipment

- Model Magic by Crayola for each group, in assorted colors.
- Flip chart and markers.

Area Setup

Table for each group.

Process

1. State that good learning has a social base. Interacting with others is a means to learn more. This activity will provide the opportunity for small groups to pool their collective knowledge and ideas to create an ideal and unique image of what the organization can become. Tell them that, to do this, each group will have 10 minutes to build something that represents the future of the organization using the Model Magic provided.

2. Form small groups of seven to ten participants. Give each group some Model Magic and begin timing the 10 minutes.

3. At the end of the 10 minutes, have each group briefly explain its creation. Lead applause after each explanation.

4. Summarize the activity with the following questions, recording the answers on a flip chart:
   - What was the most difficult part of this activity?
   - What was the easiest part of this activity?
   - What happened when you heard the presentations from the other groups? Did that change your thinking any? If so, how? What does this suggest about how to Inspire a Shared Vision?
   - What are the exciting possibilities of the future?
   - How can the ideas that were generated be used to improve the organization?
   - Where shall we start to move forward?

Linda S. Eck Mills, MBA, owns Dynamic Communication Services, a firm specializing in presenting information that has immediate and relevant implications to the work and lives of individuals by linking common everyday objects to any topic. Her work includes professional speaking, training, facilitating, and career/life coaching. Linda is the author of her self-published book *From Mundane to Ah Ha!—Effective Training Objects* and a contributor to *Trainer's Warehouse Book of Games* (Pfeiffer, 2008), *The 2009 Pfeiffer Annual: Training,* and over 160 articles.

Linda S. Eck Mills, MBA
Dynamic Communication Services
20 Worman Lane
Bernville, PA 19506
  Phone: (610) 488-7010
  Email: AhHaBook@aol.com
  Website: www.theconsultantsforum.com/eckmills.htm

DEFINING A VISION THAT OTHERS WILL FOLLOW

Submitted by Nanette Miner and Lynn Little

Objectives

- To create a clear vision for the work to be done.
- To define and communicate the vision in a way that will inspire others to follow.

Audience

Four to six participants.

Time Required

30 to 45 minutes.

Materials and Equipment

- Paper and pencils or pens for writing.
- Standard meeting room table and chairs to accommodate four to six people.

Area Setup

Because this is small-group work, the arrangement of the room is not crucial, so long as the temperature is comfortable, the lighting is adequate, and the group members can hear one another and not be disturbed by others outside their groups.

Process

1. Give group members the following instructions: Think of a project for which you are the leader or that you would like to lead for

your organization. Given the importance of inspiring a shared vision (as described by Jim Kouzes and Barry Posner) to get followers to understand the project, to be inspired by the project, and to want to give their full support to the project, how would you go about creating a clear vision for the work to be done and then defining and communicating that vision in a way that will inspire others to follow?

2. Take 5 or 10 minutes to write down the vision in a way that it will be understood by potential followers (other members of your group, in this exercise) and that it will inspire them to want to take action to achieve the vision and to follow your lead in doing so. Ensure that your vision adheres to Kouzes and Posner's guidelines:

"We define vision as a unique and ideal image of the future for the common good. To be able to inspire others you need to be able to state what's unique and distinctive about your vision of the future. You need to be able to describe it so that people can picture it in their own minds, 'Oh, I see what you're talking about!' And you need to be able to talk about the future, not just the present, in a way that is appealing to a large number of people. Your vision may be compelling to you, but if it's not attractive to others they will not move toward it."
Leadership Challenge Workbook, 2003

3. After 10 minutes, ask each individual to present his or her vision using the following guidelines:
   When you are the "leader": Present your vision to your group members. Pay attention to how they respond and to what they

and you can identify as strong points and weak points in the vision as you have presented it. Within about 5 minutes of sharing responses, reach consensus with your group members on how the vision can be improved.

When you are the "follower": Participate as a potential follower as the other group members take the leader role and go through the process of presenting their visions for their own projects. Ask challenging questions and give constructive feedback (for example, Did you mean this or this? What would that result in? Is that the best way to Inspire a Shared Vision? What if you tried_____?).

4. After each person has presented his or her vision and received feedback from the group, if time permits, facilitate a group discussion summarizing what participants have learned from this exercise.

Variation

• Allow enough time for individuals to revise their visions based on the feedback they received.

Nanette Miner, Ed.D, founded, and is the principle consultant for, The Training Doctor, LLC, an instructional design firm with offices in Connecticut and South Carolina. She is also the executive director of www.TheAccidentalTrainer.com, an online support group for workplace professionals who have found themselves thrust into the role of trainer. She is a regular contributor to industry publications and has authored or co-authored a half-dozen books in the last decade.

Lynn Little, Ph.D., has for the past dozen years taught graduate courses in leadership to students pursuing Ed.D. degrees in higher education at Nova Southwestern University. He also has written more than one hundred monthly articles on Lessons in Leadership for Magna Publications, Madison, Wisconsin, articles which he now is compiling into a book. Recently, he retired as professor and chairman of the Department of Medical Laboratory Sciences at The University of Texas Southwestern Medical Center at Dallas.

Nanette Miner, Ed.D.
The Training Doctor, LLC
Bristol, CT
   Phone: (800) 282-5474
   Email: nanette@trainingdr.com
   Website: www.trainingdr.com

Lynn Little, Ph.D.
Nova Southeastern University
Dallas, TX
   Phone: (214) 693-3309
   Email: lynn.lit@nova.edu

THE SPIRITUAL LEADER

Submitted by Mohandas Nair

Objectives

- To understand the concept of spiritual leadership through a case study dialogue.
- To explore the concept of Inspire a Shared Vision through a discussion.
- To consider one's own leadership skills for enlisting others.

Audience

Ideally, ten to twenty participants in leadership positions or in line for leadership positions.

Time Required

60 to 90 minutes.

Material and Equipment

- A copy of the case study, The Spiritual Leader: A Case for Discussion, for each participant.
- Large chart paper with colored markers.
- Masking tape.

Area Setup

A large room with plenty of light and space for small discussion groups, the ability to hang charts on the wall, and ample space for a gallery walk.

Process

1. Arrange participants into small groups of three or four participants.

2. Lead a general discussion on the fundamental concepts underlining the five practices with emphasis on Inspire a Shared Vision.

3. Distribute a copy of the case study, The Spiritual Leader, to each participant. Ask them to read it and discuss it in their small groups with the goal to arrive at a common understanding among group members on the facts of the case. Groups should discuss the case in light of the following Commitments of Leadership:
   • Envision the future by imagining exciting and ennobling possibilities.
   • Enlist others in a common vision by appealing to shared aspirations.
   Allow about 10 minutes.

4. Give each group a flip-chart page and markers. Ask the groups to explore the following:
   • What obstacles did Chinnapillai face?
   • From where did her strength emanate?
   • How does this situation resonate with your own situation at work?
   • How is it different?
   • Ask them to post responses to the four questions on the chart paper.

5. Ask each group to hang its prepared chart on the wall. Facilitate a gallery walk. Ask participants to add appropriate comments on the charts not prepared by their groups.

6. Facilitate a discussion using questions such as:
   • How do obstacles affect your ability to Inspire a Shared Vision?

- Do you draw on spirituality to overcome obstacles? If yes, how? If not, where do you get strength?
- What lessons can be implemented based on this case at your location?

7. Facilitate a discussion with the entire group on general experiences and learning from the activity. Ask each participant to share at least one takeaway from the activity.

Variations

- Ask each group to address this case as it relates to all of The Five Practices.
- During the gallery walk, post representatives of each group in front of each chart to explain their understanding and thoughts.

Mohandas Nair is a management educator, teacher, trainer, writer, and a facilitator of learning. He earned a B.Tech. (Mech.) from IIT Kharagpur, India, has a diploma in training and development, and has over thirty years of experience in industry and consultancy in the fields of industrial engineering and human resources development. He has published two books, written numerous articles, and facilitated many management development programs.

Mohandas Nair
A2 Kamdar Building
607 Gokhale Road (South)
Dadar, Mumbai – 400028
India
  Phone: 91 22 24226307; 09820935427
  Email: nair_mohandas@hotmail.com; mknair@vsnl.net

THE SPIRITUAL LEADER: A CASE FOR DISCUSSION

Chinnapillai is an illiterate farm worker from a poor village in the state of Tamil Nadu in South India. She was being presented with the Indian Merchant Chambers (IMC) Ladies wing–Jankidevi Bajaj Award for rural entrepreneurship in 2000, in the Indian capital, New Delhi. After presenting her with the award, Ms. Sumitra Kulkarni, granddaughter of Mahatma Gandhi, remarked, "Chinnapillai doesn't need our awards; she just needs us to allow her space to carry on the fantastic work she is doing."

Her work? Women's empowerment in village India, feudal India.

The diminutive Chinnapillai, a fifty-year-old landless laborer from Tamil Nadu, won the annual award for promoting a unique savings-and-loan scheme for village women in her region. The program, which she launched informally thirty-five years ago, now covers nearly fifty thousand village women in Tamil Nadu and the neighboring state of Andhra Pradesh. The movement, called *Kalanjiam* (savings, credit, self-help), now also conducts campaigns against alcoholism and child labor and runs a primary school.

"I've always been a daredevil. Perhaps that's why God has been on my side," said Chinnapillai to a journalist after the award ceremony. Not that her achievement came easily. "But can you accomplish anything in this world without a hard fight?" asks Chinnapillai, who has taken on the ferocious feudal lords, ruthless money lenders, bloody minded politicians, obstreperous bankers, and bureaucrats in her long struggle to get the downtrodden their due.

Chinnapillai's struggles started when she was thirteen. "We women would work long days in the fields but go home with only a bag full of grain, or occasionally a few rupees. It used to burn my heart. I was a leader of a group of women workers and decided to use my position to demand our due. I started calling women's meetings to discuss the issue. Everyone was terrified in the beginning, including my husband, but I persuaded them to demand a hike in wages."

Chinnapillai asked the landlord for a hike and got a kick instead. Nonetheless, she persisted until they relented and agreed to a two-rupee hike. "I felt that was a signal from God to carry on. I soon started urging the women to put aside a little money as savings. Of course, they didn't listen. How could they? They needed food for their families and liquor for their men. But again, I kept at it. Eventually, they agreed to keep aside a few rupees—not at home, where it could be spent off any minute, but safely in our *Kalajiam*.

Chinnapillai then decided that these collective savings could be used to give small loans to women at a low rate of interest—24 percent compared with the 60 to 120 percent charged by local money lenders. "My dream was to free us peasants from the stranglehold of money lenders. City people will not understand how that feels. It's like walking around with a tight noose around your neck."

She also organized the women to seek jobs in new and non-women oriented projects, too. For instance, she obtained her village women the fishing rights in the local pond (which had for decades been controlled by local landlords and corrupt politicians). "We petitioned the local government authority in this regard, and the sympathetic officer took up cudgels on our behalf."

The *Kalajiam* movement began to spread, and women from other villages joined in. As the corpus of savings grew, a local non-government organization (NGO) called DHAN (Development of Humane Action) came in to help them bank their money, liaise with officialdom, and establish local committees to disburse loans meant to pay for house construction, marriage expenses, farming materials, and seeds.

"We started with 200 rupees collected from twenty women in my village some thirty years ago; now our *Kalajiam's* savings run to several hundred thousand rupees in the local district alone and nearly fifty million rupees in the two states of Tamil Nadu and Andhra Pradesh." She smiles. "But you know I have no idea how much money Rs. 100,000 is. I still cannot count more than 100."

The crusader is still as poor as, well, an Indian peasant, earning as she does twenty-five rupees a day for four hours work in the fields. Her two sons and daughters-in-law toil all month, but Chinnapillai now works ten days a month; the rest of the time she's busy with committee meetings in various villages. She has debts totaling 35,000 rupees. But she does not intend to touch her prize money of 100,000 rupees. "It will go to the *Kalajiam*, toward helping the more needy" she stated firmly.

Small wonder, then, that when he presented her with a special award during the special Women's Empowerment Year launch function in Delhi, the then Prime Minister of India, Atal Behari Vajpayee, was sufficiently moved to bow down and touch Chinnapillai's feet.

Author's Note

In India you touch the feet of an elder to show respect. However, the prime minister of India is in a position where he or she is not constrained to do this as a formality. He or she would not touch the feet of any top business executives of any organization in the world or of any politicians. He or she would do so only in the presence of saints, sages, or spiritual leaders.

DEFINE YOUR VALUES THROUGH A VISION STATEMENT

Submitted by Steve A. Rainey

Objectives

- To identify the steps needed to develop a written vision statement.
- To write an initial vision statement.

Audience

Any size group, preferably ten to twelve participants who have never written a vision statement before.

Time Required

60 minutes.

Materials and Equipment

- Whiteboard or flip chart and markers.
- Paper and pencils for participants.
- Examples of vision statements from key leaders in history written on a flip chart or on a slide. (See Vision Statements sheet.)
- One Vision Consideration handout for each participant.
- One Kouzes and Posner Vision Consideration handout for each participant.

Area Setup

Any classroom setting. If an option, can be conducted outdoors.

Process

1. Have the vision statement of Martin Luther King, Jr. ("I have a dream") posted and visible on a whiteboard. Say: "Vision, it all starts with a dream. You must have an idea of the direction in which you want to move, that initial dream that motivates you to take action. One of the most memorable visions in history belonged to Martin Luther King, Jr., who stated his vision with the words 'I have a dream.' It is the same for any leader who wishes to motivate others to take positive action. That leader, too, must have a dream. What is it you wish to accomplish? What is that key issue you want others to rally around and work toward?"

2. Show the second example of a vision by Winston Churchill and read it. State, "Is there any doubt what Churchill meant for the people of England? They were to fight, to never accept surrender, to pay any cost for victory and that the whole of England was involved in the process. This is what a vision statement can do for you. It can rally your people, it can bind your people to each other for a common cause, and it can give them direction and unity of purpose. It can work in peace time as well as war for any company willing to invest the time to write one with conviction and sincerity."

3. Show the chart with vision statement from GE CEO Jack Welch. State, "Write down what it is you want your vision to be. What is it you want to do? Don't be afraid to be imaginative. Tell us where it is you want to take your organization, nothing too complicated, just a few sentences about the direction you want to move your organization." Give participants 5 minutes to do this.

4. Provide participants with the Vision Considerations handout.

5. State, "Let's expand on what you wrote with the guidance from the Vision Considerations handout. Include these steps while writing your expanded vision statement." Give participants 15 minutes to do this.

6. Give participants the guidance from Kouzes and Posner handout. State, "Now using the guidance from Kouzes and Posner, take 20 minutes to further expand your vision statement."

7. Once they have completed their visions, say, "Vision is the unifying statement that will energize and rally your people to take action, now and into the future. And this is your first step toward developing your skill at writing and expressing yourself in a written vision statement. Keep this product with you and use the steps outlined today to rewrite and expand upon this first version. Step back and imagine that you are twenty or even thirty years in the future and looking back at the vision statement you wrote. Would it take you and your organization to that future point in time? Don't go back and put what you wrote in a drawer and forget about it; continue to develop it until it can take you where you want to go."

8. Summarize with these questions:
   - What did you enjoy about writing your vision?
   - What was difficult about writing your vision?
   - What is your next step? How will you refine your vision?

Steve A. Rainey recently retired from the U.S. Army, having spent seventeen years with the 5th Special Forces Group in various leadership assignments. He culminated his career as a team sergeant for a military freefall team. Currently a graduate student in the strategic leadership program at Mountain State University in Beckley, West Virginia, Steve has a B.S. degree from Excelsior

College, a master certificate in organizational leadership from Villanova University, and aspires to teach adult learners upon graduation.

MSG Steve A. Rainey, U.S. Army (Retired)
548 Bryan Road
Clarksville, TN 37043
   Phone: (931) 358-0286
   Email: sar59@bellsouth.net

VISION STATEMENTS

"I have a dream."
Martin Luther King, Jr.

"We shall defend our island, whatever the cost may be. We shall fight on the beaches . . . we shall fight in the fields and in the streets . . . for each and for all.
Winston Churchill

"General Electric will be number one or number two in each of its businesses, and if it can't achieve that position it will fix, close, or sell the business."
Jack Welch, CEO, General Electric

VISION CONSIDERATION

- Keep it simple, realistic, believable. Paint a picture with words of what you want the organization to look like and how it's going to get there.
- Remember, as you write, to keep the vision statement in the present tense.
- Provide clarity to the purpose and the direction you want to provide your organization.
- Don't be afraid to assume a little risk; be bold, but don't complicate the statement with ambiguity or unnecessary language.
- Make it easy to understand.
- Provide incentive for getting people on board; provide a reason for them to commit and believe in the vision.
- Be honest, speak from the heart; you are providing a symbol to rally your people to take action.

KOUZES AND POSNER VISION CONSIDERATIONS

- What is your *ideal* work community? What do you personally aspire to create?
- What is *unique* about your hopes, dreams, and aspirations? How are they distinctive compared to all the visions of the future?
- When you project this vision into the *future* ten to fifteen years, what does it look like? What innovations and trends will influence the future? What vision will carry us forward into the future?
- What *images* come to mind when thinking of the future? What does it look like, sound like, taste like, and feel like?
- How does this vision serve the *common good*? What are the shared aspirations among all the constituents? How does the vision fulfill others' ideal and unique images of their futures?

LIGHTS, CAMERA, ACTION!

Submitted by Devora Zack

Objectives

- To gain ownership and clarity of team vision.
- To inspire a shared, upbeat commitment to vision.

Audience

Eight to fifty participants, in teams of four to six.

Time Required

45 to 60 minutes (may be longer for large groups)

Materials and Equipment

- Large display of team or organization-wide vision statement (a pre-existing vision statement or a new vision statement determined by the group prior to the start of this activity).
- Paper and pen for each participant.
- Group prize.

Area Setup

Space for each team to work independently—one large room, nearby breakout rooms, or outdoors.

Process

1. Begin with everyone in a central room or shared space. Use any method to place participants on teams of four to six participants each.

2. Tell each team to create an original commercial advertising their shared vision. They have 20 minutes to prepare. Everyone must be involved. Each team presentation can be up to 5 minutes. Presentations should include a title, jingle, and at least one tip on how to bring the vision alive. Presentations should meet the criterion of being creative and compelling—capturing the audience's attention while inspiring them to share in the vision. Teams can use any items easily gathered or created during the preparation time. Each team is assigned an independent space to work. Recommend that teams assign timekeepers to ensure they use the time well and suggest they assess individual talents and predispositions to break down tasks (writing the jingle, creating props, structuring the commercial). While they are working, circulate among the groups ensuring everyone is involved in the preparation and participating in the commercial. Ask teams their team titles and assign the order of the presentations.

3. When time is up, gather together the teams. Introduce each team by its title. Advise the other teams to pay close attention, and take notes if they like, because at the conclusion, each team will have one collective vote for its favorite commercial (not their own). After the presentations, give each team a couple of minutes to determine its first choice, write it on a piece of paper, and hand it to you to tally. The winning team receives the team prize.

4. Lead a discussion to process the experience. Discussion points can include: how the teams worked together, what was learned about teammates, how they got unstuck, what inspires increase collaboration, and what elements of this activity increased their ability to share in the group vision.

5. Summarize with a discussion about the vision:
   - How has this experience changed your thoughts about the vision?
   - How has this experience increased or decreased your feelings of a shared commitment toward the vision?
   - What's your next step regarding the vision?

Devora Zack, president of Only Connect Consulting (OOC), provides leadership development, coaching, team training, and assessments to more than seventy-five clients, including Deloitte, America Online, U.S. Patent & Trademark, OPM, Enterprise, and the U.S. Treasury. Devora has been faculty for Cornell's leadership program for thirteen years. Devora holds an M.B.A. from Cornell University and a B.A. from the University of Pennsylvania. Her certifications include MBTI and Neuro-Linguistic Programming. She is a member of Phi Beta Kappa, Mensa, and ASTD. Her designs are featured in five publications. OCC is the recipient of USDA's Woman-Owned Business of the Year award.

Devora Zack
Only Connect Consulting, Inc.
7806 Ivymount Terrace
Potomac, MD 20854
   Phone: (301) 765-6262
   Email: dzack@onlyconnectconsulting.com
   Website: www.onlyconnectconsulting.com

CLAIMING A BREAKTHROUGH

Submitted by Sherene Zolno

Objectives

- To envision a compelling future for a work team or company.
- To develop a vividly described vision story.
- To develop a breakthrough statement of commitment to achieving a vision of the future.

Audience

This process is appropriate for any size group; however, given time constraints, facilitators may want to limit the group size.

This process is appropriate for executives, leadership teams, management groups, project leaders, and trainers/consultants who will be developing leaders.

Time Required

60 minutes.

Materials and Equipment

- Claiming a Breakthrough worksheet for each participant.

Area Setup

Room setup would include an area where participants may sit at tables during the guided imagery process, and room for them to stand during the breakthrough statement process.

Facilitators may choose to use relaxing music to enhance the guided imagery process.

Process

1. Introduce the process by saying:

    "Jim Kouzes and Barry Posner, in their book *The Leadership Challenge*, say that 'the unique reason for having leaders—their differentiating function—is to move us forward. Leaders get us going someplace.' This thinking fits with research that indicates that all action is conditioned by the fact that we live in an anticipatory world of images, that our organizations exist because leaders and stakeholders envision the same possibilities for their shared future. Therefore, as a leader in your organization, inspiring a shared vision will be an important factor in your success, impacting every day's commitment to quality operations. You and your organization's members will be working together toward an image of the future.

    "Vision shapes direction, but also influences daily decision-making. In organizations, it shapes hiring, promotion, and action towards customers, partners, teammates, and investors. It conveys a *sense of direction*. It releases a *sense of discovery*. And it implies a *sense of destiny*.

    "An inspiring, shared vision helps align our espoused values with our everyday practices, ensuring our own personal congruency and that of a work team, a leadership team, and an organization. A shared vision includes two components:

    - A vision story that captures the essence of who and what we will be when we are in our desired future. The vision story is a vibrant, engaging, and specific description of what it is like when the future is achieved. It is told in the language of the senses to make the dream of the future more alive.

176

- A breakthrough statement, a succinct statement declaring the commitment that is intended to inspire the present. It is spoken using powerful language. Examples include: 'We are committed to being . . . ' '"I will . . . ' 'We will create . . . '"

Continue by saying, "Today you will:

- Use a unique guided-imagery process to envision a compelling future for your work team or company;
- Use your image of the future in the development of a vividly described story of what you saw, heard, and felt during the guided imagery process; and
- Develop a breakthrough statement of the commitment you have to achieving this vision of the future—a statement that can be shared with your team to guide your present actions."

2. Have participants find places to stand in the room where they can take a step forward and back in a safe manner with their eyes closed. Ask them to close their eyes, if they are comfortable doing so. Suggest ways for them to be more relaxed, yet erect, balanced, and with their hands at their sides.

3. Say:

"Close your eyes and imagine that a shiny, golden circle is next to you on the floor. This is the future when a breakthrough in your team's work or organization has already been achieved. Step into the golden circle, and notice that you are now at that time and that you have already achieved your breakthrough. Notice what is going on around you, see what you see and hear what you hear, and feel how resourceful, engaged, and competent you are feeling. Let your mind imagine the possibilities in all senses: visual, auditory, and kinesthetic. Even notice what you are tasting and smelling.

"Now slowly shift your posture a bit, and stand in a way that shows you have achieved your breakthrough. Think of a small gesture, but one of the tremendous resourcefulness you are experiencing, a gesture that will serve as your private anchor to this experience. Make this gesture now, as you are experiencing yourself as fully resourceful, engaged, accomplished, and successful.

"Still keeping eyes closed, step back out of the circle, leaving the future there. [pause] Now, remembering that time in the future when you achieved your breakthrough, and the resources you have then and now, think of something you will need to do in the very near future to advance your breakthrough commitment, when you will need those resources. Imagine experiencing this situation, feeling yourself in your own body, looking through your own eyes, seeing what you see, and hearing what you hear.

"As you are experiencing this time, take a step back into your circle. Make the gesture signifying your resourcefulness, and experience yourself having those resources in this situation. Notice how you are feeling even more powerful and capable in this situation, with your sense of already having achieved your breakthrough result. [pause] Now step out of the circle, open your eyes and quietly return to your seat."

4. Hand out copies of the Claiming a Breakthrough worksheet to all participants and have them take the next 7 to 10 minutes to read the top part of the worksheet and complete the sections at the bottom.

5. Have each participant tell his or her vision story to one person sitting nearby.

6. Say, "Breakthrough statements are powerful conversations for possibility. By declaring your commitment in front of the group today, you invite their active support along with the coaching you

need to be prepared to make this powerful statement before your work team or organization." Ask each person to stand and say his or her breakthrough statement, using language such as "I will," or "I commit to," and for everyone else to provide coaching on the clarity of the statement, its impact on you in terms of the power of the words used, and the congruency and commitment with which it is presented. Ask others to make any suggestions for how the statement might be spoken even more clearly, congruently, and powerfully. Lead applause for each statement.

Sherene Zolno, executive director of The Leading Clinic, and chair of the Department of Leadership and Organization Development for Leadership Institute of Seattle (LIOS), is a registered OD consultant, researcher, educator, and certified coach who works with executives and their teams in identifying strategic possibilities, improving operations, and transforming culture. Her research-based *Model for a Healthy World*™ and *Coaching Certification Program in Appreciative Inquiry and Whole System IQ*™ are the foundation for leadership development and change in several major organizations. Sherene served on ASTD's OD Professional Practice Area board. Her writing has been published by ASTD and ODN and has appeared in Pfeiffer's 2000, 2002, and 2008 *Annuals*.

Sherene Zolno
Leadership Institute of Seattle/Saybrook University and The Leading Clinic
25900 Pillsbury Road SW
Vashon, WA 98070
Phone: (206) 463-6374
Email: szolno@comcast.net
Website: www.proactionassociates.com

CLAIMING A BREAKTHROUGH

" . . . the unique reason for having leaders—their differentiating function—is to move us forward. Leaders get us going someplace."

Jim Kouzes and Barry Posner, The Leadership Challenge

"The manager has his eye always on the bottom line; the leader has his eye on the horizon."

Warren Bennis, On Becoming a Leader

Vision shapes direction, but also influences daily decision making. In organizations it shapes hiring, promotion, and actions toward customers, partners, teammates, and investors.

An inspiring shared vision conveys a sense of direction. It releases a sense of discovery. And it implies a sense of destiny. It allows you to lay claim to a breakthrough in possibility for your team or organization.

An inspiring, shared vision helps align our espoused values with our everyday practices, ensuring our own personal congruency and that of a work team, a leadership team, and an organization. A shared vision includes two components:

- A vision story that captures the essence of who and what we will be when we are in our desired future. The vision story is a vibrant, engaging, and specific description of what it is like when the future is achieved. It is told in the language of the senses to make the dream of the future more alive.

- A breakthrough statement, a succinct statement declaring the commitment that is intended to inspire the present. It is spoken using powerful language. Examples include:

  "We are committed to being . . . " "I will . . . " "We will create . . . "

Use the space below to draw an image or write words describing your vision story, answering the questions: What are you *seeing*? What are you *hearing?* and What are you *tasting, smelling,* or *feeling* in your breakthrough future?

What are you committed to now that you have envisioned the future? Write your breakthrough statement here:

CHAPTER FIVE: CHALLENGE THE PROCESS

In This Chapter

- Describe an overview of Challenge the Process.
- Discuss the corresponding Commitments of Leadership.
- Consider the importance of this practice.
- Introduce the activities for this practice.
- Present the activities for this practice.

The Leadership Challenge introduces change in the third practice, Challenge the Process. Change has become an everyday way of life for most of us. Change is easier to address with a solid foundation of values and a clear vision of the future.

Addressing change is a complex task required of all leaders in today's rapidly changing world. Managing change effectively is the single most important element in organizational success. Unfortunately, organizations and their leaders have not always been as successful as they would like. In this practice, leaders recognize that change may come unexpectedly from the outside, or it may be a planned change to seize an opportunity. No matter where it emanates, leadership is required to make the change a success.

HOW DOES A LEADER CHALLENGE THE PROCESS?

Effective change will not happen by itself. A leader needs to have a plan. The plan must translate the concepts into concrete steps so that employees can implement them. A leader needs to help carry out the plan. That requires getting everyone involved who has a stake in the change to step outside his or her comfort zone. How do leaders Challenge the Process and make things happen?

Consider the related Commitments of Leadership:

- Search for opportunities by seizing the initiative and by looking outward for innovative ways to improve.
- Experiment and take risks by constantly generating small wins and learning from experience.

Search for Opportunities

There is always room for improvement. Exemplary leaders involve everyone in identifying ways to improve. They encourage others to speak up and challenge the status quo. Leaders coach others to see a better way and encourage them to take initiative to challenge what they see.

Leaders are successful making change when they consider their ethical responsibility to the organization and the people. They are successful if they:

- Raise issues that the organization cannot raise itself.
- Conduct change efforts honestly and responsibly.
- Introduce new perspectives for consideration.
- Communicate honestly and openly.
- Listen to opposing views.
- Encourage and enable participation.

Experiment and Take Risks

To ensure that everyone is involved in challenging the process, leaders must learn how to generate small wins and learn from experience. Small wins are a must; they are easier to sell, easier to implement, and employees are more willing to accept them. Some of the most effective changes occur slowly, one step at a time. Most successful change processes are made up of small, incremental steps.

During times of change, the leader who experiments and learns along the way will be the most successful in the long run. Exemplary leaders are life-long learners. Think back to when you learned the most. It was probably an experience that was not easy and not 100 percent perfect. It is true that we learn from our mistakes. Leaders allow for learning to occur. Like the military, leaders may implement an "after-action review," which quite simply examines what went well, what did not, what was learned, and what will be done better next time.

Finally, leaders Challenge the Process using a template or model that allows them to follow a process that has been proven effective. People can gain control of change if they have a clear plan, milestones to achieve along the way, and measures that tell them they are making progress toward their objective.

WHY IS CHALLENGE THE PROCESS IMPORTANT?

Change is here to stay. It is what makes organizations more competitive. Change can bring out the best in people because they are pushed to dig deeply into their reserves and to tap into uncharted talent. Change forces people to be innovative, to experiment with new processes, and to find ways to be more effective and efficient. Change can also create havoc and produce resistance when leadership skills are not evident.

ACTIVITY INTRODUCTION

The eighteen activities in the Challenge the Process chapter are creative and exciting. You will have fun delivering any of these, and your participants will glean ideas for improving leadership skills as well as improving processes. Activities range from being a judge or a general to acting as a builder.

Several activities give actual experiences of teams challenging a process, and others provide the participants with an opportunity to practice risk-taking. Several opportunities exist for teams to construct a project. An assessment relating the causes of resistance to change provides opportunity for rich discussion. Most of the activities provide you with the means to move the notion of Challenge the Process from concept to a tangible application.

Finally, the collection of activities provides you with a mix that can be used with your current day-to-day processes or processes that have been designed specifically for the experience.

Activity List

- Game of the Generals by Elisa May Arboleda-Cuevas and Audie Bautista Masigan
- Take Off the Blindfolds by Douglas Austrom
- The Giant Skip by Peter Cheng
- Change: Feel the Pain, See the Gain by Daryl R. Conner
- Gordon's Knot by Ricky Foo
- Take a Risk! by Dennis E. Gilbert
- When Questions Are the Answer—Challenging the Process by Barbara Pate Glacel
- Toss It Around by Ann Hermann-Nehdi
- Challenge Think Tank by Amanda Crowell Itliong

- Cash Flow Exercise by Edith Katz
- Change Project Summary by Edith Katz
- Constructing a Global Team Communications Device by John Lybarger
- Identify Perceived Causes of Resistance by Consuelo Meux
- In-Basket Exercise by Alan Richter
- Challenge the Process in Real Time by L.J. Rose
- Overcoming Barriers by Darryl Sink
- You Be the Judge!™ by Karen Travis
- Assumption Reframe by Devora Zack

GAME OF THE GENERALS

Submitted by Elisa May Arboleda-Cuevas and Audie Bautista Masigan

Objectives

- To help participants see the value of experimenting and taking risks as a leader.
- To foster teamwork and team strategy toward the attainment of team goals.

Audience

Twenty-five to thirty participants, who are working on risk taking and experimenting.

Time Required

30 to 45 minutes.

Materials and Equipment

- Music of drum beats or actual drumming.
- Strips of paper for the ranks/positions created from rank table (copy and cut up).

Area Setup

A large room, but no chairs and tables are required. A park, beach, or other outdoor setting is an option.

Facilitator Note

The Game of the Generals is an educational "war chessboard game" invented by Sofronio H. Pasola, Jr., in 1970. It is also called "Salpakan" in Filipino or simply "The Generals."

Process

1. Divide participants into two battalions (teams). Ask each battalion to assign a leader. The leader will assign the ranks/ positions to members, by providing each team member with a strip of paper with a rank written on it (see below). Each person should keep his or her rank secret. The table below allows for fifteen group members (note that there are two Three-Star General strips and two One-Star General strips). *Should you opt to involve more than fifteen members, you may assign more than one of any rank, such as three Privates and three Spies.*

Five-Star General	Eliminates any lower-ranking officer
Four-Star General	Eliminates any lower-ranking officer
Three-Star General	Eliminates any lower-ranking officer
Three-Star General	Eliminates any lower-ranking officer
One-Star General	Eliminates any lower-ranking officer
One-Star General	Eliminates any lower-ranking officer
Colonel	Eliminates any lower-ranking officer
Lt. Colonel	Eliminates any lower-ranking officer
Major	Eliminates any lower-ranking officer
Captain	Eliminates any lower-ranking officer

(Continued)

1st Lieutenant	Eliminates any lower-ranking officer
2nd Lieutenant	Eliminates the sergeant and the private
Sergeant	Eliminates the private
Private	Eliminates the spy
Spy	Eliminates all officers from the rank of Sergeant up to Five-Star General

2. *Explain the* goal is for each battalion to capture as many war prisoners as it can. As the facilitator (arbiter), determine how many series of "war rounds" will occur. Tell participants the number of rounds and provide the rules:
   - No one from the other camp should know the ranks of those in the opposite camp.
   - After the first round, the leader should strategize before sending men to the battlefield based on which ranks were taken prisoner.
   - The facilitator (arbiter) will decide how many men should be sent to the battlefield and will state, "Leaders, send X troops to battle." You will select two to four each round.
   - Once sent forward, troops who take prisoners may be used again.
   - After the first round, tell the leader he or she may confer with the entire team.
   - No leader knows the rank/designation of the opposing team members. The facilitator (arbiter) identifies which battalion captures the opponent's soldiers to become war prisoners.
   - The battalion with the most number of prisoners of war at the end wins.

3. Share this example with the group.

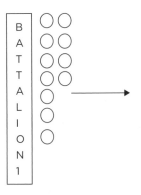

- Facilitator (Arbiter) says, "Send four troops to the battlefield!"
- Five-star general of Battalion 1 will be war prisoner of Battalion 2. (The spy takes the five-star general.)
- Private of Battalion 1 will be war prisoner of Battalion 2. (The four-star general takes the private.)
- One-star general of Battalion 2 will be war prisoner of Battalion 1. (The three-star general takes the one-star general.)
- 1st Lieutenant of Battalion 2 will be war prisoner of Battalion 1. (The major takes the 1st lieutenant.)
- In this case, each battalion was able to capture two prisoners of war.

4. Play the stated number of rounds, identifying how many members should be sent to each battle.

5. Once all rounds have been played, count up the number of prisoners. The team with the most prisoners wins.

6. Debrief the activity by asking these kind of questions:
    - How did each team feel when they were capturing their opponent's soldiers? Responses might be similar to these:
        - Sense of victory.
        - Impending celebration.
        - Strategy is working.
        - Should not be complacent at any point in time.
    - How did each team feel when they were losing their men? Responses might be similar to these:
        - Starting to lose morale.
        - Desire to continue to fight and gain the upper hand.
        - Suggest reviewing strategy.
        - Not to lose hope.
    - For the team who won, what was your strategy? Responses might be similar to these:
        - They were observant and took notes of the ranks of the opposing soldiers as they were engaged in the battlefield, based on which ranks were captured.
        - Took the risk in sacrificing some of their men to win the war.
        - Leader listened to the suggestions of his members.
        - Team members trusted and cooperated with their leader.
    - For the team who lost, what could have been done to avoid losing your men? Responses might be similar to these:
        - Better strategy.
        - Risk taking is part of the process of attaining the goal.

- Members should be willing to forward suggestions to the leader, and the leader should cultivate an atmosphere of openness.
- Learn from the mistakes of the past.
- What values did you learn from this activity and why? Responses might be similar to these:
  - Taking risks and experimenting is an integral part of leadership.
  - Goals are achieved through teamwork.
  - In the real battlefield, suggestions from everyone are most welcome.
  - You can never experience triumph without sacrifice.
- As a leader, how would you relate this to your work? Responses might be similar to these:
  - Organizations should keep abreast of current and future trends.
  - Change is a leader's best friend. It makes the organizations relevant and sustainable.
- What's the attitude of people toward change? Draw out thoughts, feelings, and sentiments and lead them into the realization that change is an organization's friend.

Elisa May Arboleda-Cuevas is a highly accomplished innovator and marketing professional with a solid track record of success in marketing and business development. Having worked with multinational corporations in the Philippines and the Asia-Pacific region (such as Nestlé, DHL, and Coca-Cola), her exposure has made her an expert dealing with the workplace and has spurred her passion to be highly committed to people development and marketing communications. Currently, she is the CEO of PeopleSparx, Inc.

Audie Bautista Masigan is a training consultant at the top training and development organization in the Philippines. He is driven by his passion to develop the most important asset of any organization—its people. His overall commitment to arrive at the desired results has made him a prominent leader in the field of organizational dynamics and development in his country. He is currently the chief operating officer and chief engineer for organizational dynamics and development of PeopleSparx, Inc.

Elisa May Arboleda-Cuevas
PeopleSparx, Inc.
7F YL Holdings Building
115 V.A. Rufino cor. Salcedo Sts.
Legaspi Village, Makati City
M.M. Philippines 1229
  TeleFax: (632) 893 0893

Audie Bautista Masigan
PeopleSparx, Inc.
7F YL Holdings Building
115 V.A. Rufino cor. Salcedo Sts.
Legaspi Village, Makati City
M.M. Philippines 1229
  TeleFax: (632) 893 0893

TAKE OFF THE BLINDFOLDS

Submitted by Douglas Austrom

Objectives

- To experience the importance of challenging the process to achieving significant breakthroughs in performance.
- To provide hands-on experience to search for opportunities and to take risks for making improvements.

Audience

Eighteen to twenty-four participants interested in developing their leadership and team effectiveness skills, divided in teams of five or six participants each.

Time Required

60 to 75 minutes, depending on how extensively you choose to debrief the exercise.

Materials and Equipment

- Four red bandanas, one blue bandana, and one white bandana for each team of six participants or four red bandanas and one blue bandana for each team of five participants.
- A construction kit in Ziploc® bags for each team containing a picture of a Tinkertoy® or similar structure and the Tinkertoys or similar parts to make the structure. Keep the construction materials out of sight until after the builders are blindfolded and the construction kits are distributed to the team leaders.
- Timer for the first round of the exercise.

- Stop watch for each team for the second round of the exercise.
- Flip chart and markers.

Area Setup

Meeting room with tables and seating for each team of five to six participants.

Process

1. Prior to starting the activity, distribute four red bandanas, a blue bandana, and a white bandana (if using) to each table of participants. Ask each person to select a bandana.

2. Begin by saying, "We will be doing a team exercise that provides an opportunity to experience the practices and commitments of leadership. Your team will have 10 minutes to build a structure. Each of you will have a specific role to play in this exercise: the people with the red bandanas will be builders; the person with the blue bandana will be the team leader; and the person with the white bandana will be an observer. The builders will be blindfolded and can only use one hand. The leader will be given a construction kit with the picture of a structure and the parts needed to build the structure. The leader can dump the parts in the middle of the table and pick up the picture. The leaders cannot touch either the construction materials or the workers. They can only give verbal instructions on how to build the structure shown in the picture. Observers, your job is to watch for examples of effective leadership and good teamwork. Once all of the builders are blindfolded, the leaders can pick up the construction kits and you will have 10 minutes to build the structure. Please clear your tables. Builders, put on your

blindfolds." *Note:* If you do not have an observer for every team, then you can also ask the observers to wander around the room and observe multiple teams.

3. As soon as all of the builders are blindfolded, tell them they will have 10 minutes. Set the timer for 10 minutes and invite the leaders to pick up their construction kits.

4. As you move about the room, remind the leaders that they cannot touch the parts. Also remind the builders that they can only use one hand.

5. When time expires, tell participants to remove their blindfolds and spend a few minutes in their groups discussing what happened, providing any examples of effective leadership and teamwork that they experienced. Very few, if any, teams will complete the structure in the allotted time.

6. After 4 or 5 minutes of team discussion, ask the observers for examples of effective teamwork and effective leadership. Usually people mention such things as the importance of clear instructions, listening carefully, cooperation among team members to put together the pieces, keeping everyone involved, and providing encouraging feedback.

7. Some of the experiences in this round of the exercise can be generalized to the participants' organizational experiences. With some gentle probing, someone will comment that their leader instructed the builders to "pick up the red piece" or some other colored part that they could not distinguish because of the blindfolds. This provides a good entree for comparing the simulation with the typical workplace; for example, "Do you or your colleagues ever feel that you receive instructions like this?"

8. Ask the builders how they felt during the exercise. Often they will admit that they felt underutilized, left out, and frustrated because they weren't sure what to do or how to contribute. Once again, comparisons can be made to how many employees feel in organizations today. Similarly, the role of the leader should be discussed. Often they report feeling considerable pressure to keep everyone working and productive, to provide useful instructions, and to complete the task within the time allowed.

9. If it is not mentioned, ask the group whether any of the leaders started their verbal instructions by describing the structure and creating a verbal picture of the structure, in other words, a vision. If not, you can then ask the builders what they thought they were building. Ask the group, "Would it have been helpful to have a verbal picture or vision of the structure?"

10. To complete the debriefing of the first round of the exercise, ask participants: "What would you do differently if you had it to do over again." Typically, participants make suggestions that would improve team functioning within the parameters of the simulation—for example, division of labor, modular construction, and clarity of instructions. They seldom challenge the blindfolds, building with only one hand, and so on. If and when they do, proceed to the discussion of how to "reengineer the process."

11. Announce the following to the group: "You have all been assigned to a task force to reengineer this process. You have a blank sheet of paper. What would you do differently to improve the process?" Record their suggestions on a flip chart, which will typically include ideas such as:
    - Take off the blindfolds.
    - Use both hands.

- Show everyone the picture.
- Divide up the task.
- Use modular construction.
  Ask the following leading questions so that they identify tactics such as planning and preparation, practice, and continuous process improvement.
- "What should you do before you start a task?"
- "In the performing arts and competitive sports, what does it take to get better and better?"
- "And in this exercise, what are we improving?"

12. Provide the following instructions for the second round: "You will have 15 minutes in your teams to plan, prepare, practice, and otherwise improve your process of building this structure. There are only two constraints: First, the observer will serve as your timekeeper and cannot participate. Second, while you can have the parts in hand, there can be no pre-assembled parts or modules. And those are the ONLY constraints. Anything else is OK. At the end of the 15 minutes, we will have all teams build the structure at the same time to see which team is fastest."

13. Distribute the stopwatches to the observers. Make a point of moving from table to table because participants will usually have questions about the constraints. Here are some of the questions you can expect. "Can we use both hands?" "Do we have to keep the blindfolds on?" "Can the leader participate?" And the answer is: "There are only two constraints: No pre-assembled parts and the observer can't participate."

14. Some teams may be inclined to over-plan the process. Encourage them to do as many timed practice runs as possible.

15. As you circulate, find out how fast the teams are building the structures and announce the fastest times. When one of the teams builds the structure in 1 minute or less, ask: "I wonder which team is going to break 1 minute first?" Usually, participants will become very engaged during this time as their performance improves. It is not unusual for teams to burst into spontaneous cheering and high-fiving when they achieve a significant breakthrough.

16. At the end of the 15 minutes, instruct the teams that all parts must be disassembled. Ask the observers to serve as timers for different teams. When the teams are ready, give them a countdown, and begin timing. Virtually all teams will complete the structure in less than 20 seconds. The fastest team will do so in under 10 seconds.

17. Initiate the debriefing of this round by noting the dramatic improvement in results between the first round and the second round, "None of the teams completed the structure in 10 minutes in the first round. All teams were able to complete it in less than 30 seconds in the second round." Depending on the audience, you may wish to comment on the importance of breakthrough improvements in performance in today's hyper-competitive business environment. Ask the group, "How did you Challenge the Process and how did challenging the process contribute to such dramatic improvements in performance between the first and second rounds?" Here is a sampling of answers that workshop participants have provided:

    • We challenged the old process by taking off the blindfolds, using both hands, sharing the picture with everyone, and testing the assumption that the leader was just there to give directions. Without these changes, we would never have been able to achieve the times we did.

- During our planning and preparation phase, we came up with an initial process and then we tried it. We continually evaluated the best way to do it. We observed where idle time existed and where people were overloaded. We revised the process to balance the workload and we tried it again.
- Everyone was actively engaged and we listened to everyone's input.
- We weren't stuck in our roles. If someone could do something better, we rotated roles.
- We paid attention to the other teams' times and challenged ourselves to do better. While we competed with the other teams, we competed with ourselves even more.
- We constantly evaluated what worked. If something didn't work, we tried something else.
- We benchmarked the other teams to get new ideas.
- Once we discovered a process that worked for us: practice, practice, practice.

18. You may wish to post these questions as a summary:
    - How did the levels of engagement and enthusiasm between the first round and the second round compare?
    - In the first round, who felt the most responsibility for the success of the team?
    - In the second round, who felt responsible for the success of the team?

19. Then ask the group, "What accounts for the significantly higher levels of engagement, enthusiasm, and sense of ownership in the second round? How were you enabled to perform? Answers from previous workshop participants have included:

- Because we had a shared goal and a shared vision because we could all see the picture, we developed a much greater sense of ownership.
- Everyone was focused on team success and we trusted others to do their parts.
- Removing the blindfolds and using two hands made us feel more capable and increased the teamwork.
- Everyone made suggestions and contributed to improving the process.
- As we tried different things, our times got better. As our times got better, everyone became more excited and enthusiastic. And the excitement was contagious.
- There was mutual encouragement.
- Every time we tried something a little bit different, we got feedback right away whether it worked or not.

20. As a parting challenge, ask the participants, "What could you do to take this level of energy and enthusiasm or even a fraction of it back to your workplace? After all, the work that you and your colleagues do is certainly more interesting and important than building the same Tinkertoy structure over and over again."

Facilitator Note

The blindfolds can be used to represent the personal paradigms, untested assumptions, and self-limiting beliefs that often get in the way of breakthroughs in performance and real change. Working with one hand is also a metaphor for the obstacles or challenges in our organizations that prevent employees from performing at their maximum.

Sharing the picture, that is, the vision, also demonstrates the second practice, Inspire a Shared Vision, and the importance of a tangible vision to the changing role of leadership. In older, more hierarchical models of leadership, the leader had sole access to the "picture," and they parceled it out to people who could not see the whole picture. The leader in the first round was, in fact, the major bottleneck in the process. In today's rapid response environment, everyone must be able to see the whole picture.

Douglas Austrom, Ph.D., is co-founder of Turning Point Associates, Inc., an organizational consulting firm that specializes in strategic planning and implementation, organizational and cultural change, leadership development, and customer satisfaction. He has over twenty-five years of consulting experience with a wide range of organizations such as AT&T, Eli Lilly and Company, Rolls Royce, E. Merck, Indianapolis Symphony Orchestra, KFC Corporation, The Nature Conservancy, RCI, and Westvaco. He is also an adjunct professor with Indiana University's Kelley School of Business, where he teaches a capstone M.B.A. course on ethical leadership.

Douglas Austrom, Ph.D.
Turning Point Associates, Inc.
217 W. 10th Street
Indianapolis, IN 46202
  Phone: (317) 633-8747
  Email: daustrom@tpaconsulting.com
  Website: www.tpaconsulting.com

EXAMPLE OF A TINKERTOY STRUCTURE

THE GIANT SKIP

Submitted by Peter Cheng

Objectives

- To instill a Challenge the Process mindset among participants.
- To experience the exemplary behaviors of a leader challenging the process with his or her team.
- To create an environment in which the participants can change, grow, and innovate their processes and apply their key learning back to the workplace.

Audience

Up to thirty people in groups of eight to ten.

Time Required

50 to 60 minutes.

Materials and Equipment

- Rock climbing rope of about 7 meters in length (21 feet) for each group.

Area Setup

Open space with no or high ceiling with plenty of room for each team.

Process

1. Form groups of eight to ten people. Provide a rope to each participating group.
2. Have two people in each group hold either ends of the rope. Tell the participants that the goal is for each group to perform twenty

205

continuous skips in full circle. State that they have 15 minutes for practice and planning and 10 minutes to reach this goal.

3. State that only two people are permitted to be the "swingers" (one on each end of the rope). The swingers will swing the rope in a complete 360-degree spin from the bottom, to the top, and back to the bottom again. The rest of the team members will line up and one at a time will skip as the rope approaches their feet.

4. The group will have to restart when the team fails to complete twenty successful skips. To restart means having to count from 1 again.

5. Give the group 15 minutes for planning and practice.

6. Announce when the 10 minutes begin for the actual demonstration. You may have all the teams conducting their process at the same time or, if there are only two groups, you may wish to have each observe the other.

7. Facilitate a debriefing session to unravel the key learning pertaining to Challenge the Process:
   • What was most helpful during the planning and practice time?
   • How did it feel to challenge the process?
   • What was your team's most innovative idea?
   • What was the greatest risk your team took?
   • How did you handle "mistakes"?
   • How does what you did in this activity relate to processes at work?
   • What have you learned that can be applied back at the workplace?

Peter Cheng has over ten years of experience and dedication to organization development, coupled with more than fifteen years of work experience in market research, sales and marketing, retail and distribution, strategic planning, business development, lecturing, and general management. Peter is an accomplished facilitator and executive coach. He is one of the first two Leadership Challenge® Certified Master Facilitators in Asia, actively facilitating The Leadership Challenge® Workshop in the regional countries. Adding to his list of credentials, Peter is also a Certified Master Coach with the Behavioral Coaching Institute (BCI). Peter holds a master of arts degree in education and human development from The George Washington University.

Peter Cheng
PACE Organization Dynamics Pte Ltd
162 Bukit Merah Central
#06-3555
Singapore 150162
  Phone: 65-62788289
  Email: petercheng@pace-od.com
  Website: www.pace-od.com

CHANGE: FEEL THE PAIN, SEE THE GAIN
Submitted by Daryl R. Conner

Objective

- To enable the leaders of an initiative to gain a deep understanding of and a shared alignment around the case for change.

Audience

Limit the group size to twenty to twenty-five people. This activity is intended for leaders of a challenging initiative, typically a major, highly disruptive organizational change. Participants in this activity, as leaders of the initiative, should have a thorough understanding of the initiative and its expected outcomes.

Time Required

Approximately 3 hours.

Materials and Equipment

- One Case for Change 2-by-2 matrix on $8\frac{1}{2}$ by 11–inch paper for each participant.
- Five or six flip charts (one for each table, plus one for the facilitator).
- Red and blue flip-chart markers for the table flip charts.
- Black flip chart markers for the facilitator (avoid red and blue for the facilitator).

Area Setup

Arrange four or five tables (preferably round) so that participants seated at each table can comfortably see the facilitator. Each table should have four or five chairs and a flip chart. Draw the Case for Change 2-by-2 matrix on each table flip chart. Place one or two flip charts where the facilitator will stand.

Facilitator Note

To realize the objectives of a major change, leaders should agree that the status quo is no longer acceptable and that there is a "burning platform" for change. In addition, leaders must enroll those who are the targets of the change in the burning platform sense of urgency. Many leaders are hesitant to share "pain messages" that the status quo is unacceptable, and often only want to share the benefits of the desired future state. If the organization does not understand the case for change and has a strong desire to maintain the status quo, then the likelihood that the organization will realize the objectives of the initiative is much lower.

A burning platform in this context represents a business imperative. The motivation for change is created when the price of maintaining the status quo is greater than the price of change. The concept is meant to illustrate the level of resolve leaders need to have before undertaking major change, not the necessity for the organization to be in crisis before major change can occur. Burning-platform type urgency (a business imperative) can surface in one or a combination of current or anticipated problems or opportunities.

Process

1. Share the objective of the session. Ask participants to spend a couple of minutes reflecting individually on the organization's case for change.

2. Provide each participant with a blank Case for Change template. Ask each participant to capture individually his or her

perspective on reasons why the organization needs to change. The participant should capture as many reasons as possible. Warn them that it is typically easier to identify problems than opportunities and ask the participants to ensure they consider every box on the template. Allow about 10 minutes.

3. Summarize the case for change in small table groups. Provide each table with a flip chart copy of the Case for Change matrix. At each table, ask participants to discuss and summarize their individual reflections into one case for change matrix for their team. Instruct them to use red and blue markers to indicate alignment. The team should use a blue marker to indicate agreement, and a red marker to indicate non-agreement. Tell them they have 30 minutes for this task.

4. Discuss and internalize the case for change. Ask one table to share information gathered for the box labeled Current Problem. Facilitate a discussion of their findings with the entire group. Ask questions to deepen the discussion on items that seem sensitive. Probe to ensure the discussion deepens into the personal pain of the change. Use these questions:
   - What compels you as an individual to embark on the change?
   - What will sustain you as an individual through the tough decisions and actions that will be part of the transformation journey?
   - What is the price to you, individually, of not changing? What will happen to you personally if this change fails?
   - Determine whether the rest of the group has anything to add. If so, note it on the flip chart of the team that is sharing. Draw a black box around this box on this team's template only to indicate the box they shared.

5. Move to another team and have them share information gathered for the box labeled Anticipated Problem. Follow the same process. Move to another team and follow the same process for the box labeled Current Opportunity. Ask the final team to follow the same process for the box labeled Anticipated Opportunity. As the teams share their results with the larger group, ensure the conversation has deepened to the personal impacts of the change. Ensure they understand and relate at an emotional level to the pain they will incur if the change is not successful. This may take as much as 90 minutes.

6. Summarize and agree on a compelling case for change.
   - With the input from the participants, capture the most compelling reasons for change identified during the discussion on your flip chart. Ensure it considers all four boxes of the Case for Change matrix, though the final case for change will not necessarily include them all.
   - Check with the leader of the initiative to ensure he or she believes the list is compelling and complete. If not, the leader should suggest what is missing and discuss it with the participants, as needed.

7. The leader of the change should then ask the participants, "Does anyone not support this as the case for change?" As needed, assist with any discussions around additional input or alignment.

8. The exercise is complete when the leader of the initiative and the participants agree they have either captured a compelling case for change, or that there is not a case for change for the initiative.

9. Ask the leader of the initiative to share the planned next steps.

Daryl Conner is an internationally recognized leader in organizational change, a dynamic public speaker, and an advisor to senior executives. In more than thirty-five years of practice, Daryl has worked with successful organizations around the world to help them achieve the full intent of their most critically important initiatives. Daryl has authored two books: *Managing at the Speed of Change* (Random House, 1993) and *Leading at the Edge of Chaos* (John Wiley & Sons, 1998).

Daryl R. Conner
Chairman
Conner Partners
Suite 1000
1230 Peachtree Street, NE
Atlanta, GA 30309
    Phone: (404) 564-4800
    Email: daryl.conner@connerpartners.com
    Website: www.connerpartners.com

CASE FOR CHANGE

On this template, list your individual view of the need to change. Consider both external and internal problems and opportunities— those that you are currently facing or that you anticipate in the future.

	PROBLEM	OPPORTUNITY
CURRENT		
ANTICIPATED		

The Leadership Challenge Activities Book
Copyright © 2010 by James M. Kouzes and Barry Z. Posner.
Reproduced by permission of Pfeiffer, an Imprint of Wiley. www.pfeiffer.com.

GORDON'S KNOT

Submitted by Ricky Foo

Objectives

- To understand the characteristics of an effective problem solver.
- To articulate the critical success factors to Challenge the Process effectively.
- To apply the critical success factors to real workplace situations.

Audience

Suitable for any group size. An even number is preferred. If there is an odd number of participants, the facilitator can join in.

Time Required

30 minutes.

Materials and Equipment

- Two ropes of different colors (for example, red and yellow), about 1 to 1.5 meters each. The ropes will need to have loops at both ends. The loop needs to be large enough to allow participants to put their hands through it.

Area Setup

Sufficient space for participants to stand and move around within a 1 to 2 square meter area.

Process

1. Ask the participants to pair up (preferably same gender if possible).

2. Distribute two ropes (one of each color; for purposes of these directions, we'll refer to them as yellow and red) to every pair.

3. Ask the person holding the yellow rope to put each of his or her wrists into one of the loops at each end.

4. Ask the second person, who is holding the red rope, to put one loop over his or her left wrist, wrap the rope around the yellow rope and put the last loop on his or her right wrist.

5. At this point, the participants are tied together with the ropes.

6. Brief the participants that the objective is to disentangle the ropes. There are two rules:
   They are not allowed to remove the loops from their wrists.
   They cannot cut or remove the knot on the rope.
   State that they will be given about 10 minutes to untangle themselves.

7. While the participants are trying to disentangle themselves, observe how they focus on the ropes, how they move around each other, but can't loosen themselves. Allow about 6 or 7 minutes before giving hints. It is important that they try various methods to solve the problem.

8. If none of the participants are able to solve the problem, demonstrate to them by using one of the pairs. Allow the participants to try to solve the problem after one demonstration and encourage those who have solved the problem to help others.

9. End the activity after about approximately 10 minutes.

10. Close with several debriefing questions:
    • What was successful during this problem solving stage?
    • What are the characteristics of effective problem solving?

- What are the critical success factors to Challenge the Process?
- How can we apply these critical success factors at the workplace?

Solution

In order to disentangle from the knot, the person with the red rope picks up the rope from the bottom and brings the rope to enter the right-hand loop of the yellow rope from the back at the wrist level. Then, a small loop can be created by using the red rope and to loop it over the right hand of the person holding the yellow rope. By switching the red rope and yellow rope at the wrist level, the red rope will be disentangled.

Ricky Foo affirms positive thinking and life-long learning. A graduate with an honors degree in business from the Nanyang Technological University, his learning journey continues as he pursues a master of arts in education and human development from The George Washington University. His passion in personal and organizational development sees him highly committed and dedicated to cover the extra miles in the journeys with his learning partners. He is an accredited Myers-Briggs Type Indicator (MBTI) administrator and a Certified Facilitator of The Leadership Challenge® workshop.

Ricky Foo
PACE Organization Dynamics Pte Ltd
Blk 162 Bukit Merah Central
#06-3555
Singapore 150162
  Phone: +65 6278 8289
  Email: rickyfoo@pace-od.com
  Website: http://www.pace-od.com

TAKE A RISK!
Submitted by Dennis E. Gilbert

Objectives

- To engage participants in a deeper understanding and exploration of risk taking.
- To discover connections to learning, innovation, and growth through reasonable risk taking.
- To identify individual attitudes or perceptions about reasonable risk.
- To discuss why risk taking is critical to Challenge the Process.

Audience

Group size may range from ten to forty participants. This activity is ideal as a session opener or used in leadership training.

Time Required

Approximately 60 minutes.

Materials and Equipment

- One copy of the Risk-Taking Mini-Assessment for each participant.
- One copy of the Risk-Taking Scoring Sheet for each participant.
- One copy of the Facilitator Assessment Debriefing Guide for the facilitator.
- One copy of the Risk-Taking Debriefing Sheet for each participant.
- Flip chart and markers for facilitator debriefing.
- Suitable writing surface and pen or pencil for participants to fill out worksheets.

Area Setup

Any room large enough for the entire group and breakout subgroups to work without disturbing each other.

Process

1. Begin by introducing the activity as an exercise to get participants engaged exploring reasonable risk taking. This activity is not about right or wrong answers but is about self-assessment and awareness as it relates to risk taking.

2. Hand out the Risk-Taking Mini-Assessment and clearly explain the directions. Allow 5 to 10 minutes and ask participants to remain quiet when finished. Stress that first reactions and honest answers yield the best results on this instrument.

3. When all participants are finished or time is called, hand out the Risk-Taking Scoring Sheet and give instructions for completing the worksheet, prompting participants for any questions before beginning. Instruct participants to carefully transfer their scores, paying close attention to reversing only asterisked items. Reinforce the thought that, regardless of their scores, this is about discovery and that one individual may view reactions to the statements in a different way than another individual does. Advise participants that sharing their scores is a personal choice and that scores will not be requested on an individual basis. Allow 5 minutes for scoring.

4. *(Optional)* You can ask for a show of hands of those in a particular scoring bracket. It is strongly advised to be cautious and sensitive about exploiting any individual scores. Only ask for a show of hands for one or two of the highest performing categories.

218

Avoiding the lower categories helps avoid discomfort of the participants.

5. Utilizing the Facilitator Assessment Debriefing Guide, explain the value or intention of each assessment statement. This will take about 15 minutes.

6. Break participants into small subgroups of four or five people per group. Have each subgroup select a recorder and a speaker. Utilizing the Risk-Taking Debriefing Sheet, have the subgroups discuss their answers to the questions. Ask one person in each subgroup to record reactions to the questions. Allow 15 to 20 minutes for subgroup interaction.

7. Reassemble the entire group and facilitate a debriefing by soliciting and recording themes from the subgroups on a flip chart. Focus on items that promote learning and innovation while also expressing the importance of risk and growth. Allow 10 to 15 minutes to debrief. While debriefing, encourage the use of audience experiences to promote and solidify how taking reasonable risk promotes growth for both individuals and entire organizations.

8. As the facilitator, reflect on why risk taking is critical to Challenge the Process. Remind participants that they have a responsibility to assess the true consequences of real risk. Sometimes we confuse real risk with perceived risk and should utilize a lead-by-example approach to risk assessment.

Dennis E. Gilbert is the president of Appreciative Strategies, LLC, a human performance improvement training and consulting business. His extensive background in management and education are the culmination of over twenty-five years of experience with both for-profit businesses and non-profit institutions of higher learning. An accomplished executive, manager, consultant, and trainer, Dennis delivers exceptional human performance improvement solutions to businesses and organizations. His focus is on leadership development, communications, and group dynamics.

Dennis E. Gilbert
Appreciative Strategies, LLC
P.O. Box 164
Montoursville, PA 17754-0164
    Phone: (570) 606-3780
    Email: dennis@appreciativestrategies.com
    Website: appreciativestrategies.com

RISK-TAKING MINI-ASSESSMENT

Instructions: Read each statement and provide your initial reaction without in-depth thought. Your facilitator will give you additional instructions shortly. Please remain quiet when finished.

Circle the number that best matches your initial reaction, with a "1" representing total disagreement and a "5" representing complete agreement.

1 = Total Disagreement 3 = Neutral 5 = Complete Agreement

Statement	Your Assessment
1. I understand the boundaries of my authority and take appropriate risks.	1 2 3 4 5
2. Taking a few risks while focusing more on safe choices is the best path for individual and professional growth.	1 2 3 4 5
3. Experiences during my life and career are valuable to me.	1 2 3 4 5
4. When I analyze a challenge, I consider action plans and results based on a one-step-at-a-time approach.	1 2 3 4 5
5. In part, confidence comes from observing numerous smaller challenges develop into a big win.	1 2 3 4 5

(Continued)

		1	2	3	4	5
6.	I pursue challenges with the correct balance of safety in my choices and real risk.	1	2	3	4	5
7.	As my confidence grows, I take more risks.	1	2	3	4	5
8.	Confidence is built by learning from both successes and failures.	1	2	3	4	5
9.	Making safe choices provides the best opportunity to learn.	1	2	3	4	5
10.	I assess risk the same during times of extreme pressure to perform, as compared with times of normal business climate.	1	2	3	4	5
11.	There is little risk involved with innovation.	1	2	3	4	5
12.	I believe in a climate that supports learning from mistakes.	1	2	3	4	5

RISK-TAKING SCORING SHEET

Instructions: Transfer your scores from the mini-assessment, reversing scores marked with an asterisk (items 2, 9, 11) according to the following scale:

5 = 1   4 = 2   3 = 3   2 = 4   1 = 5

Statement	Score	Statement	Score
1.	7.		
2.*	8.		
3.	**9.***		
4.	10.		
5.	**11.***		
6.	12.		
Total-A		Total-B	
Total A + B = your score: _____			

Assess your results by marking the appropriate block with an "X."

"X"	Score	Assessment
	54 to 60	You understand risk—go make things happen!
	45 to 53	Good general sense of risk—explore more to grow more!
	35 to 44	Probably too conservative—playing it too safe, take a risk!
	12 to 34	Start taking risks or get out of the way!

FACILITATOR ASSESSMENT DEBRIEFING GUIDE

Instructions: As the facilitator, you can offer a review and discussion of each of the assessment statements. Utilize the information provided below to begin a debriefing process.

1. I understand the boundaries of my authority and take appropriate risks.
   Discussion: This statement is provided to lay some ground rules as we consider risk. Workshop participants need to be aware of the importance and value of striving to do more and to take risks, but at the same time not to exceed the boundaries of their authority.

2. Taking a few risks while focusing more on safe choices is the best path for individual and professional growth.
   Discussion: Safe choices typically do not promote growth. When we make safe choices, we are likely not pushing far enough to achieve true growth. Remember that we learn from our mistakes and true growth comes from learning. A proper balance of risk and safe choices is important, but this statement suggests a "focus" on safe choices that would likely be counter-productive to risk and growth.

3. Experiences during my life and career are valuable to me.
   Discussion: The purpose of this statement is to reinforce the idea that growth comes from learning and that all experiences, regardless of the context of good or bad, provide value to us.

4. When I analyze a challenge, I consider action plans and results based on a one-step-at-a-time approach.

Discussion: This supports the value of "small wins." As we take on challenges, it is important to look for small wins along the way. This helps to build confidence and reassurance while also allowing for a fluid process.

5. In part, confidence comes from observing numerous smaller challenges develop into a big win.
   Discussion: Often we observe success only as the end result. We build confidence by reflecting on smaller challenges along the way. Confidence inspires us to reach for more growth since the feeling of real risk becomes less.

6. I pursue challenges with the correct balance of safety in my choices and real risk.
   Discussion: Since we are half-way through the assessment, it is time again to set the proper tone for risk. We should utilize the correct balance of safety and real risk. If we believe we can jump from a five-story building and land safely without some special equipment or safety devices, we are in for a surprise. Balance your pursuit of challenges with both safe choices and risk.

7. As my confidence grows, I take more risks.
   Discussion: Participants should find agreement with this statement. When we observe smaller successes, our confidence grows. As confidence grows, the weight of some risks appears to be less, thus promoting continuous risk taking.

8. Confidence is built by learning from both successes and failures.
   Discussion: Many would quickly attribute confidence being built from successes, but we can also improve confidence from failed experiences. A risk that has not resulted in fulfillment of our

expectations can promote the continued pursuit of options (a fluid process). If we learn from the failed experience without negative punishment (for example, being fired or demoted) for exploring, we can move forward and be more confident. We understand that reasonable risk is a safe place for us.

9. Making safe choices provides the best opportunity to learn.
Discussion: If we only make safe choices we are not "spreading our wings." Taking more risk provides the best opportunities to learn.

10. I assess risk the same during times of extreme pressure to perform, as compared with times of normal business climate.
Discussion: This statement could lead to a very lengthy and broad discussion. In brief, as leaders we need to be aware that extreme pressure to perform could upset the balance of safety in choices and reasonable risk. Occasionally, we hear a business news report of someone who broke the law or engaged in unreasonable risks when under extreme pressure to perform. We should assess risk carefully during all business climate conditions.

11. There is little risk involved with innovation.
Discussion: Innovation involves risk taking. If we are truly innovating, we are taking risks.

12. I believe in a climate that supports learning from mistakes.
Discussion: Our climate and environment need to support a culture of learning. We can learn in a variety of ways, but one important method of learning is from analyzing our failures. By taking corrective action that results in a better choice the next time, we can foster a climate of learning from mistakes. As simple as this sounds, it is often not well supported.

RISK-TAKING DEBRIEFING SHEET

Instructions: In your subgroups, offer discussion on the following three questions. At least one person in the subgroup should record combined group answers or thoughts.

1. Which statement (or statements, pick one or two) do you feel has the most relevance to reasonable risk taking and leadership growth? Why do you think that?

2. Discuss your opinions of risk taking. Do you feel most organizations support reasonable risk taking and an environment of learning from mistakes? Why or why not? Explain.

3. Your group has been charged with promoting an environment that utilizes a proper balance of safety in choices and risk taking. What advice would you give to support this balance and to create a culture of learning from mistakes?

4. Why is risk taking critical to Challenge the Process?

WHEN QUESTIONS ARE THE ANSWER— CHALLENGING THE PROCESS

Submitted by Barbara Pate Glacel

Objectives

- To provide practice in asking questions, suspending judgment, and being open to outcome.
- To use a process that results in better decision making and synergistic problem solving.
- To discuss items of leadership interest.
- To practice question as a way to challenge the process.

Audience

Groups of six to eight participants are ideal. Multiple groups of six to eight can perform the exercise simultaneously.

Time Required

The activity should take approximately 2 1/2 hours. It is important not to shorten the discussion section in order to force the practice of using questions.

> Facilitator lecturette and setup 30 minutes
> Discussion 60 minutes
> Formulating the answer 15 minutes
> Determining the winner 5 minutes
> Debriefing 30 to 45 minutes

Materials and Equipment

- A copy of the When Questions Are the Answer Lecturette material for the facilitator.

- A copy of the When Questions Are the Answer Guidelines for each participant.
- A copy of the Leadership Questions for each group.
- Fake $50 bills—make one page per participant and cut into bills.
- Talking stick *(optional)*.

Area Setup

Each group should be at a table (preferably round) or in a circle with sufficient space between groups so that they can conduct lively discussion without bothering the group adjacent to them. Groups may also use separate breakout rooms if available.

Process

1. Begin with a discussion of what it means to Challenge the Process and what questioning techniques are effective in making a challenge. Use the Lecturette to guide the discussion. This will take about 30 minutes.

2. Present the roles and rules for the discussion and explain rewards and fines. Provide the Guidelines to each participant.

3. Within each group, tell participants to appoint an observer to monitor the rules, keep time, and be the banker. All others will be discussants, competing to end with the most money.

4. Each discussant will begin the process with $500 in fake $50 bills (ten bills each). The observer will hold the remaining fake $50 bills.

5. Give each table group a leadership topic for discussion listed on the Leadership Questions handout. The topic may be assigned, the group can choose from the list, or a relevant and timely topic may be selected.

6. For the next 60 minutes, have the groups discuss the topics. In accordance with the rules, no one may make a statement except in answer to an open-ended question, and no closed questions may be asked. Discussants may only ask open questions that do not reflect their opinions, but are intended to solicit more information. When the rules are not followed, the observer collects fines. When the discussants are entitled, the observer awards rewards.

7. At the end of discussion time, the group decides on a brief statement as an answer to the leadership topic question that was assigned.

8. The observer makes the final awards and the "winner" is announced.

9. Conduct a debriefing of the process to determine what the groups learned. Allow 30 minutes for the discussion and select from these questions:
   - What would you describe as the series of things that took place during your 60-minute discussion?
   - What did you find difficult?
   - Was there a leader? How did you know? What did the leader do?
   - What frustrated you?
   - Describe the level of participation. Who participated? Who did not? What impact did that have?
   - What did you learn about leadership that you did not know or had not considered before?
   - Who had influence? How did that person influence you?
   - What do you think about the answer your team developed? How does it compare to what you were thinking at the beginning of the discussion?

- What did you learn about how a team works together?
- What went particularly well for you and your team during the discussion?
- What did not go well for you and your team during the discussion?
- What behaviors would you choose to repeat in a different team setting?
- What would you do differently to be more effective the next time?
- What can questions accomplish for you?
- How does the use of questions drive Challenge the Process?
- Complete the following sentences:
  - I learned that . . .
  - I learned that I . . .

Barbara Pate Glacel, Ph.D., is principal of The Glacel Group of Washington, D.C., and Brussels, Belgium. She is co-author of a business bestseller on teams. She works with individuals, teams, and organizations in the Fortune 500 and not-for-profit arenas. She has over thirty years of experience in executive coaching and leadership development at all levels of organizations. An author and public speaker, she has coached and consulted with executives around the world.

Barbara Pate Glacel, Ph.D.
The Glacel Group
12103 Richland Lane
Oak Hill, VA 20171
  Phone: (703) 262-9120
  Email: BPGlacel@glacel.com
  Website: www.glacel.com

WHEN QUESTIONS ARE THE ANSWER LECTURETTE

Challenge the Process

Jim Kouzes and Barry Posner present five key practices of exemplary leadership:

- Model the Way
- Inspire a Shared Vision
- Challenge the Process
- Enable Others to Act
- Encourage the Heart

The third practice, *Challenge the Process*, is all about seeking innovative ways to change, grow, and improve. The effective leader is always seeking ways to move beyond the status quo, to step into the unknown. There is evidence all around us that those organizations deemed "excellent" twenty-five years ago have either fallen from grace or look different today than they looked a quarter of a century ago. To maintain organizational excellence requires leadership that looks at new ways of performing and enabling success.

Innovation is based on one's ability to LISTEN. That may seem counterintuitive to what is expected of the leader. Doesn't the leader direct, tell, guide, inform? Perhaps yes, under the right circumstances. However, innovation comes from listening more than telling. The leader's contribution to innovation, according to Kouzes and Posner, includes the recognition of good ideas, the support of those ideas, and the challenge to create new and better products, processes, services, and systems. The leader does not have to come up with all the good ideas because often the best ideas live throughout the organization.

This means that leaders must be learners. Learning unlocks the door to opportunity. What better way to learn than to ask questions?

Leaders often fall into the trap of thinking that, because they are in charge, they should know all the answers. That false belief sometimes belies the insecurity of the leader who is reluctant to say, "I don't know." However, the more senior a person rises in the organizational hierarchy, the less it is possible to know everything because of the vast number of people working on many projects dealing with endless information. Therefore, leaders must know the right questions because they do not have all the answers.

Questions serve a multitude of purposes:

1. Questions solicit information without passing judgment.
2. Questions allow people to come up with their own ideas.
3. Questions provide an avenue for cooperation without creating entrenched positions.
4. Questions hold up a mirror allowing one to reflect on what the answer really means.
5. Questions allow one to test assumptions, especially when the wrong assumption might prove embarrassing.
6. Questions create a situation in which people can get to know one another and build trusting relationships.
7. Questions facilitate a deeper understanding by digging beneath the surface.
8. Questions protect one who does not want to give away information.

9. Questions guide one's thinking in order to sell an idea and get another's buy-in before announcing a concrete decision.

10. Questions provide answers when other people just don't know.

Often, one asks a question just to confirm what is already known or to gain approval. The frequently asked closed-ended questions (that can be answered with a yes or no) simply imply a solution or put the respondent on the spot to agree or disagree. These questions do not elicit innovation and allow learning. In fact, they limit those opportunities, even when they may be seen as efficient.

When one challenges the process, the question must truly open up the conversation. The leader must go into this conversation being open to an outcome that is not known, not agreed, nor even apparent at the time. The effective question to enable learning and innovation suspends all judgments and makes no assumptions. Therefore, effective questions must be open-ended questions that truly inquire.

Open-ended questions begin with words such as:

- How
- Why
- What
- Where
- To what extent
- When
- Who

WHEN QUESTIONS ARE THE ANSWER GUIDELINES

One person is selected as the observer/banker/timekeeper. That person is responsible for:

1. Monitoring the time period as follows:
   Discussion 60 minutes
   Formulating the answer 15 minutes
   Determining the winner 5 minutes
   Facilitating the debriefing 30 minutes
2. Enforcing the rules as listed below
3. Distributing awards
4. Collecting fines

All other members of the group are discussants.

Rules

1. Only one person may speak at a time. (If a talking stick is utilized, only the holder of the talking stick may speak.)
2. Declaratory statements are only allowed as an immediate response to a question.
3. Closed-ended questions (those that can be answered with a "yes" or "no") may not be asked.
4. The leadership question may not be finally answered during the 60-minute discussion period. The final answer may only be determined when the observer calls "time" and allows 15 minutes to determine the final answer.

5. If a person is out of money, it is possible to borrow from the bank at a 10 percent interest rate to be repaid at the end of the discussion.

Fines and Rewards

1. All fines are in multiples of $50. The observer may determine the amount. Fines are collected for the following offenses:
   - Interrupting or speaking when another is talking.
   - Making a declaratory statement at any time during the discussion period (except as a direct answer to an open-ended question).
   - Asking a question that can be answered with "yes" or "no."
   - Trying to answer the leadership question during the discussion period.
   - Talking too much and not allowing others to participate.
   - Not participating.
   - Asking questions that "lead the witness."
   - Belittling or criticizing the comments of others.

2. All rewards are in multiples of $50. The observer may determine the amount. Rewards are presented for the following behaviors:
   - Influencing others to think with different mental models (Challenge the Process).
   - Asking open-ended questions that advance the conversation (Model the Way).
   - Changing your mind (Challenge the Process).
   - Building on another's idea that was not yours (Enabling Others to Act).
   - Supporting another's stand (Encouraging the Heart).
   - Arriving at a synergistic answer to the question (Inspiring a Shared Vision).
   - Reaching true consensus, not voting (Inspiring a Shared Vision).
   - Demonstrating effective teamwork (Enabling Others to Act).

LEADERSHIP QUESTIONS

1. How can leaders be effective role models?

2. How do leaders create a vision that is shared and aligned throughout the organization?

3. What is the best way for a leader to challenge the organization's conventional wisdom?

4. How do leaders enable others in the organization to act effectively?

5. What is effective leadership behavior that encourages the hearts of those in the organization?

6. What role does a leader play in the development of others?

7. What is the best way to teach leadership skills in an organizational environment?

8. How does an organization select leaders to assure success?

9. What are the leadership skills that are called on in times of crisis?

10. What do leaders do that might be different from what managers do?

11. The group may choose its own relevant and timely leadership question. The question must be posed as an open-ended question and must not have an obvious answer.

The Leadership Challenge Activities Book
Copyright © 2010 by James M. Kouzes and Barry Z. Posner.
Reproduced by permission of Pfeiffer, an Imprint of Wiley. www.pfeiffer.com.

Challenge the Process

TOSS IT AROUND

Submitted by Ann Hermann-Nehdi

Objectives

- To personally experience a challenge in a group to demonstrate behaviors that can be reviewed against the Challenge the Process practice.
- To observe others' behaviors in the activity and explore your reaction to those behaviors.

Audience

Ideal: twelve to fifteen per group. This will work with up to thirty people per group or break into smaller groups. Minimum group size should be eight to ten to increase the level of the challenge.

Time Required

20 to 40 minutes, depending on group size (larger takes longer).

Materials and Equipment

- Six Koosh® balls or other easy-to-toss balls such as tennis balls, per group.
- A method of timing the activity.

Area Setup

Open space with enough room for people to stand in a circle (or circles depending on group size).

Process

1. Have participants stand forming a circle (or circles). Tell the group that their challenge is to first learn a process, then to improve (challenge) that process once they have mastered it.

2. Ask one person to start with the Koosh ball by naming a particular person in the circle and throwing/tossing the ball across the circle to him or her. Model this by demonstrating: say the name of the person you are tossing to (out loud) and toss the ball across the circle to that person. The person tossed to must catch the ball without dropping it and then name another (different) person in the circle and toss the ball across to him or her while saying the person's name out loud. That person catches it without dropping it and does the same until every person has tossed the ball and it returns to the first person who threw it. Repeat the process, ensuring that the same order is used every time: everyone will consistently receive the ball from the same person and throw it to the same person. (that is,, "A" always throws the ball to "C" and "C" always throws it to "G," and so on). This requires remembering the sequence (and everyone's names if this is a newly formed group).

3. Once the participants have completed Step 2 successfully, add a second ball right after the first and repeat the motion. Then go to three balls, four balls, and up to six (time allowing).

4. Congratulate the group on successfully learning the process and indicate that they now need to *improve the process* by reducing *the pass time* to as short as possible without losing accuracy or quality (ball dropping). Indicate that they should try to beat the "world record" for this activity getting it down *to seconds* per toss. They

will typically struggle for a few minutes trying different ways, often not listening to each other. If there is more than one group, you can up the ante by putting competitive pressure between the groups; however, do not tell them that they cannot observe each other and learn from the other group. They will often compete rather than learn from each other—although learning from each other is allowed and is not considered "cheating."

5. Ultimately, a good solution to achieve the fastest speed is to have the group line up in the order of the sequence and hand the balls down the line. Even faster is to have the group form a circle (in the correct sequence and all touch the ball at the same time by placing it in the center of the circle and saying the names in sequence, replacing ball 1 with ball 2, 3, 4, 5, and 6 when done (this may require the facilitator to hand the balls to the group as they finish each one). Be sure to have a timer available to measure the average pass time.

6. Debrief by asking the group to the following:
   • How open were you and how did you react to others' suggestions about ways to innovate and change the process?
   • If there was more than one group, did you look outside your group to find different ideas?
   • How willing were you to experiment with changes in format and to try other approaches?
   • How did you feel in general about the challenge to test out new ideas?
   • How willing were you to learn as part of the process versus "take over" and ensure your ideas were heard?
   • If you were the leader of a group, how did your behavior demonstrate your willingness to Challenge the Process? If you

were a follower, how would you feel about the behaviors you
demonstrated here?

- What behaviors are most beneficial to Challenge the Process?
- How can you ensure these beneficial behaviors are
  implemented on the job?

Ann Herrmann-Nehdi is CEO of Herrmann International, a global
learning and development company and publisher of the Herrmann
Brain Dominance Instrument (HBDI). Ann has led the company's
applied research on thinking and the brain, using the company's Whole
Brain® Thinking model and database of over one million assessments
to help organizations *get better results through better thinking* and
do more with less. Author of many articles and chapters, Ann is
currently working on a book to be released in 2010.

Ann Herrmann-Nehdi
Herrmann International
794 Buffalo Creek Road
Lake Lure, NC, 28746
　Phone: (828) 625-9153
　Email: ann@hbdi.com
　Website: www.hbdi.com; www.HerrmannInternational.com

CHALLENGE THINK TANK

Submitted by Amanda Crowell Itliong

Objective

- Create a safe and easy way for leaders to practice overcoming challenges by seeking ideas and input from others.

Audience

Any total group size with participants divided into small groups of four or five. Groups should be as mixed up as possible based on the types of work everyone in the group does.

Time Required

25 minutes.

Materials and Equipment

- Blank note cards (two for each participant).
- Pens for writing.

Area Setup

Have participants sit either at small tables with four or five chairs each or in circles of chairs with four or five people in each circle.

Process

1. Have each participant think of two current challenges he or she is facing at work that are not yet solved. Give each participant two note cards.

2. Have each participant write one challenge on the front of each note card. Tell them to remove all personal information or details that might make the challenge inappropriate to share.

3. Once everyone has finished writing, explain that sometimes solutions can be hard to find when we are too personally involved and invested. Often we can Challenge the Process by sharing our challenges with others outside of the project who might have simple, creative, outside solutions to recommend.

4. In each small group, have one person read one of his or her cards out loud and describe the challenge to the members of the small group.

5. Each person in the small group should offer the first idea or possible solution that comes to mind for the challenge. The person who shared the challenge should listen politely and write his or her favorite possible solutions on the back of the card.

6. Repeat this process for everyone in the group once. If there is leftover time, go around the circle again for those who have another challenge for which they would like to receive ideas.

7. At the end of the activity, have everyone thank others in his or her group for the creative ideas.

8. Ask the participants to reflect on the following questions:
    - Did you hear anything you haven't thought of yourself?
    - In your daily life, who else could you ask for possible solutions for your challenges?
    - Where else could you look for ideas for these particular challenges?
    - What is challenging for leaders who Challenge the Process?
    - How will you think differently about challenges in the future?

Amanda Crowell Itliong is the student development and leadership programs director at Stanford University's Haas Center for Public Service, where she teaches and advises emerging leaders in public service. She has spent the last ten years training and creating curriculum for students, faculty, community volunteers, and nonprofit leaders on topics related to service-learning, social justice, and leadership. She holds a B.A. degree in human services from The George Washington University, an Ed.M. from Harvard's Graduate School of Education, and a certificate in dialogue, deliberation, and public engagement from Fielding Graduate University.

Amanda Crowell Itliong
Haas Center for Public Service–Stanford University
562 Salvatierra Walk
Stanford, CA 94305
  Phone: (650) 724-9233
  Email: akc@stanford.edu
  Website: www.haas.stanford.edu

CASH FLOW EXERCISE

Submitted by Edith Katz

Objectives

- To participate in a process-improvement exercise and experience the associated behaviors.
- To experience the dynamics of Challenge the Process, which then can be used as a reference point for the future.

Audience

Minimum of five or six participants; if you have fifteen or more, you can break the group into two smaller groups.

Time Required

20 minutes.

Materials and Equipment

- Flip chart with a chart drawn on the page that has two columns titled "Estimated Time" and "Actual Time"; rows should be labeled "Run 1," "Run 2," and "Run 3."
- Markers.
- Clock with a second hand or a stopwatch.

Area Setup

An open area large enough for all participants to form a circle standing.

Process

1. Ask participants what behaviors are associated with Challenge the Process. Record their responses on a flip-chart page (not the prepared page).

2. State that they will have an opportunity to apply the practice through an activity called Cash Flow.

3. Ask participants to form a circle. Ensure that they have elbow room.

4. Produce a quarter. Place it on the back of your hand. State the following:
   - These monies must pass completely around the circle.
   - Everyone in the system must "touch" the monies moving through. No downsizing!
   - Regulations prevent us from allowing anyone to secure the funds passing through. (You can only have contact with the quarter with the back of your hand.)
   - The funds must flow continuously.
   - If the funds are dropped, you must begin the process over.

5. Ask the participants to estimate a time, to set a goal, for successful completion of the task.

6. Record this figure on the chart in the square that is Run 1, Estimated Time.

7. Conduct the first run. Time the participants. Record the actual time it takes for the quarter to pass all the way around the circle. Record the time in the square that is Run 1, Actual Time.

8. Ask the participants whether they think they can improve on their performance. Clarify the rules as necessary. Allow 3 or 4 minutes for discussion about performance improvement.

9. After participants have developed a new plan, ask them for a new estimated time. Record this time, allow the second run, and compare estimated to actual.

10. Continue to challenge the group to improve its effectiveness. It is possible to complete it in "n" seconds where "n" equals the number of participants. If their faith wanes, share this timing information with the group. Allow a couple more trials.

11. Debrief using these questions:
    • What specifically did you do that enabled you to improve your productivity? (Possible answers may be: brainstormed ideas, listened to all ideas, modeled the way, worked as a team, consider change, broke the process into smaller parts.)
    • How can you apply these behaviors in your role at work?

Edith Katz is the manager of employee development at Brooks Health System, where she facilitates an eleven-part Leadership Challenge series. The series includes a lab session the week after each practice has been introduced. In the lab session, each participant presents his or her application assignment to the class and a discussion is opened to provide feedback, ideas, and suggestions. This *active learning* component helps each participant to apply the knowledge to his or her real-life work challenges and allows participants to learn from others as well.

Edith Katz
Brooks Health System
3901 University Boulevard South, Suite 103
Jacksonville, FL 32216
    Phone: (904) 858-7334
    Email: edith.katz@brookshealth.org

CHANGE PROJECT SUMMARY

Submitted by Edith Katz

Objective

- Participants will participate in an *action learning* activity wherein they learn from each other about how others challenge the process.

Audience

Group of ten or fewer can use this in smaller breakout groups.

Time Required

45 to 60 minutes.

Materials and Equipment

- One copy of the Change Project Worksheet for each participant.

Area Setup

An open area large enough for all participants to form a circle standing.

Process

1. Ask participants to identify a specific opportunity from their department/team/workplace that they want to change.
2. Hand out a Change Project Worksheet to each participant. Give them 15 minutes to complete it.
3. Have each person share his or her change project outline with the class. After each is shared, open the floor for comments, suggestions, and questions from the rest of the group.

4. Summarize by asking:
   - What did you learn in general about Challenge the Process?
   - What will you do in the future when needing to improve a process?

Variation

- You may wish to ask participants to identify best practices related to each project in other organizations between classes or sessions.

Edith Katz is the manager of employee development at Brooks Health System, where she facilitates an eleven-part Leadership Challenge series. The series includes a lab session the week after each practice has been introduced. In the lab session, each participant presents his or her application assignment to the class and a discussion is opened to provide feedback, ideas, and suggestions. This active learning component helps each participant to apply the knowledge to his or her real-life work challenges and allows participants to learn from others as well.

Edith Katz
Brooks Health System
3901 University Boulevard South, Suite 103
Jacksonville, FL 32216
   Phone: (904) 858-7334
   Email: edith.katz@brookshealth.org

CHANGE PROJECT WORKSHEET

Name of Change Project _____

Current State	Desired Future State	Action Steps
(describe in bullets)	(describe in bullets)	(describe in bullets)
•	•	•
•	•	•
•	•	•
•	•	•
•	•	•

Best Practice Research

Include research about best practices in other high performing organizations that relate to this opportunity (this may be home-work between sessions).

CONSTRUCTING A GLOBAL TEAM COMMUNICATIONS DEVICE

Submitted by John Lybarger

Objectives

- To introduce the basic concept of Challenge the Process.
- To communicate how Inspire a Shared Vision supports Challenge the Process.

Audience

Ideally, a group of twenty-five to thirty with participants in teams of five.

Time Required

60 to 90 minutes.

Materials and Equipment

- The Classic Tinkertoy® Construction Set (102 pieces) Available at Toys R Us or online at www.hasbro.com (one for each team).
- One chart with team objective and guidelines hung on the wall or written on a flip-chart page.

Area Setup

Room set with tables and chairs for teams.

Process

1. State that two exemplary leadership practices—Inspire a Shared Vision and Challenge the Process—go hand-in-hand.

Ask participants to form teams of at least five people to discover how these two practices are related. If necessary, ask teams to clear off their tables so that they have a clean workspace.

2. State that you will give each team construction materials for this project. Distribute one Classic Tinkertoy Construction Set (102 pieces) to each team.

3. Ask participants to review the objective and guidelines with you. Refer to the chart.

4. State, "Your planning time begins now. In 20 minutes I will ask for a team to volunteer to present its project while the other groups observe. Each team will have 5 minutes to present its project." Give a 5-minute warning before the end of the time.

5. When the construction time has ended, call a halt and ask for a volunteer team. Welcome them to the front of the room and remind them they have 5 minutes for their presentation. Following the team's presentation, ask the large group to critique the project in terms of meeting the required characteristics. Allow the team to respond to questions and observations made by the group.

6. Repeat this process with each team. Following each team's presentation, give thunderous applause and invite another volunteer team to present.

7. Facilitate a large group debriefing by using these questions:
   • What did you learn from participating in this activity?
   • What was most challenging for you or for your team?
   • What was most rewarding for you or for your team?
   • How did you Challenge the Process with your construction project and presentation? (Some responses may include:

We had to think differently about the Tinkertoys to build something "green." We had to be imaginative and think "outside the box" to create something new with multiple applications.)

- How did Inspire a Shared Vision support Challenge the Process during the construction? (Some responses may include: working together we created a shared team vision that was really made up of parts of each of our individual ideas. We realized that our team result was more productive and more creative than it would have been if we had created it individually.)
- What do you see as the relationship between Inspire a Shared Vision and Challenge the Process?
- Why do you need both to be successful?
- Did you see yourself applying your strengths from your LPI in this activity?
- Did you see any of your growth areas from the LPI come into play in this activity?
- What will you do as a result of this discussion?

Variation

- You may also choose observers from the group to assist in observing the teams. Observers would add to a large group discussion by sharing their observations about how the teams executed the team objective and followed the guidelines. This works well if you have an uneven number of team members or a group of more than thirty participants.

John Lybarger, Ph.D., has twenty-three years of experience working with federal agencies including the Defense Department, Treasury, Office of Personnel Management, and Justice Department, and private-sector companies such as Qwest, AT&T Broadband, Ryder, Frito-Lay, Procter & Gamble, The Home Depot, and Charles Schwab. He has been an adjunct at the Center for Creative Leadership and the Graduate School USDA and has conducted more than nine hundred coaching sessions and delivered more than nine hundred training programs with more than eleven thousand participants, from front-line employees to senior executives. He is a certified facilitator for The Leadership Challenge® Workshop.

John S. Lybarger, MBA, Ph.D.
Lybarger & Associates Inc.
8489 W 95th Drive
Westminster, CO 80021-5330
   Phone: (303) 421-8080
   Email: john@lybargerassociatesinc.com
   Website www.lybargerassociatesinc.com

OBJECTIVE AND GUIDELINES

Team Objective: Construct a Global Team Communications Device

Team Ground Rules

1. All team members must participate.
2. The Global Team Communications Device must have these characteristics:
    *   Mobility
    *   Balance
    *   Multiple methods of communicating globally
    *   Security
    *   Green construction
3. 20 minutes' construction time
4. 5-minute presentation

IDENTIFY PERCEIVED CAUSES OF RESISTANCE

Submitted by Consuelo Meux

Objectives

- To assess reasons for perceived resistance to change.
- To identify potential systemic organizational causes for employee resistance.

Audience

Eight to twenty employees in an organization addressing change.

Time Required

Approximately 1 1/2 hours for group assessment and discussion.

Materials and Equipment

- One copy of Identify Perceived Resistance to Change: A Primer for the facilitator, to be read prior to session.
- One copy of the Resistance to Change Assessment for each participant.
- Whiteboard or flip chart and markers.

Area Setup

A U-shaped arrangement of desks/tables if room allows.

Facilitator Note

This exercise should only be used when resistance to change has already surfaced. For best results, use the assessment with no fewer than eight employees to ensure confidentiality.

Process

1. Before the session, read Identify Perceived Resistance to Change: A Primer and prepare a few remarks appropriate for the group.

2. Provide each participant with a copy of the Resistance to Change Assessment. Review the directions and tell them it will take 15 to 20 minutes to complete. Emphasize that, although participants may want to select more than one item in each section, they must select the one that is most prevalent. Provide a 5-minute notice before the end of the time.

3. Have participants score their own assessment and read the descriptors.

4. List A through H vertically on a flip chart. Have each person go to the chart and fill in his or her score for each letter. Once everyone has finished, quickly tally the score for each letter.

5. Review the results of the assessment to understand the potential areas of conflict. Ask the following questions:
   • In which of the eight centers of conflict did you expect to see the highest score?
   • Where is the actual center of the conflict according to your assessment?
   • What do you think is the root cause?

6. Put participants into small groups of four to five participants and ask them to respond to this question:
   • What steps can be taken to alleviate the conflict and resolve the problems?
   Allow about 15 minutes.

7. Ask each group to share ideas with the large group. Post them on the flip chart.

8. Summarize the group ideas and state what will happen next.

Expected Results

Although this exercise should only be used to identify the underlying causes of resistance to change, sometimes other positive actions occur, including these:

The discussions often create a more positive and supportive atmosphere for employees.

Understanding what could be causing conflict may lead to a reassessment of specific areas in the organization.

The responses may lead to an examination of ambiguous company policies.

The results and discussions may unearth discrepancies between stated and actual policies, practices, and procedures in the organization, giving leaders a chance to correct the differences.

Variations

- The scoring grid could be posted on a flip chart for participants to mark their specific questions.
- Have leaders available to respond when the group reports out their ideas in Step 7.
- The assessment can be given to all employees in a department and the consolidated responses analyzed.

Consuelo Meux, Ph.D., is a strategic mentor to women in leadership and a Certified Mastermind Executive Coach. She is the president and founder of the International Alliance of Women

Leaders (IAW Leaders) and is a speaker and trainer on leadership and business issues.

Consuelo Meux, Ph.D.
International Alliance of Women Leaders
P.O. Box 4326
Paso Robles, CA 93447-4326
   Phone: (805) 227-4964
   Email: Consuelo@consuelomeux.com
   Website: Http://www.iawleaders.com

IDENTIFY PERCEIVED RESISTANCE TO CHANGE: A PRIMER

Change in organizations is inevitable. Some change is evolutionary and some is deliberate. All change defines and determines how employees function in the organization (Schein, 1997). Organization leaders must take a more active role in managing the effects of change on employees as the demographics of employees becomes more diversified. They must take a more holistic role to develop and maintain valuable employees. "If you have the wrong people, it doesn't matter whether you discover the right direction; you won't have a great company" (Collins, 2001, p. 13).

Keeping the right people offers new challenges to leaders. Traditionally, organization leaders did not always feel obligated to communicate their intentions to employees or to participate in employee development. Now, "senior leaders need to provide visible, consistent support and necessary resources. And they need to communicate clearly with managers at all levels about their role as talent leaders" (Rezak, 2008, p. 92).

Providing a New View of Change Management

When implementing change, leaders must consider the effect this change may have on both the organization's culture and on the organization's employees. Employees will have a sense of disruption, and sometimes the disruption may be interpreted as resistance to change by the organization's leaders. This is particularly relevant when the change disrupts the organization's culture. In a well-established organization, the culture "develops over long periods of time and is socially complex" (Hitt, Freeman, & Harrison, 2001,

261

p. 173). Although it can take years or even decades to develop and firmly entrench a culture into an organization, "that culture can be destroyed very quickly by senior managers in a firm, making decisions that are inconsistent with that culture" (p. 173).

When organization leaders implement changes, employees may display behavior that looks like a form of resistance. This apparent resistance may occur at any level of the organization: individual, groups, departments, or organization-wide (Jones, 2004). However, organizational studies have found that employees do not always resist change for itself. In fact, many applaud changes. What may be missed by leaders is that, during the change process, a disruption in any aspect of the organization could also disrupt other aspects of the organization, including the culture, processes, or other systemic areas. This disruption could highlight covert issues between employees and leaders that already existed. With a systems view of the organization, leaders appreciate that what happens in one part of the system will inevitably have an effect on all of the other parts of the system.

Care for Employees

To support employees, leaders need to understand the root cause for their apparent "resistance." For example, issues may be blamed on diversity or cultural problems, when in fact, they may be due to employees' natural response to a change. The issue is whether leaders have a tool to accurately identify what employees may be experiencing and to pinpoint what is causing the frustration. If leaders have a dependable way to identify the root cause of the behavior, it may not be labeled as resistance. The assessment in this activity is such a tool.

Root Cause in the System: A Case

One department director felt his administrative assistants continually resisted his directives to make changes in the department. He had experienced similar problems with three employees in the same position, all of whom had finally either left his department or quit the company. While the situation seemed to be a diversity issue, further probing suggested that the problem wasn't personal but systemic:

1. None of the employees had been provided with a clear description of his or her job functions and authority.

2. None of the employees had been appropriately socialized into the organization.

3. No instructions were available to assist the employees, who were often left to figure things out on their own, as the director was often away from the office immediately after hiring the person.

This resulted in frustrations and behavioral problems. The root cause was a lack of organization support (job descriptions and proper orientation). Once this was discovered and remedied, the department director was able to make the adjustments and retain the employee he had recently hired.

Organization managers and leaders have a tendency to focus solely on the behavior of employees and do not recognize that the root causes of some problems are in the organizational systems.

Potential Results of the Assessment

The Resistance to Change Assessment assists leaders to better understand employees' views. This is especially important when considering whether change is a personal issue or systemic in nature.

The assessment identifies the sources of resistance or areas of conflict in the organization to help leaders find effective solutions to organizational problems.

A limited view of possible resistance may be a reason that organization leaders hesitate to initiate change, initiate change poorly, or appear to miss important elements when implementing change. The assessment helps to develop a systemic understanding of resistance to change by highlighting reasons why employees may seem to resist change.

The assessment could be helpful in allowing organization leaders to determine where problems actually exist in the leader-employee relationship instead of having to make assumptions. All relationships go through some need for socialization either formally or informally. The effectiveness of this socialization at the beginning of the employment of any employee becomes a pivotal point on how well each is assimilated into the organization and its culture. In other cases, this assessment can point out areas that still need more socialization and discussion.

While personality conflicts certainly exist, this assessment can show that not all organization issues are related to personal or behavioral issues. Any type of change strategy in an organization can raise problems.

Using this assessment can help to bring about a shared vision among employees and leaders about potential centers of conflict in the organization. With this knowledge, steps can be taken toward resolutions that bring harmony within the organization.

References

Collins, J. (2001). *Good to great*. New York: HarperCollins.

Hitt, M.A., Freeman, R.E, Harrison, J.S. (Eds.) (2001). *Handbook of strategic management*. Oxford, UK: Blackwell Business.

Jones, G.R. (2004). *Organizational theory, design, and change* (4th ed). Englewood Cliffs, NJ: Prentice Hall.

Rezak, C.J. (2008). Beyond talent management: Manager as talent leaders. In Robert C. Preziosi (Ed.), *The 2008 Pfeiffer annual: Management development*. San Francisco: Pfeiffer.

Schein, E.H. (1997). *Organizational culture and leadership* (2nd ed). San Francisco: Jossey-Bass.

Tidd, J., Bessant, J., & Pavitt, K. (2005). *Managing innovations: Integrating technological market and organizational change* (3rd ed). Hoboken, NJ; John Wiley & Sons.

RESISTANCE TO CHANGE ASSESSMENT

Instructions: Review the statements in each section. Circle the statement in each group that most reflects your feeling related to organization life. Then complete the scoring.

Section 1

a. Many experience limitations in resources to do the job in my department.

b. I feel anxious about expressing a new point of view for changes in the organization.

c. I believe that employees feel the competitive nature of the workplace hinders advancement opportunities.

d. I am confused about the organization culture (norms, values, behaviors).

e. I feel the organization rules and regulations are not clear.

f. The centralized operations structure is too restrictive.

g. I have gaps in my job functions/job description.

h. I don't understand the politics of the organization.

Section 2

a. I personally lack the necessary resources to do my job.

b. I feel my personal contributions to the job are not valued.

c. I need more training in order to effectively do my job.

d. I feel employees are given responsibility for tasks without the authority to complete them.

e. I feel that the organization rules and regulations cause stress.

f. The decentralized operational structure is too cumbersome.

g. Other employees in my department have gaps in their job functions/job descriptions.

h. The politics of the organization determine advancements and opportunities.

Section 3

a. The distribution system for resources is a source of frustration.

b. I feel that my personal values are questioned at work.

c. I feel there are gaps between my job knowledge and job duties and need more training and development.

d. I believe the changes in the organization will mean my job is no longer needed.

e. I am not sure about the dress code expectations at work.

f. The organizational structure makes access to technology (hardware, software) needed to do my job limited or unavailable.

g. The process to get a response to a request, inquiry, or question is long and cumbersome.

h. Changes in the organizational system would prevent me from having an influence over others in my department.

Section 4

a. There are not enough financial resources to properly meet job expectations.

b. I don't feel that I am thought of as an individual in the workplace.

c. I feel that my position is not secure because of a lack of training and development.

d. I see a big difference between what organization leaders say and how they act.

e. I feel the work hours are not flexible enough to meet the reality of employee lifestyles.

f. The structure of the organization makes access to technology (hardware, software) to do my job too restrictive.

g. It is difficult to contact a leader to listen to an employee's point to view on proposed changes.

h. Changes in the organizational system would alter my ability to have an influence throughout the organization.

Section 5

a. There is a shortage of necessary supplies to complete the job.

b. I feel people should make more effort to get along with each other as colleagues in this organization.

c. I feel the organization should provide the training and development employees need to advance in the organization.

d. Employees do not have enough information to make good decisions.

e. I am not clear about the chain of command in the organization.

f. The way the organization is structured keeps me from reaching my personal goals.

g. Leaders should listen to what employees have to say about the proposed changes.

h. Certain leaders in the organization will lose their power if the suggested changes are implemented.

Section 6

a. There is a need for more human resources to fill necessary positions to complete tasks.

b. I believe there are conflicts between my values and the organization's culture.

c. There is a need to expand access to training opportunities to all employees.

d. I see a difference between what duties are said to be valuable and what is actually rewarded.

e. The communication system prevents leaders and employees from freely discussing issues.

f. The organizational structure makes reaching department goals difficult.

g. I worry about how changes will affect how things get done in the organization.

h. Opportunities to promote are influenced by organizational politics.

Section 7

a. I need more supplies and resources to do my job well.

b. I feel the organization's management and staff are not sensitive to issues related to diverse employees.

c. I am not certain that I am always doing my job correctly.

d. I believe the suggested organizational changes will have a negative effect on the culture of the organization.

e. I feel communication is limited and employees don't know what's going on.

f. The structure of the organization hinders interactions with people in other departments.

g. The process to submit suggestions to leadership is unclear or unknown.

h. An unequal distribution of organization power limits my ability to attain my goals.

Score the Assessment

Use the following grid to score your assessment:

1. Mark the letter circled in each section.
2. Count the letters and place the total at the bottom of the column.
3. Move to the next section and put the total for each letter next to the section names.
4. Review the information on the Centers of Conflict to understand the potential areas of conflict in your organization.
5. Review and work through the debriefing questions.

Section	a	b	c	d	e	f	g	h
1								
2								
3								
4								
5								
6								
7								
Total								

Put the total number of times each letter was circled in each of the blanks below. If you have two or more areas with high scores, consider how they might be related.

    a. _____ Necessary Resources
    b. _____ Personal Identity
    c. _____ Training and Development
    d. _____ Organization Practices
    e. _____ Policies
    f. _____ Organization Structure
    g. _____ Processes
    h. _____ Political Factors

Review the Potential Centers of Conflict

This section explains the different Centers of Conflict used in the assessment. Review these categories to understand where a conflict is potentially centered instead of making assumptions about how to act on a conflict in the organization.

a. Necessary Resources

A lack of resources causes feelings that management has unrealistic expectations to get a job done without the support to do so. Resources include any organizational support that an employee needs to complete a job. These include money, office supplies, information, additional employees on the task, and ability to access resources.

b. Personal Identity

Employees may feel they are not appreciated as individuals in the workplace. Additionally, employees may not feel comfortable being authentic in expressing ideas, problems, or suggestions, even when their knowledge would be helpful to alleviate an issue. The employees may feel a lack of acceptance or be confused about the culture in the workplace and how things function. This area could also include conflicts based on diversity and cultural issues.

c. Training and Development

Conflict can arise when employees feel they are expected to perform duties when they do not have the proper training in an area. This causes excess stress and resistance. A lack of consistent training can lead to competition. Employees may feel everything is competitive so developing friendships is difficult. Employees may feel lost and directionless, that there are gaps between what they know and what is expected. This creates feelings of anxiety and fear that jobs are in jeopardy. The resistance shown might actually be a lack of understanding what to do.

d. Organization Practices

Areas of conflict in organization practice can arise when employees feel they have been given responsibility without the authority to get something done or when promotion opportunities are limited, possibly because of political maneuvering in the organization or the wrong use of power. Some people resist change because they are comfortable with the way things are and any change would mean disrupting that level of comfort. Others feel that not enough information is shared with employees, leaving a feeling of fear about the changes.

e. Policies

Organizational policies can generate conflicts and apparent resistance to change when the rules and regulations are not clear, are so restrictive that they cause stress, or are perceived as unreasonable policies that do not meet the reality of employee lifestyles. This can include a lack of understanding about such daily policies as dress codes, use of the chain of command, and communication systems.

f. Organizational Structure

What can seem like resistance to change could be a misunderstanding about the organization's structure and how the organization functions. Areas to note could be how operations are centralized or decentralized, the availability of and access to organization-wide technologies, including information systems to do the job, and even the organizational structure. Employees could be concerned about the effects of change in one section of the organization and how these would have an effect in other organization sections.

g. Processes

Gaps in job descriptions and expected job functions are known areas of potential conflict in the workplace. Additionally, employees could be affected by gaps within entire departments related to job functions that make completing tasks difficult. Some employees feel uninformed about upcoming changes and fear sets in about how the change will affect their jobs, departments, or the entire organization. They long to have leaders listen to their points of view because they are the ones working on the front lines.

h. Political Factors

Employees are often confused about the politics of the organization. They need mentoring on how politics influence advancement and other opportunities. Changes in the organization could shift the major players, resources, and other dynamics. Some employees fear that their entire departments will be in jeopardy due to political maneuverings during the change process. Even the external environment can affect internal outcomes.

IN-BASKET EXERCISE

Submitted by Alan Richter

Objectives

- To test the validity, value, or efficacy of a particular leadership strategy, approach, or methodology.
- To think from the opposite point of view to challenge any organizational process or strategic approach.

Audience

Up to twenty-five participants divided into teams of four to seven people.

Time Required

Approximately 1 hour.

Materials and Equipment

- An in-basket memo for each team. Two samples have been provided, but you are free to customize your own.
- Flip chart and markers for debriefing the activity.

Area Setup

Tables set up for teams.

Process

1. As you prepare, decide on the strategy, approach, or methodology that needs to be challenged. Write a short memo that states (fictitiously) that the organization will cease with that approach

(see sample handouts on using diversity and ethics). Other topics you might select include leadership development, performance management, risk management, change management, quality assurance, balanced scorecards, or customer service.

2. Provide a copy of your memo to each team. Tell them that their task will be to read the memo and then collectively shape a response in memo or bullet format.

3. Allow 20 to 30 minutes for the groups to complete their responses.

4. Ask each group to share its response. Track responses on a flip chart, gathering themes or categories. Compare all responses and discuss them.

5. Review the learning and efficacy of this approach to Challenge the Process.
    • How were your responses in synch with the Kouzes and Posner guidance?
    • How could your response be improved?
    • What lesson are you taking from this activity?

Alan Richter, Ph.D., the founder and president of QED Consulting, has consulted to organizations for many years and specializes in the areas of leadership, values, culture, and change. He has designed and developed innovative curricula, as well as award-winning games, videos, software, and case studies such as the Global Diversity Game©, the Global Diversity Survey© and both the Global Ethics and Integrity and Global Diversity and Inclusion Benchmarks©. Alan has consulted extensively in Africa, Asia, Europe, and North America. He has an M.A. and a B.A.B.Sc. from the University of Cape Town and a Ph.D. from Birkbeck College, London University.

Alan Richter, Ph.D.
President
QED Consulting
41 Central Park West
New York, NY 10023
   Phone: (212) 724-3335
   Email: alanrichter@qedconsulting.com
   Website: www.qedconsulting.com

SAMPLE MEMO ON ETHICS

Memo from: _____

To: Everyone at the meeting

Date: _____

Subject: Our Ethics Program

After much debate and soul-searching we have decided, effective immediately, to end our Ethics Program throughout the organization.

We have taken this bold step for the following reasons:

We believe that we are an ethical organization and do not need the bureaucracy and training to support it;

- Ethics is simply not a strategic business issue; and
- We are simply too busy to spend time and resources on relatively new and non-strategic initiatives.

Ethics is not being singled out; other initiatives and programs may also be cut.

We apologize for any inconvenience we've caused you in the creation of the ethics office and the helpline, but these activities will cease henceforth. Our code of conduct will not be affected.

We appreciate your compliance.

SAMPLE MEMO ON DIVERSITY

Memo from: _____

To: Everyone at the meeting

Date: _____

Subject: Our Diversity Initiative

After much debate and soul-searching we have decided, effective immediately, to cease completely with our diversity initiative throughout the organization.

We have taken this bold step for the following reasons:

- We believe that we are diverse enough, and we do not necessarily want more diversity;
- Diversity is not a strategic initiative; and
- We are simply too busy to spend time and resources on relatively new and non-strategic initiatives.

Diversity is not being singled out; other initiatives and programs may also be cut.

We apologize for any inconvenience we've caused you in the creation of the diversity committee and in planning, but all diversity initiatives will cease henceforth.

We appreciate your compliance.

CHALLENGE THE PROCESS IN REAL TIME

Submitted by L.J. Rose

Objectives

- To use informal coaching as a vehicle to apply Challenge the Process to real issues.
- To move Challenge the Process from concept to tangible application.
- To use core elements of Challenge the Process as a framework to generate robust next steps in a short period of time with a coaching buddy.
- To give participants a model to use in their workday so they can actively apply the practice to real issues in a short period of time.

Audience

This activity can be done with ten people or hundreds of people. It can also be adapted to intact teams and/or blended learning settings.

Time Required

Approximately 90 minutes.

Materials and Equipment

- One Challenge the Process on a Real-Time Issue worksheet for each participant.
- PowerPoint slides or flip-chart pages with instructions.
- PowerPoint slides or flip-chart pages with Tips to Apply Outsight and Actions to Generate Small Wins
- PowerPoint slides or flip-chart pages with questions from worksheet, with one question per/page or slide.

- Watch or timer.
- Flip chart or projector to display instructions.

Area Setup

This activity can be done during meetings or workshops or injected into blended-learning adaptations. Coaching partners will need to be shoulder to shoulder during the workshop activity or have access to one another in a blended-learning application.

Facilitator Notes

If you're doing a Leadership Challenge workshop, this process comes nicely after you've provided some details on outsight and small wins. These are two essential drivers for Challenge the Process. You do not need to spend long describing them but long enough so participants will be able to generate ideas during the activity. If you're not doing an in-room workshop, this activity can be framed as an application tool for Challenge the Process and adapted accordingly. Feel free to innovate!

Coaching in this context is used to help participants get comfortable with being coached and coaching someone.

If a trio is necessary, huddle with them to see how they want to manage their time during the activity.

Process

1. In a workshop setting, let the group know they will be applying Challenge the Process in three steps: reflection, coaching, and action planning.

2. Hand out the worksheet and give everyone 8 minutes to come up with general answers for each question. Let them know they will

have time with coaching partners to be more specific. These are the questions they'll be addressing:

- What's your challenge and idea for improvement?
- What makes this challenge meaningful to you?
- Specifically, how can you exercise outsight to strengthen your idea?
- What are two small wins you can generate to gain and maintain momentum?

3. Once participants have completed the worksheet, have people find partners in the room. Have participants move to sit next to their partners. If possible, encourage them to pull their chairs away from the table so they can huddle together better.

4. Ask the partners to decide who will be the coach first and then ask the coaches to raise their hands to ensure a decision has been made. Before they start coaching, ask the whole group: "What are some characteristics of a great coach?" They'll shout out words and adjectives that you can use to reinforce what is about to unfold.

5. Mention to the group that compressed time is often an advantage to Challenge the Process if focus is present. Let them know they will have a short period of time to address the questions in order to find their essential points. Also let them know that you will be managing time and helping them stay focused on one question at a time.

6. Use a PowerPoint slide or a flip chart to present each of the four worksheet questions, one at a time. Put the first question up and tell participants to take the full 2 minutes to answer question 1 on their worksheet. Coaches should be instructed to listen only and not give any coaching yet.

7. Set your timer and let them go for 2 minutes.

8. After 2 minutes say "Okay, stop that's time!" or "Heads up, everybody!" or something that gets their attention. Emphasize that you'll be keeping track of time and when you indicate that it's time to stop they should imagine the elevator door opening and the conversation ending wherever it is.

9. Instruct all the coaches to take 1 minute and mirror back what they heard to confirm accuracy.

10. When moving to question 2, instruct the partners that they should now shift into discussion mode. Reveal question 2 and tell the group they have 2 minutes.

11. After 2 minutes have passed say, "Okay, heads up everybody. Time to stop." Ask the group to be aware of whether they're able to converse or whether someone is dominating the discussion. If so, suggest that they be aware of that as they answer the next question.

12. Present the Tips to Apply Outsight and review them quickly. Present question 3 and tell them they have 4 minutes to address outsight and really stretch one another beyond the obvious ideas.

13. After 4 minutes say, "Okay, heads up everybody. Time to stop."

14. Present the last question and emphasize that they should be as specific as possible with generating some "small wins" for the participant's issue. Present the "Actions to Generate Small Wins" information and review quickly. Tell them they have 4 minutes and to begin.

15. After 4 minutes, say, "Okay, heads up everybody. Time to stop."

16. State that the partners will switch roles. Return to step 6 and conduct the process through step 15 again.

17. Have the partners think about two additional aspects of Challenge the Process, defying the critics and enabling failures to lead to success.

18. Have them talk together for 5 minutes about what they expect from the "critic" audience and whether they have specific ways to address their concerns. Also have them talk about what support mechanisms they'll need to put in place in order to maintain momentum when things don't go as expected.

19. Summarize the activity with these questions:
    • How did this activity go for you?
    • What did you learn while being coached?
    • What did you learn while coaching?
    • How could you use informal coaching in your normal work day?

Variations

• To save time, the worksheet could be completed before the session.
• Formal coaches can also use this worksheet for phone or in-person coaching discussions.

L.J. Rose has over twenty years of experience in the public, private, and non-profit sectors. She is currently a keynote speaker and Master Facilitator of Kouzes and Posner's Leadership Challenge® Workshop. Passionate about ideas, talent, and results, L.J. facilitates learning experiences for emerging leaders and executive teams. Since 2000 she has worked with employees at numerous organizational levels in functions as varied as finance, IT, sales, marketing, R&D, engineering, operations, manufacturing, HR, and customer support. In addition to being active in the world of work, L.J. is also a world traveler.

L.J. Rose
Leadership Challenge Master Facilitator
San Francisco, CA
  Phone: (415) 929-9090
  Email: Ljroseconsulting@aol.com
  Website: www.leadershipchallenge.com

APPLYING CHALLENGE THE PROCESS TO A REAL-TIME ISSUE

Two Commitments of Challenge the Process:

- Search for opportunities by seizing the initiative and by looking outward for innovative ways to improve.
- Experiment and take risks by constantly generating small wins and learning from experience.

What's your challenge and idea for improvement?

What makes this challenge and idea meaningful to you?

Specifically, how can you exercise outsight to strengthen your idea?

What are two small wins you can generate to gain/keep momentum?

Activity Instructions for Applying Challenge the Process

Decide who will be coached FIRST

☐ 2 minutes: DESCRIBE your Challenge and Idea.

☐ 2 minutes: DISCUSS what makes this Challenge and Idea meaningful to you.

☐ 4 minutes: DISCUSS ways to exercise Outsight to Strengthen your Idea—BE SPECIFIC.

☐ 4 minutes: DISCUSS two small wins you can generate to gain/ keep momentum.

Tips to Apply Outsight

☐ Arrange a field trip to stimulate thinking.

☐ Read magazines from fields you know nothing about.

☐ Call customers and ask what they would like to see you do that you are not doing.

☐ Shop at a competitor's store or website.

☐ Ask a client to share ideas at a planning meeting.

☐ Observe a customer or client using your product or service.

Actions to Generate Small Wins

☐ Break It Down

☐ Make a Model

☐ Keep It Simple

☐ Do the Easy Parts First

☐ Accumulate Yeses

☐ Experiment

☐ Give/Receive Feedback

☐ Celebrate

OVERCOMING BARRIERS

Submitted by Darryl Sink

Objectives

- To identify and prioritize problems associated with a change or process improvement.
- To suggest alternative solutions for removing or reducing these problems or barriers.

Audience

Three to five individuals per group, with a minimum of three groups. There should be the same number of groups as problems/barriers to be resolved. Usually not more than five problems/barriers are selected.

Time Required

60 to 75 minutes.

Materials and Equipment

- Flip chart and markers.
- Five envelopes.
- A stack of blank 3 by 5 index cards for each team.
- Paper and writing utensils.

Area Setup

One round table with chairs for each team of three to five people.

Facilitator Note

Leaders and managers spend a fair amount of time introducing new corporate initiatives such as new technologies, processes, products, and strategies. Often they are working with a team of people during the execution of a new initiative. Often, even though a team gets excited initially about the new ideas/initiatives, there is usually a *yeah-but* stage people go through. This activity is empowering for participants. The activity engages participants to identify ways to overcome the *yeah-but* stage on their own.

Process

1. Divide participants into teams of three to five people each.

2. Tell participants that this activity is designed to help them identify and prioritize problems associated with a change—a shift from how things were to a new way—and to develop strategies for removing or reducing these problems. Describe for the teams the shift that they will be using in this activity.

3. Explain that the teams are to brainstorm and to list other possible problems associated with the shift. Ask each team to brainstorm for 5 minutes and to prepare a list of five critical problems.

4. Ask the teams to take turns calling out one of the problems on their lists. Prepare a combined list on a flip chart. Facilitate the discussion to ensure that the teams avoid redundant items. Continue this procedure until the flip chart contains about ten problems. Number the items in order, 1 through 10.

5. Ask each team member to select his or her top priority from the combined list and to write down its number. Tabulate by a show

of hands how many people voted for each problem on the flip chart. Circle the problem with the most votes. Repeat the process. Everyone writes down the next-most-important problem. Again tabulate the results and circle the second problem. Continue until your group feels they have the top three to five problems. During this process, if there is a tie among problems, do not check off any problem for that round. Ask each team to take a minute to explain its rationale for the choice of that particular problem before proceeding to another round of voting.

6. Generate problem envelopes by writing each of the top three to five problems on the face of a different envelope. Distribute one envelope to each team. Ask the participants to study the problem statement on the envelope and to come up with criteria for evaluating alternative solutions. Examples might include such criteria as easy to implement, most effective, or cost is low. Announce a time limit for this activity (3 to 5 minutes). Ask the teams to write down their criteria on a separate sheet of paper.

7. Ask each team to pass its problem envelope to the next team. Ask the teams to study the problem and to come up with suitable solutions. Announce an appropriate time limit (5 minutes) and ask each team to write down each of their solutions (ways to respond to the barrier) on one side of a 3 by 5 card. So if they generate seven solutions, there would be seven cards.

8. Ask the teams to put the solution cards inside the problem envelopes and to pass them to the next team. Each team now reads the new problem and (without looking at the solutions inside the envelope) identifies their solutions within the 5-minute time limit. Have participants write one possible solution per index card and place them inside the envelope.

9. Repeat this procedure until the problem envelopes return to the original teams (which had earlier set up the criteria for evaluating alternative solutions).

10. Ask the teams to evaluate the solutions. The teams will open the envelopes and review the solution cards. Each team compares the different solutions to the same problem and uses their criteria written earlier in Step 6 to select their top three choices.

11. Ask each team to read the problem statement on the envelope and their top three solution cards. It is even more useful to have them write the problem/barrier on a flip chart page with the three solutions or ways to respond to the barrier. Have them post the page on the wall and present it to the rest of the group.

12. Summarize this activity by asking:
    - What are the advantages to this process?
    - When could this process be used?
    - What did you experience during the activity that could be useful in other situations?
    - How is this process useful for implementing Challenge the Process?
    - When might you be able to use this process?

Darryl Sink, Ed.D., is president of Darryl L. Sink & Associates, Inc. (DSA). with twenty-eight years of designing great learning experiences. He is the recipient of International Society for Performance Improvement (ISPI) Professional Service Award and three times has been awarded the Outstanding Instructional Product of the Year Award by ISPI. Darryl authors the monthly *Learning and Performance Tips* newsletter available at www.dsink.com as well as various chapters in professional books.

Darryl Sink, Ed.D.
Darryl L. Sink & Associates, Inc.
1 Cielo Vista Place
Monterey, CA 93940
 Phone: (831) 649-8384
 Email: darryl@dsink.com
 Website: www.dsink.com

YOU BE THE JUDGE!™

Submitted by Karen Travis

Objectives

- To advance participants' ability to rate the effectiveness of a process.
- To help participants communicate their criteria for effective and ineffective behaviors.
- To have participants gain fresh insights from other participants that can be applied to their own performance.
- To utilize a tool for implementing Challenge the Process.

Audience

Participants should have a common interest in the process to be challenged. Any number of groups of four to six.

Time Required

About 1 hour for one scenario. Additional 45 minutes for each extra scenario.

Materials and Equipment

- Scenarios appropriate to the process being judged, scripted and printed for each participant; typically one or two pages. (See the Sample Scenario for an example.) If you are using multiple scenarios, to avoid confusion with the ratings, you may wish to label the scenarios as Round A, B, and C (do not use numbers).
- A rating mechanism for each participant and the facilitator. You could use any of the following:
    - A pre-prepared set or rating cards (ten index cards numbered 1 through 10)

- Blank index cards (one for each process/scenario used) and a marker; participants would simply write their rating for each process/scenario
- A mini whiteboard and Dry Erase pen (and something to wipe the board with); again, participants would simply write their ratings for each process/scenario on the whiteboard
- *(Optional)* Audio recordings of the scenario(s) to be judged.
- Pen and paper for note-taking.

Area Setup

Participants should be seated in table groups of four to six people.

Facilitator Note

This activity can be used with participants who have already learned the process being discussed or as a way to help a group refine or improve a process that may not be clearly defined.

Process

1. Ask participants, "Have you ever wanted to be an Olympic judge? Here's your chance." Distribute the rating cards (or whatever rating mechanism you're using) to each participant.

2. Show participants your own rating mechanism. Explain that in this activity, "You will learn from each other by rating the process we are about to review. 1 is the lowest rating and 10 is the highest possible rating."

3. Lead a practice round by saying, "We are going to start by rating something that you are all familiar with. When I tell you what we are rating, you should take a few moments to individually rate

it. Then, at the count of three, I want you to hold your rating up high. Arms straight up!"

4. Quickly ask, "How effective is the chair you are sitting on?" Do not pause or answer any questions.

5. Remind them, "This is an individual rating, no need to confer with your neighbor."

6. Loudly say, "One — two — three, ratings please!" Encourage the slow movers to raise their rating cards and for everyone to keep those scores held up high or "higher," if you can't see the ratings.

7. Ask the participant with the highest rating to explain what he or she finds effective about his or her chair. Ask, "How is the chair effective?" If he or she starts to list pros and cons, ask him or her to hold the thoughts on what was ineffective. Later in the process you can give participants more leeway, once they understand the judging process.

8. Ask the participant with the lowest rating to explain why he or she finds the chair ineffective. Again, if the participant lists what he or she thought was effective, ask him or her to focus on what was ineffective to support the low score.

9. Ask two or three other participants at the high and low end of the ratings to explain their rating. [*Note:* Be careful about using synonyms for "rating"—stick with rating or scoring. Avoid using words like ranking or voting.]

10. Explain how the activity will continue by saying, "Now that we know how the judging works, let's use the rating system to evaluate our processes." Before you begin the judging process, it might be a good opportunity to review the process being evaluated.

11. Ask the group for key indicators they will look for. For example, in the sample scenario in which a manager attempts to calm an upset CSR, participants might say "The manager should be brief, not be defensive, acknowledge the CSR's frustration, let the CSR talk more than the manager, don't blame others, et cetera." For the sample scenario provided, you could continue with, "Specifically, we're going to rate how effective the manager is at calming the angry CSR."

12. Distribute the scenario you have prepared. If you have recorded the scenario, play the scenario once everyone has a handout. Encourage the participants to "just listen" the first time you read (or play) the scenario.

13. When the scenario is finished, say, "On your own, please rate how effective the [person being assessed] was." (In the sample scenario, participants would be evaluating the manager.) Give the group approximately 20 seconds or ask folks to look at you when they are ready.

14. Ask participants to raise their rating cards. Looking for the high and low ratings again, ask several participants to explain, in detail, their rating. Specific examples from the scenario should be encouraged. If you use additional scenarios/rounds, vary whether you start randomly or with the highest or lowest rating. Don't always start with the highest rating. Also, if you notice that certain individuals are always providing a high or low score, be sure to call on other participants so the same people are not speaking each time.

15. Ask the group, "Please identify what the [person being evaluated] said that was ineffective in. . . ." *Note:* In your session, you

would insert the name or title of the person being evaluated and complete the sentence by indicating the task. So for the sample scenario, you'd be asking what the manager said that was ineffective in calming the CSR. Be sure to keep the group focused on the process and not evaluate other aspects of the scenario that may not be relevant to the process you are evaluating. Try to avoid having anyone present a laundry list of pros and cons; you could guide the discussion by saying, "Let's hear one effective and one ineffective step in the process." The more people that can participate and add their perspective, the better.

16. Identify one or two of the statements the group identified as ineffective. Ask, "Would anyone like to share how they would modify the statement?" If participants start to rationalize or explain, ask them to use the specific words they would use. Repeat as appropriate but do not "fix" every statement. A few examples will suffice. Rather than rework, it is also acceptable for a participant to suggest that a statement be eliminated.

17. *Note:* As the facilitator/leader, allow participants to learn from one another. Refrain from commenting on the scenarios, adding to or clarifying participants' comments. Rely on the discovery process to maximize the participants' learning and "Ah ha's." Participants will learn from each other; you are guiding, not driving the conversation. Facilitate learning by encouraging participants to speak up. Limit your participation to thought-provoking questions, if needed! For example, with the sample scenario, you might use the following questions:
   • How could the manager be briefer? (If a participant raised this issue, do not ask it again!)

- Did anything the manager say seem defensive or as though he was taking the customer's side?
- Who talked more—the CSR or the manager?

18. To wrap up this round, ask volunteers to share some Ah ha's. Since these rating rounds tend to move rather quickly with little time for reflection, you may want to provide 30 or 45 seconds for participants to consider what they have learned from this scenario. Ask participants to write down their Ah ha's and decide how they will proceed differently the next time they encounter the situation in the scenario.

19. *(Optional)* If you are conducting multiple rounds, you may ask participants to write down their "Ah ha's" but do not share them publicly. Then, after you have finished all the rounds of judging, ask participants to share their biggest "Ah ha."

20. *(Optional)* Conduct a second round using a different but related scenario, either written or recorded. Tell participants, "Do not compare this scenario to the first round. Simply rate this scenario on its own merits." We suggest that the facilitator always have a printed copy of the scenario, even though the participants may not receive the handout in this round. Debrief using the format above, from Step 13 to Step 19. [*Note:* The elimination of a hard copy challenges participants to listen more carefully.]

21. *(Optional)* For the third scenario, debrief as above, but change the format by asking participants: "On the count of 3, raise those hands high and show your rating." Confirm everyone has revealed his or her score. Say, "Thank you. Now that you've individually rated this scenario, please work at your table groups to reach a consensus rating." Allow about 5 minutes. Ask each

group to select a representative to share the group's answer when you ask. The representative will provide the team score, as well as the range of scores at the table (highest rating and lowest rating). Once you hear the team ratings, start with the group that gave the highest or lowest rating. As with the other rounds, focus the teams on identifying what behavior(s) was effective or ineffective in the process.

22. If time permits, ask for individuals to comment by asking, "Was there any new learning by asking you to reach consensus and come up with a rating representing the entire group?"

23. There is no need to debrief the activity any further. Thank participants for their participation and move on. Resist the urge to add your own thoughts or to summarize and rehash what has happened!

Variations

- Typically "You Be the Judge" involves up to three rounds of scenarios, which allows the participants to critique several iterations of related processes. It is also possible to conduct several shorter rounds over the course of a day to provide a change of pace in a training session. In any event, be sure to vary the order of the scenarios if you use this methodology on a regular basis. Do not always move from the worst to better and best. Sometime it is appropriate to have no "good" scenarios presented.

- In a training situation, ideally "You Be the Judge" would be followed by opportunities for participants to role play the scenarios and receive feedback from their peers. Using trios is the preferred methodology, for example, a manager, a CSR, and an observer. Participants would rotate roles, taking turns in each role.

- This activity may be conducted with one small group of five to eight people, for example, as part of a staff meeting or a "lunch-and-learn" series. Once participants know the methodology, it is easy to use this technique on an ongoing basis.
- This technique can be used on almost any process, depending on the scenarios you choose. Scenarios might cover coaching effectiveness for team leaders, calming an angry customer, handling customer objections in the sales process, a long-time employee doing poorly in a new assignment, or a newly implemented process causing customers to pay more than double for shipping and handling due to a "system error."
- If you only have scripted scenarios, you can provide "audio" by asking a participant (or another manager) to read through the scenarios. The facilitator should always play the person who is NOT being judged. Videos are okay, if available, but be sure to remind participants they need to focus on relevant behaviors—not on the artwork on the manager's office wall, unless it is relevant to the issue.
- This activity may be conducted as part of an online webinar. It is most helpful if participants have a way to submit their ratings, with their names attached. Committing to their individual ratings, by sharing them with everyone in writing, is an important part of the design. This prevents participants from changing their ratings on the fly as others begin to share their own thoughts. If your online meeting software does not support this type of public polling, you could ask participants to submit their ratings in a chat window. Be sure to send participants at least one scenario for them to print and "bring with" them to the webinar.

Karen Travis is the president and CEO of Sigma Performance Solutions. A professional trainer, consultant, and frequent keynote speaker, Karen graduated from Cornell University with a bachelor's degree in business management and The Johns Hopkins University with a master's degree in applied behavioral science. Sigma provides training, coaching, and consulting for organizations worldwide in high-tech, healthcare, and financial services, using LIST® and other tools to leverage technical expertise with productive conversations to improve and sustain business results.

Karen A. Travis
Sigma Performance Solutions, Inc.
660 Kenilworth Drive #104
Baltimore, MD 21204
   Phone: (410) 667-9055
   Email: karen@sigmatraining.com
   Website: www.sigmatraining.com

YOU BE THE JUDGE!: SAMPLE SCENARIO

In this scenario, Mike Forsythe, a call center manager at Premiere Storage, receives a call from one of his best CSRs, Sara Smith. Mike knows two things. First, a key client has escalated his project over the last week because the client had to delay testing a new computer system at City Hospital because the customer's data center had inadequate power to support the new system. Second, Premiere's on-site service professional helped the client schedule an electrical contractor to install an additional power supply tomorrow morning.

Call Center Manager: Premiere Storage. Mike Forsythe here.

CSR: Hi, Mike, this is Sara. Remember, you assigned me to the City Hospital Project?

Call Center Manager: Yes. Hi, Sara, how can I help you?

CSR: What you can do is tell me exactly what is going on! I just got blindsided by the customer that the new equipment is not even plugged in; the floor is still wide open and the power connectors are sticking out in the air, obviously UN-plugged. Unless I'm mistaken, we were supposed to be powered up and testing today! We're already two days behind schedule; now add another.

Call Center Manager: Yes . . . [pause, to see if Sara continues venting]. There's been a slight delay while we wait for the additional power supplies to be replaced first thing tomorrow morning.

CSR: Slight delay? By whose definition? And why exactly are you talking about adding additional power after the testing was supposed to be underway? Someone should have figured this out days ago? I know that Ted, your most senior technician, has been on site at least four times since the power was hooked up last week. Don't try to convince me that he didn't notice the problem until today! And worse, I have to learn it from the client. I've always had a great relationship with Jose at the hospital, and now he is hopping mad. That's a capital M – A – D.

Call Center Manager: When we went to power up the system we discovered that the breakers had too low an amp rating and we need to add the new power supplies.

CSR: This is absolutely ridiculous. Excuses don't help me. Why didn't our QA processes catch this? I expect my teammates to detect problems before they affect me and most definitely before they delay a deadline! Do I have to handle everything? I bet this will be an excuse for you to delay the final cutover!

Call Center Manager: Sara?

CSR: Yes?

Call Center Manager: I do NOT want to delay the cutover.

CSR: Well, finally some good news.

Call Center Manager: I'm sorry you were blindsided.

CSR: Good. I expect the system to be running properly VERY soon. I should have been advised immediately when this problem was detected. I detest surprises.

Call Center Manager: Me, too. Unfortunately, some surprises are almost inevitable in this business, but our clients can count on us to help them recover when they do happen.

CSR: "Inevitable?" I don't think so! These days it's become SOP. Did you hear a word I said? Why don't we get it right the first time? I've tried to stay calm through all the changes and I've always thought we had a good relationship, but it seems like things are just falling apart. This is not the first time we've had the conversation. How can I support from my side if you plan on making mistakes?!?

Call Center Manager: Sara, I hear you. I appreciate your patience.

CSR: Well, it's starting to wear thin.

Call Center Manager: Things have been rough.

CSR: You've got that right. [Pause] It's late and I'm sure you want to get home; maybe we can talk about some solutions tomorrow?

Call Center Manager: Okay.

ASSUMPTION REFRAME

Submitted by Devora Zack

Objectives

- To reveal and address assumptions.
- To challenge the thought process of making decisions and discovering solutions.
- To identify a small win to keep the process improvement in motion.

Audience

Four to fifteen participants.

Time Required

40 to 60 minutes (depends on depth of issues discussed and number of participants).

Materials and Equipment

- Self-sticking flip-chart paper on sturdy easel and markers—black and red (or another color).
- Timer or stopwatch.

Area Setup

Participants seated where they can see each other and the easel.

Facilitator Note

Sometimes a team is stymied because team members cannot move beyond obvious assumptions in a process. This activity eliminates the assumptions so the team can move forward and continue to Challenge the Process.

Process

1. Have the participants select a current, real challenge they collectively face (a decision, project, or opportunity).

2. Have participants take turns (no more than 2 minutes per person) describing the situation and potential responses using stream-of-consciousness. They should not edit or question each other, and comments need not follow those of the person speaking prior. Group determines a timekeeper and a scribe. As participants speak, the scribe captures comments by writing clearly on the flip-chart paper with the black marker, keeping as many as possible of the precise words used.

3. Two other participants come forward and underline any assumptions they can identify in red marker. The rest of the group can assist them in this process. (Example: We must handle this as expediently as possible. Everyone knows the basic structure of our shared vision so it makes sense to expand our customer base.) The group need not be in agreement as to what is considered an assumption. If even one person requests an underline, it should be made. Groups are typically surprised with how much of what was written is underlined. Rather than providing parameters of assumption or challenge to the group in advance, let them discuss and determine their definitions, with assistance from the facilitator.

4. Ask a new participant to come forward. This person leads the group in replacing assumptions. (Example: This is an area to examine and address, so we will make it a priority. We will begin by ensuring we have a shared understanding of our

department's vision. Then we will conduct a needs analysis to determine whether it makes sense to expand our customer base and/or explore alternative options.) While it may be impossible to eliminate any words that one could potentially challenge as assumptions, the emphasis at this point should be a thoughtful revision and conscious strategy based on challenging the standard process of workplace strategies.

5. Based on this work together, have the team identify one to three immediate action steps, or small wins, to keep their process in motion.

Devora Zack, president of Only Connect Consulting (OOC), provides leadership development, coaching, team training, and assessments to more than seventy-five clients, including Deloitte, America Online, the U.S. Patent & Trademark Office, OPM, Enterprise, and the U.S. Treasury. Devora has been on the faculty for Cornell's leadership program for thirteen years. Devora holds an M.B.A. from Cornell University and a B.A. from the University of Pennsylvania. Her certifications include MBTI and Neuro-Linguistic Programming. She is a member of Phi Beta Kappa, Mensa, and ASTD. Her designs are featured in five publications. OCC is the recipient of USDA's Woman-Owned Business of the Year.

Devora Zack
Only Connect Consulting, Inc.
7806 Ivymount Terrace
Potomac, MD 20854
   Phone: (301) 765-6262
   Email: dzack@onlyconnectconsulting.com
   Website: www.onlyconnectconsulting.com

CHAPTER SIX: ENABLE OTHERS TO ACT

In This Chapter

- Overview Enable Others to Act.
- Discuss the corresponding Commitments of Leadership.
- Consider the importance of this practice.
- Introduce the activities for this practice.
- Present the activities for this practice.

The Leadership Challenge presents compelling evidence about why collaboration is a critical competency for achieving and sustaining high performance. At the base of this practice is the need to build trust between the leader and employees as well as build trust between employees. Trust is one of those elusive characteristics that may often be described as "I'll know it when I see it." Every leader needs to identify ways to build trust and facilitate trusting relationships throughout the organization.

HOW DOES A LEADER ENABLE OTHERS TO ACT?

To enable others to act, leaders must be relationship-oriented from two perspectives. First, they must provide a climate that is conducive to building positive interaction throughout the group. Second, they must build individuals' capacity within that positive climate.

311

Consider the related Commitments of Leadership:

- Foster collaboration by building trust and facilitating relationships.
- Strengthen others by increasing self-determination and developing competence.

Foster Collaboration

A collaborative atmosphere begins by building trust throughout the organization (or team). How can leaders build trust? Leaders must trust before they can expect to be trusted. There are generally four behaviors that build and strengthen a trusting relationship:

- *Honesty and candor*. Leaders say what they mean. You will never wonder what they are "really" thinking.
- *Accessibility and openness*. Leaders tell you what works for them. They keep their agendas open and you know who they are. They share information and resources.
- *Approving and accepting*. Leaders value people and diverse perspectives. You can count on being heard without judgment or criticism, making them easy to talk to. They facilitate relationships with others.
- *Dependable and trustworthy*. Leaders do what they say they will do. They keep their promises and you know that you can count on them.

Related to building trust is facilitating relationships by developing cooperative roles and goals. Leaders structure projects to promote teamwork, use "we" more often than "I," listen, take advice, and ultimately transform their followers into leaders themselves.

Strengthen Others

Excellent leaders Enable Others to Act by ensuring that everyone feels competent, capable, and confident. Malcolm Knowles made it clear that adults come to any experience expecting to be treated with respect. That holds true for every day at work. When others are treated with respect, they exude a deep sense of being in control of their own lives.

Leaders can strengthen others and ensure that they feel in control by providing choices within their jobs and by designing jobs that offer them an opportunity to make decisions and foster accountability. *The Leadership Challenge* recommends monthly coaching conversations between leaders and each of their direct reports.

WHY IS ENABLE OTHERS TO ACT IMPORTANT?

In a world that is caught up in doing more with less and faster, collaboration is a critical competency. Achieving and sustaining high performance is possible with a collaborative atmosphere that is built on trust and positive relationships. Unfortunately, competition is still the way in much of the world. By strengthening every individual on the team, a leader strengthens the team.

ACTIVITY INTRODUCTION

A potpourri of activities address a wide variety of skills and characteristics that Enable Others to Act, such as resilience, making decisions, influencing, empowerment, and building trust and trustworthiness.

Activities demonstrate the benefits of fostering collaboration, present ways to strengthen team performance, and encourage career coaching between leaders and their direct reports. Many of the activities are appropriate for a variety of group sizes up to several hundred. Time varies from a few minutes to a couple of hours.

Activity List

- What Would YOU Do in My Shoes? by Geoff Bellman
- Enabling Cross-Functional Leadership by Christopher Chaves
- Building Resilience for Change by Daryl R. Conner
- Enabling with Style by Ann Hermann-Nehdi
- Currency Exchange by Cindy Huggett
- Team Competency Development Plan by Edith Katz
- Career Conversations: Cues for Developing Others by Beverly Kaye
- Double Overlapping Strategic Cross by Sharon Landes
- What Makes You Trust Someone? by Sherri Dosher
- Trust-Building Discussion by Doug Leigh
- Human Trust Knot by Jan Miller and Denise Knight
- Trust and Communication by Jan Miller and Denise Knight
- Share Fair by Marilyn Myers
- No Easy Way Out by Mona Lee Pearl
- Coaching Versus Telling by Lou Russell
- Empowerment Force Field Analysis by Cindy Taylor
- Inflated Actions by Lorraine Ukens
- Activate to Motivate by Devora Zack

WHAT WOULD YOU DO IN MY SHOES?

Submitted by Geoff Bellman

Objectives

- To gather ideas that help make decisions and lead others.
- To model learning and humility.
- To cause others to think as leaders.

Audience

Group size can vary from two to two hundred; the design is adjusted to the group and becomes more structured with more involved. An actual organizational leader facilitates the group.

Time Required

30 minutes to 1 hour.

Materials and Equipment

- A pen and paper for you, the leader
- An easel, flip-chart paper, and markers (with five to twenty-five participants).
- Writing materials for teams (with twenty-five to two hundred participants).
- Paper and bold marker for each participant.

Area Setup

Tables for groups of five to eight.

Process

1. Briefly explain the issue, opportunity, or problem facing you—one that calls for you to make a decision. Check with participants for their understanding of the issue.

2. Make it clear to the group that you really need their help on this issue. Ask individuals to write down their answers to the question: What would YOU do in my shoes? Have them write their answers with bold markers on 8.5-by-11 inch paper, one answer per sheet.

3. For larger groups, ask them to share their answers at their tables and come up with what their table groups think are the best answers.

4. Collect the responses and spread them out on the floor for all to see and discuss.

5. Lead a discussion about the solutions. State your appreciation for what they have contributed, show your interest in it, and commit to getting back to them with your final decision.

6. State that you just engaged them in a process that regularly faces you in your role as leader. Emphasize how useful it is to have them think as leaders too.

7. Summarize with these questions:
   - How did this process go for you?
   - How useful was it?
   - How enjoyable was it? Why or why not?
   - What did you experience about leadership during the activity?
   - Did the activity change your thoughts about leadership in any way? If so, how?
   - What might you do, think, or say differently as a result of what you experienced?

8. Once your decision has been made, inform the group of your decision and thank them again. (*Note:* Keep in mind that this process does not require you to make a decision at the time responses are offered. Quite the contrary, it asks you to not decide and to hear the group. You are the leader; you can hold the decision to yourself if you choose—but make a better decision with their input.)

Variation

Collect responses after Step 2 for later review.

Geoff Bellman has consulted with and written about leadership for forty years. His more widely read books include *Getting Things Done When You Are Not in Charge* (Berrett-Koehler, 2001) and *Extraordinary Groups: How Ordinary Teams Achieve Amazing Results* (Jossey-Bass, 2009).

Geoff Bellman
1444 NW Woodbine Way
Seattle, WA 98177
    Phone: (206) 365-3212
    Email: geoffbellman@gmail.com
    Website: See Facebook

ENABLING CROSS-FUNCTIONAL LEADERSHIP

Submitted by Christopher Chaves

Objectives

- To define leadership as a process whereby anyone in the organization, regardless of title, can influence across functions to produce positive change.
- To establish that effective leadership requires functional expertise and cross-functional understanding and engagement.
- To demonstrate the role questions can play in enabling others to act.

Audience

Five to twenty participants.

Time Required

90 to 120 minutes.

Materials and Equipment

- Paper and pencils or markers.
- Copy of Understanding Cross-Functional Leadership for each participant.
- Copy of Action Case Scenarios for each participant.
- Flip chart and markers.

Area Setup

Workspace with tables and enough space for small team discussion and collaboration without interrupting other teams.

Facilitator Note

The idea of "leadership" has been reconceptualized to mean the process of influencing individuals and situations during the course of events designed to achieve organizational goals; leadership is no longer the sole province of managers. It is especially necessary for individuals operating within flatter organizations to have a wider span of influence on operational processes. However, many individuals working within flat, hierarchical, organic, or mechanistic organizations fail to employ necessary leadership due to their lack of a systems perspective concerning their organizations. The following exercise can help an individual or a group of employees develop a new form of cross-functional leadership perspective and the subsequent confidence in using appropriate leadership actions to help solve organizational problems.

Process

1. Divide the group into four teams of five members each (fewer teams if you have fewer than twenty participants). Once they have arranged themselves in their team locations, state that each team will examine a scenario from a different organization facing a different problem. Say that Enable Others to Act requires working together in a collaborative manner. This means that individuals understand what others do in various parts of the organization.

2. Explain to participants that they will receive a mini-MBA orientation that includes essential information about the four major organizational line functions: marketing and sales; design and engineering; production and assembly; and accounting and finance. Give one copy of the Understanding Cross-Functional

Leadership handout to each participant. Ask participants, "Do any of the four major line functions outlined relate in any way to your current or previous work?" It is important to find out how much knowledge and experience participants offer to the group and to their respective teams relating to general organizational functions. Make use of participants' experiences during the following discussion.

3. Explain each of the line functions. Invite participants to take notes during the discussion.

    *   Begin by explaining that generally within the marketing and sales (M&S) function, market research is accomplished and the marketing mix involving the product, its price, the place to offer it, and its promotional strategies is developed and subsequently deployed. Additionally, explain that the sales force must be continuously trained about product or service knowledge related to the benefits and features associated to the company's offerings. Ask, "Are there any questions about this function?"

    *   Second, explain that the design and engineering (D&E) function collaborates with M&S about what market research results indicate and mean to new product or service development. Using this data and information, D&E will draw up conceptual designs that conform to customers' desires related to the benefits and features they want in a product or service. Should it be a physical product, explain that engineers will determine what tangible available technologies can make the desired benefits and features possible; explain also that the role of key suppliers and production and assembly (P&A) is crucial at this stage of product or service development.

Ask, "Are there any questions about this function or its role with M&S?"

- Third, explain the function and collaboration that production and assembly (P&A) generally undertakes with respect to M&S and D&E, that "M&S must provide P&A with sales (demand) forecasts for given periods of time into the future. Further explain that P&A needs information from D&E regarding product/service concept design and development." Continue explaining that P&A will in essence implement the design specifications developed by D&E on an assembly line system, which may include a manufacturing assembly process or a services-based operation (e.g., hospitals, banking). Ask, "Are there any questions about this function or its impact on D&E or M&S?"

- Finally, explain that the accounting and finance (A&F) function is generally responsible for accounts receivable and payable processes, tax issues, and budget development and monitoring, in addition to the role that finance undertakes in raising funds, issuing equity and corporate bonds, and managing customer credit. Encourage questions from participants at this point.

4. Explain to participants that the model speaks primarily to private-sector organizations, but various aspects of it may have application to public-sector and non-profit organizations. Ask participants, "What other functions within the organization are missing?" Document participants' feedback on a flip-chart sheet under the appropriate enterprise line function for future reference.

5. Hand out the Action Case Scenarios. Assign each team one of the scenarios: A, B, C, or D. Briefly review each of the scenarios,

including the industry, the organization, the product or service, customers, and the problem the organization is facing.

6. Explain to the teams that they are to imagine that they are the leadership of the organization and that they will identify what actions they might take to solve the problems. On each team, participants should:
   - Select a team leader.
   - Assign one person as a subject-matter expert to each of the four functional areas: Sales and Marketing; Design and Engineering; Production and Assembly; and Accounting and Finance. The team leader can also be assigned a subject-matter expert role. These individuals are responsible for their specific areas during the exercise: role, responsibility, accountability. They will focus on their organizational roles as the teams explore the problems. (*Note:* If there are fewer than five people on a team, some individuals can play dual roles.)
   - Read the scenario and the list of questions. The questions are meant as examples of what a leader might want to know to resolve the problem.
   - Complete the requested information as a team.

7. Each team should focus on how they can Enable Others to Act throughout the scenario, for example:
   - How can they foster collaboration?
   - How can they build trust across functions?
   - How can they facilitate relationships?
   - What responsibility do they have to develop competencies in each other?

Each team should be prepared to report out on both "what" they might do, as well as "how" they might do it. Tell them they have 45 minutes.

8. After 45 minutes, call time and ask each team to report out on its scenario. Ask each team to:
   - Provide examples of other questions.
   - State how the leader could best Enable Others to Act cross-functionally.

9. Wrap up the exercise by asking:
   - What makes it difficult to collaborate across functions? Can you provide examples?
   - How do the natural functional roles in an organization make it difficult to build trust? Facilitate relationships?
   - What is your greatest take-away from this activity?
   - What will you do as a leader in your organization as a result of what you learned during this activity?

10. State that enabling and empowering individuals to act on and solve future organizational challenges requires both developmental opportunities and experiences to prepare and empower individuals to do what they need to do. State that Enable Others to Act is not just about their roles as leaders, but about how they will prepare the next leaders to do the same thing.

Christopher Chaves, Ed.D, is assistant professor and deputy chief for faculty and staff development at the Joint Forces Staff College in Norfolk, Virginia. He offers nearly twenty-five years of professional experiences, including with the U.S. Air Force, entrepreneurship, non-profit organizations, educational organizations, economic development agencies, and university-level teaching, toward his scholarship and writing efforts. He holds an undergraduate degree in education, training, and development from Southern Illinois University, Carbondale; a master's degree in business administration (M.B.A.) from Western International University; and a doctoral degree in education from the University of Southern California.

Chris Chaves, Ed.D.
Joint Forces Staff College
7800 Hampton Boulevard
Norfolk, VA 23511-1702

UNDERSTANDING CROSS-FUNCTIONAL LEADERSHIP

Marketing and Sales (M&S)

- Conduct market research
- Determine product pricing
- Develop a promotional strategy
- Conduct sales training
- Share market research with Design and Engineering
- Share sales forecasts with Production and Assembly

Concerns: _____

Design and Engineering (D&E)

- Design conceptualization and specifications
- Identify benefits and features to meet customers requirements
- Build supplier relations
- Share sales design specifications with Production and Assembly

Concerns: _____

Production and Assembly (P&A)

- Implement design specifications developed by D&E
- Use either manufacturing or service operation to produce the product or service
- Maintain communication with Marketing and Sales regarding timeline

Concerns: _____

Accounting and Finance (A&F)

- Pay suppliers
- Invoice customers
- Address tax and budget issues

Concerns: _____

Concerns Across Functions That Enable Others to Act

- Maintaining good communication
- Building trust
- Fostering collaboration
- Facilitating relationships
- Developing and improving competencies
- Understanding other departments' challenges

ACTION CASE SCENARIOS

Scenario A

The Greenburg Hybrid Car Company has not met its sales goals for the last two years and lost market share during the fuel crisis of 2008. As the director of Marketing and Sales, what questions would you ask of yourself and your cross-functional team members concerning actions you would recommend to respond to slumping sales in what should be a growing and lucrative vehicle market? The M&S leader might begin by asking the following questions:

- Did we invite the right demographic group to our survey and focus group sessions?
- Did our market research and focus group facilitators ask the right questions?
- Did we allow our survey and focus group participants to volunteer information about the benefits and features they desired in the hybrid vehicle?
- As compared to the "best in class" (competition) in the hybrid vehicle industry, what benefits and features are we not offering in our hybrid vehicle models?
- Were our hybrid models competitively priced?
- Did we offer our showcase vehicle models in accessible and convenient venues for potential customers?
- Did our e-commerce strategy work effectively?
- Was our choice of advertising media (Internet, radio, print) deployed using the right strategy?
- Was our sales force adequately trained to effectively communicate the pertinent benefits and features that each customer was looking for?

- Was there collaboration and partnership between M&S, D&E, and key suppliers about hybrid vehicle design features and benefits?
- Was P&A apprised early enough about M&S's sale forecasts (customer demand)?
- Did A&F adequately fund the M&S campaign?
- Did A&F provide adequate and equitable access to credit to current and potential new customers?
- What other questions might the leader ask?
- How can the leader foster collaboration across functions?
- What might you do in this scenario? How?

Scenario B

Rodriguez Mobility Scooter Manufacturing designs and engineers various mobility scooter models for disabled workers; the mobility scooters for the disabled must be of a workplace-friendly design for ease of operation in various occupational work settings. However, serious complaints from current customers are streaming in about one of the models, the Max Mobility Scooter. The complaints address the model's lack of ease of mobility in tight spots, its short battery life, the navigation toggle unit, and lack of sitting comfort over an eight-hour work day. As the director of Design and Engineering, what questions would you ask of yourself and your cross-functional team members concerning what actions you would recommend to respond to what seem to be design and engineering flaws in the Max Mobility Scooter? The D&E leader might begin by asking the following questions:

- Did we receive adequate information and recommendations from M&S concerning the Max Mobility model's market research results and customer desires about its benefits and features?
- Did D&E incorporate the timely input from its key suppliers concerning various pieces of raw or assembled technologies?

- Did we make adequate use of our computer-aided design software and hardware resources to align design specifications with engineering tolerances and limitations?
- Did we have the timely input from P&A regarding the assembly-line technologies for required lean assembly?
- Did A&F under-fund the Max Mobility Scooter project due to faulty information?
- What other questions might the leader ask?
- How can the leader foster collaboration across functions?
- What might you do in this scenario? How?

Scenario C

For the last three years, MacArthur Good Samaritan Hospital (MGSH) has been experiencing a steady increase in customer complaints regarding influenza vaccination treatment, its lack of availability, and the general customer service experience. While the demand for healthcare services in general has been increasing due to the aging population and job layoffs, the hospital's doctors, nurses, and administrators have been unable to reasonably predict and plan for future demand of this seemingly common annual vaccination requirement. As the director of Primary Care Services (Production and Assembly) for MacArthur Good Samaritan Hospital, what questions would you ask of yourself and your cross-functional team members concerning what actions you would recommend to respond to what seems to be failure to prepare and respond to annual winter influenza vaccination requirements? The P&A leader might begin by asking the following questions:

- Does MacArthur Good Samaritan Hospital (MGSH) have formal contract relationships with more than one key influenza vaccination supplier in the industry for just-in-time deliveries?

- Did the M&S department at MGSH provide key influenza vaccination suppliers with historical customer demand data along with quantitative estimates related to possible future demand of multiple vaccine types?
- What month of the year does M&S launch its marketing campaign to inform the public about the up-and-coming flu season?
- Did the Primary Care Services department order influenza vaccinations as early in the year as possible?
- Are medical assistants partnering and communicating with physicians, nurses, or local vaccination clinics about vaccination walk-ins and/or appointments?
- Does the Primary Care Services department offer walk-in convenience on the weekends or through vaccination zones (such as city neighborhoods)?
- Are there adequate Primary Care Services storage facilities to hold supplies of influenza vaccination?
- Has A&F provided for adequate "charity funds" to vaccinate those patients without insurance or an ability to pay?
- Is the billing for influenza vaccinations adequately documented for reimbursement purposes and for patient records accuracy?
- How can an enterprise resource planning system better align MGSH's influenza vaccine orders with key supplier deliveries?
- What other questions might the leader ask?
- How can the leader foster collaboration across functions?
- What might you do in this scenario? How?

Scenario D

The White Clothing Manufacturing Company (WCMC) designs, assembles, and distributes quality-made clothing items for children and working men and women. Due to the recent worldwide recession, many of WCMC retail operation partners have been unable to offer adequate corporate credit lines to customers and, as a consequence, have the level of clothing orders from the WCMC has dramatically dropped. Prior to the recession, many young working-class families used credit cards to make purchases, but due to banks increasing interest rates on credit cards accounts, many of these families have lost or canceled their credit card accounts hoping for other forms of credit access. The A&F leader might begin by asking the following questions:

- Did the accounting and finance (A&F) department at WCMC recently restrict customer credit qualifying terms, and, if so, why?
- Does the A&F department at WCMC offer a layaway plan, through its retail operation partners, for customers based on certain income criteria?
- Does the WCMC A&F department utilize an accounting software program? If so, which kind?
- Does the WCMC ship its fully assembled clothing items directly to its retail partners, or does it market them through wholesale operations?
- How can savings be achieved for the customer through the use of internal and external e-commerce?
- What other value chain activities can achieve great efficiencies to afford customers greater savings?
- What other questions might the leader ask?
- How can the leader foster collaboration across functions?
- What might you do in this scenario? How?

BUILDING RESILIENCE FOR CHANGE
Submitted by Daryl R. Conner

Objectives

- To help individuals learn to understand and manage their own responses to change.
- To identify how resilience is important to enable others to act.
- To identify specific actions that individuals and teams can take to strengthen resilience.

Audience

An intact work group or team, which could range from small (three or four people) to moderately large (twenty to twenty-five people).

Time Required

45 to 90 minutes, depending on the size of the group and the depth of the discussion.

Materials and Equipment

- Flip chart and markers for the facilitator.
- LCD projector *(optional)*.
- A prepared handout or PowerPoint slide that summarizes the characteristics of resilience (see Characteristics of Resilience sheet).
- Two or three images depicting situations inside or outside the workplace for which resilience could be applied, for example, individual in a wheelchair confronting a flight of stairs or a house that has burned down. If images are not available or are

inappropriate, short written scenarios could serve as a substitute, for example, uncertainty that accompanies a restructuring in the wake of a merger or the disruption of being faced with a new, demanding boss.

Area Setup

If the group is small, members should be seated around a table together. If the group is larger, it could be broken up into several smaller groups around tables set up so that participants are facing each other but oriented toward the facilitator.

Process

1. Briefly set the stage by acknowledging that change is challenging, sharing an example of a time when you faced disruptive change and found it difficult, and affirming that each member of the group has the ability and responsibility to manage his or her own response to change.

2. Invite the group to think about people they know who are resilient—able to bounce back effectively from disruptive change without compromising the achievement of important personal and organizational goals. Ask them to identify the attributes that contribute to their resilience. Record these on a flip chart.

3. Share the resilience characteristics that have been identified as contributing to effective responses to change, providing a handout for reference, and relating them to the attributes the group identified.

4. Show an image of a potentially disruptive situation. Then ask participants to discuss how some or all of the resilience characteristics might be applied to help the individual effectively

address the challenge. As desired, additional situations could be presented and discussed. The goal is for the participants to become familiar with the basic resilience characteristics and their application to challenging situations.

5. Ask the group to work in triads. Have them identify how the five characteristics of resilience are important to Enable Others to Act. Allow 15 minutes and ask each group to report on its discussion.

6. Ask individuals to work in pairs to identify and share one or more resilience characteristics that are personal strengths, and one or more areas for which they would like to develop their capabilities further. Allow 5 to 10 minutes.

7. Combine pairs to form groups of four. Have them work together to identify next steps for strengthening their own resilience. These could include:
   • Finding potential coaches from within the group who could help them work on one of the resilience characteristics— these could be mutual coaching relationships (e.g., I help you with Focused, you help me with Flexible) or one-directional, depending on the composition of the group.
   • Choosing specific actions they could take to strengthen one of the characteristics—this could include beginning a new practice (e.g., using a day planner for the Organized characteristic, starting an appreciation journal for the Positive characteristic), taking a course, or some other related activity.

8. Bring the entire group together. Ask for examples of how they will strengthen one of the characteristics. Summarize with these questions:
   • What role does resilience play in Enable Others to Act?

- How does resilience play a part in being the leader you are?
- What's your next "go do" based on this activity?

9. Ask the group to agree on a future time and place to gather and check in on progress. Ideally, this topic would become part of the ongoing conversation within an intact work group.

Daryl Conner is an internationally recognized leader in organizational change, a dynamic public speaker, and an advisor to senior executives. In more than thirty-five years of practice, Daryl has worked with successful organizations around the world to help them achieve the full intent of their most critically important initiatives. Daryl has authored two books: *Managing at the Speed of Change* (Random House, 1993) and *Leading at the Edge of Chaos* (John Wiley & Sons, 1998).

Daryl R. Conner
Chairman
Conner Partners
Suite 1000, 1230 Peachtree Street, NE
Atlanta, GA 30309
  Phone: (404) 564-4800
  Email: daryl.conner@connerpartners.com
  Website: www.connerpartners.com

CHARACTERISTICS OF RESILIENCE

- **Positive**—Display a security and self-assurance that is based on a view of life as complex but filled with opportunity. (This enables people to engage their energy in addressing challenges, rather than retreating from them.)
- **Focused**—Have a clear vision of what one wants to achieve. (This enables people to direct energy toward their most important goals, rather than diffusing it across too many options.)
- **Flexible**—Demonstrate a special pliability when responding to uncertainty. (This enables people to open up a wide range of options and resources, rather than limiting themselves to the familiar.)
- **Organized**—Develop structured approaches to managing ambiguity. (This allows people to apply structure and discipline to generating effective plans, rather than working unsystematically.)
- **Proactive**—Engage change rather than defend against it. (This allows people to experiment with action in the face of uncertainty rather than holding back until everything is clear.)

The Leadership Challenge Activities Book
Copyright © 2010 by James M. Kouzes and Barry Z. Posner.
Reproduced by permission of Pfeiffer, an Imprint of Wiley. www.pfeiffer.com.

ENABLING WITH STYLE

Submitted by Ann Hermann-Nehdi, with input from Travis Felton, CBA-GLOBAL

Objectives

- To increase success with the "others" in Enable Others to Act practice by developing empathy for the others' way of doing (which may be different than the leader's).
- To apply a whole-brain approach to be more effective in allowing others to choose *how* to do their work.

Audience

Any size—ideally an even number of participants.

Time Required

20 to 30 minutes.

Materials and Equipment

- A timer or watch to monitor time.
- An LCD projector and computer (for slides) and screen or slides may be printed out as separate pages and used as handouts.

Area Setup

In a way that allows people to work in pairs.

Process

1. Have people pair off, preferably with those who are not like them (mix functions, area of expertise etc.). Show slide 1. Each member of the pair selects one of the four phrases that he or she prefers to

use to explain to his or her partner how he or she would approach one of the following tasks. They select one task only and each member needs to select a different phrase:

- Achieving the Bottom Line
- Building a Great Plan
- Developing Rapport and Friendship
- How to Be Creative and Spontaneous

2. Have pairs find spaces to work and show slide 2. Instruct participants to follow the guidelines for their selected phrase to create a description that will last for 2 minutes. They must keep talking for the full 2 minutes. They have 1 minute to prepare. Review briefly the four options. State that, depending on their selection:

- They must describe Achieving the Bottom Line as a Motivational Speaker, Counselor, or Teacher would, using only "we" and caring, thoughtful approaches, making good eye contact throughout, and "checking in" with the other person throughout to make sure the person is following and understands.

- They must describe Building a Great Plan as an Artist or Entrepreneur would, using only visual terminology and metaphors, starting with the end of the plan and working backward, sketching out on paper as they are talking. If possible, use props or anything available to make the description "come alive."

- They must describe Developing Rapport and Friendship as a CFO or Engineer would, using precise business terminology, technical and quantitative or financial lingo only. Demonstrate that they have done their homework and share their analysis. Be efficient and direct in the process and take out any unnecessary chit chat or emotion.

- They must describe How to Be Creative and Spontaneous as a Quality Control Manager or Drill Sergeant would, in a formal numbered sequence of steps, in clear finished sentences, with very clear directions at each step and no pauses, options, or variance. Do not digress. Minimize any hand gestures and maintain a consistent tone throughout. Make sure to be well organized and very thorough.

3. After 1 minute of preparation, ask the first person to begin explaining his or her task to his or her partner using the stated guidelines. After 2 minutes, call time and have the other member of the pair describe the task he or she has chosen using the stated guidelines.

4. Show slide 3 and explain that this exercise used opposing styles of the Whole Brain Model to show why it is important to let others choose how to do their work in Enable Others to Act. The selected topic (often closer to the individual's preference) was in one style and the guidelines were in an opposing style. State that A (blue) and B (green) are more left-brained styles; C (red) and D (yellow) are more right-brained styles.

5. After much laughter, bring their attention back to the large group.

6. Use slide 4 to ask the following debriefing questions:
   - How did it feel to be told HOW to do the assigned task?
   - How effective were you? Would you have been more effective if you could have done it *in your own way*?
   - How does this relate to your approach to the Enable Others to Act practice?
   - What can you learn and how will you change as a result of this exercise?

Ann Herrmann-Nehdi is CEO of Herrmann International, a global
learning and development company and publisher of the Herrmann
Brain Dominance Instrument (HBDI). Ann has led the company's
applied research on thinking and the brain, using the company's Whole
Brain® Thinking model and database of over one million assessments
to help organizations *get better results through better thinking* and
do more with less. Author of dozens of articles and chapters, Ann is
currently working on a book to be released in 2010.

Ann Herrmann-Nehdi
Herrmann International
794 Buffalo Creek Road
Lake Lure, NC, 28746
　Phone: (828) 625-9153
　Email: ann@hbdi.com
　Website: www.hbdi.com; www.HerrmannInternational.com

SLIDE 1: ENABLING WITH STYLE: STEP 1

Enabling with Style: Step 1

In pairs, each person selects ONE of the four phrases below **that you prefer to use to explain to your partner how you would approach this task.** You may select only one phrase and each partner **must select a different phrase.**

1. **Achieving the Bottom Line**
2. **Building a Great Plan**
3. **Developing Rapport and Friendship**
4. **How to Be Creative and Spontaneous**

SLIDE 2: ENABLING WITH STYLE: STEP 2

Enabling with Style: Step 2

> You are required to use the following guidelines to create your description <u>that will last for 2 minutes; you must keep talking for the full 2 minutes.</u> You have 1 minute to prepare. Decide who is going first and who is going second. If you selected:

Developing Rapport and Friendship:

Describe this as a CFO or engineer would, <u>using precise business terminology, technical and quantitative or financial lingo only.</u> Demonstrate that you have done your homework and share your analysis. Be efficient and direct in the process and avoid any unnecessary "chit chat" or emotion.

How to Be Creative and Spontaneous:

Describe this as a quality control manager or drill sergeant would, <u>in a formal numbered sequence of steps, in complete sentences, with very clear directions at each step, and no pauses, options or variance.</u> Do not digress. Minimize any hand gestures and maintain a consistent tone throughout. Make sure you are well organized and very thorough.

Building a Great Plan :

Describe this as an artist or entrepreneur would, using only visual terminology and metaphors, <u>starting with the end of the plan and working backward</u>, sketching out on paper as you are talking. If possible, use props or anything available to make your description "come alive."

Achieving the Bottom Line:

Describe this as a motivational speaker or teacher would, using only "we" and caring, thoughtful approaches, making good eye contact throughout and <u>"checking in" with the other person as you progress</u>, to make sure he or she is following and understands.

SLIDE 3: ENABLING WITH STYLE: STRETCHING YOUR STYLE BY USING OPPOSING QUADRANTS OF THE WHOLE BRAIN MODEL

Enabling with Style: Stretching *Your Style* by Using Opposing Quadrants of the Whole Brain® Model

A Quadrant Style (Blue) Describe this as a CFO or engineer would, <u>using precise business terminology, technical and quantitative or financial lingo only.</u> Demonstrate that you have done your homework and share your analysis. Be efficient and direct in the process and avoid any unnecessary "chit-chat" or emotion.	***D Quadrant Style (Yellow)*** Describe this as an artist or entrepreneur would, using only visual terminology and metaphors, <u>starting with the end of the plan and working backward</u>, sketching out on paper as you are talking. If possible, use props or anything available to make your description "come alive."
Describe this as a quality control manager or drill sergeant would, <u>in a formal, numbered sequence of steps, in complete sentences, with very clear directions at each step and no pauses, options or variance</u>. Do not digress. Minimize any hand gestures and maintain a consistent tone throughout. Make sure you are well organized and very thorough. ***B Quadrant Style (Green)***	Describe this as a motivational speaker or teacher would, using only "we" and caring, thoughtful approaches, making good eye contact throughout and <u>"checking in" with the other person as you progress</u>, to make sure he or she is following and understands. ***C Quadrant Style (Red)***

SLIDE 4: ENABLING WITH STYLE: OUR PREFERENCES IMPACT HOW WE APPROACH A TASK

Enabling with Style: Our Preferences Impact How We Approach a Task

1. How did it feel to be told HOW to do the assigned task?

2. How effective were you? Would you have been more effective if you could have done it *in your own way*?

3. How does this relate to your approach to the Enable Others to Act practice?

4. What did you learn and how will you change because you did this exercise?

CURRENCY EXCHANGE

Submitted by Cindy Huggett

Objective

- To visibly demonstrate the benefits of fostering collaboration.

Audience

Works with any size audience. Two volunteers are needed for the demonstration.

Time Required

25 minutes.

Materials and Equipment

- Two pieces of currency (such as two dollar bills or two quarters).
- One index card per participant.
- One writing utensil per participant.

Area Setup

No special setup is needed.

Process

1. Casually ask participants, "Who has a dollar bill?" Substitute local currency (euro, yen, or other currency) as needed. For added flair, search through your own wallet as if you're looking for change, so that participants don't immediately realize this is a learning activity.

2. Select two participants who answer "yes," and invite them to the front of the room. Ask them to bring their dollar bills with them.

3. In view of all participants, ask the volunteers to exchange dollar bills. (Participant A gives his or her dollar bill to Participant B. Participant B gives his or her dollar bill to Participant A.)

4. Narrate the action by saying that the participants have just exchanged dollar bills.

5. Ask the group the following questions:
   • Is either participant richer now that they've exchanged bills? (Anticipated response, no, they each started with one dollar and ended with one dollar.)
   • What if these dollar bills represented *ideas*? Participant A had an idea, Participant B had an idea, and they exchanged them. Now would either participant be richer?
   • How are they each richer? (Anticipated responses, they each started with one idea, now they have their original idea plus another idea for a total of two ideas, therefore they are both richer than they were before the exchange.)
   • What does this tell us about sharing ideas? (Anticipated responses, sharing ideas is a good thing because it makes us richer.)

6. Thank the volunteers and ask them to return to their seats.

7. Distribute one index card to each participant. Ask participants to write down one idea they have to improve their workplace.

8. Ask all participants to stand, holding their index cards.

9. Have each participant exchange index cards with someone else in the room and discuss the ideas on the cards. (Person A gives an index card to Person B. Person B gives an index card to Person A.

Each keeps the other person's index card.) Allow no more than 2 minutes for the discussion.

10. Have participants exchange index cards again with different people in the room and explain the ideas. (Person A gives an index card to Person C. Person C gives an index card to Person A. Each keeps the other person's index card.)

11. Repeat Steps 9 and 10 for several rounds until all participants have exchanged cards with several others in the room.
    - Keep this activity moving at a brisk pace. If the audience is small (fewer than twelve), stop the exchange after just a few rounds.
    - By the time you have finished this step, participants should have seen and exchanged many different index card ideas.
    - Depending on the size of the room and number of participants, you may choose to keep participants standing for the debriefing discussion. Otherwise, ask participants to return to their seats at this time.

12. Ask the following questions:
    - How many ideas did you start with? (Anticipated response, one.)
    - How many ideas did you encounter during this activity? (Anticipated response, many.)
    - What insights did you gain during this activity? (Anticipated responses, there were some good ideas generated, I think we should do several of the ideas, I learned new ideas, and This was helpful/useful.)
    - What are the benefits of fostering collaboration when we Enable Others to Act? (Anticipated responses, we consider multiple perspectives, we have more than one idea to work with, and we benefit from collaborating.)

Variations

- If you chose a topic relevant to the participants and there is time and energy around processing the ideas generated, have participants get into small groups to discuss the feasibility of these new ideas, with the goal of creating post-class action plans.
- If only one person in the audience has a dollar bill, the facilitator can act as the second volunteer to exchange bills.
- If no one in the audience has dollar bills, the facilitator can ask for two volunteers and provide each one with a dollar bill to exchange.
- Other currency amounts can be substituted for the dollar bill.
- In Step 7, choose a topic relevant to the participants. For example, if a business problem has previously been discussed, ask participants to write down an idea for solving that specific problem.

Cindy Huggett is a Certified Professional in Learning and Performance (CPLP) with over sixteen years' experience in organization development, performance management, leadership, program design, classroom facilitation, and adult learning. She's passionate about leadership, learning, and training trainers. In addition to her consulting practice, Cindy is a training performance consultant for AchieveGlobal. She's also the 2009–2010 chairperson of ASTD's National Advisors to Chapters and serves on the national ASTD board of directors.

Cindy Huggett, CPLP
128 Benedict Lane
Raleigh NC 27614
   Phone: (919) 349-4589
   Email: chuggett@gmail.com
   Website: www.atrainerslife.com

TEAM COMPETENCY DEVELOPMENT PLAN

Submitted by Edith Katz

Objective

• To obtain feedback on developing team competencies.

Audience

Group of ten participants or fewer; you can also use this activity in smaller breakout groups.

Time Required

45 to 60 minutes.

Materials and Equipment

One Team Competency Development Plan template for each participant.

Area Setup

Depending on the size of the room, a U-shape or small table groups.

Pre-Work

Before the session, ask participants to write plans to develop their team competencies over the next six months. Their plans should have goals, action steps, and timelines. Have participants bring enough copies of their plans for every person in the group. A template is included with this activity.

Process

1. Begin by stating that a critical part of Enable Others to Act is to ensure that others have the skills and knowledge required to

act. Strengthening others by developing their competencies is an important leadership commitment. Continue by saying that collaboration is also an important aspect of Enable Others to Act and that this activity will give everyone an opportunity to collaborate.

2. Have each person share their Team Competency Development Plans with the other participants. Open the floor for comments, suggestions, and questions.

3. Summarize by asking participants:
   - What changes will you make in your plans based on suggestions from others?
   - What was the most valuable learning for you today?
   - How many ideas are you leaving with?

Edith Katz is the manager of employee development at Brooks Health System, where she facilitates an eleven-part Leadership Challenge series. The series includes a lab session the week after each practice has been introduced. In the lab session, each participant presents his or her application assignment to the class and a discussion is opened to provide feedback, ideas, and suggestions. This *active learning* component helps each participant to apply the knowledge to his or her real-life work challenges and allows participants to learn from others as well.

Edith Katz
Company Brooks Health System
3901 University Boulevard South, Suite 103
Jacksonville, FL 32216
   Phone: (904) 858-7334
   Email: edith.katz@brookshealth.org

TEAM COMPETENCY DEVELOPMENT PLAN

Skill or Knowledge	Action Steps	Timeline

CAREER CONVERSATIONS: CUES FOR DEVELOPING OTHERS

Submitted by Beverly Kaye

Objectives

- To help leaders understand the importance of career coaching in their organization.
- To engage leaders in conversations with their direct reports that lead to realistic lists of career actions and questions.

Audience

Any size, ideally between twenty and twenty-five participants.

Time Required

Approximately 60 minutes (more time can be allowed if participants are engaged in the conversations and brainstorming discussions).

Materials and Equipment

- One copy of the Career Conversations Coaching Skills handout for each participant.
- One copy of the Career Conversations Cues—Taking Action handout for each participant.
- Flip chart or PowerPoint slide with the 1 to 5 scale noted in the process.

Area Setup

Any arrangement will do; however, clusters of four to six participants are preferred for maximizing conversations.

Facilitator Note

People are the most important asset of today's organizations. Given the fierce competition for qualified talent, organizations must be able to offer a rewarding future. At the same time, individuals must prepare themselves to meet the challenges of new strategic directions in the workplace. Managers as career coaches play a critical role in this process by finding the common ground between the career aspirations of the individual and the organization's goals. The following exercise can stimulate conversations and actions for leaders to begin creating a development culture.

Process

1. Provide the Career Conversations Coaching Skills handout to participants.

2. Ask each participant to read the content and the questions at the end of each paragraph and rate how effective leaders are at these activities using the following scale. Specify whether participants should be rating a leaders at the department, business unit, or organization level. Show this scale on a flip chart or PowerPoint slide.

3. When everyone has finished, review each of the five questions, allowing participants time to share their answers and their ratings. Ask the following questions:
   • Why is coaching for development an essential aspect of being a good leader?

- What prevents managers and leaders from having coaching conversations with employees?
- How can barriers be removed? How can coaching conversations be encouraged?

4. Distribute the Career Conversation Cues—Taking Action handout and remind participants of the five coaching skills associated with the questions they answered.

5. Divide the group into two teams. Have one group create a list of realistic actions leaders could take to start creating a development culture. Have the other group generate questions that leaders could ask in conversations with their employees to be more effective in their coaching area.

6. Have groups share their ideas with each other. Ask participants:
   - Which questions resonate with you?
   - Which actions are you likely to try?

7. Ask each leader to commit to one coaching action for the next thirty days. You may wish to schedule a follow-up session to discuss successes and challenges.

Beverly Kaye, Ph.D., is an internationally recognized authority on career issues and on retention and engagement in the workplace. As founder and CEO of Career Systems International, and a best-selling author on workplace performance, Beverly has worked with a host of organizations to establish cutting-edge, award-winning talent development solutions. With the fourth edition of *Love 'Em or Lose 'Em: Getting Good People to Stay* (Berrett-Koehler, 2008), a best-seller she co-authored, she once again proved to be a pioneer in addressing one of the most pressing workplace problems of the 21st century: retaining and engaging employees. In her follow-up companion best-seller, *Love It, Don't Leave It: 26 Ways to Get What You Want at Work* (Berrett-Koehler, 2003), she and her co-author show employees how they can find greater satisfaction in their current work lives.

Beverly Kaye, Ph.D.
Career Systems International
3545 Alana Drive
Sherman Oaks, CA 91403
  Phone: (818) 995-6454
  Email: Beverly.kaye@careersystemsintl.com
  Website: www.careersystemsintl.com

CAREER CONVERSATIONS COACHING SKILLS

There are many ways and opportunities for leaders to help people develop their careers. These actions can be divided into five basic skill areas, each of which is summarized below. Each area describes behaviors and conversations managers can use at different stages of the career development process. Rate your leaders on each of the five skills and place a score from 1 (not very effective) to 5 (very effective) in each box.

LISTEN: Effective listening requires that you go beyond the words and try to understand what really matters to your people. The aspect of listening in career conversations means being effective in inquiring or asking good questions. Leaders who listen create opportunities for people to discuss their career concerns and clarify what is most important to them. It is not critical that you have all the answers. It is most important that you truly understand your team.

> *How well do our leaders talk to their direct reports to understand their individual talents, career desires, and capabilities?* _____

LEVEL: Your direct reports need to know how you see them. Leaders who are honest provide candid feedback regarding performance. However, they help people see beyond performance to how substance, style, and reputation collectively influence career options and career choices. Leveling means not being afraid to tell the truth, whether positive feedback or about developmental needs.

> *How well do our leaders provide honest viewpoints regarding their employees' image, professional style, performance, and potential?* _____

356

LOOK AHEAD: What's happening in your department, the organization, your business unit, the industry, this country, or the world at large that can impact the decisions your people make today about their careers? Leaders who look ahead help people spot and understand emerging trends and new developments that affect their career prospects. They relate the strategic business initiatives to the competencies required for the future.

How well do our leaders communicate information about the trends (economic, political, demographic) affecting our organization? _____

LEVERAGE: Leaders can become involved and help people create a set of simultaneous options for movement and/or development. People expand their thinking when they identify multiple options. That way, if one path becomes blocked, they have other ways to continue to grow and identify realistic career goals from a variety of potentially desirable options.

How well do our leaders help employees identify multiple goals (current and future) that are realistic? _____

LINK: This involves matching the needs of the individual to specific resources in the organization. Leaders can arrange useful contacts with people in other areas of the industry, organization, or profession. Leaders serve as advocates on behalf of those seeking information or opportunities and speak to their reputation and worth. They link people with the resources they need to implement career management plans.

How well do our leaders discuss with employees how to continue to take action on their careers and development plans? _____

357

CAREER CONVERSATIONS CUES—TAKING ACTION

"Effective leaders give team members the self-confidence to act and to take charge of their responsibilities rather than merely perform assigned tasks. In short, leaders create leaders!"

Coaching Skill	Questions	Actions
Listen		
Level		
Look Ahead		
Leverage		
Link		

DOUBLE OVERLAPPING STRATEGIC CROSS

Submitted by Sharon Landes

Objectives

- To observe one's own leadership behavior and the behavior of the team in an unscripted situation.
- To determine which personal leadership behaviors facilitate successful task accomplishment and which get in the way.
- To practice enabling others while overcoming communication barriers.

Audience

Twenty to twenty-four participants, divided into four teams, each with the same number of people.

Time Required

50 to 60 minutes, including debriefing.

Materials and Equipment

- Masking tape or painters tape to lay out the grid.
- One copy of Instructions for Field Locations for each participant (excluding Executive Team Members).
- One copy of Instructions for Headquarters: Teams A and B for the Executive Team members from Teams A and B.
- One copy of Instructions for Headquarters: Teams C and D for the Executive Team members from Teams C and D.

Area Setup

See preparation notes. You'll need a large enough space for the four teams to stand in the grid and a separate room/space for the leaders' headquarters. Leaders and teams should not be able to see each others' areas.

Facilitator Note

This is a variation on Strategic Cross/Traffic Jam that allows for more leadership and team dynamics to surface than in the standard version.

Preparation

Set up the Strategic Cross grid. You may want to do this in a separate room, or in some way keep the group from being able to see the grid before you're ready to begin the activity. Use brightly colored surveyor's tape to lay out the grid, which creates excitement. Alternatively, you can use masking tape or have participants stand on sheets of paper.

Lay out the Strategic Cross by creating two segments that overlap in the shape of a + and share the same open center space. (Not counting the open center space, the number of squares required for each of the two segments of the + is one half the number of people in the group, minus two, with half of those squares on either side of the open center space. You don't need an even number of people. If you have an odd number, you'll have an extra square on one side of the open center square.) In the example, there are twenty people in the group—sixteen in the field and four (one from each team) on the Executive Team. Thus, to figure out the number of squares, you take the group size (twenty), divide by half (ten), subtract two (eight), and then put half that number on either side of the center square, so four squares are on either side, as shown in the sample grid.

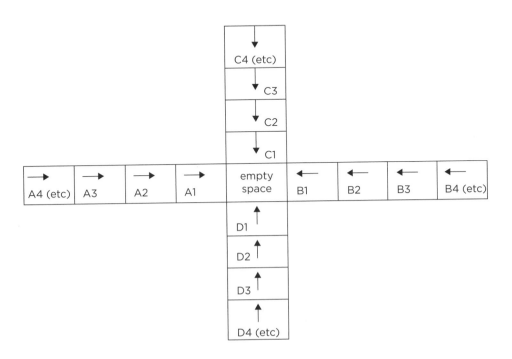

Process

1. Divide the group into four sub-teams, A through D.

2. Ask each sub-team to nominate one person to be on the Executive Team and have the Executive Team move to the side.

3. Describe the task in very broad terms, creating a scenario that makes sense to the participants with whom you are working. You may choose to add complexity by blindfolding a few people at random on each of the sub-teams (blindfolds will need to stay on throughout the activity).

4. Leave the Executive Team where they are and bring the rest of the group to where the grid is laid out.

5. Arrange the sub-teams on the grid, facing each other. Distribute the Instructions for Field Locations only and let them know that the "clock is starting and you'll have 30 minutes." Do not answer any questions.

6. Go back to the Executive Team and distribute both Instructions for Headquarters sheets to the appropriate Executive Team Members and let them know that the "clock has already started and all the information you need is on your instruction sheets." Do not answer any questions.

7. Travel back and forth between the Executive Team and the Field as the exercise progresses to observe their process. Intervene only if the group seems ready to blow off the rules; do so in a way that will be in sync with the context you've created. (Although you should give them a chance to self-monitor before you step in.)

8. As time is running out, you can offer some extra time, up to 10 minutes, but leave that up to a consensus of the group. (Their decision can be an interesting element to debriefing.)

9. Debrief using these questions:
   - What happened during the exercise?
   - What communication barriers occurred?
   - How is this activity related to Enable Others to Act?
   - What leadership practices did you note?
   - What leadership behaviors facilitated task completion?
   - What natural behavioral tendencies surfaced for you? Were these helpful? Why or why not?
   - What would you change if you could do this activity again?
   - How can you transfer what you learned to your work situation?

Variation

- The activity can be used to highlight all of the Five Practices, as a post-LPI experience to focus the work for the remainder of the workshop, or at any point that you want to give participants a chance to observe their own behavior.

Insider's Note

A single strategic cross is completed by starting with A1 moving in one direction to the empty space followed by B1 moving two spaces in the other direction. A1 moves up one space, allowing B2 to move from the other direction, and so on. Then begin to move in descending order once people start arriving at their final positions.

There are issues galore that will come up—communication, support, cooperation versus competition, ethics, shared vision, the best role/function for executives to take on, creativity and initiative, who gets heard and why, the interplay between leadership and followership, speaking up, checking out, and others. ENJOY!

Sharon Landes has been working with individuals and organizations in the United States and abroad to help them clarify their core principles and beliefs, develop their leadership skills, work effectively in teams, and advance their communication and relationship-building skills for over twenty-four years. She is adept at establishing open and safe environments, eliciting candid disclosure from group members, and guiding a flexible process for learning and discovery. She brings to bear both her consulting experience across a wide range of clients and industries and her experience as a leader and manger inside organizations.

Sharon served as a visiting member of the faculty and lecturer in leadership communication at the Haas Graduate School of Business, University of California, Berkeley. Sharon is a TLC Master Facilitator, working directly with clients and in training other facilitators. She delivered her first TLCW in 1990.

Sharon Landes
20 Mosswood Road
Berkeley, CA 94704
    Phone: (510) 548-6945
    Email: shlandes@comcast.net

STRATEGIC REALIGNMENT INSTRUCTIONS FOR HEADQUARTERS: TEAMS A AND B

The Goal: The task is complete when all team members in the field locations complete the objective of moving from their initial positions to their final positions.

Constraints:

- Only one representative from the Executive Team may serve as a liaison with each field team at any given time.
- All but the liaison must remain in the HQ designated area.
- This paper may not leave the HQ designated area.
- The time limit for the task is 30 minutes.

Initial Positions

>>>	>>>	>>>	>>>	empty	<<<	<<<	<<<	<<<
A4 (etc)	A3	A2	A1	space	B1	B2	B3	B4 (etc)

>>> and <<< denote facing direction

FINAL POSITIONS:

<<<	<<<	<<<	<<<	empty	>>>	>>>	>>>	>>>
B1	B2	B3	B4 (etc)	space	A4 (etc)	A3	A2	A1

<<< and >>> denote facing direction

STRATEGIC REALIGNMENT INSTRUCTIONS FOR HEADQUARTERS: TEAMS C AND D

The Goal: The task is complete when all team members in the field locations complete the objective of moving from their initial positions to their final positions.

Constraints:

- Only one representative from the Executive Team may serve as a liaison with each field team at any given time.
- All but the liaison must remain in the HQ designated area.
- This paper my not leave the HQ designated area.
- The time limit for the task is 30 minutes.

Initial Positions

INITIAL POSITIONS:

>>> C4 (etc)	>>> C3	>>> C2	>>> C1	empty space	<<< D1	<<< D2	<<< D3	<<< D4 (etc)

>>> and <<< denote facing direction

FINAL POSITIONS:

<<< D1	<<< D2	<<< D3	<<< D4 (etc)	empty space	>>> C4 (etc)	>>> C3	>>> C2	>>> C1

<<< and >>> denote facing direction

STRATEGIC REALIGNMENT INSTRUCTIONS FOR FIELD LOCATIONS

You are a sub-team located in a Field Location, and will be so for the next 30 minutes.

You might take time to discuss how you want to work together. You must follow the guidelines below.

1. There are only two legal ways to move.
   - You may move into an empty space directly in front of you.
   - You may move around one person if that person is facing you and there is an empty space directly behind that person.

2. No one may turn around or move backward.

3. If the team reaches an impasse, you must start over from the beginning.

4. Only one person may move at a time.

5. Only one person may occupy a square at a time.

WHAT MAKES YOU TRUST SOMEONE?

Submitted by Sherri Dosher

Objectives

- To discuss the importance of trust in effective leadership.
- To discuss the impact of trust on relationships and results in the workplace.
- To identify behaviors that promote trust and relate to Commitment 7.

Audience

Any number who are currently supervisors/managers or a group of aspiring leaders.

Time Required

20 to 30 minutes, depending on time allowed for discussion.

Materials and Equipment

- Flip chart with markers.
- One Trust Worksheet for each participant.
- Pens or pencils.
- Paper for participants.

Area Setup

Participants seated in small groups at tables.

Process

1. Hand out copies of the Trust Worksheet. Have each participant think of two people in leadership positions (now or in the past), one he or she trusts and one he or she does not trust.

2. Have participants complete their worksheets individually. Under the positive column, tell participants to list the traits or behaviors that lead them to trust that person. Under the negative column, they should list the traits or behaviors that prevent them from trusting that person. On the effects row, ask them to list the impact of the person's behavior on them, their work, or the results. Allow about 5 minutes.

3. Once individual worksheets are complete, have participants discuss their results with others at their tables, identifying common themes. Allow about 10 minutes.

4. Have participants record common themes to share with large group. Ask each group to share their themes with the large group. Record these themes on the flip chart.

5. Ask participants how these themes relate to Commitment 7: foster collaboration, building trust and facilitating relationships. *Note:* If the group is large, over thirty, discussion can take place at tables and then be shared with the larger group.

6. Summarize with these questions:
    *   How important is trust in a leader?
    *   What is the impact of a lack of trust in the workplace?
    *   What is the impact of solid trust in the workplace?
    *   What behaviors will you polish to promote trust when you return to the workplace?

Sherri Dosher coordinates instructional design and delivery of curriculum, design, and maintenance of the university website and coordination of the online learning program and multi-media authoring initiatives. Sherri is an adjunct instructor for John Tyler

Community College in connection with Chesterfield's School of Quality and Continuous Improvement. Sherri holds a B.S. degree in education from the University of North Alabama and is currently pursuing a master's degree in instructional technology from Virginia Tech.

Sherri Dosher
Chesterfield County, Chesterfield University
9901 Lori Road, Room 303
Chesterfield, VA 23832
Phone: (804) 717-6614
Email: Doshers@chesterfield.gov
Website: www.chesterfield.gov

TRUST WORKSHEET

	Trusted and Positive+	**Did Not Trust Negative-**
Traits		
Effects		

The Leadership Challenge Activities Book
Copyright © 2010 by James M. Kouzes and Barry Z. Posner.
Reproduced by permission of Pfeiffer, an Imprint of Wiley. www.pfeiffer.com.

TRUST-BUILDING DISCUSSION

Submitted by Doug Leigh

Objectives

- To differentiate trust, distrust, and trustworthiness.
- To describe three rules of trust building.
- To explain how to generate worthy trust within leadership.

Audience

Any size audience can be supported, so long as small discussion groups of three to four participants can be formed.

Time Required

1 hour. This time can be increased to permit greater elaboration and discussion, but should not be adjusted downward.

Materials and Equipment

- Participants should have read *The Leadership Challenge*, and refresh their memory of Chapter 9 (Foster Collaboration) within Practice 4 (Enable Others to Act).
- A whiteboard or three flip charts set up near the facilitator.
- Dry Erase marker (for whiteboard) or markers (for flip chart).

Area Setup

Nothing special.

Process

1. Begin by saying, "Within Jim Kouzes and Barry Posner's *The Leadership Challenge*, the practice of enabling others to act

depends on fostering collaboration. This begins with creating a climate of trust. Authentic leaders demonstrate integrity, character, and honesty and, in doing so, enhance their reputation for trustworthiness. Conversely, those who do not or cannot disclose and live by a clear set of values, ethics, and standards tend to be viewed with suspicion. Trust in one's leader, Jim and Barry argue, both increases risk taking and reinvigorates organizational momentum."

2. Create three columns on a whiteboard (or use three different flip charts) with "trust" at the top of one, "distrust" on another, and "trustworthiness" on the third. Ask participants how they define trust, distrust, and trustworthiness. Capture their comments.

3. Ask participants how they differentiate trust and distrust from trustworthiness. Allow discussion.

4. Explain that Russell Hardin of New York University is one of the preeminent thinkers and researchers on the topic of trust. In his 2004 book, *Trust and Trustworthiness*, he offers that trust is a rational choice that we make about others' dependability to do what they say they will (or will not) do. From this perspective, demonstrating this dependability both encourages and rewards trusting. Trustworthiness begets trust. A leader's trustworthiness encourages followers to develop trust in the leader and serves as a motivation for cooperation. Trustworthy leaders, then, "pull" trust from their followers.

5. Explain that participants will explore the three truths about trust offered by Hardin and discuss their implications to leadership.

6. In groups of three or four, ask participants to develop a list of "anyone they trust with everything and in every way." After

373

5 minutes, ask groups to report back and list these on the whiteboard (or flip chart). Do not anticipate large numbers of people to be identified.

7. Explain that—with the exception of the supernatural and perhaps the most intimate of relationships—we do not trust or distrust others universally. On top of this, the question of whether we or our followers "trust most people most of the time" seems to indicate little more than whether we or they are willing to take small risks with those we do not yet know well. Rarely if ever do we trust without question, limitation, or qualification—and when we do, more than likely it's faith or hope at play, not trust. In reality, we tend to trust certain people only with certain things, or under certain circumstances. Trust typically operates such that "Person A trusts Person B to do (or not do) X." Thus, Person A might trust Person B with X, but not trust him or her with Y or Z. Explain that this is the first of the three truths about trust: that it exists as a "three-part relationship" in which "A trusts B to do (or not do) X."

8. Ask participants what benefits, if any, might exist for Person A as well as Person B in not trusting "anyone with everything." Anticipate that the conversation will address issues of avoiding over-commitment, over-reliance, and under-delivery.

9. In the same small groups, have participants imagine that they are in a situation in which they are certain that they trust or distrust someone else. Reiterate that trust is distinct from faith or hope, then ask the participants to list what it is like to experience trusting or distrusting another person. Emphasize that this is not a question of how one knows whether or not

374

someone is trustworthy, but rather about the ways in which they know that they are experiencing trust or distrust. After 5 minutes, lead discussion based on comments from the groups.

10. Explain that trust is a cognitive act, but not one that we can choose or un-choose. Henry Ford is said to have proffered that "no matter whether you think you can or can't, you're right." In the same vein, while we may know or believe that something is true or false, we do not choose for that thing to be true to us; it simply *is*. While love may be blind, trust is not. Trust and distrust are assessments we make about others. While we may either be unsure or convinced, our belief is never arrived at by voluntary decision making; rather we discover or are somehow convinced that we trust or distrust another. The corollary of this is that if someone distrusts you, there's no convincing the person not to do so. Instead, the person must feel that he or she has enough reason to believe that the risk of trusting you is worth the potential reward for doing so. Explain that this is the second of the three truths about trust: that even though it relies on evidence, trust is something that is subjectively understood, rather than something that is decided upon.

11. Ask participants what the saying "fool me once, shame on you; fool me twice, shame on me" means in this light. Follow up by asking participants how they know that *they themselves* are or are not seen as trustworthy.

12. Ask participants to return to their small groups to list situations in which they cooperate with those either whose trustworthiness is *uncertain* or whose untrustworthiness *is certain*. After 5

minutes, ask groups to report back and track these discussions on the whiteboard (or flip chart).

13. Explain that trust operates as an "encapsulated interest": I'll scratch your back if I believe that you feel it advantageous to scratch mine. We trust others, in part, because we believe they have an interest in fulfilling our trust. In other words, people trust one another only so long as it's apparent that it's mutually beneficial to do so. We expect those we trust to act in accordance with the belief that they too see a benefit in being concerned with our interests. Explain that this is the last of the three truths about trust: whether we trust "Person B" to do or to not do X, we do so because we believe that that Person B feels it is in his or her best interest to attend to *our* interests.

14. Ask participants why people cooperate with those they don't trust. Anticipate that the conversation will surface issues of power, obligation, and benefit of the doubt.

15. Sum up by recapping the three truths of trust and their implications.
    - First, trust exists as a "three-part relationship" in which "A trusts B to do (or not do) X." The implication of this is that leaders should not seek to demonstrate their trustworthiness to all people in all ways. Rather, leaders should clarify and communicate the types of things for which they wish to be known as someone to be counted on. Leaders should consistently, reliably, and publicly demonstrate their dependability for specifically stated behaviors.
    - Second, even though it relies on evidence, trust is something that is subjectively understood, rather than something we

decide. The implication of this is that since leaders cannot control their followers' assessments of them, leaders should generate evidence that they are trustworthy through regular interactions with others. It is impossible to compel another to trust you. Further, trust is not open-ended. If you fail to follow through on those matters for which you wish to be known as someone to be counted on, expect to lose your followers' trust. Since a mountain of evidence can be overturned by a single fact, regaining lost trust is more difficult than establishing it in the first place.

- Third, whether we trust "Person B" to do or to not do X, we do so because we believe that the person feels it is in his or her best interest to attend to *our* interests. The implication of this is that others are wary of trusting us if they can't see why it's beneficial for us to both have and to reciprocate their trust. Without this encapsulated interest, followers are liable to disengage because of the sense that their trust is neither important nor necessary to the leader's plans.

16. Ask participants what they will do to generate trustworthiness as leaders.

Doug Leigh, Ph.D., is an associate professor with Pepperdine University's Graduate School of Education and Psychology. His research, publication, and consulting interests concern cause analysis, organizational trust, leadership visions, and alternative dispute resolution. Doug has co-authored several books and scores of articles on these are related topics. He has served as chair of the American Evaluation Association's needs assessment topic interest group and as editor-in-chief for the International Society for Performance Improvement's (ISPI) journal, *Performance Improvement*. A lifetime member of ISPI, Doug has most recently served as chair of its research committee.

Doug Leigh, Ph.D.
Pepperdine University
Graduate School of Education and Psychology
6100 Center Drive
Los Angeles, CA 90045
   Phone: (310) 568-2389
   Email: doug@dougleigh.com
   Website: www.dougleigh.com

HUMAN TRUST KNOT

Submitted by Jan Miller and Denise Knight

Objectives

- To build trust within the group.
- Explore trust as it relates to Enable Others to Act.

Audience

Fifteen to twenty participants.

Time Required

15 to 30 minutes.

Materials and Equipment

- None required.

Area Setup

Large enough area for the group members to stand in a circle.

Process

1. Have participants stand in a circle shoulder to shoulder.
2. Have each participant reach across and grab two different participants' hands.
3. After every participant is holding hands with two different people, the group will detangle the "human knot" without releasing hands.
4. It can be untangled, but it will take time, effort, and trust!

5. Have participants return to their seats. Ask these follow-up questions:
   - What is trust?
   - How does a leader build trust?
   - How certain were you that the human knot could be untangled?
   - How is the knot activity like the real world?
   - What is critical about leadership and trust?
   - Why does Enable Others to Act require trust?
   - How does this activity help you better understand your own needs for trust?

Jan Miller, Ed.D., currently serves as an assistant professor at the University of West Alabama in the College of Education–Instructional Leadership Department. She has twenty-two years of public school experience in the state of Mississippi. During those years, Jan has taught numerous grade levels, served as a lead teacher, and supervised two schools as principal. She earned a B.S. degree in elementary education from Livingston University, an M.Ed. in elementary education from Livingston University, an Ed.S. in elementary education from Mississippi State University, and an Ed.D. in educational leadership from NOVA Southeastern University.

Denise Knight, Ed.D., currently serves as an assistant professor at the University of West Alabama in the College of Education. She has twenty-three years of public school experience in the state of Mississippi. Denise has taught numerous grade levels, taught talented and gifted, served as a district-wide director of federal programs and elementary curriculum, and served as an elementary principal. She earned a B.S. degree in elementary education from Mississippi State University, an M.Ed. in elementary education from Livingston University, an M.Ed. in school administration from the University of West Alabama, an Ed.S. in curriculum and instruction from Mississippi State University, and an Ed.D. in educational leadership from NOVA Southeastern University.

Jan Miller, Ed.D.
University of West Alabama
Station #34
Livingston, AL 35470
    Phone: (205) 652-3445
    Email: jmiller@uwa.edu

Denise Knight, Ed.D.
University of West Alabama
Station #34
Livingston, AL 35470
    Phone: (205) 652-3801
    Email: dknight@uwa.edu

TRUST AND COMMUNICATION

Submitted by Jan Miller and Denise Knight

Objective

- To build trust and facilitate relationships.

Audience

Any size.

Time Required

20 minutes.

Materials and Equipment

- Paper.
- Markers.

Area Setup

Tables and chairs so that participants can work with partners.

Process

1. Ask each participant to use the paper and markers to illustrate his or her version of trust.

2. Have participants pair up with other participants. Tell them they should not share their pictures of trust.

3. Have partners sit with their backs against each other.

4. Have each partner describe his or her view of trust to the other partner (not the picture itself). The listening partner creates the image based on the participant's verbal description only.

5. Repeat the cycle with the other person's version of trust.

6. Allow the partners to face each other and compare the original pictures of trust with what the partners heard each other say.

7. Wrap up with these questions:
   - How similar were the drawings?
   - Why do you suspect there were differences?
   - How does communication affect trust?
   - How does trust affect communication?
   - How will you as a leader depend on trust to Enable Others to Act?

Jan Miller, Ed.D., currently serves as an assistant professor at the University of West Alabama in the College of Education–Instructional Leadership Department. She has twenty-two years of public school experience in the state of Mississippi. During those years, Jan has taught numerous grade levels, served as a lead teacher, and supervised two schools as principal. She earned a B.S. degree in elementary education from Livingston University, an M.Ed. in elementary education from Livingston University, an Ed.S. in elementary education from Mississippi State University, and an Ed.D. in educational leadership from NOVA Southeastern University.

Denise Knight, Ed.D., currently serves as an assistant professor at the University of West Alabama in the College of Education. She has twenty-three years of public school experience in the state of Mississippi. Denise has taught numerous grade levels, taught talented and gifted, served as a district-wide director of federal programs and elementary curriculum, and served as an elementary principal. She earned a B.S. degree in elementary education from Mississippi State University, an M.Ed. in elementary education from Livingston University, an M.Ed. in school administration from the University of West Alabama, an Ed.S. in curriculum and instruction from Mississippi State University, and an Ed.D. in educational leadership from NOVA Southeastern University.

Jan Miller, Ed.D.
University of West Alabama
Station #34
Livingston, AL 35470
  Phone: (205) 652-3445
  Email: jmiller@uwa.edu

Denise Knight, Ed.D.
University of West Alabama
Station #34
Livingston, AL 35470
  Phone: (205) 652-3801
  Email: dknight@uwa.edu

SHARE FAIR

Submitted by Marilyn Myers

Objectives

- To foster collaboration to improve performance.
- To develop competence and confidence in individual employees and the team.

Audience

Ten to one hundred participants, plus four to six presenters.

Time Required

1 to 2 hours.

Materials and Equipment

Whatever each presenter needs to present.

Area Setup

Breakout rooms or areas. If separate rooms are not possible, then break the room into sections where small groups can have designated spaces. Each presenter should have a table so groups can rotate to them.

Process

1. Identify internal employees who are performing above level in some part of their jobs. Ask them to prepare 15-minute demonstrations or presentations.

2. Invite the rest of the organization to the Share Fair. Have participants gather around each presenter in somewhat equal-sized small groups.

3. Every 15 minutes, have the participants switch to a different presentation until they have visited all of the learning opportunities.

4. End each presentation with a heartfelt round of applause.

5. Bring everyone together at the end and use questions like these to wrap up:
   • What unique things did you learn?
   • How might you be able to implement some of these ideas in your area?

Variations

• For a schoolhouse meeting, every month I identify a different group of teachers to present their great work that reinforces the wide variety of skills. Each "Share Fair" has a different group of presenters to ensure that a variety of employees are being recognized for their hard work and given the ability to lead their teams to a higher level of success.

• This activity could also be used to build capacity in the Encourage the Heart practice.

Marilyn Myers, Ph.D., currently serves in the capacity of instructional leader at Florida Virtual School (FLVS). Her leadership mirrors the FLVS culture of student centeredness, teamwork, positive relationships, innovation, and growth. Marilyn received her Ph.D. in educational leadership from Capella University. Reflecting her desire for creating positive change, her doctoral dissertation research examined the business processes that define, promote, and reinforce a vision of excellence and service in urban educational leadership. She recently was honored for her work with "At Promise" Students as the 2009 Best Practices Administrator of the Year Award by the Reaching at Promise Students Association.

Marilyn Myers, Ph.D.
Florida Virtual School
2145 Metro Center Boulevard, Suite 200
Orlando, FL 32835
   Phone: (904) 233-3572
   Email: mmyers@flvs.net
   Website: www.flvs.net

NO EASY WAY OUT

Submitted by Mona Lee Pearl

Objectives

- To demonstrate teamwork in making difficult decisions.
- To demonstrate healthy debate in slaying "sacred cows."
- To demonstrate thought processes that occur at all levels of the organization.
- To demonstrate the importance of open communication in making and announcing decisions.

Audience

Works for any size group of four people or more. Groups larger than eight will operate in teams of four to eight.

Time Required

From 1 to 2 hours, depending on time available and the desired depth of discussion and debate.

Materials and Equipment

- Flip-chart pads on easels with markers.
- Mini flip-chart pads with markers.
- A small group, especially an intact team, could benefit from use of a "magic wall" and 5-inch by 8-inch note cards with markers or large Post-its and a clear wall.
- One Scenario handout for each participant.
- A card with a role written on it for each member of the team: board member, executive, manager, or staff.

- For the facilitator's reference only, a handout recapping Kouzes and Posner's Five Practices of Leadership (taken from *The Leadership Challenge* website)

Area Setup

Groups should work in the round. If there are multiple groups in one room, allow space for work areas for each small group.

Process

1. If there are more than eight people in the group, divide the larger group into teams of four to eight people and assign roles:
   - The four roles are board member(s), executive(s), mid-level manager(s), and staff. Provide each team with an evenly distributed number of role cards, ensuring that each team has at least person in each role.
   - For simplicity and equity, have team members draw cards with roles written on them.

2. Assign work space to each team and have each team select a leader.

3. List the five Kouzes and Posner leadership practices and remind the group they are doing the exercise to strengthen their skills in leadership in general and leading through change in particular. Tell them that it is also critical for them to think about involvement and how to Enable Others to Act in this situation. *Note:* Add further explanation if you believe participants need a refresher on the practice.

4. Describe the scenario, then give a copy of it to each team member. After each member has read the scenario, ask whether

participants have questions. They have the flexibility to let the process unfold as they wish, so answers to questions are not prescribed in this description. Make sure that ambiguity about the assignment is eliminated to the greatest extent possible. Some members of the group will notice that there is hardly any detail that would be helpful to creating a solution. When that happens, tell the teams to begin the exercise by making a list of the information they will need and the assumptions they will make to reach the optimal decision.

5. Remind the team(s) that they must choose a spokesperson—a board member, executive, manager, or staff member—who will deliver the news to the entire group in the room as though the group represents the stakeholders of Hillydale Hospital.

6. With the dilemma clear and a leader for each team appointed, remind the participants that they are to act and think in the roles they have been assigned. Give the group 30 to 45 minutes (or longer, if time is available and helpful) to craft a solution to the dilemma. Leave time for each team to "deliver the message."

7. Remind the team(s) to get started by listing the data they will need before crafting possible solutions. (Each team can make up the data they believe they need in order to reach a conclusion.) While the teams work, observe the way the process unfolds and any specific interactions that will make good discussion.

8. Be available and engage where necessary to keep the process moving forward. Answer questions, make observations, suggest breaks—whatever will help the group stay on task. Advise the group at the halfway point and when there are 15 and 5 minutes remaining. At the 10-minute mark, make sure the teams are

working on their presentations of the chosen solution. Watch for and be ready to comment later on:

- Role ambiguity as participants attempt to think differently from their daily roles
- Frustration or even anger
- Collaboration and building trust
- Inclusion
- Disengagement
- Great ideas that are outside the standard way of thinking about change
- Other elements specific to the situation and goals of the group being facilitated

9. At the end of the time allotted, have each team spokesperson deliver his or her team's solution to the rest of the group as though they are the stakeholders involved. If there is only one team, you can role play the stakeholders. It is important to the exercise for the spokesperson to be required to "deliver the news" and to answer questions from the stakeholders.

10. Debriefing questions should include:
- How did you decide on your solution?
- How important was it for the group leader to demonstrate inclusiveness so that all members of the group felt welcome to participate?
- What insight did you gain about how people at other levels in the organization think about dilemmas?
- How effective is your organization at:
  - Using insight from all levels of the organization?
  - Getting information about change to all levels of the organization as quickly as feasible and advisable?

- What problems might be caused by not sharing enough information early enough?
- What problems might be caused by sharing too much information too soon?
- In deciding how to deliver the news, by what means or words did your team decide to inspire the vision for the change among all stakeholders (staff, community, clients, etc.)?
- What methods would you employ to Enable Others to Act, that is, to carry out the decision while retaining autonomy and authority in implementing the change?

Mona Lee Pearl teaches seminars and works with employee groups, boards of directors, and community nonprofit organizations in setting goals and creating programs. As a facilitator and trainer, her seminars include gender communication, decision making, change management, and leadership. She holds a certificate in organization development from Linkage™ Inc. and an ASTD certificate in facilitating organizational change. Her bachelor's degree is from the University of Missouri at Kansas City and her master's degree is from Lesley University.

Mona Lee Pearl
Align® Organizational Development and Training,
a division of Western States Learning Corporation
1401 Airport Parkway, Suite 300
Cheyenne, WY 82001
Phone: (307) 772-9001; 800-999-6541, ext 9001
Email: pearl@wslc.com
Website: www.alignwslc.com

SCENARIO

Due to the building of a new hospital in a metropolitan area sixty miles away, demand for all services at the Hillydale Memorial Hospital has dwindled and cannot be renewed in the near future. The one-hundred-bed hospital must cut its operating budget, which means either closing one of three clinics, with a loss of four positions, or eliminating some services.

The clinics, which charge for their services, require appointments, and are open weekdays, are located in:

- Redtown—employing one physician, two registered nurses, and one support person.
- Bluesville—employing one physician, one nurse practitioner (a registered nurse trained in primary health care; a nurse practitioner can diagnose and treat minor illnesses), one registered nurse, and one support person.
- Greenburg—employing one physician, one registered nurse, one licensed practical nurse, and one support person.

The services that could be eliminated are:

- Home health care—in-home care provided by registered nurses and certified nursing assistants.
- Community wellness programs—annual health fair, flu shot clinics, and wellness education.
- Weekend walk-in clinic in Hillydale—a clinic open only on weekends for people with non-emergency care needs; there is a charge for these services.

The board will choose an option for reducing operating costs and management will relay the information to staff.

THE FIVE PRACTICES OF EXEMPLARY LEADERSHIP® SUMMARY

The Five Practices of Exemplary Leadership® resulted from an intensive research project to determine the leadership competencies that are essential to getting extraordinary things done in organizations. To conduct the research, Jim Kouzes and Barry Posner collected thousands of "Personal Best" stories—the experiences people recalled when asked to think of a peak leadership experience.

Despite differences in people's individual stories, their Personal-Best Leadership Experiences revealed similar patterns of behavior. The study found that, when leaders are at their personal best, they:

Model the Way

Leaders establish principles concerning the way people (constituents, peers, colleagues, and customers alike) should be treated and the way goals should be pursued. They create standards of excellence and then set an example for others to follow. Because the prospect of complex change can overwhelm people and stifle action, they set interim goals so that people can achieve small wins as they work toward larger objectives. They unravel bureaucracy when it impedes action; they put up signposts when people are unsure of where to go or how to get there; and they create opportunities for victory.

Inspire a Shared Vision

Leaders passionately believe that they can make a difference. They envision the future, creating an ideal and unique image of what the organization can become. Through their magnetism and quiet persuasion, leaders enlist others in their dreams. They breathe life into their visions and get people to see exciting possibilities for the future.

Challenge the Process

Leaders search for opportunities to change the status quo. They look for innovative ways to improve the organization. In doing so, they experiment and take risks. And because leaders know that risk taking involves mistakes and failures, they accept the inevitable disappointments as learning opportunities.

Enable Others to Act

Leaders foster collaboration and build spirited teams. They actively involve others. Leaders understand that mutual respect is what sustains extraordinary efforts; they strive to create an atmosphere of trust and human dignity. They strengthen others, making each person feel capable and powerful.

Encourage the Heart

Accomplishing extraordinary things in organizations is hard work. To keep hope and determination alive, leaders recognize contributions that individuals make. In every winning team, the members need to share in the rewards of their efforts, so leaders celebrate accomplishments. They make people feel like heroes.

COACHING VERSUS TELLING

Submitted by Lou Russell

Objectives

- To choose questions for the best way to coach each unique individual.
- To redefine leadership as *growing the strong and capable* versus *telling the weak what to do.*

Audience

Ten to one hundred participants, divided into teams of three or four members each.

Time Required

30 minutes.

Materials and Equipment

- Chunks puzzle handout—one per team of three or four.
- One Hint sheet for each coach—one per team.
- One Solution sheet for each coach—one per team.

Area Setup

This works best with round tables for each three-or-four-person team. It is also easily done by turning chairs together or using different corners of a square table.

Process

1. Place participants into groups of three or four. Ask for the following volunteers: one Coach, one Coachee, and one or two observers for each team.

2. Ask the coaches to meet you in the front of the room or in the hall—someplace the others can't hear. Explain that the coach will help the coachee solve the three puzzles. Each "chunk" contains three characters (between the brackets). The chunks must be rearranged to create a meaningful statement. Show them how the punctuation (for example, the period indicates the end of a sentence) can give clues. Make sure they can explain the puzzle to their coachees.

3. Quickly give each coach a sheet of hints and then a sheet of answers. Avoid answering any questions about their use (I usually say something like "you decide" if I'm pushed) and instruct them to return to their coachee quickly, as they will only have 5 minutes to solve as many puzzles as possible.

4. Instruct the observers to only observe—they cannot help solve the puzzle in any way.

5. Amplify the pressure by announcing the time every minute (example, "4 minutes left!").

6. Debrief by attempting to get the group to notice that, most of the time, the coach decides, with no input from anyone, how much help to give the coachee, and as pressure mounts, spends more time TELLING and less time ASKING. Very few people start with "I have the hints, and I have the answers. How much help would you like me to give you?" as a leader. It is better to get someone in the group to observe this, so:

- Ask the observers to share the things they saw that showed great coaching.
- Ask the observers to share the things they saw that could have been improved in terms of coaching.
- Ask the coachees the same questions.
- Ask the coaches the same questions.

If no one comes to the conclusion that no coaching was taking place, ask the coachees to raise their hands if any of the coaches told them they had hints and answers. Then continue to discuss the different situations and level of help required. For example, if there is a fire, it's not a good time to ask people if they'd like help learning how to escape.

Lou Russell is a CEO, consultant, speaker, and author whose passion is to create growth in companies by guiding the growth of their people. She is committed to inspiring improvement in three sides of the optimization triangle: leadership, project management, and individual learning. Lou is the author of six popular and practical books: *IT Leadership Alchemy* (Prentice Hall, 2002); *The Accelerated Learning Fieldbook* (Pfeiffer, 1999); *Training Triage* (ASTD Press, 2005), *Leadership Training* (Pergamon, 2006); *Project Management for Trainers* (ASTD Press, 2000); and *10 Steps for Successful Project Management* (ASTD Press, 2007).

Lou Russell
Russell Martin & Associates
6326 Rucker Road, Suite E
Indianapolis, IN 46220
  Phone: (317) 475 - 9311
  Email: lou@russellmartin.com
  Website www.russellmartin.com or www.lourussell.com

CHUNKS[1]

Each of the items below is a sentence cut into three-character chunks (including the spaces and punctuation marks). The chunks are arranged in alphabetical order. The coachee has 5 minutes to solve these three puzzles with the coach's help.

Chunks 1

[DO] [FL] [JU] [DON] [EE,] [FIG] [FLO] [HT,] [N'T] [ST] ['T]
[W!]

Chunks 2

[EV] [WI] [WI] [A C] [ERY] [ESS] [IN] [LIC] [NO] [NS] [NS!]
[ONE] [ONE] [ONF] [T,] [UNL]

Chunks 3

[AR] [EA] [PR] [TH] [. Y] [CAN] [CON] [CT] [CTS] [E L] [EDI]
[EM.] [ENT] [FLI] [IKE] [KES] [M O] [NOT] [OU] [QUA] [R P]
[REV] [RTH] [THE]

[1]"Chunking" was created by Thiagi. www.thiagi.com

HINTS

Chunks 1

The first word is "Don't."

Chunks 2

One of the words is "unless."

Chunks 3

The last word is "them."

SOLUTIONS

Chunks 1

Don't fight, don't flee, just flow!

Chunks 2

In a conflict, no one wins unless everyone wins!

Chunks 3

Conflicts are like earthquakes. You cannot predict them or prevent them.

EMPOWERMENT FORCE FIELD ANALYSIS

Submitted by Cindy Taylor

Objectives

- To discuss the dynamics of empowerment.
- To plan strategies for obstacles to empowerment.

Audience

Works best with those who are currently supervisors/managers, although the activity can also be used with a group of aspiring leaders. Can be done with large or small groups.

Time Required

20 to 30 minutes, depending on length of discussion.

Materials and Equipment

- Whiteboard or flip chart with appropriate markers.
- Sharpies® for participants.
- Pads of 5 by 3 self-sticking notes (ten sheets per participant).

Area Setup

Participants seated in small groups.

Process

1. Discuss a definition of empowerment. Ask for and give some of your own examples of empowerment.
2. Have participants brainstorm three things that are good about empowered employees (driving forces) and three things that are

negative about empowerment (restraining forces). Have them record one idea per sticky note. As they are recording these, have participants designate a "+" for positive items and a "−" for negative items on each sticky note.

3. Draw a large T grid on the whiteboard or flip-chart pad with one side for positive (+) driving forces and one for negative (−) restraining forces. Have participants place each of their sticky notes on the appropriate positive or negative side.

4. have the participants continue to generate what's positive or negative about empowered employees. Have them post the ideas on the appropriate side of the grid. State that they have created a Force Field Analysis grid.

5. Discuss what appears on each side. Some questions to consider:
   - Are some items appearing as both driving and restraining forces? Why is that?
   - What can you do to overcome any obstacles to empowerment?
   - What can you do to reinforce the positive aspects?

6. Tie discussion points to Commitment 8:
   - Strengthen people by giving power away.
   - Provide choice
   - Develop competence
   - Assign critical tasks
   - Offer visible support

7. Summarize by asking participants what they will do with what they have learned when they return to the job. Note their ideas on the flip chart. Have them develop action plans if desired.

Cindy Taylor has twenty-five years of human resource management experience in the federal and local government, with a focus on employee relations and organization development and training. She is certified in conducting the Myers-Briggs Type Indicator, an International Public Management Association for Human Resources (IPMA-HR) Certified Professional, and a trained mediator. She is a contributing author in the recently published *Leadership Secrets of Local Human Resource Officials*, a cooperative effort between ORACLE and IPMA-HR.

Cindy Taylor
Chesterfield County, Chesterfield University
9901 Lori Road, Room 303
Chesterfield, VA 23832
   Phone: (804) 748-1552
   Email: taylorc@chesterfield.gov
   Website: www.chesterfield.gov

INFLATED ACTIONS

Submitted by Lorraine Ukens

Objectives

- To analyze team behaviors and actions under competitive conditions.
- To explore how planning and leadership affect overall team results.

Audience

Twelve to eighteen participants.

Time Required

30 to 45 minutes.

Materials and Equipment

- One large cardboard box (large enough to hold all balloons).
- Three medium cardboard boxes.
- Eighteen to twenty-four assorted size (5 inches to 9 inches) balloons, inflated.
- Timer.

Area Setup

A large open-space area, with the biggest box situated in the center and the three medium boxes equidistant from the center box and each other. Place all the inflated balloons into the large box.

Process

1. Divide the group into three teams of four to six persons each and direct each team to stand by one of the medium boxes. Randomly assign one person in each team to act as leader.

2. Read the following directions to the group: "The balloons in the center large box represent clients/sales/products [select as appropriate], and each team is one unit within an organization. The goal is for each team to get the most balloons into its own box within a set 2-minute time limit. At any point, you also may take balloons from another team's box. However, you are not allowed to touch another participant and you may not run. Your team will have 1 minute to discuss your planned approach before the contest begins."

3. Allow 1 minute for the planning stage, and then announce the start of the contest. Time the action for 2 minutes while observing how the participants interact within their own teams and with members of the other teams. Make special note of behaviors involving competition and leadership.

4. At the end of the 2-minute period, call time and ask each team to return to its box. Count the number of balloons in each box and announce the "winner."

5. Direct a discussion of the activity using the following questions:
   • How did you as individuals feel throughout the course of the activity? Why was that?
   • What happened during the team's planning process? What role did the leader take?
   • What behaviors and actions occurred during the actual contest? How did these affect the end results?

- How well did the initial planning process support your team's actions during the contest? What factors influenced the resulting behaviors?
- How effective was the assigned team leader? Why was he or she effective or not effective? Did any informal leaders emerge?
- What were some of the constraints encountered during the contest (for example, distance between boxes, boxes too small to hold balloons, different sized balloons, balloons floating away)? Did your team take any creative approaches to overcoming these conditions (for example, move boxes, deflate balloons, combine all boxes)?
- How successful was your team in meeting its goals? What factors made the biggest impact on the results?
- What could your team have done differently to be more effective? Were you able to learn anything by observing other teams? If so, what?
- What might have happened if the teams had fostered collaboration?
- What learning points can you take with you as a result of this activity?

6. Conclude the session by pointing out that, although teams may be divided within an organization, they still represent one large entity that is trying to meet its goals. Teams can use competition to strive to do their personal best, but they also need to cooperate with other teams to reach organizational goals. Coordination, planning, and support for teamwork come from exemplary leaders. They foster collaboration and build trust among peers, managers, customers and clients, suppliers, citizens—all those who have a stake in the vision.

Lorraine Ukens is a performance improvement consultant who specializes in team building and experiential learning. She has written several activity books, consensus simulations, and a training game. She was the editor of *What Smart Trainers Know* (Pfeiffer, 2001) and wrote a chapter on team training. Her B.S. in psychology and M.S. in human resource development are from Towson University in Maryland. She was an adjunct faculty member in the graduate division at Towson for eight years, until her move to Florida.

Lorraine Ukens
Team-ing With Success
25252 Quail Croft Place
Leesburg, FL 34748
   Phone: (352) 365-0378
   Email: Ukens@team-ing.com
   Website: www.team-ing.com

ACTIVATE TO MOTIVATE

Submitted by Devora Zack

Objectives

- To brainstorm creative, low-cost ways to motivate others.
- To energize a group through collaboration.
- To encourage participants to connect motivation and having fun to the effort to Enable Others to Act.

Audience

This activity is successful with groups from six to two hundred. Six is the minimum because this activity requires at least three teams with at least two people each. Larger groups can be divided into up to fifteen teams. It is not necessary that groups be equal size. This activity works for a diverse range of audiences.

Time Required

Depending on group size (larger groups require slightly more time), the activity requires approximately 30 minutes.

Materials and Equipment

- Paper and a writing utensil for each team.
- A team prize, such as a bag of chocolates.

Area Setup

Teams need to be seated in discrete groups. This can be achieved by separate tables or simply pushing chairs together. This activity can be adapted as an outside event.

Process

1. Divide participants into teams using any method. Tell them they have 10 minutes to brainstorm as many ideas as possible on how to motivate others at work. Ideas should be low to no cost. Depending on the circumstance, the facilitator or group can define "low cost." Explain that the winning team will have the most, and most creative, ideas. Say that you will explain how this will be determined following the brainstorming. This activity can be preceded by a discussion of brainstorming techniques and guidelines if desired.

2. Tell groups to select recorders to write all ideas on a piece of paper (not on a large easel pad). This person should be able to write quickly and legibly.

3. While the teams are brainstorming, go around the room encouraging them to continue thinking of new ideas when teams seem to slow down. Keep track of time, providing 5- and 2-minute reminders.

4. When brainstorming time is over, invite one team representative per team to come to the front of the room with the list and pen or pencil, standing all team reps in a row facing the rest of the group. For example, if there are six groups of seven participants each, you will have six people at the front of the room. Tell them the representatives will take turns, from left to right, each sharing one idea from the group. Representatives should speak loudly and clearly. For large rooms, a hand-held microphone can be passed down the line. The rules are as follows:
    *   Representatives may not repeat any idea that has already been shared. Often ideas are very similar so the part of the group

seated, collectively, must determine whether an idea is a repeat (such as "free movie pass" verses "cinema gift certificate"). They are allowed to cross items off their lists as others are speaking to avoid repeating ideas.

- Representatives may not alter ideas that are written or add new ideas that occur to them as they stand in front of the group (if someone says "mentor low performers" and the idea is on another participant's list, that participant can't change the same idea to "give plenty of positive reinforcement").
- Long delays between ideas shared as representatives go down the line are not allowed. Give them a maximum of 5 minutes.
- If a team representative has no more ideas left on his or her list (that haven't already been shared), he or she sits down.
- The winning representative is the last one standing and brings his or her group the team prize.

5. Debrief the activity, including a selection of these points: many motivators are not high cost, brainstorming without boundaries allows many ideas to be solicited, stretching beyond typical solutions enhances our brains' elasticity (the ability to think creatively), and working together is an efficient, energizing way to move into action.

6. Summarize by asking, "How do motivation, collaboration, and having fun affect a leader's ability to Enable Others to Act?"

Devora Zack, president of Only Connect Consulting (OOC), provides leadership development, coaching, team training, and assessments to more than seventy-five clients, including Deloitte, America Online, the U.S. Patent & Trademark Office, OPM, Enterprise, and the U.S. Treasury. Devora has been faculty for Cornell's leadership program for thirteen years. Devora holds an M.B.A. from Cornell University and a B.A. from the University of Pennsylvania. Her certifications include MBTI and Neuro-Linguistic Programming. She is a member of Phi Beta Kappa, Mensa, and ASTD. Her designs are featured in five publications. OCC is the recipient of USDA's Woman-Owned Business of the Year.

Devora Zack
Only Connect Consulting, Inc.
7806 Ivymount Terrace
Potomac, MD 20854
  Phone: (301) 765-6262
  Email: dzack@onlyconnectconsulting.com
  Website: www.onlyconnectconsulting.com

CHAPTER SEVEN: ENCOURAGE THE HEART

In This Chapter

- Overview Encourage the Heart.
- Discuss the corresponding Commitments of Leadership.
- Consider the importance of this practice.
- Introduce the activities for this practice.
- Present the activities for this practice.

The Leadership Challenge recognizes the importance of rewarding and recognizing individuals and celebrating in the spirit of community. Recognition for a job well done is a crucial motivator for employee performance. Many leaders immediately translate this to forms of recognition that increase employees' paychecks—raises and promotions. Yet employees are more often motivated by personal, thoughtful recognition that shows true appreciation for a job well done—unique recognition "over and above" the norm of the workplace.

HOW DOES A LEADER ENCOURAGE THE HEART?

How do leaders achieve this very important practice? First, they expect the best from everyone, because individuals tend to act consistently with others' expectations of them. This means that high expectations will lead to equally high performance.

413

Cash awards have the advantages of being easy to administer, understood by all, and desirable. The drawbacks of cash awards are that there is no lasting value (that is, no "trophy effect"), they are not exotic, they lack creativity and personalization, cannot be enhanced, and they tend to become an "expected" award.

Consider the related Commitments of Leadership:

- Recognize contributions by showing appreciation for individual excellence.
- Celebrate the values and victories by creating a spirit of community.

Recognize Contributions

Before a leader recognizes contributions, conditions must be established that create an environment in which people can earn the recognition. Included in these behaviors are things a leader can do: expect the best, set clear expectations and goals, provide feedback, and create conditions for success.

The most powerful motivators for people are personalized, instant recognition from leaders, including such things as:

- Personal congratulations.
- Personal notes about good performance.
- Promotions based on performance.
- Public recognition for good performance.
- Gatherings to celebrate successes.

What can a leader do to recognize employees in creative, personalized ways? How can a leader thank others for contributions and going the extra mile? There are literally thousands of things that can be done for recognizing employees and team leaders as well as colleagues. Don't forget, the best thing is to just say, "thank you."

Celebrate the Values and Victories

Leaders who create a spirit of community to celebrate successes enhance productivity, psychological well-being, and even the physical health of their employees. Having fun together is healthy.

It isn't all about fun and laughter. The exemplary leader becomes personally involved and displays honest caring for employees. He or she reinforces a sense of not being alone but part of a team that cares both about others and about accomplishing the goal. Celebrations are an opportunity to reinforce core values.

WHY IS ENCOURAGE THE HEART IMPORTANT?

Everyone wants to feel that he or she is a part of the team and that his or her contributions are valuable. Feeling a part of the team improves communication, decreases misunderstandings, and increases productivity. In addition, Encourage the Heart has been proven to be healthy for employees—both physically and mentally.

ACTIVITY INTRODUCTION

The fewest number of activities were submitted for this practice. That does not make it less important than the others, but is another reminder that too often both leaders and trainers run out of time for this leadership practice or, worse yet, take it for granted. In fact, we could probably make a case for making this practice the most important.

The activities in this section are some of the most fun—as they should be to Encourage the Heart. Here are a couple titles: Hip-Hip-Hooray! You're Making Me Blush! and Refreshing Frescos. Doesn't that make you want to turn to the next pages to read more about them? Participants will foster an atmosphere of inclusion, show appreciation for fellow participants, encourage others, break down barriers and build intimacy, and achieve a positive mood.

Several of the activities in this section are excellent closing activities for your training session. However, don't forget to expand them out and use them outside the learning setting.

Activity List

- Accelerating Change-Readiness by Herb Cohen and Bruce Fern
- Thank You Card by Ricky Foo
- Complimentary Closer by Michael Gerlach
- Positive Bombing by Jonas Hansson
- Conundra by Brian Jackson
- Writing and Receiving Class Affirmations by Edith Katz
- A Rewarding Activity by Lorraine Kohart
- You're Making Me Blush! by Jan Miller and Denise Knight
- Hip-Hip-Hooray by Jan Miller and Denise Knight
- Creating Your Team's Celebratory Crest by Anne Reilly and Homer Johnson
- Gifts by Kris Taylor
- Refreshing Frescos by Devora Zack

ACCELERATING CHANGE-READINESS

Submitted by Herb Cohen and Bruce Fern

Objectives

- To help leaders motivate employees and stimulate change-readiness, a prerequisite to large enterprise-wide strategy shifts.
- To explore options for recognition and support that are available to use with employees.
- To understand the change-readiness levels that encourage and reinforce individuals.

Audience

Any size group divided into smaller groups of five people. Levels and situations might include:

- Executives who need to help the division operate differently for more effective strategy adoption and execution.
- Middle managers who need to earn the commitment and motivation to a specific company change initiative, strategy shift, or new way of doing business.
- First-line supervisors who need to help employees change their behavior in order to adopt new roles and tasks.

Time Required

60 to 90 minutes.

Materials and Equipment

- One copy of Handout 1: Assessing Change-Readiness for each participant.

- One copy of Handout 2: Accelerating Change-Readiness for each participant.
- Paper and pencils/pens for each participant.

Area Setup

Tables with room for approximately five people per table.

Facilitator Note

The fourth practice is Enable Others to Act. The fact is that change-readiness is a prerequisite to empowerment. Feeling empowered, capable, and powerful all require unique ways of thinking and acting. For people who already live their lives this way, no change is required. However, for people who do not approach their business challenges from a position of empowerment, significant changes in thinking and behavior are required.

The fifth practice is Encourage the Heart. This requires a certain degree of trust and openness between leaders and the people they work with. The Change-Ready Model (discussed in Handout 1) creates a dialogue platform in which honest discussions can take place about the employee's conceptual and emotional reactions to change.

Process

1. Welcome leaders. Explain that the objective of this leadership activity is to help them increase their employees' readiness to change and to reinforce their support. Refer to the objectives in the activity description.

2. Ask and discuss why people have a hard time changing. You may wish to post the responses on a flip chart.

3. Ask about and discuss the specific changes the leaders would like their people to make to better support the direction they would like to take their businesses.

4. Ask participants to list, on their own sheets of paper, the initials of three people who work for them and an example of a behavior for each that reflects a change that each leader desires. (Use initials rather than names to protect employees' privacy.)

5. Explain that the primary determinant of whether these people will make the changes required of them is *not* whether they are motivated to change but rather whether they are *ready* to change. Further explain that people progress through *five levels of readiness* when considering a change.

6. Provide Handout 1 to each participant. Review the handout by using some of your own examples. Ask for and answer questions. Ask leaders to think of each person and the designated behavior they listed and to assess each person's level of readiness for that behavior.

7. Have participants discuss their answers at their tables and provide evidence for their ratings. (Again, emphasize that participants should refer to employees by initials only; don't use actual names.) Allow about 15 minutes, depending on the group size.

8. Ask for a few examples from the entire group. Explain that once one knows a person's level of readiness, one can better determine the strategies to use to encourage that person and accelerate his or her readiness to change.

9. Hand out and overview Handout 2. Ask for and answer questions. Have leaders return to their lists of three people and, for each, identify a strategy to increase that person's readiness based

on the information in the handout. Have them discuss their answers at their tables and provide rationales for their strategy suggestions.

10. Bring the large group together. Respond to any questions.

11. Summarize with these questions:
    - What is significant about this model and how you reward or do not reward employees today?
    - What is the most valuable nugget of information that you gained? Why is it of value to you?
    - In what situations will you use what you have learned?

Variations

Either handout may be used as a stand-alone activity or resource. Applications might include these situations:

- Getting the workforce aligned with the company's strategic priorities and critical business goals.
- Helping employees change their behavior to better fulfill the company's brand promise and service imperative.
- Providing appropriate behavioral support for an employee's growth and development.

Herb Cohen, chairman of Performance Connections, is responsible for executive consulting, business development, distributor management and specializes in working with retail clients. Prior to working in the performance improvement industry, Herb was president of Miles Shoes, a senior executive at Melville Corp/CVS, VP at Meldisco, and VP of Stores at CVS. He was one of the original principals of MOHR Development, CEO of MOHR Learning Systems, and Provant

Group President. Herb is a past president of ISA and is on the faculty at NYU and the Ritz Carlton Leadership Institute.

Bruce Fern is the president and founder of Performance Connections International, which specializes in customer and employee engagement and retention. Prior to this, Bruce was an executive with Blessing White/MOHR, Citibank, and MHT/Chase Bank. Bruce is considered an engagement and retention opinion leader, having consulted on engagement and retention internationally. He is in the top fifty honorees in HR Workplace Who's Who list, in Strathmore's Who's Who, and is an assistant professor at NYU. At Performance Connections, Bruce is responsible for executive consulting, solution development, and managing domestic/international consultants.

Herb Cohen
Chairman, Performance Connections International, Inc.
39 Brook Farm Road
Bedford, NY 10506
    Phone: (914) 244-0400
    Email: herb.choen@performanceconnections.com
    Website: www.performanceconnections.com

Bruce Fern
President, Performance Connections International, Inc.
39 Brook Farm Road
Bedford, NY 10506
    Phone: (914) 244-0400
    Email: bruce.fern@performanceconnections.com
    Website: www.performanceconnections.com

HANDOUT 1
ASSESSING CHANGE-READINESS

The Change-Ready™ Model, developed by Performance Connections International, Inc., is based on Prochaska and DiClemente's Transtheoretical Model of Change (1983), applied to personal medical health management (smoking, medication compliance, etc.) The research has been adapted for business, resulting in the user-friendly Change-Ready™ Model.

This powerful model reveals the secrets behind why some employees seem to embrace change and others resist it. Classic thinking on behavior change presumed that an employee's willingness to change was most correlated with his or her motivation to change. This is only partly true. An employee's ability to change is, in fact, most correlated with the person's readiness to change. Readiness and motivation are not the same.

Your ability to grow your business is dependent on your ability to identify each employee's level of readiness to embrace strategic behavior change and then accelerate that readiness.

Traditional change-management approaches fall short of managing behavior change effectively because they espouse a one-size-fits-all approach to behavior change. The Change-Ready™ Model helps us realize that behavior change is personal and must be tailored to each employee who is short of the behavior being a habit.

The Performance Connections model defines the five levels of readiness to change a specific behavior.

1. **Zero Intent**—At this level, the employee, team, or entire organization has no intention of changing behavior. There is absolutely no commitment to change.

   Example: A software development team manager has been told about a new "agile" software development process called Scrum that takes him out of a leadership role and puts him in more of a mentor role. He has absolutely no intention of transitioning his team to this process because of his concerns about his role change.

2. **Contemplating Change**—At this level, the person in question considers changing his or her behavior, but has not yet decided to do so. He or she is less resistant than at the zero intent level, but there is still no commitment to changing.

   Example: A financial sales professional is told she needs to begin discussing insurance needs with her clients. She is not comfortable with the idea but realizes its potential value both to her and her clients, so she is thinking about it.

3. **Planning and Preparation**—At this level, the person in question has decided that it probably makes sense to change and he or she is thinking through *how* he or she might make the change.

   Example: A call center manager has been told he needs to monitor the calls his reps make and then sit down and coach them using the recorded calls as a coaching tool. In the past, he claimed he was too busy to take the time to do this. He now realizes that coaching his people goes to the core of his job and that he must make time for this. He begins to go through his calendar to determine when he would coach, for how long, with which employees, and on what topics.

The Leadership Challenge Activities Book
Copyright © 2010 by James M. Kouzes and Barry Z. Posner.
Reproduced by permission of Pfeiffer, an Imprint of Wiley. www.pfeiffer.com.

4. **Visible Action**—At this level, the employee has made the behavior change. The evidence is that you can observe, document, and record the behavior. Most people might be tricked into thinking that the goal has been achieved. One of the most revealing aspects of the research on behavior change tells us that there is a significant risk that the employee will "bungee back" into old behavior patterns.

    Example: A healthcare manager has been asking her nurses to put more energy into collaborating more effectively with each other. They do a great job of taking care of their own patients but have historically not supported each other very well. During the first part of the month, she sees them demonstrating effective levels of mutual support. In the latter part of the month, the patient load increases significantly, everyone becomes stressed, and collaboration falls apart.

5. **Habit**—At this level, the behavior is now second-nature. The person in question consistently performs the behavior and has settled into new behavior patterns that reflect the targeted behavior.

    Example: A retail store manager has been trying to conduct brief "Daily Line-Up" meetings to celebrate service success from the previous day and discuss service goals for today. In the past, she conducted these meetings inconsistently. Currently, she has them every day without fail.

Reference

Prochaska, J.O., & DiClemente, C.C. (1983). Stages and processes of self-change of smoking: Toward an integrative model of change. *Journal of Consulting and Clinical Psychology, 51*, 390–395.

HANDOUT 2
ACCELERATING CHANGE-READINESS

Once a leader understands the change-readiness level of a person, team, or entire division of an organization, he or she can apply certain strategies to accelerate that readiness. Below is a description of some of the Do's and Don'ts for each level of readiness.

Level of Readiness	General Strategy	
Zero Intent	**Do**	**Don't**
	These people need *information and options* in order to get them unstuck from their current resistant positions. *Data, facts, and benchmarking information* can help them take their heads out of the sand by realizing that the requested change has meaningful benefits attached to it. If we give them several different *alternatives* concerning *how* they might implement the change, it can help them at least consider the change seriously. A sense of control increases flexibility.	Don't mandate change at this level of readiness. People at this level are likely to find excuses for not doing the behavior or simply hide from your scrutiny. Forcing change will lead to resentment and, even if you get the desired behavior change, it will disappear when you stop looking.

(Continued)

Level of Readiness	General Strategy	
Contemplating Change	**Do**	**Don't**
	Ask the person to consider the pros and cons of making the change. Conduct an objective analysis with the person to shed light on hidden benefits of changing and less obvious disadvantages of staying the same. Ask the person to consider his or her image in this analysis and what public statements he or she is making by changing or not changing. Also have the person consider the consequences of not changing and its affect on him or her personally.	Don't ask for an action plan on how the person will make the change just yet. He or she is still considering the change and "pushing" too fast can lead to "pushback."
Planning and Preparation	**Do**	**Don't**
	It is at this point of readiness that individuals are most responsive to a request for commitment. They are on the cusp and asking for commitment can propel them into the next level of readiness. Note that the research indicates that if you ask for commitment to change at levels earlier than this, it is likely to fall on deaf ears.	Don't assume that a well-thought-out plan will lead to guaranteed action. The person is trying to build change momentum but doesn't have it yet. Be sure to help the person follow through on plans to change.

Level of Readiness	General Strategy	
Visible Action	**Do**	**Don't**
	Focus on making it easier for them to turn this new behavior into a habit. Reward and reinforce the behavior change and positive results that come from it. Remove environmental impediments to performing the behavior on a regular basis, and set up support groups that encourage the employee to "keep it up."	Don't assume that when you see the behavior once it is now a habit. It takes a significant amount of energy to develop new habits, and you must support the employee to develop new routines and set new patterns in place. Don't move on to other pressing priorities and forget about this. See this through to the Habit level of readiness.

In summary, this powerful model will help any leader accelerate change-readiness, increase organizational agility, and manage change organically and, in fact, much more rapidly than mandated change, which often takes months if not years to take hold.

THANK YOU CARD

Submitted by Ricky Foo

Objectives

- To demonstrate the practice of Encourage the Heart.
- To show appreciation to fellow participants in the workshop using written words of encouragement.

Audience

Suitable for any group size.

Time Required

10 minutes.

Materials and Equipment

- Cards of post-card size with the title "Thank You" printed on them. The logo of the client, the title of the workshop, and other words can be printed on them too. Participants can also decorate the cards as part of the process, but must leave sufficient space for writing.
- Markers or pens of different colors.

Area Setup

Participants sit in a circle facing each other.

Process

1. This activity is usually conducted near the end of the workshop. State that the workshop is coming to an end, and this activity is

for participants to show appreciation to each other and to model Encourage the Heart.

2. Distribute one card to each participant (more cards can be given if there is time).

3. Have everyone write his or her name on a piece of paper and place the pieces of paper in a bag or box. Have each person draw a name. Ask everyone who drew a name to write words of encouragement to the participant whose name was drawn. Allow about 3 to 5 minutes for everyone to write.

4. After everyone has written a card, ask participants to stand up together. At the count of 3, ask everyone to go to the person they have written to and give that person the card!

Variation

- To make the activity more interesting, simple goodies such as chocolates or candies can be given to each participant to be given together with the thank you card.

Ricky Foo affirms positive thinking and life-long learning. A graduate with an honors degree in business from the Nanyang Technological University, his own learning journey continues as he pursues a master of arts degree in education and human development from George Washington University. His passion in personal and organization development sees him highly committed and dedicated to the journey. He is an accredited Myers-Briggs Type Indicator (MBTI) administrator and a Leadership Challenge® Certified Facilitator.

Ricky Foo
PACE Organization Dynamics Pte Ltd

Blk 162 Bukit Merah Central
#06-3555
Singapore 150162
  Phone: +65 6278 8289
  Email: rickyfoo@pace-od.com
  Website: www.pace-od.com

COMPLIMENTARY CLOSER

Submitted by Michael Gerlach

Objectives

- To demonstrate a way to encourage and compliment co-workers or team members.
- To break down barriers, build unity, and build intimacy.

Audience

Any size group, department, or team that has or is working together.

Time Required

10 to 15 minutes.

Materials and Equipment

- Thank you cards.
- One pen for each participant.

Area Setup

Enough room to gather the entire group around tables, with enough space to write.

Process

1. Give everyone a thank you card with his or her name on the front and a pen.

2. Have everyone hand his or her card to the person seated to the right.

3. Instruct participants that they have 15 seconds to write an encouraging "one-liner" about the persons whose cards they are currently holding. Every 15 seconds instruct the group to pass the cards to the right.

4. Once all the cards have gone around the table, allow participants to read their cards.

5. Wrap up the activity with these questions:
   • How did you feel when we started the activity (expect that some might respond negatively, "hokey," "uncomfortable").
   • How did you feel as the activity continued?
   • How are your feelings related to the fifth practice, Encourage the Heart?
   • What will you do as a result of participating in this activity?

Facilitator's Note

This activity is a great way to get co-workers to compliment one another. Some participants keep their cards to look at when they have an occasional bad day at work. Here is an example of how this has worked:

The author led focus groups to address low morale. Groups consisted of one representative from each department. They meet once a month to develop and implement various programs to raise employee morale. The facility is split into two different levels, which hinders employees/departments from interacting with one another on a regular basis. After the group's first meeting, a "complimentary closer" session was used to end the meeting. Each participant received a personalized encouragement card to take back to his or her work area. Some examples of encouragement words were "team player," "always smiling," "infectious laugh," "leader," "warrior," "encourager," "willing to stand in the gap," "watches my back," and "MVP."

Michael Gerlach is an outreach referral coordinator for the Tennessee Orthopaedic Alliance in Nashville, Tennessee. He is a certified athletic trainer and EMT. He has an M.S. degree in physical education from Middle Tennessee State University, Murfreesboro, Tennessee, and is the only person in his family with a college degree. He is currently a member of Toastmasters International.

> **Michael Gerlach**
> Outreach Referral Coordinator
> Tennessee Orthopaedic Alliance
> 301 21th Avenue North
> Nashville, TN 37203
>   Phone: (615) 416-3742
>   Email: gerlachmr@toa.com
>   Website: www.toa.com

POSITIVE BOMBING

Submitted by Jonas Hansson

Objectives

- To achieve a positive mood in the group.
- To focus on positive features.

Audience

Five to ten participants who are members of any group that has been working together.

Time Required

45 minutes.

Materials and Equipment

- Paper and pens or pencils for each participant.

Area Setup

A place for a feedback recipient to sit while receiving feedback.

Process

1. Begin by saying, "Today we are going to conduct a feedback activity. We will focus on positive features." Tell participants to prepare themselves by writing positive features about everyone else in the group. State that they should not complicate the instructions, but to keep it simple by listing ordinary things the group members do or skills they have that contribute to the process.

2. Ask for a volunteer to be first to receive feedback. Have the volunteer sit on a chair with his or her back toward the group. Tell the group that if the receiver of the feedback does not look at the group, he or she will listen much better to the words the group is delivering.

3. Ask each member of the group to provide positive feedback to the volunteer on the chair. You can either go around or let the group members improvise. It depends on the group's maturity. Do not let the receiver respond to the feedback. He or she may just say, "Thank you for the feedback."

4. When the first volunteer has received feedback, ask for a second volunteer. Continue until everyone has received feedback.

5. Complete a quick summary with these questions:
   - How did it feel to give the feedback?
   - How did it feel to receive the feedback?
   - How can you use this concept in your team situation?

Variation

- This is a very good activity to end the work week.

Jonas Hansson is a consultant at the Centre of Leadership in Umeå, Sweden. His work is at Umeå University as a teacher in the police program. He became a police officer in 1993 and is teaching conflict management communication and self-protection, group processes, leadership, and human rights. He relies on his experience in practical police work as well as being a member of a team. Jonas' vision is to receive a university degree and conduct research in the future.

Jonas Hansson
The Centre of Leadership in Sweden
Ledarsskapscentrum
Box 7978
907 19 Umeå
Sweden
  Phone: 0046730234415
  Email: jonas.hansson@ledarskapscentrum.se
  Website: www.ledarskapscentrum.se

CONUNDRA

Submitted by Brian Jackson

Objectives

- To encourage participants to capitalize on their own, and one another's, skills and strengths.
- To celebrate by creating a spirit of community.
- To foster an atmosphere of inclusion, exploration, and fun.
- To ultimately realize the shortcomings of a win-lose strategy.

Audience

Eight to one hundred participants.

Time Required

Approximately 60 minutes.

Materials and Equipment

- One Conundra handout for each participant.
- One prepared bag per team, filled with:
  - Two 3-ft lengths of rope (¼-inch nylon works best) with a simple overhand knot tied in the middle of each
  - Six wooden dowel rods of equal length, each about 8 inches long
  - Six golf pencils
  - Twelve index cards.
- One Scoring Key for the facilitator.

Area Setup

If working indoors, have each team seated at its own work table. Alternatively, if planning to work outdoors, mark out one 12-ft. by

12-ft. area per team on the ground/grass using masking tape or survey tape approximately 30 feet from one another, but well within seeing/talking distance.

Facilitator Note

Typically, teams assume this project is competitive and never consider challenging the process by collaborating—to the obvious detriment of all.

Process

1. Assign participants to teams. State that they will play Conundra, in which teams will earn as many points as possible by solving a diverse collection of unrelated problems: some easy, some hard; some word-based, some mathematical; some logical, some illogical; some hands-on, and some abstract. Tell them that each problem has specific points assigned to it, and there are additional points possible for speed of completion.

   If outside, when approaching the general area where Conundra is set up, stop the group, immediately divide up into the appropriate number of teams, and then quickly point out the different areas marked out to everyone. Introduce the project along the lines of:

   "In this immediate vicinity are several large square areas marked out on the ground—one per team. Within each of these areas you will find a bag containing information and resources that will be helpful to you in successfully completing this project. However, please do not open the bag until your whole team is inside the boundary line. Time starts immediately. Good luck!"

If working indoors at tables, modify your words appropriately. Either way, note the start time as soon as the last team opens its bag.

2. Circulate during the project, initially in purely an observational capacity, and then consider assisting each team in some small way (via subtle hints!) so that, you will know that each problem has been solved by at least one of the groups.

3. Provide a 2-minute warning before the end of the time.

4. When time is up, pull all the teams together and quickly go through each problem in a light-hearted manner, inviting solutions from the different teams in turn. Stress using an honor system, and ask each team to keep track of its own score that will be shared later. While this process is underway, mentally note whether every problem was solved by at least one team.

5. It is important to first run through the answers to enable teams to move on from a problem-solving mode to processing their effectiveness. After doing so, acknowledge everyone's efforts, and have teams publicly announce their point scores.

6. Process the experience as a large group. Be sure to focus on some positive elements of individual and group dynamics prior to raising the issue of collaboration. Select any of the questions that are most pertinent to your teams. Some possible questions and categories follow.
    *   Individual Focus
        *   What were the different strategies you used when tackling this project?
        *   In what ways did you identify and capitalize on individual strengths and skills?

- What can we learn about appreciating individual differences and valuing diverse contributions?
- How did team members encourage others?
- Team Focus
  - How clear were you about organizing yourselves and planning effectively to meet your objectives?
  - How pleased are you with the way you developed ideas together and maximized your resources?
  - How flexible and creative were you when faced with difficulty in finding solutions rapidly?
  - In what ways could you have more successfully completed this project, and why?
  - Did individuals use reward or recognition to encourage others on the team?
- Organizational Collaboration Focus
  - What false assumptions/artificial constraints did you place on yourself? Why did you do that?
  - In what ways could you have been more pro-active in sharing ideas, resources, and solutions across all teams—thereby developing a win/win scenario for all?
  - How does the practice of Encourage the Heart create a win/win for an organization?
  - What are some helpful insights, parallels, and/or reminders that you can take forward from this experience back to your work environment?

7. Add some of the following comments to summarize the activity:
   - The issue of assumptions is important; teams assume this project is competitive. They don't notice the distinction between "getting as many points as possible for your team"

with "being the team with the most points." Where the former invites collaboration, the latter spurs competition. Clarity of purpose is critical here, and the distinction is significant within organizations.

- Even if teams are not overtly competitive, they assume they cannot talk to or approach one another. This is an entirely erroneous and self-imposed constraint. Often, even if a team member suggests talking to another team, he or she is dissuaded from doing so by teammates. Despite the incentives for rapid problem solving, teams tend to work harder, not smarter, reinforcing the silo mentality.
- Accordingly, there are ample opportunities to challenge the (self-imposed) process—both inter- and intra-team, to confess ignorance/ineptitude and thereby ask for help or insight, and to capitalize productively on individual talents. Above all, this Conundra project offers the opportunity to exercise good leadership.

8. Summarize by inviting examples from participants of parallels within their own organizations. Ask for volunteers to state what they have learned from this activity.

Variation

- Alternatively, consider having teams conduct their own debriefings initially, using some "teaser" questions on PowerPoint to get their conversations started. Then move to a large group debriefing, during which you can begin to raise the issue of collaboration. Some sample questions follow:
  - What were the different strategies you used in tackling this project, and how effective were these?

- In what ways did you identify, capitalize on, and encourage individual strengths and skills?
- How clear were you about organizing yourself and planning proactively to meet your objectives?
- How pleased are you with the way you developed ideas together and maximized your team's resources and talents?
- How well did you listen to one another or think outside the box?
- What example of Encourage the Heart did you hear?
- In what ways could you have more successfully completed this project? How? Why?

Brian Jackson is the founder and director of The Orion Trust. He is a leader in designing and facilitating experience-based organizational performance programs for corporate clients throughout the United States and elsewhere, with a primary focus on leadership and team development. Because of his thirty years of international experience, Brian's expertise is sought by other nationally recognized providers of experiential development programs to enhance the quality and effectiveness of the services that they, in turn, offer to their own clients.

Brian Jackson
The Orion Trust
P.O. Box 521389
Longwood, FL 32752
   Phone: (407) 320-1881
   Email: bj@oriontrust.com
   Website: www.oriontrust.com

CONUNDRA

The purpose of this project is to enable you to get to know one another better, and to encourage both personal leadership and effective teamwork among all of you.

Your objective is to earn as many points as you can for your team (the maximum possible is a score of 265) within the next 20 minutes by correctly solving as many of the various challenges outlined below as possible. TIME STARTS NOW.

A bag of resources/equipment is provided for your team. Please monitor your own scoring, and we will confirm your responses at the conclusion of this project. Good luck, and make haste—there are bonus points for speed of completion!

A. Using just the six sticks provided, create four equilateral triangles simultaneously without bending, cutting, or damaging these sticks in any way. For the purposes of this particular project, an equilateral triangle is defined as "any triangle with its three internal angles equal, as well as its three sides being of equal length, and each side being the **full** length of a stick."
   In order to qualify, one of your team members must be ready to demonstrate your solution.
   Points earned for correct solution: 20

B. Assume you have two bills in your pocket, making a total of $101. One of them is **not** a $1 bill. What denominations are they (if any)?
   In order to qualify, you must be prepared to announce your solution in public.
   Points earned for a correct solution: 5

C. You are deep in the dungeon of an old deserted castle, where there are three identical, unmarked light switches. All are currently in the "OFF" position. Each switch independently controls one of three different light bulbs situated two floors above you (and out of sight from the dungeon). You may flip any of the switches to try to find out which one works which bulb. However, if you can only go upstairs just once to look, how can you discover—definitively—which switch works which light?

To qualify, your solution and explanation must be written down on paper for public presentation.

Points earned for correct solution: 15

D. A man shows you a photograph of one of his relatives, and says, "Brothers and sisters have I none; this man's father is my father's son." Who exactly is in the photograph?

In order to qualify, your solution must be written down for explanation/presentation.

Points earned for the correct solution: 15

E. Using one of the lengths of rope provided, you are to begin with the rope stretched out straight in front of you and containing no knots whatsoever. Your challenge is to end up with a simple over-hand knot (as in the early stages of tying a shoelace, and as per the sample/s provided) tied in the middle of the rope, and with a hand on each end of the rope. However, you are to envision that—before initially picking a rope up—you have "Superglue" on both hands, so that the moment you touch the rope, you are permanently stuck to it. Furthermore, in attempting to tie this knot, you must begin by grasping each end of the rope **simultaneously** with your hands.

In order to qualify, **one** of your team members must be ready to demonstrate your solution.
Points earned for a qualified solution: 30

F. You have just two hourglasses, a 4-minute glass and a 7-minute glass. However, you need to measure exactly **nine** consecutive minutes from the moment you touch either one of these hourglasses. How do you do this by using just the two hourglasses provided?
To qualify, your answer must be written down on paper.
Points earned for a correct solution: 15

G. A traveler arrives at a fork in the trail and does not know which path to take to reach her destination. She sees two people at the fork—one of whom is widely known to always lie, while the other always tells the truth. However, the traveler does not know which person is which. She can ask only **one** of these two people just **one** question to enable her to unequivocally identify the correct path to take. What is this question, and which person should she ask?
The question, and to whom it is addressed (as well as your explanation), must be written down to qualify.
Points earned for correct solution: 25

H. Identify the next four letters in this sequence: **O, T, T, F, F, ...**
In order to qualify, your solution and explanation must be written down for public presentation.
Points earned for a qualified solution: 25

I. You have eight ancient cannonballs that all look and weigh the same—except that one is only **marginally** heavier. The only means of measurement you have available to you is an old-fashioned weighing (or balance) scale; however, you may use it **only twice**

for weighing purposes. Within this constraint, how can you identify the slightly heavier cannonball?

In order to qualify, your answer must be written down on paper.

Points earned for the correct solution: 15

Note: Rapid planning and implementation of this project will be rewarded with bonus points. Your team's bonus is directly correlated to the total time your team takes to successfully complete this project on the following basis (that is, if you are able to identify **correct** solutions to **ALL** nine problems):

Completion within 18 minutes: 25 pts.
Completion within 16 minutes: 50 pts.
Completion within 14 minutes: 75 pts.
Completion within 12 minutes: 100 pts.

CONUNDRA SCORING KEY

A. Build a pyramid up from a triangulated base.
    Points: 20

B. The **other** is a $1 bill. Or two utility bills. Or two $50s and some change
    Points: 5

C. Turn Switch 1 on for a while—about 5 minutes or so—and then turn it off. Turn Switch 2 on, and now go up and inspect. The hot bulb—although off—is controlled by Switch 1, the lit bulb is controlled by Switch 2, and the unlit and cold bulb is controlled by the untouched Switch 3.
    Points: 15

D. It's a photograph of his son.
    Points: 15

E. Fold arms first, then take hold of the ends of the rope and unfold arms.
    Points: 30

F. Start both hourglasses simultaneously. When the 4-minute glass runs out, turn it over immediately (4 minutes now have elapsed). When the 7-minute glass runs out, turn it over immediately (7 minutes now have elapsed). When the 4-minute glass runs out this time (8 minutes have now elapsed), the 7-minute glass has been running for exactly 1 minute. Turn it over immediately once again. When it stops, 9 minutes have elapsed.
    Points: 15

G. The traveler can ask either person "Which way would your buddy send me?" and then always take the opposite road from the one indicated.
   Points: 25

H. *S, S, E, N* (The first letters of the numbers written as words.)
   Points: 25

I. Start by weighing any three and three. If they are equal, then weigh the remaining two. If the first "three and three" are unequal, weigh any two from the heavier side. If they are equal, the heavier ball is the one that was removed. Alternatively, if one side goes down, that is the heavier ball.
   Points: 15

If teams are able to identify correct solutions to ALL of these problems, bonuses as follows:

Completion within 18 minutes: 25 pts.
Completion within 16 minutes: 50 pts.
Completion within 14 minutes: 75 pts.
Completion within 12 minutes: 100 pts.

WRITING AND RECEIVING CLASS AFFIRMATIONS

Submitted by Edith Katz

Objective

- Participants will experience writing and receiving affirmations from each other, as an example of Encourage the Heart.

Audience

No limitations.

Time Required

10 minutes, plus extra time for facilitator to compile affirmations after class.

Materials and Equipment

- Customize the Affirmations Worksheet with all participants' names (one copy for each participant).
- One copy of the Class Affirmation Story for the facilitator.

Area Setup

None.

Process

1. Read the Class Affirmations Story out loud to the group.
2. Provide each participant with an Affirmations Worksheet with all participants' names listed. Share the directions with them, asking

each participant to write one to three affirmations or something special about every other person in the group.

3. Collect all worksheets and compile a composite of all shared affirmations for each participant. Give to each participant at a later date. Depending on the group, you may wish to frame the affirmations or print them on special paper.

Edith Katz is the manager of employee development at Brooks Health System, where she facilitates an eleven-part Leadership Challenge series. The series includes a lab session the week after each practice has been introduced. In the lab session, each participant presents his or her application assignment to the class and a discussion is opened to provide feedback, ideas, and suggestions. This active learning component helps participants to apply the knowledge to their real-life work challenges and allows participants to learn from others as well.

Edith Katz
Brooks Health System
3901 University Boulevard South Suite 103
Jacksonville, FL 32216
   Phone: (904) 858-7334
   Email: edith.katz@brookshealth.org

CLASS AFFIRMATIONS STORY

One day a teacher asked her students to list the names of the other students in the room on two sheets of paper, leaving space between names. Then she told them to think of the nicest thing they could say about each of their classmates and to write it down. It took the remainder of the class period to finish their assignment, and as the students left the room, each one handed in his or her paper.

That Saturday, the teacher wrote down the name of each student on a separate sheet of paper and listed what everyone else had said about that individual.

On Monday she gave each student his or her list. Before long, the entire class was smiling. "Really?" she heard whispered. "I never knew that I meant anything to anyone!" and "I didn't know others liked me so much," were most of the comments.

No one ever mentioned those papers in class again. She never knew whether they discussed them after class or with their parents, but it didn't matter. The exercise had accomplished its purpose. The students were happy with themselves and with one another. That group of students moved on.

Several years later, one of the students was killed in Vietnam and his teacher attended the funeral of that special student. She had never seen a serviceman in a military coffin before. He looked so handsome, so mature. The church was packed with his friends. One by one those who loved him took a last walk by the coffin. The teacher was the last one to bless the coffin. As she stood there, one of the soldiers who acted as pallbearer came up to her. "Were you Mark's math teacher?" he asked. She nodded, "Yes." Then he said, "Mark talked about you a lot."

After the funeral, most of Mark's former classmates went together to a luncheon. Mark's mother and father were there, obviously waiting to speak with his teacher. "We want to show you something," his father said, taking a wallet out of his pocket. "They found this on Mark when he was killed. We thought you might recognize it." Opening the billfold, he carefully removed two worn pieces of notebook paper that had obviously been taped, folded, and refolded many times. The teacher knew without looking that the papers were the ones on which she had listed all the good things each of Mark's classmates had said about him.

"Thank you so much for doing that," Mark's mother said. "As you can see, Mark treasured it." All of Mark's former classmates started to gather around.

Charlie smiled rather sheepishly and said, "I still have my list. It's in the top drawer of my desk at home."

Chuck's wife said, "Chuck asked me to put his in our wedding album."

"I have mine too," Marilyn said. "It's in my diary."

Then Vicki, another classmate, reached into her pocketbook, took out her wallet, and showed her worn and frazzled list to the group. "I carry this with me at all times," Vicki said, and without batting an eyelash, she continued: "I think we all saved our lists."

That's when the teacher sat down and cried. She cried for Mark and for all his friends who would never see him again. The density of people in society is so thick that we forget that life will end one day. And we don't know when that one day will be. So please, tell the people you love and care for, that they are special and important. Tell them, before it is too late.

Remember, you reap what you sow. What you put into the lives of others comes back into your own.

AFFIRMATIONS WORKSHEET

As in the story you have just read, all members of our group have given you a gift by sharing their knowledge, gifts, and talents. On the lines below each person's name, write one to three affirmations or something special you learned about this person during this workshop.

We will compile all of the comments for each person and give them to you at our group celebration.

Name: _____

_____
_____
_____
_____
_____

Name: _____

_____
_____
_____
_____
_____

Name: _____

_____
_____
_____
_____
_____

Name: _____

_____
_____
_____
_____
_____

Name: _____

_____
_____
_____
_____
_____

Name: _____

_____
_____
_____
_____
_____

Name: _____

_____
_____
_____
_____
_____

Name: _____

_____

_____

_____

_____

_____

Name: _____

_____

_____

_____

_____

_____

Name: _____

_____

_____

_____

_____

_____

A REWARDING ACTIVITY

Submitted by Lorraine Kohart

Objectives

- To recognize desired behaviors.
- To identify spontaneous rewards to encourage desired behaviors.

Audience

Ten to one hundred participants.

Time Required

45 to 60 minutes.

Materials and Equipment

- A flip chart and markers for each group.

Area Setup

A room large enough for participants to break into smaller groups.

Process

1. Explain to your audience that rewards come in many different ways. But most importantly, the feeling of being rewarded stirs the emotions of appreciation and pride of accomplishment. It makes someone want to repeat a behavior. Although one's typical expectation for rewarding employee-preferred behavior is through financial compensation, Dr. Gerald Graham found otherwise. Through experimentation, he found that the most powerful motivator is instant, on-the-spot recognition. In this activity,

participants will learn how to identify behaviors worth repeating and how to support them through spontaneous rewarding.

2. Place the participants into groups of five to seven. Have each group convene into an area with a flip chart and markers. Have each group select a recorder and a spokesperson. Ask the groups to identify fifteen behaviors they would like to reward. These could be a smile to a co-worker from an otherwise dour person, someone restocking the copier paper, or answering the phone in a polite, positive manner. Even someone taking the initiative to be the spokesperson in a breakout group! Give them 10 minutes.

3. Reconvene the entire group. Have the spokespeople speak for their groups about their lists of desired behaviors. If the group is large, ask each group to select one or two of the behaviors to report out.

4. Have groups re-form into their original groups. (Or if you would like to combine this into a get-to-know-you activity, have them reconvene into new groups.)

5. Tell the participants that they will have 10 minutes to identify fifteen creative ways to spontaneously reward the desired behaviors they thought of. Examples would be to stop and smile at someone, shake someone's hand for a job well done, or compliment an action in front of someone they respect. Tell them they may be specific for each behavior or just give general suggestions.

6. After time is up, reconvene all the participants and ask each group to list their five favorite suggestions.

7. Debrief the activity with these questions and use some of your own:
   • Why is it important to first recognize what behaviors you would like to encourage?
   • How do you feel when someone recognizes your efforts?

- How do you feel when giving someone a compliment?
- What is a handshake? What relationship does this have in rewarding comments?
- How does rewarding the positive promote desired outcomes?
- What has someone done for you lately that has made you feel good and made you want to do more of what the person was appreciating about you?
- What have you done for someone that reaped an unexpected favorable response?
- What types of behaviors would you like to promote?
- How will you use what you have learned by doing this activity in the workplace? At home?

Lorraine Kohart, president of Archie and Associates, Inc., has been in the training field for the past ten years. She is a published author, provides marketing research, designs training materials, and currently provides editorial support for the Pfeiffer *Annuals*. She has held leadership positions in various non-profit organizations. Lorraine is an active member of Toastmasters International and the Cape Henry Rotary Club, International.

Lorraine Kohart
President, Archie and Associates, Inc
908 Abingdon Road
Virginia Beach, VA 23451
   Phone: (757) 404-1651
   Email: lorrainekohart@yahoo.com

YOU'RE MAKING ME BLUSH!

Submitted by Jan Miller and Denise Knight

Objective

- To recognize and appreciate the many talents and values of each participant in the group.

Audience

Sixteen to twenty participants.

Time Required

25 to 30 minutes.

Materials and Equipment

- Chart paper.
- Markers.
- Scrap-booking stickers, paper, letters, and other items.
- Hobby supplies such as felt, embroidery floss, yarn, buttons, sequins, glitter glue, and other items you may have.
- Scissors.
- Tape.
- Glue.

Area Setup

Tables and an area where each participant can share his or her Encourage the Heart poster.

Process

1. Write a list of the names of all the participants. Cut the list into individual strips and place them in a container.

2. Have each participant select one name from the container, being sure not to take his or her own.

3. Say that each participant will create an Encourage the Heart poster for the person whose name he or she drew from the container. Have participants take a flip-chart page and any of the supplies they desire for decorating the poster. Give people about 10 minutes.

4. Once the posters are complete, ask each participant to share his or her poster with the group *without disclosing who the poster is about.*

5. After all posters have been shared, ask group members to guess who each poster represents based on the characteristics on the poster.

6. Once the person has been identified, lead applause for the designer. Continue around the group until all the posters have been delivered to their rightful owners.

Jan Miller, Ed.D., currently serves as an assistant professor at the University of West Alabama in the College of Education–Instructional Leadership Department. She has twenty-two years of public school experience in the state of Mississippi. During those years, Jan has taught numerous grade levels, served as a lead teacher, and supervised two schools as principal. She earned a B.S. degree in elementary education from Livingston University, an M.Ed. in elementary education from Livingston University, an Ed.S. in elementary education from

Mississippi State University, and an Ed.D. in educational leadership from NOVA Southeastern University.

Denise Knight, Ed.D., currently serves as an assistant professor at the University of West Alabama in the College of Education. She has twenty-three years of public school experience in the state of Mississippi. Denise has taught numerous grade levels, taught talented and gifted, served as a district-wide director of federal programs and elementary curriculum, and served as an elementary principal. She earned a B.S. degree in elementary education from Mississippi State University, an M.Ed. in elementary education from Livingston University, an M.Ed. in school administration from the University of West Alabama, an Ed.S. in curriculum and instruction from Mississippi State University, and an Ed.D. in educational leadership from NOVA Southeastern University.

Jan Miller, Ed.D.
University of West Alabama
Station #34
Livingston, AL 35470
  Phone: (205) 652-3445
  Email: jmiller@uwa.edu

Denise Knight, Ed.D.
University of West Alabama
Station #34
Livingston, AL 35470
  Phone: (205) 652-3801
  Email: dknight@uwa.edu

HIP-HIP-HOORAY

Submitted by Jan Miller and Denise Knight

Objective

- To celebrate the values and victories of The Leadership Challenge® Workshop.

Audience

Twenty-five to thirty participants.

Time Required

20 minutes.

Materials and Equipment

- A container with six word cards (make one card for each of the following words): CELEBRATION, ACHIEVEMENT, RESPONSIBILITY, KNOW THYSELF, TEAMWORK, LEADERSHIP

Area Setup

A large common area for performance.

Process

1. Divide the group into six smaller groups.

2. Ask each small group to select a word card.

3. Based on the word card selected, the group will create and present a cheer or chant to the larger group. Tell them they have 5 minutes for planning.

4. Ask for one group to volunteer to go first. After their cheer, lead a loud round of applause and cheering. Go through each team's chant or cheer in the same way.

5. This is an excellent activity to conclude The Leadership Challenge® Workshop.

Jan Miller, Ed.D., currently serves as an assistant professor at the University of West Alabama in the College of Education–Instructional Leadership Department. She has twenty-two years of public school experience in the state of Mississippi. During those years, Jan has taught numerous grade levels, served as a lead teacher, and supervised two schools as principal. She earned a B.S. degree in elementary education from Livingston University, an M.Ed. in elementary education from Livingston University, an Ed.S. in elementary education from Mississippi State University, and an Ed.D. in educational leadership from NOVA Southeastern University.

Denise Knight, Ed.D., currently serves as an assistant professor at the University of West Alabama in the College of Education. She has twenty-three years of public school experience in the state of Mississippi. Denise has taught numerous grade levels, taught talented and gifted, served as a district-wide director of federal programs and elementary curriculum, and served as an elementary principal. She earned a B.S. degree in elementary education from Mississippi State University, an M.Ed. in elementary education from Livingston University, an M.Ed. in school administration from the University of West Alabama, an Ed.S. in curriculum and instruction from Mississippi State University, and an Ed.D. in educational leadership from NOVA Southeastern University.

Jan Miller, Ed.D.
University of West Alabama
Station #34
Livingston, Alabama 35470
  Phone: (205) 652-3445
  Email: jmiller@uwa.edu

Denise Knight, Ed.D.
University of West Alabama
Station #34
Livingston, Alabama 35470
  Phone: (205) 652-3801
  Email: dknight@uwa.edu

CREATING YOUR TEAM'S CELEBRATORY CREST

Submitted by Anne Reilly and Homer Johnson

Objectives

- To create a symbol (crest and motto) that represents a team accomplishment.
- To develop a sense of identity with, and commitment to, the team or organization.

Audience

Groups, teams, and organizations that are in the process of celebrating success.

Time Required

45 minutes.

Materials and Equipment

- Flip chart and different colors of markers.
- Paper and pens.
- Copies of blank crest and motto template for each participant.
- Stickers.
- Small symbols and simple line drawings to trace.
- Colored paper.
- Embroidery floss.
- Felt.
- Fabric scraps.
- Buttons.

- Glue.
- Scissors.

Area Setup

Workplace with a table for the team to work. If working with multiple teams, a larger space with room for several tables is required.

Process

1. Begin by saying, "In Heraldic times, groups, families and principalities developed a crest, shield, or banner to represent their shared vision, purpose, values, and identity. Crests were often placed near the front door of the house or above the mantel of the central fireplace to inform visitors of the shared identity of the family that lived in the house. The crest said, 'This is who we are, this is what we stand for, and these are our values.' The crest was their identity. In many cases, the crest also included a brief motto below the symbolic crest, further emphasizing the family's shared identity. Crests also appeared on battle shields carried by soldiers and warriors. These battle shields represented the identity of the warriors, the principality, or country. Moreover, these symbolic shields also appeared on battle flags and banners. The banners or flags often marked the winner's spoils. We continue to use crests, shields, mottos, and flags to provide symbols of who we are. For example, most countries have national flags—the United States has the Stars and Stripes; army units have arm patches that represent their units; and universities and colleges have crests. Can you think of any more examples of crests or shields?" You may wish to write the examples on a flip chart.

2. Continue by saying, "What we are going to do is develop a crest, shield, and motto that represent our celebration (win, good fortune, or whatever the team is celebrating). It will be a crest that says 'This is who we are. This is our purpose and what we are celebrating. This is what we stand for as a team.' You are to end up with one single crest and motto that represents this celebration. However, your task is more complicated in that the crest must contain *symbols*, not words. Thus, you will have to think up symbols to represent your celebration. For example, on the American flag, the fifty stars represent the fifty states, and the stripes represent the original thirteen colonies."

"There are many common symbols that you may choose to represent a particular value. For example, a lion is often used in heraldry to represent courage, a dove may represent peace, an outstretched hand represents giving or friendship, a heart symbolizes love, a cross symbolizes Christianity, and clasped hands might represent working together or teamwork. What are some other symbols that we often use?" List responses on a flip chart.

3. Continue with, "To assist you, I have made copies of a blank crest." Pass out copies of the blank crest. "Note that this is the typical design of a crest or shield. It is divided into four parts, which often is done so people might use four symbols. However, you can design your crest any way you want. Don't feel required to use this model. At the bottom is a space for a motto. If you can think of a motto that represents your group's celebration, you might put it in there. But again, don't feel required to come up with a motto."

"A final note on crests: they often contain symbols not only about who we *are*, but also who we would like *to be*. For example, the lion appeared on many battle shields. The lion symbolized that the warriors wanted to be courageous in battle; it was an aspiration, rather than a reality. And the stars on the American flag represent a vision of the fifty states, each independent, but all united. Are there any questions as to the task or crests?"

4. State, "Before designing your crest, it might be helpful to develop a list of what you might want to include to represent your celebration. First, think of your celebration/win/award. Brainstorm ideas about what symbols represent that celebration. You may identify lots more than four values or ideas; this means you must prioritize and decide which of these many possibilities are most representative." Tell them that there are other art supplies available that they can use such as fabric, stickers, and colored paper. "After you have designed your crest, you might think of a motto that symbolizes your team, or this celebration, and put that in the blank under the crest. This motto might verbalize a shared desire to be the best."

5. Typically, teams plunge into the task without any need for help. Be available if needed. Emphasize that it is the team's celebration and that the team can design the crest any way it wants.

6. Once the team has completed the crest, ask whether everyone is satisfied with it.

7. Make colored copies of the crest so that each person can have his or her own.

Variation

- Enlarge the crest or draw a larger one on a flip-chart page and hang it in a prominent place in the workplace.

Anne Reilly, Ph.D., is a professor of management in the Graduate School of Business at Loyola University Chicago. Her research interests are organizational change, gender and career issues, and teaching development. She has published extensively on these topics for both academic and managerial journals.

Homer Johnson, Ph.D., is a professor in the Department of Management, School of Business Administration, at Loyola University Chicago where he teaches courses on values-based leadership, often using *The Leadership Challenge* materials. He is a frequent contributor to the Pfeiffer *Annuals* and is the co-author (with Linda Stroh) of the recent best-selling book on consulting skills titled *Basic Principles of Effective Consulting* (Lawrence Erlbaum Associates, 2005).

Anne H. Reilly, Ph.D.
Department of Management
Loyola University Chicago
820 North Michigan Avenue
Chicago, IL 60611
  Email: areilly@luc.edu

Homer H. Johnson, Ph.D.
Department of Management
Loyola University Chicago
820 North Michigan Avenue
Chicago, IL 60611
  Email: hjohnso@luc.edu

Encourage the Heart

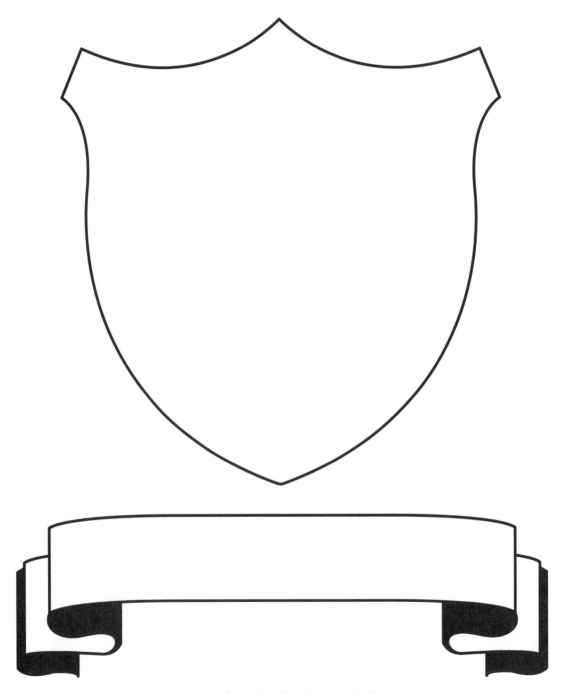

GIFTS

Submitted by Kris Taylor

Objectives

- To create a sense of unity and purpose.
- To identify, share, and celebrate individual strengths.
- To challenge common beliefs about strengths.

Audience

This activity requires at least five to six participants. It has been successful with groups up to one hundred.

Time Required

60 minutes.

Materials and Equipment

- A copy of the What Strengths Do You Bring to Work? handout for each participant.
- Pre-cut paper quilt pieces. Cut these from colored paper and have at least three quilt pieces per person. Scrapbook paper or old wallpaper samples are good for this because you can find coordinating papers with small background designs. Choose a simple quilt pattern to assemble, such as Nine Block, Grandmother's Flower Garden, Pinwheel, Dresden Plate, or Eight-Pointed Star. Patterns are easily found on the Internet or in a fabric shop.
- A pre-assembled quilt block (from the paper pieces) as a guide.
- Sharpie® pens in dark colors.
- Masking tape.

- *The Quiltmaker's Gift* by Jeff Brumbuau and Gail de Marcken (Orchard Books, 2000).
- Flip-chart pages (*optional,* if wall space does not accommodate assembling quilt blocks).

Area Setup

Tables where natural work teams or groups can sit together. Ideally, enough open wall space to create the quilt squares. If there is not enough open wall space, quilt squares can be assembled onto poster board or on a flip chart easel and taken back to the work areas.

Process

1. Explain that they are going to explore and share the strengths they bring to work. State that too often we can list our weaknesses, but not our strengths. Ask the group why they believe that happens and explore the comments. Possible comments include:
   - Our culture focuses on weaknesses and flaws.
   - We are socialized not to brag.

   Provide some examples. Many participants can relate to their teachers and parents focusing on the bad grades and not the good ones. Or perhaps when they did feel pride in something, they were given the message not to get "too big for your britches."

2. Describe some common myths that we carry about strengths:
   - Anyone can learn to be competent in anything with enough hard work and practice.
   - Practice makes perfect.
   - You have the greatest room for growth in your area(s) of weakness.

3. Explain that research is finding that when individuals operate in their areas of strength, many positive things happen. Highlight what has been learned about high performance and using individual strengths.
   - Every person's talents, gifts, and strengths are enduring and unique. They are a result of early learning and innate abilities.
   - People learn more readily in areas of strength.
   - People perform at a higher level in their areas of strength.
   - People are more fulfilled when working with strengths.

4. Use an example that the audience will relate to. One you might use is Michael Phelps, the Olympic swimmer. Michael's body is uniquely built for powerful swimming.
   - At 6 feet, 4 inches Phelps has the length in the pool he needs.
   - An arm span of 6 feet, 7 inches gives him incredible pulling power in the water.
   - He has the torso of a 6 foot, 8 inch man, which aids his reach.
   - Phelps' torso is hydrodynamic (low drag), being long and thin and triangular shaped.
   - He has the legs of a 6-foot-tall man, giving him a stouter kick, power in the turn, and a hydrodynamic lower half.
   - Phelps' hands are huge and can grab a lot of water. In addition, they are slightly webbed.
   - His feet are even larger (size 14) and act as flippers.
   - Plus, Michael Phelps is double-jointed, which lets him whip his arms, legs, and feet through a greater range of motion than most.
   - Just his body alone is not the only differentiator. He has the internal discipline to practice hard and has developed his skills over time.

5. Define the differences between talent, knowledge, and skills and how they apply to strengths.
   - *Talent:* naturally recurring patterns of thought, feeling, or behavior. Talents are innate.
   - *Knowledge:* facts and lessons learned; book learning.
   - *Skill:* the ability to complete specific actions or steps within a process.
   - *Strength:* the outcome of developing a natural talent through acquiring knowledge, acquiring skills, and focused practice.

6. Note that skills and knowledge can be acquired through learning and practice. Strengths are built when you apply knowledge, learn skills, and practice your talent—that turns it into a strength. Review these descriptors that indicate how easily you might turn your talents into a strength:
   - You learn to do this—in a variety of situations.
   - You learn rapidly.
   - You derive great satisfaction from doing it.
   - It comes easily and naturally to you.
   - You gain positive energy from it; it is intrinsically rewarding.

7. Share a personal story. This can be of a talent you have identified and developed into a strength. You can also share a powerful story about your frustration in trying to learn or perform in areas of weakness for you.

8. Explain that participants are going to have an opportunity to identify and to share the strengths that each person brings to the team. Give each participant the handout What Strengths Do You Bring to Work? Ask participants to check five strengths they possess.

9. After 5 minutes, ask participants to share their strengths with the other participants at their tables. Allow 15 minutes for sharing.

10. Debrief the exercise by asking the larger group:
    - What did you learn by doing this activity?
    - How did it feel to discuss your strengths?
    - Is it harder to share your weaknesses or your strengths? Why?
    - Did others see strengths that you bring that you did not identify?
    - How often do you use your strengths at work?
    - What is the value of knowing your own strengths?
    - What is the value of knowing the strengths of others?
    - How can you use this information to work better as a team?

11. Hand out three paper quilt pieces and a Sharpie pen to each participant. Ask participants to write their names and one strength they possess clearly on each quilt piece.

12. Have each person come, one at a time, to the front of the room and share the strengths they bring and how they use these strengths at work. Once they have shared, provide them with masking tape for the backs of the quilt pieces and begin to assemble the quilt pieces on the wall. If there is not enough wall space, quilt pieces can be glued to pages of flip-chart paper.

13. Read aloud the book, *The Quiltmaker's Gift*.

14. State that a quilt is a good metaphor for combining individual strengths into a strong organization. Ask, "Why did I pick the metaphor of a quilt for today as we talk about pooling or putting together our strengths?" Possible answers include:
    - A quilt is made of many individual pieces, just as many individuals make an organization.

- When stitched together, quilts are strong, warm, and vibrant. Organizations are stronger than individuals and can achieve what one person cannot.
- Each quilt is unique—just as an organization is.

15. Ask, "As we look at the wonderful merging of talents, gifts, and strengths that make up our organization how are we unique? Why does that matter? What is our organization's gift to the world? What is your piece in that?"

Kris Taylor is the president of K. Taylor & Associates; a consulting group that has enabled over twenty-five organizations to successfully implement and sustain large-scale, strategically focused change. Change works include mergers and acquisitions, ERP and technology solutions, and performance optimization. She has deep expertise in organizational change, workplace learning and performance, and general business, including fifteen years with a Fortune 200 company and ten years in non-profit organizations.

Kris Taylor, CPLP, SPHR
K. Taylor & Associates, LLC
4710 S 100 East
Lafayette, IN 47909
    Phone: (765) 477-6015
    Email: kris@ktaylorandassoc.com

WHAT STRENGTHS DO YOU BRING TO THE WORK?

Instructions: Review the list of strengths listed below. Check the top five strengths that you possess. This is not an all-inclusive list. Feel free to add other strengths at the bottom of the form.

☐ **Ability to Deal with Ambiguity.** I can effectively cope with change and can comfortably handle risk and uncertainty.

☐ **Achievement Oriented.** I have a need for achievement. I must achieve something tangible every day to feel good about myself. I am productive and full of energy.

☐ **Action Oriented.** I have energy and drive and am willing to act with a minimum of planning.

☐ **Adaptability.** I live in the moment. I don't resent sudden requests or unforeseen events. I am flexible and can stay productive, even where there are multiple demands.

☐ **Analytical.** I am objective. I like data, patterns, and connections. I am logical and rigorous.

☐ **Approachable.** I am easy to approach and talk to. I am warm, pleasant, gracious, and a good listener.

☐ **Command Skills.** I am looked to for direction in a crisis as I am energized by tough challenges and am able to face adversity head on.

☐ **Compassion.** I show concern for others' problems, both work and non-work related, and am willing to help when needed.

☐ **Competition.** I like to outperform my peers. I like to win. I am invigorated by competition.

477

- ☐ **Composure.** I handle stress well and stay cool under pressure.

- ☐ **Conflict Management.** I can read situations quickly, am good at focused listening, and can settle conflict and achieve cooperation with little noise.

- ☐ **Creativity.** I come up with many new and unique ideas and am seen by others as original and value-added during brainstorming sessions.

- ☐ **Customer Focus.** I establish and maintain effective relationships with customers, am dedicated to meeting the customer's needs, and I act with my customers in mind.

- ☐ **Decision Quality.** I am sought out by others for advice and solutions, as I make good decisions that are based on a mixture of analysis, wisdom, experience, and judgment.

- ☐ **Delegation.** I trust people to perform their jobs and delegate both routine and important tasks and decisions.

- ☐ **Directing Others.** I am a clear communicator and am able to establish clear directions and lay out work in a well-organized manner.

- ☐ **Empathetic.** I can sense the emotions of others around me. I may not agree with others' perspectives, but I can understand how they feel.

- ☐ **Focus** I am clear about where I am headed. I set goals. I have clear priorities and stay focused on them.

- ☐ **Fostering Harmony.** I seek areas of agreement. I seek to keep conflict and friction to a minimum. I find common ground with others.

- ☐ **Inclusiveness.** I include other people and make them feel part of the group. I cast few judgments.

☐ **Informing.** I provide the necessary information in a timely manner so that people can do their jobs, make accurate decisions, and feel good about being members of the team.

☐ **Integrity and Trust.** I am seen as a direct, truthful individual who keeps confidences and admits my mistakes.

☐ **Interpersonal Savvy.** I build constructive and effective relationships by relating well to all kinds of people—up, down, sideways, inside, and out of the organization.

☐ **Listening.** I am an attentive listener and have the patience to hear people out. I can accurately restate the opinions of others, even when I have a differing opinion.

☐ **Organizing.** I can round up the resources to get things done, use my resources effectively and efficiently, and orchestrate multiple tasks at once to accomplish a goal.

☐ **Perseverance.** I pursue everything with energy, drive, and a need to finish. I seldom give up before finishing, especially in the face of resistance or setbacks.

☐ **Planning.** I set objectives and goals, break work down into process steps, develop schedules, measure performance against my goals, and evaluate results.

☐ **Problem Solving.** I use method and logic to solve problems and look beyond the obvious for answers.

☐ **Relationship Builder.** I turn strangers into friends. I love to be around my close friends. My relationships are deep and genuine.

☐ **Responsibility.** I take psychological ownership for anything I commit to. I follow through. Excuses are unacceptable.

☐ **Self-Assurance.** I know I am able. I make my own decisions. No matter what the situation, I know what to do.

☐ **Time Management.** I use my time effectively and efficiently, and I get more done in less time than others.

☐ **Timely Decision Making.** I am able to make quick decisions under pressure and tight deadlines.

☐ **Verbal Communication.** I can explain things clearly. I like to speak in public. I like to tell stories. People like to listen to me.

☐ **Written Communication.** I can explain ideas and concepts clearly in writing. I like to write. People ask me to help craft written documents.

List other strengths you have here.

REFRESHING FRESCOS

Submitted by Devora Zack

Objectives

- To Encourage the Hearts of participants through sincere appreciation.
- To engage participants in a creative activity requiring teamwork and eloquence.

Audience

Eight to one hundred participants (equal-sized groups of four to eight, resulting in an even number of teams).

Time Required

30 minutes. An excellent closing for a program or project conclusion.

Materials and Equipment

- A large piece of flip-chart paper and several thick, multi-colored markers per team.
- Tape to put frescos on wall (unless self-sticking flip-chart paper is provided).

Area Setup

Each team needs enough space to work standing or sitting around a large sheet of paper.

Process

1. Give each team a letter or name and assign neighboring team partnerships, for example. Teams A + B, C + D, and E + F. Teams

remain physically discrete, yet able to see the partnering team's members. Each team has 15 minutes to draw an image (an anchor, a battery pack, a vista, dynamite, explanation point, etc.) that somehow represents each of the other team's members. Do not provide examples; let teams interpret the instructions freely. Some teams will link their images together; others will make separate pictures. When completed, ask the teams to hang their frescos on the wall.

2. Teams invite their partners to view the frescos while explaining the symbolism and what observations led them to select the images for each person.

3. With the entire group back together, lead a brief discussion. Ask participants whether they want to share any aspect of the activity with the group, such as the process, particular images, or the emergence of unexpected talent or creativity. Discuss the impact of expression through pictures. It is a near guarantee that the image drawn of each person will stay with him or her longer than anything else discussed that day.

Devora Zack, president of Only Connect Consulting (OOC), provides leadership development, coaching, team training, and assessments to more than seventy-five clients, including Deloitte, America Online, the U.S. Patent & Trademark Office, OPM, Enterprise, and the U.S. Treasury. Devora has been faculty for Cornell's leadership program for thirteen years. Devora holds an M.B.A. from Cornell University and a B.A. from the University of Pennsylvania. Her certifications include MBTI and Neuro-Linguistic Programming. She is a member of Phi Beta Kappa, Mensa, and ASTD. Her designs are featured in five publications. OCC is the recipient of USDA's Woman-Owned Business of the Year.

Devora Zack
Only Connect Consulting, Inc.
7806 Ivymount Terrace
Potomac, MD 20854
   Phone: (301) 765-6262
   Email: dzack@onlyconnectconsulting.com
   Website: www.onlyconnectconsulting.com

CHAPTER EIGHT: OVERARCHING ACTIVITIES

In This Chapter

- Describe the overarching activities.
- Discuss how these activities could be used.

   The Leadership Challenge presents The Five Practices of Exemplary Leadership®, including:

- Model the Way
- Inspire a Shared Vision
- Challenge the Process
- Enable Others to Act
- Encourage the Heart

LEADERSHIP OVERARCHING ACTIVITIES

The response to the solicitation for activities for this book was overwhelming. Once we sorted through the stacks, a number of activities did not fit in one of the above five categories. They were too good to eliminate, so we decided to include them in their own separate chapter.

HOW TO USE THESE ACTIVITIES

This chapter contains activities that could be used in several ways. Since they address all five of the practices or could if designed with that feature, you could use the activities in this chapter to:

- Introduce The Five Practices.
- Review a completed workshop.
- Review a section of a workshop.
- Refresh leaders between sessions.
- Coach a small group as follow-up to a training session.
- Send with participants as a resource for them to use.
- Conduct a follow-up workshop.
- Provide additional support for any specific topic.

ACTIVITY INTRODUCTION

This chapter contains fifteen overarching activities. They will most likely be used as written. Each activity covers all five practices. A couple of the activities could be used as introductions to the topic of leadership or even as icebreakers. One invites participants to get engaged in the training session.

Activity List for Overarching Activities

- Dinosaurs by Douglas R. Bender, Sr.
- A Night at the Oscars by Michelle Poché Flaherty
- Confirmation Cards by Beth High
- Winning by Steve Houchin
- Exemplary Leadership Practices Pictionary by Andy Jefferson and Cal Wick
- Who Are Your Favorite Leaders? by Sherri Dosher
- Skit in a Box by John Lybarger and William P. van Bark
- Engagement and Risk by Andy Meyer
- Hit the Deck by Janet Morano

- Leadership in Action by Travis L. Russ
- The Leadership Challenge® Workshop Follow-Up by Charles Stump
- The Leadership Race by Richard T. Whelan
- Leadership Questions by Valarie Willis
- The Five Practice Drill Down by Valarie Willis
- The Five Practices: I Know 'em When I See 'em by Donna Yurdin

DINOSAURS

Submitted by Douglas R. Bender, Sr.

Objectives

- To increase participants' awareness of the need to examine a leadership strategy.
- To compare and contrast individual leadership experiences within a group.
- To allow participants to share their past learning about leadership effectiveness in a simple and creative way.

Group Size

Ten to twenty participants.

Time Required

30 to 45 minutes, depending on the number of participants and level of sharing within the group.

Materials and Equipment

- Several wood puzzles of about fifty pieces each (one for each table of participants); some should be missing pieces.
- Pens and paper for each participant.
- Flip-chart page(s) for each table.
- Markers for each table.
- Masking tape.

Area Setup

A room with chairs and tables on which participants can spread out and work on their flip-chart pages.

Process

1. Divide the group into small table teams of three to five participants each. Give all participants paper and pencils for taking notes.

2. Announce the objectives of the activity, briefly explaining that the leadership strategies we utilize come from experiences we have had. Say that participants will have an opportunity to discuss and reflect on those experiences in a fun and engaging way. Like the dinosaurs, some things we believe and do reflect archaic and extinct thinking.

3. Give each table team a puzzle. Have participants try to complete the puzzles at their tables and let them know they have 5 minutes to complete the task.

4. Once the participants have completed the effort (or after time has run out) have them discuss at each table their thoughts about the exercise for 5 to 10 minutes. Ask them to:
   - Compare putting the puzzle together to leadership.
   - Identify things they believe about leadership that should go the way of the dinosaur.
   Have each team list its observations on a sheet of flip-chart paper.

5. Once all teams have completed the task, have them hang their sheets on one of the walls of the room with masking tape.

6. Ask each team, one at a time, to share thoughts about what they have written.

7. Once all table teams have reported out, debrief the activity by having the group compare and contrast the different experiences that were shared.

489

8. Conclude with a discussion about the impact it has on leadership effectiveness when pieces of the puzzle are missing and when inappropriate thinking dominates the efforts of the group, organization, or team. Encourage participants to think about the influence they have on their organizational relationships. Address the following questions:
   - What leadership practices did you observe?
   - Examine other teams' lists. What leadership behaviors could we put in the place of those listed?
   - How are these related to the most significant efforts that contributed to your success?
   - In what ways might we actively impact leadership within an organization using this exercise as a metaphor?
   - What will you do back on the job as a result of experiencing this exercise?

Douglas R. Bender has appeared in a number of regional, national, and international Who's Who publications. He has also written and self-published a book entitled *The ABCs of Leadership,* which received a 2008 Axiom Business Book Awards Bronze Medal. He is currently president and CEO of Paladin Consulting Services, Inc., and is also founder and managing partner of a newly developed HR consulting consortium called ONYX Global HR in Southern California. Doug is a guest writer and management consulting expert for the highly successful web incubator for business startups www .perfectbusiness.com.

Douglas R. Bender, Sr.

Paladin Consulting Services, Inc.

P.O. Box 5673

Orange, CA 92863

Phone: (626) 405-9127

Phone: (714) 724-2424

Email: dbender@paladinconsulting.us

Website: www.paladinconsulting.us

A NIGHT AT THE OSCARS

Submitted by Michelle Poché Flaherty

Objectives

- To witness behavioral models of what The Five Practices look like in action, both on the part of the leader and on the part of others who respond favorably to the leader's actions.
- To relate at a human level to characters—some believable, everyday leaders and some spectacularly inspirational leaders—who successfully demonstrate one or more of The Five Practices.

Audience

Any size audience can participate. This is effective as a large group exercise to incorporate into an overall presentation on The Five Practices.

Time Required

90 to 120 minutes to cover The Five Practices and all of The Ten Commitments. If you're only discussing a segment of the practices, plan to spend 20 to 30 minutes on each practice.

Materials and Equipment

- A collection of DVDs that feature scenes from movies or television shows in which a leader demonstrates one or more of The Five Practices and/or The Ten Commitments you wish to describe in your workshop. Select examples that reflect ethnic and gender diversity (see list provided).

- A DVD player and monitor (for small groups) or a laptop computer with a drive that plays DVDs, with a projector, screen, and adequate sound projection system (for large groups).
- A public performance license for each of the films you wish to show. The Federal Copyright Act requires such licensing. Information about licensing can be obtained from the Motion Picture Association of America on their Internet website at www.mpaa. org/Public_Performance.asp

Area Setup

Any seating arrangement that allows participants to comfortably view and hear the film clips.

Facilitator Note

It is helpful to have an assistant who cues up each film clip for you on your equipment while you are presenting, so that your audience doesn't have to wait for you to find the right scene.

Process

1. Introduce the first practice and commitment you wish to describe. Spend about 5 minutes explaining the practice and commitment to your audience.

2. Show a 3- to 10-minute film clip that illustrates the practice and commitment you've just described.

3. Lead a discussion about how the character(s) demonstrated leadership, and the practice/commitment in particular. Helpful questions for starting discussion might include:
   - What did we see?

- Would you agree that [character's name] was an effective leader? Why or why not?
- How did [character's name] demonstrate [practice/commitment]?

If the example isn't as obvious to your audience as it is to you, you may need to provide some of the answers for your group by saying something like, "Did you see the way he/she . . . ? And did you see how [other characters, followers] responded to him/her?"

4. The goal is to illustrate the impact of the practice and/or commitment by not only depicting a compelling leader, but also showing how surrounding characters respond favorably to these leadership behaviors. Such examples bring to life The Five Practices in a much more tangible way than simply describing them. Summarize with these questions:
   - How did this scene relate to situations you face as a leader?
   - What similarities and/or differences did you see?
   - How can you transfer the learning from this clip to your leadership situation?

Variation

- This activity can easily be supplemented with small group breakout discussions as desired.

Michelle Poché Flaherty is the organizational development manager for the City of Rockville, Maryland. With nearly twenty years of experience in federal, state, and local government settings, she has held a variety of senior leadership positions, including assistant county manager for Washoe County, Nevada; regional director for the Trade and Commerce Agency of the State of

California; and acting deputy chief of staff for the U.S. Department of Transportation.

Michelle Poché Flaherty
City of Rockville, Maryland
111 Maryland Ave.
Rockville, MD 20850
  Phone: (240) 314-8118
  Email: mpocheflaherty@rockvillemd.gov
  Website: www.rockvillemd.gov

A NIGHT AT THE OSCARS

Descriptions of Recommended Scenes to Illustrate The Five Practices Through Film

Model the Way

1. **Find your voice by clarifying your personal values.** *Up Close and Personal:* Scene 4. Promotion (9 min.)
   After struggling with stage fright and focusing on herself as the center of attention, aspiring television reporter Tally Atwater (Michelle Pfeiffer) **finds her voice** by learning that she is simply a vehicle for the news story. She learns this when she relates her own values to those of the subject of the news story. Her boss, Warren Justice (Robert Redford), coaches her through this learning process by **enabling her to act**.

2. **Set the example by aligning actions with shared values.** *Peaceful Warrior:* Scene 15. Responsible for Your Actions (3 min.) Dan Millman (Scott Mechlowicz) learns from his wise mentor Socrates (Nick Nolte) the true meaning of **walk your talk** in this humorous scene in which muggers ask for their money, and Socrates suggests they also take their watches, coats, and more, because he believes, "the ones who are hardest to love are the ones that need it the most."

Inspire a Shared Vision

1. **Envision the future by imagining exciting and ennobling possibilities.** *Braveheart:* Scene 10. Are You Ready for War? (speech at Stirling) (7 min).
   William Wallace rallies a ragtag and outnumbered army of his fellow Scotsmen to fight (successfully, it turned out!)

496

against the British by **describing the possibility** of freedom.

Alternative recommendations for inspiring speeches include the St. Crispin's Day speech in Kenneth Branagh's *Henry V*; Martin Luther King, Jr.'s "I Have a Dream" speech; John F. Kennedy's "Ask not what your country can do for you" inaugural address; or any number of speeches offered by coaches to their teams before the big comeback scene in your favorite basketball or football film.

2. **Enlist others in a common vision by appealing to shared aspirations.** *Stripes:* Scene 17. Three-Hour Cram (11 min.) John Winger (Bill Murray) appeals to a self-deprecating aspect of patriotic pride to reveal a **shared sense of teamwork** among the members of his failing platoon. This comedy is particularly effective and refreshing when shown immediately after a serious "General to his troops" speech from *Braveheart* or *Henry V*.

Challenge the Process

1. **Search for opportunities by seeking innovative ways to change, grow, and improve.** *Men in Black:* Scene 6. Jeebs (fast-forward to exit from elevator) (6 min.)
   NYPD Det/Sgt. James Edwards demonstrates **thinking outside the box** through his unorthodox approach to bureaucracy and crime fighting and is rewarded by being selected to become Agent Jay.

2. **Experiment and take risks by constantly generating small wins and learning from mistakes.** *Star Trek Voyager Episode 118 Elogium:* Scene 7. Aggressive Posturing (4 min.)
   Captain Kathryn Janeway (Kate Mulgrew) exemplifies a confident, strong leader in a military environment while she openly

learns from mistakes in front of her crew and **enables others to act** by welcoming advice from all without appearing weak or indecisive.

Enable Others to Act

1. **Foster collaboration by promoting cooperative goals and building trust.** *Remember the Titans:* Scenes 7/9/11 (5 min.) Football coach Herman Boone (Denzel Washington) **builds teamwork** between white and African American football players forced onto the same team through desegregation. He creates an environment that enables them to **build trust** by getting to know each other as people and through harsh honesty. Team members call upon each other to **model the way** and **share power**.

2. **Strengthen others by sharing power and discretion.** *Camelot:* Scene 10. Might for Right (6 min.) The fabled King Arthur (Richard Harris) has an epiphany in which he envisions and articulates the value of **sharing power and discretion** by creating the Knights of the Round Table. (While the scene does not explicitly show others responding favorably to the proposal, the legend of King Arthur speaks for itself.)

Encourage the Heart

1. **Recognize contributions by showing appreciation for individual excellence.** *Dead Poets Society:* Scene 3. Understanding Poetry (6 min.) English professor John Keating (Robin Williams) lights up the faces of his high school students as he **encourages their hearts** by asking each of them, "What will your contribution be?" Your class discussion will no doubt point out that he also exhibits a

readiness to **challenge the process** and **inspires a shared vision.**

This is a powerful example because it does not feature a simple thank you or an award; it is an example of appreciating the potential for individual excellence in each team member and inspiring them to believe in themselves.

2. **Celebrate the values and victories by creating a spirit of community.** *Dave:* Scene 15. Money Management (5 min.) Everyman Dave Kovic (Kevin Kline), while impersonating the President of the United States, leads his cabinet to a **spirit of celebration** after challenging them to **come together** to do something that is difficult for each participant individually. This is a powerful example because it does not simply portray a victory party of some kind; it shows how a spirit of community can be created through the "doing" of difficult work, or overcoming a challenge, together.

CONFIRMATION CARDS

Submitted by Beth High

Objectives

- To help participants recognize their leadership values.
- To give participants an opportunity to acknowledge and encourage leadership in others.
- To articulate their own values as leaders and to acknowledge others.
- To give participants an opportunity to link their values with their visions.

Audience

Any sized group can participate. Adjust the presentation to fit the time available.

Time Required

5 to 30 minutes.

Materials and Equipment

- Two 3 by 5 index cards per participant.
- One pen or pencil for each participant.

Area Setup

This activity is ideally done in a circle where all are equal and all can see each other. If the room doesn't allow this, then each participant should stand (at the front of the room if possible).

Process

1. At the beginning of the workshop, have each participant take two index cards. On one, have each person write the following: "I want to be known as a leader who _____." Have them write on a second card: "I see you _____, as a leader who _____. I say this because _____." Let the participants know that by the end of the workshop they will be able to fill out the first card for themselves and the second card for others they work with whom they will acknowledge when they return to work.

2. Near the end of the workshop, have participants make their leadership declarations. This can be done in a circle. It can be done personally, or you can collect all the cards and distribute them randomly so that no one reads his or her own. This can be beneficial if you have an intact group and you want to reinforce the leadership potential within the group. Having participants read their own cards has the benefit of making statements of commitment. If time permits, in a subsequent round, you can have each participant read what he or she has written as an acknowledgement of someone else. This has the benefit of giving them practice in saying it and it also gives them lots of ideas around the types of people who can be acknowledged and what that acknowledgement might sound like. The cards can be collected, compiled, and distributed as well.

3. Ask participants to share their reactions to this process.
   - What stood out to you?
   - What ideas did you obtain?
   - What did you learn about yourself as a leader?
   - What leadership practices were evident in others?
   - What leadership practices were missing?

Beth High is a Leadership Challenge® Master Facilitator. Her consulting work specializes in the development and implementation of customized programs focused on continuing practice for leaders. These include the use of podcast and social media. Beth has worked with organizations in many different sectors including SAS (software development), the University of North Carolina (education), UBS (banking), and the Veterans Administration (government). Beth finds equal opportunity in each of these arenas to identify and encourage leadership potential.

Beth High
HighRoad Consulting
300 Ray Road
Chapel Hill, NC 27516
   Phone: (919) 261-7920
   Email: highroadconsulting@gmail.com
   Website: www.onleadershipoline.com

WINNING*

Submitted by Steve Houchin

Objectives

- To demonstrate the potentially negative impact that internal competition, rather than collaboration, has on enterprise results.
- To show that trust and collaboration are essential to building strong relationships.
- To explore how leadership can influence results.

Audience

Twenty to twenty-four leaders or individual contributors.

Time Required

45 to 60 minutes, including the debriefing.

Materials and Equipment

- One Winning Score Sheet for each team.
- A copy of the Winning Score Sheet on a slide or overhead transparency.
- Projector for slide or transparency.
- Flip chart and markers.

Area Setup

Space for teams to break out into four areas.

---

*This activity is based on the classic Prisoner's Dilemma *(Handbook of Structured Experiences for Human Relations Training,* Vol. 3. San Francisco: Pfeiffer, 1974).

Process

1. Divide the participants into four distinct partnerships, teams, or departments of five or six people each. The four partnerships constitute the group.

2. The four partnerships should create enough physical space between them to allow for their partnership discussions to be private.

3. Give each participant a Winning Score Sheet. Also project the score sheet so everyone can see it.

4. Have each partnership designate a "liaison person" to communicate with the other three partnerships when requested by the facilitator.

5. Tell participants that the basic goal is to win as much money as possible as a result of a strategy determined by the partnership, selecting either X or Y over a series of ten rounds. (If you are asked whether winning is on a partnership basis or the total group basis, explain that they will decide for themselves.)

6. Tell participants that the amount of money that each team wins in each round is determined by the overall pattern of X's and Y's selected by all four partnerships. For example, if two partnerships select X's and two select Y's, the two partnerships selecting X's win $200 each while the two partnerships selecting Y's lose $200 each. The possible combinations are in the box at the top of the page. The partnership's balance at the end of each round is the accumulative total of money won and money lost through each round. State that each partnership should keep its own score. (This may be confusing, so plan to walk the group through the first two rounds using the illustration.)

7. Give each partnership 2 minutes to discuss its strategy privately, and then select an X or Y for Round 1. Be precise on time limits.

8. Instruct the liaison person from each partnership to meet to exchange selections, which should be written down by each liaison person. This is the only communication allowed among the liaisons at this time. The liaison person returns to his or her respective partnership and advises the partnership of the selection pattern. Based on the overall pattern, the partnership determines the amount won or lost for that round and the new balance (which may be negative).

9. After balances are tallied, partnerships have 1 minute to decide their strategies for the next round, repeating Steps 7 and 8.

10. Prior to rounds 5, 8 and 10 (bonus rounds), the liaison people may meet for 3 minutes (if they desire) to discuss whatever they wish. The opportunity is to determine a group strategy that will benefit all four partnerships. In other words, they may decide to cooperate. However, as the facilitator, do not lead them in that direction. Let them make their own decisions. After the 3-minute discussion, tell them to return to their respective partnerships, which then have 1 minute to determine their strategies for that round. *Note:* The partnership may decide to overrule the agreement made by their liaison team. This becomes a great debriefing point!

11. *Bonus Rounds:* The amount won or lost in rounds 5, 8, and 10 are multiplied by 3, 5, and 10, respectively, before calculating the new balance. For example, if a partnership loses $100 in round 5 as a result of the overall pattern, the loss for the round is increased to a minus $300 when figuring the new balance. *Note:* Once during the rounds (before round 5 is a good time), record each partnership's balance on a flip chart. Add the four balances to get

a group total. Do the same after round 10 to publicly determine whether the trend consists of more winning (signifying more trust and cooperation), or more losing (signifying lack of trust and cooperation). The two possible extremes, based on cooperation versus competition are:

- If the four partnerships cooperate in all ten rounds by selecting all Y's, each partnership will win $2500, so the group wins $10,000.
- If one partnership never cooperates (always selects X), but the other three teams attempt to cooperate by always selecting Y's, the partnership always selecting X would win $7,500, but the three team selecting Y's will each lose $2,500, so the group wins $0.

12. To close the exercise, debrief using these questions:
    - How close to the potential of $10,000 did the group come?
    - What were the behaviors that contributed or detracted from the result?
    - The debriefing centers on cooperation versus competition and trust. Lack of cooperation and trust within a team or company reduces results. What was prevalent: competition or cooperation?
    - What did mistrust look and feel like during this exercise?
    - What does mistrust look and feel like in the workplace?
    - How do teammates respond to mistrust or lack of cooperation?
    - What do trust and cooperation look and feel like? How do teammates respond?
    - What leadership behaviors occurred in your partnership?
    - Which of The Five Practices were observed?
    - What influence do leaders have over collaboration?
    - What leadership learning can you take back to your workplace?

Steve Houchin is managing partner of International Leadership Associates, a leadership development firm that has presented The Leadership Challenge® Workshop to organizations, large and small, for more than twenty years. His passion is making a difference in the lives of individuals and organizations by releasing the leader that dwells within us. His knowledgeable, dynamic facilitation style, in conjunction with eighteen years of executive experience, instills the leadership values, skill set, and commitment to create collaborative environments that encourage associates to commit their best efforts and creativity to their organization's mission.

Steve Houchin
Managing Partner
International Leadership Associates
8114 Paul Manors Drive
West Chester, OH 45069
  Phone: (513) 755-7112
  Fax: (513) 755-7120
  Email: shouchin@i-lead.com
  Website: www.i-lead.com

WINNING SCORE SHEET

Directions: For ten successive rounds, you and your partners will choose either an X or a Y. The payoff for each round depends on the pattern or choices made in your group.

Strategy: You are to confer with your partners on each round and make a group decision. Before rounds 5, 8, and 10, you will confer with the other partnerships in your group.

4 Xs	Lose $100 each
3 Xs 1 Y	Win $100 each Lose $300
2 Xs 2 Ys	Win $200 each Lose $200 each
1 X 3 Ys	Win $300 Lose $100 each
4 Ys	Win $100 each

	Round	Strategy Time Allowed	Confer with	Choice	$ Won	$ Lost	Balance
	1	2 minutes	partners				
	2	1 minute	partners				
	3	1 minute	partners				
	4	1 minute	partners				
✓ 3X	5	3 minutes 1 minute	group partners				
	6	1 minute	partners				
	7	1 minute	partners				
✓ 5X	8	2 minutes 1 minute	group partners				
	9	1 minute	partners				
✓ 10X	10	2 minutes 1 minute	group partners				

✓ Bonus Round—use indicated multiplier

EXEMPLARY LEADERSHIP PRACTICES PICTIONARY

Submitted by Andy Jefferson and Cal Wick

Objectives

- To make one or more of The Five Practices of Exemplary Leadership® visible.
- To connect specific practices to exemplary leaders participants have known.
- To identify one or more practices participants would like to emulate.

Audience

Five to thirty-five participants in teams of five.

Time Required

- 30 to 45 minutes.

Materials and Equipment

- A piece of flip-chart paper hung on an easel or wall, or laid on a table for each team.
- A supply of markers in multiple colors for each team.

Area Setup

An area large enough so the flip-chart paper can be hung on walls around the room, on easels, or laid on a table, around which each team of five can work.

Process

1. Assign each team one of The Five Practices. Tell participants that their task is to draw a picture that best represents the specific exemplary practice they have been assigned. Say, "Your picture should capture the expertise, passion, energy, and best practices of exemplary leaders using the leadership practice that you have been assigned."

2. Say that they will be given bonus applause if part of the picture their team draws includes elements showing how leaders they have known actually used the practice and during the debriefing can tell the story of that leader.

3. After 10 minutes of drawing, have each team hang or display its picture. Have the teams then go on a "gallery walk" to view the drawings of the other teams. Tell them that their task is to say aloud what they see in the pictures by first identifying the exemplary practice being illustrated and then calling out what they see in that picture.

4. After others have made their comments, the team that did the drawing can add commentary about what was missed or unclear. Finally, the person who has a specific leader drawn into the picture can briefly tell the story of the leader and the actions that he or she took that made visible the leadership practice. After each story offered, give the owner of the story a raucous round of applause.

Variation

- Each participant at the conclusion of the gallery walk declares the specific leadership practice he or she would like to emulate.

Andy Jefferson is the chief executive officer of the Fort Hill Company in Wilmington, Delaware, the global leader in follow-through management technology and know-how. Andy is an accomplished executive with a career spanning both operational and legal roles. He has significant line management expertise and is experienced in strategic planning, sales and marketing, productivity, and technology development in large and small corporate environments. Andy is a co-author of *The Six Disciplines of Breakthrough Learning: How to Turn Training and Development into Business Results* (Pfeiffer, 2006) and *Getting Your Money's Worth from Training and Development* (Pfeiffer, 2009).

Cal Wick is the founder and chairman of Fort Hill Company and a nationally recognized consultant, educator, and researcher on improving the performance of managers and organizations. Cal is co-author of the highly acclaimed *Six Disciplines of Breakthrough Learning: How to Turn Training and Development into Business Results* (Pfeiffer, 2006) and *Getting Your Money's Worth from Training and Development* (Pfeiffer, 2009).

Andy Jefferson
Fort Hill Company
1013 Centre Road, Suite 102
Wilmington, DE 19805
   Phone: (302) 651-9223
   Email: jefferson@forthillcompany.com
   Website: www.forthillcompany.com

Cal Wick
Fort Hill Company
1013 Centre Road, Suite 102
Wilmington, DE 19805
  Phone: (302) 651-9223
  Email: wick@forthillcompany.com
  Website: www.forthillcompany.com

WHO ARE YOUR FAVORITE LEADERS?

Submitted by Sherri Dosher

Objectives

- To discuss characteristics of successful leaders.
- To compare a list of leadership characteristics to The Five Practices and Ten Commitments.

Audience

Any number of participants. The activity works with those who are currently supervisors/managers or a group of aspiring leaders.

Time Required

20 to 30 minutes, depending on the amount of discussion.

Materials and Equipment

- Whiteboard or flip chart with markers.
- One Favorite Leaders worksheet for each participant.

Area Setup

Tables for participants to be seated in small groups of five to seven.

Process

1. Provide a Favorite Leaders worksheet to each participant and have everyone complete the worksheets individually. Tell participants to first list the qualities and skills they expect of leaders within their organization. Next, they are to identify leaders who have demonstrated the qualities and skills they

513

have listed. State that these can be historical figures, colleagues, family members, past supervisors, or others. Allow about 5 minutes.

2. Have each table group combine its lists, creating a composite list for that group to share with the large group.

3. Use a round-robin process to have each group share one quality at a time. Record leadership qualities for all to see on a flip chart or whiteboard. Highlight the traits that relate most closely to The Five Practices and Ten Commitments if you wish.

4. Summarize with the following questions:
    *   How similar were your lists to those of others?
    *   How similar were your lists to the Kouzes/Posner qualities and skills?

5. Ask for examples of leaders who demonstrate the qualities and skills listed on the flip chart. Ask participants to go to the flip chart and write in their examples.

6. Post the list in the room after the activity so it can be referenced during the rest of the session.

Variation

*   If group is large (more than fifteen), discussion can take place at tables and then be shared with the larger group.

Sherri Dosher coordinates instructional design and delivery of curriculum, design and maintenance of the university website, and coordination of the online learning program and multi-media authoring initiatives. Sherri is an adjunct instructor for John Tyler Community College in connection with Chesterfield's School of Quality and Continuous Improvement. Sherri holds a B.S. degree in education from the University of North Alabama and is currently pursing a master's degree in instructional technology from Virginia Tech.

Sherri Dosher
Chesterfield County, Chesterfield University
9901 Lori Road, Room 303
Chesterfield, VA 23832
  Phone: (804) 717-6614
  Email: doshers@chesterfield.gov
  Website: www.chesterfield.gov

FAVORITE LEADERS

1. List qualities and skills you expect of leaders within your organization.

    •

    •

    •

    •

    •

    •

2. Identify leaders who have demonstrated the qualities and skills you listed above (historical figures, colleagues, family members, past supervisors, or others).

-

-

-

-

-

-

The Leadership Challenge Activities Book
Copyright © 2010 by James M. Kouzes and Barry Z. Posner.
Reproduced by permission of Pfeiffer, an Imprint of Wiley. www.pfeiffer.com.

SKIT IN A BOX

Submitted by John Lybarger and William P. van Bark

Objectives

- To describe the basic concepts of The Five Practices of Exemplary Leadership®.
- To communicate a practical application of one of The Five Practices of Exemplary Leadership® through a group presentation.

Audience

Ideally, a group of twenty-five to thirty, with participants equally divided among five teams.

Time Required

60 minutes.

Materials and Equipment

- Five plastic boxes, each labeled for one of The Five Practices of Exemplary Leadership®.
- Miscellaneous props that can be used creatively to act out a skit that teaches one of The Five Practices. Each box should contain: scissors, tape, colored paper, notebook paper, markers, stapler, Styrofoam cups, and glue sticks.
- Additionally, add these separate items to the labeled boxes:
  - **Model the Way**: modeling clay, Play Dough™, lighthouse picture or model, flashlight, lantern.

- **Inspire Shared Vision**: binoculars, telescope, camera, pictures, large sunglasses, kaleidoscope.
- **Challenge the Process**: word puzzles, jigsaw puzzles, maze, rope, Slinky™.
- **Enable Others to Act**: pens, pencils, toy cell phones, calendars, toy vehicles, toy computers.
- **Encourage the Heart**: Party favors, ribbons, medals, trophies, candy, certificates.
- Flip chart or PowerPoint slide listing the activity directions.

Area Setup

Hang the posters of The Five Practices around the training room. Place a large sticky note or other noticeable designation next to Practice One on the first poster, Practice Two on the second poster, and so on.

Process

1. Begin the activity by saying, "I have posted five posters around the room listing The Five Practices of Exemplary Leadership®. Each poster highlights a different practice. In a moment, I am going to ask you to stand up and walk over to the poster with the practice that you would like to learn how to put it into practice in your own daily leadership activities. We need five equal teams, so let's try to distribute ourselves equally among the five poster groups. Please select your poster now."

2. State, "We know that one of the fastest ways to learn something is to teach it to someone else. I have a box of props

for each group. You will have 20 minutes to work as a team to complete this activity. Here are the activity directions." Show the Activity Directions on a flip chart or PowerPoint slide. Read them aloud.

- Every team member must participate in some way.
- Your team will teach the definitions of the assigned leadership practice and its two commitments to the large group.
- Your team will use a skit, song, poem, role play, or some other form of acting to illustrate how your assigned leadership practice can be applied in the daily activities of leadership.
- You will have 20 minutes to plan and practice.
- You will have 5 minutes to make each presentation.

3. Tell participants that their planning time begins now. They may remain in the room or use one of the available breakout rooms for planning and practice. State that, if they leave, they must return in 20 minutes to deliver their presentations and observe the other groups deliver their presentations.

4. When the 20 minutes are up and all groups have returned, ask for a volunteer team. Welcome them to the front of the room and remind them they have 5 minutes for their presentation. Following their presentation, give thunderous applause and invite another volunteer team. Repeat until all 5 teams have presented.

5. For a large group debriefing, ask the following questions:
- What did you learn from participating in this activity?
- How did you see yourself applying The Five Practices of Exemplary Leadership® in carrying out this activity beyond what you taught in the presentation?

- What was most challenging for you or for your team?
- What was most rewarding for you or for your team?
- Did you see yourself applying your strengths from your LPI in this activity?
- Did you see any of your growth areas from the LPI come into play in this activity?
- How will you implement some of the ideas presented?

John Lybarger, Ph.D., has twenty-three years of experience working with federal agencies, including The Defense Department, the U.S. Treasury, Office of Personnel Management, and Justice Department, and private-sector companies including Qwest, AT&T Broadband, Ryder, Frito-Lay, Procter & Gamble, The Home Depot, and Charles Schwab. He has an M.B.A. and is a Certified Facilitator for The Leadership Challenge® Workshop. John has been an adjunct at the Center for Creative Leadership and the Graduate School USDA and has conducted more than nine hundred coaching sessions and delivered more than nine hundred training programs with more than eleven thousand participants, from front-line employees to senior executives.

In his work as a coach and advisor, **William P. van Bark** has helped senior executives and high-potentials identify and develop key leadership behaviors. His areas of expertise are emotional intelligence, leadership development, and organizational change. Bill is a licensed psychologist and holds a Ph.D. in counseling psychology from the University of Denver.

John S. Lybarger, Ph.D.
Lybarger & Associates Inc.
8489 W 95th Drive
Westminster, CO 80021-5330
  Phone: (303) 421-8080
  Email: john@lybargerassociatesinc.com
  Website: www.lybargerassociatesinc.com

William P. van Bark, Ph.D.
van Bark Consulting
5910 S. University Boulevard
Suite C-18
Greenwood Village, CO 80121
  Phone: (303) 797-6557
  Email: wvb@vanbarkconsulting.com
  Website: www.vanbarkconsulting.com

ENGAGEMENT AND RISK

Submitted by Andy Meyer

Objective

- To challenge participants to fully engage in upcoming activities.

Audience

Essentially any group preparing to participate in important training, development, planning, or other group activity.

Time Required

15 to 30 minutes.

Materials Needed

- One How Engaged? handout for each participant.
- Pens.
- Flip chart and markers.

Process

1. Provide each participant with the How Engaged? handout and ask everyone to rate the four engagement questions.

2. Once individuals have completed the assignment, point out that these questions rate their level of engagement, risk, and investment in the session. Instruct all participants to briefly discuss their responses with the individuals seated next to them.

3. Conduct a full group discussion:
   - What did you learn about your responses?
   - How will what you learned affect your learning for this session?

523

4. Encourage participants to invest themselves in the session to gain the most from it. *Note:* The questions confront people with the nature of their participation in the meeting. Embedded in the questions is the belief that the participants will create the experience they are about to have. It is important to challenge participants to be candid with themselves and each other in developing their ratings. Also insert a bit of tension-reducing humor to help facilitate the process.

Variation

- Lengthen or shorten the discussion, depending on the depth and complexity of the tasks that will follow this exercise.

Andy Meyer, Ph.D., is the director of the Business Solutions Group at Innovative Productivity, Inc., in Louisville, Kentucky. He provides extensive coaching support for implementation of *The Leadership Challenge* with both the U.S. Navy and commercial client companies.

Andy Meyer, Ph.D.
Innovative Productivity, Inc.
401 Industry Road, Suite 500
Louisville, KY 40208
Email: ameyer@mttc.org

HOW ENGAGED?

Rate the following questions on a scale from 1 to 7, with 1 being low and 7 being high. Be as candid with yourself as possible.

1. How valuable an experience do you plan to have in this session or this effort—not what kind of experience you *want,* but what kind you plan to have?

2. How engaged and active do you plan to be?

3. How much risk are you willing to take?

4. How invested are you in the quality of the experience of those around you? What is your level of concern about the well-being of the larger group?

HIT THE DECK

Submitted by Janet Morano

Objectives

- To review leadership course material.
- To generate team enthusiasm and building knowledge.

Audience

Any number divided evenly into two teams.

Time Required

Less than 10 minutes.

Materials and Equipment

- Paper.
- Pencils or pens.
- Deck of playing cards.
- A timing device.

Area Setup

No need to rearrange. Teams gather around the facilitator at the front of the room.

Process

1. Ask each participant to write one question with its answer on a piece of paper. The question should be from material that they have just learned. Collect all the questions. Divide the group into two teams. Have the teams go to the front of the room with one

team standing at each side. Place the deck of playing cards on the table between the two teams.

2. Ask for two volunteers, one from each team. The two volunteers draw one card each from the deck of cards on the table. Have the volunteers return to their teams.

3. Select one of the questions and read it aloud.

4. Tell the teams that if they know the answer they should shout "Hit the Deck." They have 30 seconds to answer.

5. If a team answers correctly, that team keeps the card that was drawn and the other team replaces its card in the deck. If a team gets the answer wrong and the other team answers correctly, the first must give its card to the other team.

6. Repeat until all questions are asked. The team with the most cards wins.

Janet Morano's philosophy is, "Life is my school and I learn something new every day." She is currently a branch manager, but her passion is teaching. For the past eleven years she taught at Sheridan College. She has her Adult Education Certification from Brock University. With over twenty years of experience in client services, education, and curriculum development, Janet has skills to share and enjoys standing in front of a room as a keynote speaker or as the teacher.

Janet Morano
Morano and Associates
Educational Consultant
Burlington, Ontario L7M 4P2
Canada
Phone: (416) 402-1387
Email: janet.morano@ipcsecurities.com

LEADERSHIP IN ACTION

Submitted by Travis L. Russ

Objectives

- To review The Five Practices of Exemplary Leadership®.
- To identify diverse individuals who exhibit The Five Practices.

Audience

Fifteen to thirty participants divided into five subgroups.

Time Required

Approximately 30 minutes.

Materials and Equipment

- Five sheets of flip-chart paper (one for each group).
- Five different dark-colored markers (one color for each group).
- The Five Practices of Exemplary Leadership® Reference Handout for each participant.

Area Setup

Post five sheets of flip-chart paper around the room. The room should be arranged to allow for small groups of participants to easily rotate among the sheets.

Process

1. Divide participants into five small groups (three to six individuals per group). Direct each group to a different sheet

of flip-chart paper. Assign each group a different practice of exemplary leadership: (1) Model the Way, (2) Inspire a Shared Vision, (3) Challenge the Process, (4) Enable Others to Act, or (5) Encourage the Heart. Give each group a different color of marker. Instruct groups to write their assigned leadership practice atop their sheets of flip-chart paper. Distribute the Five Practices of Exemplary Leadership® Reference Handout to each participant.

2. Tell participants that they will complete five rounds of activities. They should keep their specific colored markers with them throughout the five rounds.

- *Round 1:* Instruct groups to identify at least three business leaders who epitomize their assigned practice of exemplary leadership. Have groups record their choices on their assigned sheet of flip-chart paper. Time limit: 3 minutes.

- *Round 2:* Instruct groups to rotate clockwise to the next sheet of flip-chart paper hanging on the wall. Point out that they are now working with a new practice of exemplary leadership (written atop the sheet of paper). Explain that groups must identify at least three television/movie characters who epitomize this newly assigned practice of exemplary leadership. Time limit: 3 minutes.

- *Round 3:* Repeat the previous rotation process wherein groups move clockwise to another sheet of flip-chart paper. Explain that groups must now identify at least three politicians who epitomize their newly assigned practice of exemplary leadership. Time limit: 3 minutes.

- *Round 4:* Repeat the previous rotation process. This time groups must identify at least three sports figures who epitomize their newly assigned practice of exemplary leadership. Time limit: 3 minutes.

- *Round 5:* Repeat the previous rotation process. Explain that groups must identify at least their entertainment celebrities who epitomize their newly assigned practice of exemplary leadership. Time limit: 3 minutes.

3. Have the groups return to their original sheets of flip-chart paper. Have each group circle three individuals on their flip-chart sheets who they feel best epitomize the practice of exemplary leadership written on the flip-chart paper. Stress that groups must be able to justify their choices.

4. Have each group present its "top three" selections to the rest of the group, along with a brief justification for the chosen individuals.

5. Explain that the objective of this activity was to help participants review The Five Practices as well as aid them in identifying diverse icons who exhibit these behaviors. Debrief this exercise by asking the following discussion questions:
   - Which practice is most important to being an effective leader and why? (This question is designed to raise the point that all of The Five Practices are equally important.)
   - Which of The Five Practices do you feel is a strength of most leaders in your organization and why?
   - Which of The Five Practices do you feel is an improvement opportunity for most leaders in your organization and why?

6. Go around the room (or have participants work in groups) and have each person share which leadership practice is a strength for him or her and which leadership practice is an improvement opportunity for him or her.

Travis L. Russ, Ph.D., is an assistant professor of communication in the School of Business Administration at Fordham University. He teaches graduate and undergraduate courses in management communication, organizational communication, intercultural communication, and learning and development. As a consultant, he designs and facilitates learning solutions for a wide variety of clients in the corporate, educational, and non-profit sectors. His expertise includes organizational change, workplace communication, leadership, and diversity.

Travis L. Russ, Ph.D.
Assistant Professor
School of Business Administration
Fordham University
1790 Broadway, Office #1304
New York, NY 10019
   Phone: (212) 636-6354
   Fax: (212) 586-0575
   Email: russ@fordham.edu
   Website: www.travisruss.com

FIVE PRACTICES OF EXEMPLARY LEADERSHIP® REFERENCE HANDOUT

Model the Way

Establishing norms for setting goals, achieving short- and long-term progress, and maintaining respect and dignity.

Inspire a Shared Vision

Appealing to other's values, interests, and needs to gain support and commitment.

Challenge the Process

Demonstrating creativity and taking risks to disrupt the status quo and introduce improvements and innovations.

Enable Others to Act

Involving others by relinquishing power, fostering collaboration, building trust, and facilitating teamwork.

Encourage the Heart

Recognizing and celebrating individual and team achievements to bolster motivation and reinforce expectations.

Source: The Leadership Challenge by James M. Kouzes and Barry Z. Posner

THE LEADERSHIP CHALLENGE® WORKSHOP FOLLOW-UP

Submitted by Charles Stump

Objectives

- To sustain momentum from the workshop of focusing on The Five Practices of Exemplary Leadership®.
- To identify specific behaviors and successes related to implementation of The Five Practices.

Audience

Past Leadership Challenge® Workshop attendees.

Time Required

5 to 10 minutes each month for ten months.

Materials and Equipment

- Follow-up questions for The Leadership Challenge® Workshop.

Area Setup

None.

Process

1. This follow-up activity takes little time, but it is a great way to remind participants to keep learning and growing.

2. Email questions (see attached list) each month for ten months to attendees. Ask attendees to email responses within seven business days.

3. Collate the data and use it to:
   - Share with the other participants in the group.
   - Share with your leaders.
   - Develop customized examples for your next classes.

Charles Stump graduated from Colorado State University with a B.S. degree and from the University of Northern Colorado with an M.A. He spent twenty-three years as a psychotherapist in Colorado, Nebraska, and Kansas. Charles joined Cessna in 1996 as a human resource generalist. In 2001, he returned to the Wichita facility to become an instructor in the learning and development department and in 2006 he was promoted to senior instructor.

Charles Stump
Cessna Aircraft Company
2 Cessna Boulevard
Wichita, KS 67215
   Phone: (316) 517-0476
   Email: ccstump@cessna.textron.com

FOLLOW-UP QUESTIONS FOR THE LEADERSHIP CHALLENGE® WORKSHOP

Email one of the following questions to workshop attendees each month for ten months, requesting that they respond within seven business days.

Month 1

- What have you done in the past thirty days to continue to practice *The Leadership Challenge* key practice Model the Way?

Month 2

- Tell us a story about a success you had with *The Leadership Challenge* key practice Model the Way.

Month 3

- What have you done in the past sixty days to continue to practice *The Leadership Challenge* key practice Inspire a Shared Vision?

Month 4

- Tell us a story about a success you had with *The Leadership Challenge* key practice Inspire a Shared Vision.

Month 5

- What have you done in the past sixty days to continue to practice *The Leadership Challenge* key practice Challenge the Process?

Month 6

- Tell us a story about a success you had with *The Leadership Challenge* key practice Challenge the Process.

Month 7

- What have you done in the past sixty days to continue to practice *The Leadership Challenge* key practice Enable Others to Act?

Month 8

- Tell us a story about a success you had with *The Leadership Challenge* key practice Enable Others to Act.

Month 9

- What have you done in the past thirty days to continue to practice *The Leadership Challenge* key practice Encourage the Heart?

Month 10

- Tell us a story about a success you had with *The Leadership Challenge* key practice Encourage the Heart.

THE LEADERSHIP RACE

Submitted by Richard T. Whelan

Objectives

- To create a task that gives participants the opportunity to plan, review, evaluate, delegate, mentor, create, compete, and test a finished product.
- To create situations to discuss anticipated problems.
- To explore the ramifications of spending valuable time on troubles that never happened.

Audience

Ten to twenty-five participants in groups of five.

Time Required

Minimum of 90 minutes; actual time may vary based on number of groups.

Materials and Equipment

- Six shoeboxes or similar-sized boxes/containers.
- Six unsharpened pencils.
- A pack of 3 by 5 index cards.
- Cellophane tape.
- Tape measure.
- Lego® building pieces, enough to build at least one vehicle for each group.
- Completed Lego car as a model.
- Note pads and pencils for each group.

- Small trash can.
- Cardboard running ramp for toy cars.

Area Setup

Place a long table in the front of the room. On the table place the six containers (arranged side-by-side), each holding Lego pieces. The pieces are to divided so that similar sizes and shapes are in each box, such as tires and wheels in one, axles in another, flat slabs in a third, various sized blocks in the fourth, components to build a driver in the fifth, and miscellaneous parts, such as doors, windshields, steering wheels, etc. (which may never be used) in the sixth.

Tables and chairs for the participants placed in the room so each person may be easily seen by other groups, allowing enough room for participants to stand and walk around their tables and to walk around to other tables, if they so choose.

Process

1. Prior to the activity, write the prices of each Lego piece-type on an index card. The prices should vary, and do not need to reflect any accurate market value. For example, tires may be $50 each, wheels $100, axles $200, etc. Prices on all parts in each container should be on one card, so there is one card for each container.

2. Evenly divide the group, so there are about five participants at each table. If a table has one more or less, that won't matter. If possible, place people who work together at separate tables. You may wish to have all males or all females at one table. This may well create some interesting competition, which can later be processed with all the participants. Say that Oliver Wendell Holmes once said, "I have had a thousand troubles in my life,

most of which never happened." One major responsibility in leadership is to keep errors from occurring (or re-occurring), solve problems, and prevent problems so the goal/activity may be successfully accomplished.

3. Hold up the model car you have built so all the participants can see it. Do not let them handle it, as it is only a rough example. Instruct them that their task is to create a free-moving vehicle that is to slide down the ramp (which you have placed on the trash can, ending on the floor). Say that the group that makes the car that costs the least and travels the farthest wins. Slide your model vehicle down the ramp to demonstrate the completed task.

4. Instruct the groups to each to choose a leader, an accountant, a builder, an architect, and an observer. The leader will make the final decisions and demonstrate the completed task by sliding the vehicle down the ramp.

5. Invite representatives of each group to come up and examine the Lego pieces. While they are at the parts table, show them the index cards with the prices written on them. Tell them their accountant is to purchase needed pieces and keep an account of the prices paid. If they should decide a purchased piece is not needed, they may return it, but only receive 50 percent of the purchase price. Additional pieces may be purchased at the listed prices.

6. While telling them this information, tape the price cards to the pencils and tape the pencils to the containers. Leave the tape dispenser, extra index cards, and unused pencils on the table in plain sight.

7. Standing at the table, tell everyone only items HERE may be used to create the vehicle. Emphasize the word "HERE," but do not point at the Legos. They will most likely think you mean only

the Legos, but they may also use any other item on the table, such as index cards, tape, or other items in the room. This allows for demonstration of true leadership and ingenuity. Tell them they have 40 minutes to plan and build their vehicles.

8. Have them return to their respective tables. Review the roles by telling them that all members will provide design ideas. The architect will draw out what is planned, and the accountant will purchase the needed parts. The observer will keep notes on what each member is doing, especially the leader. Additionally, the observer may go to other tables to see what those groups are doing and report back to their group leaders. Tell them that when all the groups have created their vehicles, each accountant is to report the cost of the vehicle to all.

9. After 40 minutes, call time. Have each leader place the vehicle at the top of the ramp and prepare to let it slide down. You can ask whether the leader wants to leave the ramp and trash can where they are or move them. For example, if the can and ramp have been placed on a carpet, they can be moved to a tile floor where the car will travel faster and farther. Do not suggest this, just ask.

10. Before each vehicle is let go, have the leader show it to all participants and state how it was designed to make it slide as far as possible. The vehicle will then be released down the ramp, and its distance traveled measured by you. After all cars have been demonstrated, announce the winning team and begin processing the task and leadership roles that were observed..

11. Review the activity, asking about the following:
    *   What materials did you use? Why did you choose them?
        Notes: When you said, "Use only items HERE" without specifying the Legos, it allowed participants to be creative with

540

other items in the room, such as attaching an index card and pencil to their vehicle as a sail. If there is a fan in the room, it can be placed behind the vehicle to add power or team members may create their own fans. Slick cellophane tape can be placed on the axles to lessen resistance, allowing the vehicle to travel farther. Only the teams' imagination and creativity limit the possibilities.

- How did the make-up of each team affect success?
  Note: A male table and a female table may create a competitive venue, which may add some interesting spark to the creative process. This should definitely be discussed if it occurs.
- What errors occurred?
- In hindsight, could they have been prevented?
- How did you anticipate problems? Did you ignore problems that were not likely o become an issue? How did you know the difference?
- Which of The Five Practices did you observe "in practice"?
- How will you translate what happened back to the workplace?

Richard T. Whelan, M.A., is a comprehensive human resource coordinator, certified mental health counselor, and a published freelance writer. He designs, develops, and delivers human resource and technical workshops for businesses, organizations, and agencies in public and private sectors, nationally and internationally.

Richard T. Whelan
Chesney Row Consortium for Learning & Development
4 East DeHart Avenue
Clayton, NJ 08312
  Phone: (856) 881-1157
  Email: MrPerker@aol.com

LEADERSHIP QUESTIONS

Submitted by Valarie Willis

Objectives

- To receive immediate feedback on a leadership question.
- To use the knowledge of leadership and The Five Practices of Exemplary Leadership® to answer questions.
- To add a sense of relevancy to the workshop by connecting participants' leadership questions to The Five Practices.

Audience

Twelve to twenty-five participants.

Time Required

40 to 60 minutes, depending on group size.

Materials and Equipment

- Index cards.
- Pens or pencils.

Area Setup

Works best when the room is arranged in circles or pods. For large audiences or classroom seating, have the group work in triads or pairs.

Process

1. Distribute index cards to all participants.
2. Have each participant write a leadership question or situation that is important to him or her on the front of the card.

542

3. On the back side of the index card, ask participants to write which of The Five Practices they think their questions address.

4. Divide the group into teams of four or five participants and have each team locate a space in which to work. Tell participants to take turns presenting their questions to their teams.

5. Each team member will provide coaching on questions. State that, while the other team members are making suggestions, the participant with the question must not say anything negative, but simply write notes on his or her index card. When finished, move on to the next participant. Limit the time to address each question to 5 to 7 minutes to be sure each person has an opportunity to share.

6. When all questions have been answered or reviewed, the group should consider whether common practice areas were presented. Ask the groups which practice had the most questions. You may wish to compare that to the group's composite LPI to see whether there are any correlations between the lowest practice score and where the questions originate. Ask how the exercise went. Reaffirm that the leaders need to use each other as resources for their business problems.

Variation

• This exercise can be done as part of pre-work or as a working lunch activity. Giving the assignment ahead of time or as an evening activity is a possibility.

Valarie Willis is a speaker, consultant, author, and facilitator who understands the complexity of business. With humor and a commitment to helping organizations solve problems, Valarie has built a reputation as a thought-provoking speaker and consultant. Throughout her career she has held management, leadership, and consulting roles of significant scope. Valarie is the author of the self-published book *Words for Women—from A to Z*, and is a contributing author in *Leading the Way to Success* (Insight Publishing, 2009). She has an M.B.A. from Xavier University and a B.A. from Wilmington College.

Valarie Willis
Valarie Willis Consulting
9698 Stonemasters Drive
Loveland, OH 45140
  Phone: (513) 677-5637
  Email: val@valariewillisconsulting.com
  Website: www.valariewillisconsulting.com

THE FIVE PRACTICE DRILL DOWN

Submitted by Valarie Willis

Objectives

- To reinforce The Five Practices of Exemplary Leadership®.
- To add relevancy to The Five Practices.

Audience

Fifteen to twenty-five participants.

Time Required

60 minutes.

Materials and Equipment

- PowerPoint slide (see Preparation).
- Flip-chart paper for each group.
- *(Optional)* Create a 5 by 7 colored card for each of the five practices. Have these cards laminated so they can be reused.

Area Setup

Works best when each team has its own space in which to work.

Preparation

Create a PowerPoint slide that has the following (or write on a flip chart):

- For the practice that you have been assigned, discuss the following:
  - Why is this practice important for your organization?

- What changes in organizational structure or procedures would make it easier to apply this practice?
- Identify specific ways to implement the practice into the day-to-day routine within your organization.
- Each person should decide on one or two action items.

Process

1. Remind the group that leadership should not be item number 101 on their to-do list; leadership should be integrated into their day-to-day routines. Tell them they will have an opportunity to bring what they know about leadership (common sense) into action on a more frequent basis (common practice). Continue by saying that, in order to move from common sense to common practice, they need concrete examples of how to live the practice out in their organization. Each organization is different and has a unique culture, so they will take a look at each practice as it relates to their organizational culture.

2. Create five teams by having the group count off in fives, or any other method that you prefer to use. There will be one team per practice.

3. Move from team to team and ask each to select one of the five laminated cards. The card that the group has chosen becomes the practice that they will explore. *Note:* If not using cards, just assign each table a practice.

4. Tell teams to discuss the questions on the screen (or flip chart) as they relate to the practice they have been assigned.

5. Ask each team to create a flip chart highlighting the major changes that need to occur and five or six ideas that they identified. Allow about 20 minutes.

546

6. Have each team report out to the larger group. Encourage discussion from the rest of the participants.

7. Summarize the activity by reminding the participants that they are the ones responsible for leadership in their organizations. Suggest that they have influence over their span of operation and that they should focus on making changes in their areas of responsibility. Say that change often comes as a result of many small changes.

8. Wrap up by asking each person to name one or two actions that he or she will do back on the job as a result of the discussion today.

Valarie Willis is a speaker, consultant, author, and facilitator who understands the complexity of business. With humor and a commitment to helping organizations solve problems, Valarie has built a reputation as a thought-provoking speaker and consultant. Throughout her career she has held management, leadership, and consulting roles of significant scope. Valarie is the author of the self-published book *Words for Women—from A to Z*, and is a contributing author in *Leading the Way to Success* (Insight Publishing, 2009). She has an M.B.A. from Xavier University and a B.A. from Wilmington College.

Valarie Willis
Valarie Willis Consulting
9698 Stonemasters Drive
Loveland, OH 45140
Phone: (513) 677-5637
Email: val@valariewillisconsulting.com
Website: www.valariewillisconsulting.com

THE FIVE PRACTICES: I KNOW 'EM WHEN I SEE 'EM

Submitted by Donna Yurdin

Objectives

- To help participants identify The Five Practices as they may be articulated by a leader.
- To help participants confirm their understanding of The Five Practices.

Audience

Ten to twenty-five participants.

Time Required

25 to 45 minutes.

Materials and Equipment

- One copy of President Barack Obama's inaugural address per participant.

Area Setup

Tables for five or six participants each.

Process

1. Tell participants this is an opportunity to review all five practices.
2. Give each participant a handout of the Obama inaugural address.

3. Have each participant take 10 minutes to read the Obama speech and circle a sentence or paragraph that elicits one of The Five Practices. For more coverage of the speech, assign different pages to different people.

4. Have participants form groups of four to six. Ask them to discuss what they have found in their individual reading. Allow 10 minutes.

5. Debrief the entire group by asking some or all of the following to confirm the group's understanding of The Five Practices and how they can be verbally expressed:
   • What practices did you find in the speech and where?
   • Where did you find the best use of each practice?
   • For those of you who listened to the speech or have read it previously, did it occur to you that The Five Practices were incorporated into the speech?
   • What effect do you think the utilization of the practices had on the listeners?
   • What images did the speech conjure up?
   • What does this tell you about your ability to incorporate The Five Practices into your own work day?

Donna Yurdin is the president of Credo Management Consulting, a firm specializing in transforming good organizations into great organizations. Her expertise is in the design of innovative solutions to improve the talent management processes that lead to high-performing organizations. She has worked in designing competency-based selection systems, on-boarding processes, and mentoring programs for new hires. Donna has thirty years of experience in facilitating leadership development.

Donna Yurdin
Credo Management Consulting
4000 West End Avenue, Suite 205
Nashville, TN 37205
  Phone: (615) 579-0607
  Email: donna@credomc.com
  Website: www.credomc.com

BARACK OBAMA'S INAUGURAL SPEECH

My fellow citizens:

I stand here today humbled by the task before us, grateful for the trust you have bestowed, mindful of the sacrifices borne by our ancestors. I thank President Bush for his service to our nation, as well as the generosity and cooperation he has shown throughout this transition.

Forty-four Americans have now taken the presidential oath. The words have been spoken during rising tides of prosperity and the still waters of peace. Yet, every so often, the oath is taken amidst gathering clouds and raging storms. At these moments, America has carried on not simply because of the skill or vision of those in high office, but because We the People have remained faithful to the ideals of our forebears, and true to our founding documents.

So it has been. So it must be with this generation of Americans.

That we are in the midst of crisis is now well understood. Our nation is at war, against a far-reaching network of violence and hatred. Our economy is badly weakened, a consequence of greed and irresponsibility on the part of some, but also our collective failure to make hard choices and prepare the nation for a new age. Homes have been lost; jobs shed; businesses shuttered. Our health care is too costly; our schools fail too many; and each day brings further evidence that the ways we use energy strengthen our adversaries and threaten our planet.

Barack Obama was sworn in as the 44th president of the United States and the nation's first African-American president on January 21, 2009. This is a transcript of his prepared speech.

The Leadership Challenge Activities Book
Copyright © 2010 by James M. Kouzes and Barry Z. Posner.
Reproduced by permission of Pfeiffer, an Imprint of Wiley. www.pfeiffer.com.

These are the indicators of crisis, subject to data and statistics. Less measurable but no less profound is a sapping of confidence across our land—a nagging fear that America's decline is inevitable, and that the next generation must lower its sights.

Today I say to you that the challenges we face are real. They are serious and they are many. They will not be met easily or in a short span of time. But know this, America: They will be met.

On this day, we gather because we have chosen hope over fear, unity of purpose over conflict and discord.

On this day, we come to proclaim an end to the petty grievances and false promises, the recriminations and worn-out dogmas, that for far too long have strangled our politics.

We remain a young nation, but in the words of Scripture, the time has come to set aside childish things. The time has come to reaffirm our enduring spirit; to choose our better history; to carry forward that precious gift, that noble idea, passed on from generation to generation: the God-given promise that all are equal, all are free, and all deserve a chance to pursue their full measure of happiness.

In reaffirming the greatness of our nation, we understand that greatness is never a given. It must be earned. Our journey has never been one of shortcuts or settling for less. It has not been the path for the fainthearted—for those who prefer leisure over work, or seek only the pleasures of riches and fame. Rather, it has been the risk-takers, the doers, the makers of things—some celebrated, but more often men and women obscure in their labor—who have carried us up the long, rugged path toward prosperity and freedom.

For us, they packed up their few worldly possessions and traveled across oceans in search of a new life.

For us, they toiled in sweatshops and settled the West; endured the lash of the whip and plowed the hard earth.

For us, they fought and died, in places like Concord and Gettysburg; Normandy and Khe Sahn.

Time and again, these men and women struggled and sacrificed and worked till their hands were raw so that we might live a better life. They saw America as bigger than the sum of our individual ambitions; greater than all the differences of birth or wealth or faction.

This is the journey we continue today. We remain the most prosperous, powerful nation on Earth. Our workers are no less productive than when this crisis began. Our minds are no less inventive, our goods and services no less needed than they were last week or last month or last year. Our capacity remains undiminished. But our time of standing pat, of protecting narrow interests and putting off unpleasant decisions—that time has surely passed. Starting today, we must pick ourselves up, dust ourselves off, and begin again the work of remaking America.

For everywhere we look, there is work to be done. The state of the economy calls for action, bold and swift, and we will act—not only to create new jobs, but to lay a new foundation for growth. We will build the roads and bridges, the electric grids and digital lines that feed our commerce and bind us together. We will restore science to its rightful place, and wield technology's wonders to raise health care's quality and lower its cost. We will harness the sun and the winds and the

The Leadership Challenge Activities Book
Copyright © 2010 by James M. Kouzes and Barry Z. Posner.
Reproduced by permission of Pfeiffer, an Imprint of Wiley. www.pfeiffer.com.

soil to fuel our cars and run our factories. And we will transform our schools and colleges and universities to meet the demands of a new age. All this we can do. And all this we will do.

Now, there are some who question the scale of our ambitions—who suggest that our system cannot tolerate too many big plans. Their memories are short. For they have forgotten what this country has already done; what free men and women can achieve when imagination is joined to common purpose, and necessity to courage.

What the cynics fail to understand is that the ground has shifted beneath them—that the stale political arguments that have consumed us for so long no longer apply. The question we ask today is not whether our government is too big or too small, but whether it works—whether it helps families find jobs at a decent wage, care they can afford, a retirement that is dignified. Where the answer is yes, we intend to move forward. Where the answer is no, programs will end. And those of us who manage the public's dollars will be held to account—to spend wisely, reform bad habits, and do our business in the light of day—because only then can we restore the vital trust between a people and their government.

Nor is the question before us whether the market is a force for good or ill. Its power to generate wealth and expand freedom is unmatched, but this crisis has reminded us that without a watchful eye, the market can spin out of control—and that a nation cannot prosper long when it favors only the prosperous. The success of our economy has always depended not just on the size of our gross domestic product, but on the reach of our prosperity; on our ability to extend opportunity to every willing heart—not out of charity, but because it is the surest route to our common good.

As for our common defense, we reject as false the choice between our safety and our ideals. Our Founding Fathers, faced with perils we can scarcely imagine, drafted a charter to assure the rule of law and the rights of man, a charter expanded by the blood of generations. Those ideals still light the world, and we will not give them up for expedience's sake. And so to all other peoples and governments who are watching today, from the grandest capitals to the small village where my father was born: Know that America is a friend of each nation and every man, woman and child who seeks a future of peace and dignity, and that we are ready to lead once more.

Recall that earlier generations faced down fascism and communism not just with missiles and tanks, but with sturdy alliances and enduring convictions. They understood that our power alone cannot protect us, nor does it entitle us to do as we please. Instead, they knew that our power grows through its prudent use; our security emanates from the justness of our cause, the force of our example, the tempering qualities of humility and restraint.

We are the keepers of this legacy. Guided by these principles once more, we can meet those new threats that demand even greater effort—even greater cooperation and understanding between nations. We will begin to responsibly leave Iraq to its people, and forge a hard-earned peace in Afghanistan. With old friends and former foes, we will work tirelessly to lessen the nuclear threat, and roll back the specter of a warming planet. We will not apologize for our way of life, nor will we waver in its defense, and for those who seek to advance their aims by inducing terror and slaughtering innocents, we say to you now that our spirit is stronger and cannot be broken; you cannot outlast us, and we will defeat you.

For we know that our patchwork heritage is a strength, not a weakness. We are a nation of Christians and Muslims, Jews and Hindus— and nonbelievers. We are shaped by every language and culture, drawn from every end of this Earth; and because we have tasted the bitter swill of civil war and segregation, and emerged from that dark chapter stronger and more united, we cannot help but believe that the old hatreds shall someday pass; that the lines of tribe shall soon dissolve; that as the world grows smaller, our common humanity shall reveal itself; and that America must play its role in ushering in a new era of peace.

To the Muslim world, we seek a new way forward, based on mutual interest and mutual respect. To those leaders around the globe who seek to sow conflict, or blame their society's ills on the West: Know that your people will judge you on what you can build, not what you destroy. To those who cling to power through corruption and deceit and the silencing of dissent, know that you are on the wrong side of history; but that we will extend a hand if you are willing to unclench your fist.

To the people of poor nations, we pledge to work alongside you to make your farms flourish and let clean waters flow; to nourish starved bodies and feed hungry minds. And to those nations like ours that enjoy relative plenty, we say we can no longer afford indifference to suffering outside our borders; nor can we consume the world's resources without regard to effect. For the world has changed, and we must change with it.

As we consider the road that unfolds before us, we remember with humble gratitude those brave Americans who, at this very hour, patrol far-off deserts and distant mountains. They have something to tell us today, just as the fallen heroes who lie in Arlington whisper through the ages. We honor them not only because they are guardians of our liberty, but because they embody the spirit of service; a willingness to find meaning in something greater than themselves. And yet, at this moment—a moment that will define a generation—it is precisely this spirit that must inhabit us all.

For as much as government can do and must do, it is ultimately the faith and determination of the American people upon which this nation relies. It is the kindness to take in a stranger when the levees break, the selflessness of workers who would rather cut their hours than see a friend lose their job which sees us through our darkest hours. It is the firefighter's courage to storm a stairway filled with smoke, but also a parent's willingness to nurture a child, that finally decides our fate.

Our challenges may be new. The instruments with which we meet them may be new. But those values upon which our success depends—hard work and honesty, courage and fair play, tolerance and curiosity, loyalty and patriotism—these things are old. These things are true. They have been the quiet force of progress throughout our history. What is demanded then is a return to these truths. What is required of us now is a new era of responsibility—a recognition, on the part of every American, that we have duties to ourselves, our nation and the world; duties that we do not grudgingly accept but rather seize gladly, firm in the knowledge that there is nothing so satisfying

557

to the spirit, so defining of our character, than giving our all to a difficult task.

This is the price and the promise of citizenship.

This is the source of our confidence—the knowledge that God calls on us to shape an uncertain destiny.

This is the meaning of our liberty and our creed—why men and women and children of every race and every faith can join in celebration across this magnificent mall, and why a man whose father less than sixty years ago might not have been served at a local restaurant can now stand before you to take a most sacred oath.

So let us mark this day with remembrance, of who we are and how far we have traveled. In the year of America's birth, in the coldest of months, a small band of patriots huddled by dying campfires on the shores of an icy river. The capital was abandoned. The enemy was advancing. The snow was stained with blood. At a moment when the outcome of our revolution was most in doubt, the father of our nation ordered these words be read to the people:

> "Let it be told to the future world . . . that in the depth of winter, when nothing but hope and virtue could survive . . . that the city and the country, alarmed at one common danger, came forth to meet [it]."

America. In the face of our common dangers, in this winter of our hardship, let us remember these timeless words. With hope and virtue, let us brave once more the icy currents, and endure what storms may come. Let it be said by our children's children that when we were tested, we refused to let this journey end, that we did not turn back, nor did we falter; and with eyes fixed on the horizon and God's grace upon us, we carried forth that great gift of freedom and delivered it safely to future generations.

CHAPTER NINE: LEADERSHIP TOOLS AND OTHER TIMES AND OTHER PLACES

In This Chapter

- Describe the Leadership Tools activities.
- Describe the Other Times and Other Places activities.
- Discuss how these activities could be used.

LEADERSHIP TOOL ACTIVITIES

The Leadership Challenge presents The Five Practices of Exemplary Leadership®. There are a number of skills a leader requires that are not specifically called out. Several of *The Leadership Challenge* proponents recognized that and submitted activities that address some of these skills. These tools will certainly enhance leaders' skills beyond The Leadership Challenge® Workshop sessions.

HOW TO USE THESE ACTIVITIES

The tool activities could be used in numerous ways. They certainly could be used exactly as they are written in any workshop. They could also be used:

- To enhance specific skills for small groups or individuals.
- As tools to coach an individual leader.

- As a basis for a brown-bag discussion.
- As a starter for supplemental leadership training.
- To supplement a Leadership Challenge course.
- To refresh leaders between sessions.
- To coach a small group as follow-up to a training session.
- To send with participants as a resource for them to use after the session.
- To provide additional support for any specific topic.

ACTIVITY INTRODUCTION

This chapter contains eleven leadership tool activities. The activities cover the following specific topics/tools:

- Conducting a virtual meeting
- Networking
- Leadership prospective model
- Delegation
- Team building
- Emotional intelligence
- Listening skills
- Change management
- Reflection interviews
- Focusing

The chapter also includes four Other Times and Other Places activities. All of these activities were just too good to pass up. Because they don't fit into the normal learning format, we have included them in this chapter. One occurs during lunch and another occurs in a horse pasture. (See what we mean?)

Activity List for Leadership Tools

- Leading from a Distance: How to Conduct an Effective Virtual Meeting by Debra A. Dinnocenzo
- Measure Your Networking Quotient by Michael Dulworth
- The Leadership Perspective Model by Peter R. Garber
- Cross Your Arms by Jonas Hansson
- Beat the Clock: Make Delegation Work for You! by Deborah Spring Laurel
- Building Leadership by Linda S. Eck Mills
- Emotional Intelligence for Exemplary Leadership by Dominique Parrish
- Using the Mind Screen Technique for Focus by Carole E. Pearce
- Listening Deeply as a Leader by Mary Stelletello
- My Way or the Highway by Joanne G. Sujansky
- Challenge Leadership Through Structured Reflection Interviews by Gary Wagenheim

Activity List for Other Times and Other Places

- What Leaders Do to Inspire (or Uninspire) Followers by Michael Kroth and Marty Yopp
- Walking the Talk by Nancy Lowery
- The Roving Lunch by Anntoinette "Toni" Lucia
- This Would Really Help Me by Robert Morris

LEADING FROM A DISTANCE: HOW TO CONDUCT AN EFFECTIVE VIRTUAL MEETING

Submitted by Debra A. Dinnocenzo

Objectives

- To learn the key components of an effective virtual meeting.
- To practice through simulation the process for conducting a virtual meeting.

Audience

Leaders of virtual/dispersed/global teams; group size is variable and scalable.

Time Required

1 hour.

Materials and Equipment

- Flip chart and markers.
- One copy of the Guide to Distance Dialog for each participant.
- One copy of the Guidelines for Effective Virtual Meetings for each participant.
- One copy of the Virtual Meeting/Planning Worksheet for each participant.
- One copy of the Virtual Meeting/Observation and Feedback Worksheet for each participant.
- One copy of the Virtual Meeting Checklist for each participant.

Area Setup

Use moveable chairs that can be located away from tables and arranged in small groups. Chairs should be arranged in circles for small group simulation and discussion, with chairs arranged so that participants are facing AWAY from each other (with their backs to each other to avoid eye contact and to simulate distance).

Process

1. Introduce the exercise by asking for examples of ways people are meeting from a distance. Capture these on a flip chart.

2. Discuss the following points to provide an overview of the challenges and issues involved in effectively leading virtual or distance meetings.
   - Increases in geographically dispersed workforces, telecommuting, and other forms of virtual work have had a significant impact on how leaders communicate, coach, build a team, and achieve results.
   - In spite of geographic separation, time differences, and greater dependence on technology for communication, teams must remain productive although no longer co-located.
   - This trend is likely to continue as it pervades and redefines the virtual workplace.
   - Therefore, it is imperative that leaders become competent and confident in leading from a distance through effective virtual meetings.

3. Explain the importance of the exercise by addressing these points:
   - This exercise provides leaders with the opportunity to learn and model effective skills for conducting productive virtual meetings.

563

- Working within a virtual team poses some unique challenges to anyone who feels that having face-to-face interactions is the only way to communicate effectively. While no one would dispute that *live* interactions usually are preferable, these are fast becoming a luxury.
- Mergers, acquisitions, and global competition have resulted in a geographically dispersed workforce and a growing number of distance workers. As part of this trend, it is critical that leaders become expert in conducting productive virtual meetings.
- While there is some loss of the communication subtleties gleaned from eye contact, body posture, gestures, and voice tone, virtual meetings can be enhanced in ways that minimize the negative effects of distance dialog.

4. Distribute the Guide to Distance Dialog and discuss how many of the virtual meeting options are currently being used by participants.

5. Seek from the group some quick examples of problems associated with virtual meetings. Capture these examples on a flip chart.

6. Distribute the Guidelines for Effective Virtual Meetings to provide an overview of effective virtual meeting planning.

7. Introduce the virtual meeting simulation by distributing the following items:
   - Virtual Meeting/Planning Worksheet
   - Virtual Meeting/Observation and Feedback Worksheet

8. Begin the virtual meeting simulation by following these steps.
   - Ask participants to move into small groups of three to five members.

- One member of the group begins by simulating a meeting leader who will conduct a virtual meeting.
- The leader should complete the Planning Worksheet and review with other group members the elements of the meeting plan.
- When ready to begin the discussion, group members should turn their chairs away from each other in a circle, remaining close enough to hear each other speak.
- Remind participants that:
  - They should avoid eye contact during the simulation.
  - They should limit the discussion to 10 minutes.
  - Following the discussion, the small groups should discuss the effectiveness and challenges of the discussion, using the Observation and Feedback Worksheet to structure their debriefing.

9. Repeat the simulation as time permits, allowing each small group member an opportunity to lead a virtual meeting.

10. Reconvene the entire group to conclude the exercise. Ask participants to quickly highlight:
- Major challenges/obstacles in leading the virtual meetings.
- Effective techniques utilized.
- Key learning points that will help them in leading virtual meetings in the future.

Capture their responses on the flip chart.

11. Reinforce the key learning points and the importance of effectively planning and conducting virtual meetings.

12. Distribute the Virtual Meeting Checklist as a job aid to assist in planning, conducting, and supporting successful virtual meetings.

Debra A. Dinnocenzo is an author, speaker, and educator with expertise in virtual workplace issues including virtual leadership, virtual teams, tele-work, and work/life balance. She is president of VirtualWorks!, which specializes in the human side of the virtual workplace, helping people connect more effectively through technology when they work together from a distance. Debra has published numerous books on the virtual workplace, including *How to Lead from a Distance* (The WALK THE TALK Company, 2006), *101 Tips for Telecommuters* (Berrett-Koehler, 1999), and *Managing Telecommuters* (Mancini-M'Clintock Press, 2008).

Debra A. Dinnocenzo
VirtualWorks!
10592 Perry Highway, Suite 201
Wexford, PA 15090
  Phone: (724) 934-9349
  Email: debra@debradinnocenzo.com
  Website: www.VirtualWorksWell.com

GUIDE TO DISTANCE DIALOG

Distance Dialog Options	Distance Dialog Advantages
• Email and instant messaging • Text messaging • Voice mail • Teleconference • Videoconference • Web meeting • Satellite broadcast • Web-based connections	• Saves time • Expands information shared • Can include more people • Improves clarity • Saves cost • Can be activated quickly

Email and Voice Mail Guidelines

• Keep it brief • Use proper netiquette	• Best for dissemination of documents and information • NOT a conversation

Teleconferencing

Use when:	Success keys:
• More than two people • Discuss an issue or problem • Documents previously shared • Include a remote participant in a meeting	• Purpose and outcomes clear • Everyone can hear/be heard • Participants state identity when commenting • Discussion stays on track • Acknowledgment/involvement of all participants

Videoconferencing

Use for:	Obstacles:
• "Seeing" when unable to meet live • Initial meeting of virtual teams or new project teams • Interviews, customer meetings • Displaying a tangible item or action	• Limited access to necessary technology • Incompatible technology resources • Poor video quality

567

Web Meeting	
Capabilities:	Challenges:
• Disseminates visual content to a large, geographically dispersed audience • Cost-effective way to deliver information around the globe • Live and replay video streaming without videoconference equipment • Interactive tools, such as Q&A, polling, easily included	• Incompatible browsers affect graphic displays • Various connection speeds impact downloads • Mix of audio-only and audio and web-connected participants • Potential for distractions and boredom dictate compelling delivery of content
Best Option Considerations	
• Number of people involved • Type of data to be exchanged • Cost/time constraints • Nature of subject/context • Technology accessibility • Can be activated quickly • Discussion stays on track • Acknowledgment/involvement of all participants	

GUIDELINES FOR EFFECTIVE VIRTUAL MEETINGS

Technology tools provide multiple ways for meetings to be held within the virtual workplace. Utilizing the best technology resources, along with effective meeting planning and virtual interaction, allows for distance meetings that:

- Save time
- Broaden the scope of information conveyed
- Expand the number of people included in the communication loop
- Improve communication clarity

It is often necessary to combine the use of different technologies to facilitate productive meetings of geographically dispersed teams. Survey participants to determine the best way to get the agenda to them: use videoconferencing if a visual component is necessary, use teleconferencing if voice-to-voice is sufficient, combine Internet conferencing for graphics with a conference call for the audio link, etc.

Remember, also, that introducing meeting participants to technology for meetings may require a focused effort on technical training, procedural issues, or basic etiquette for courtesy, offering input, and asking questions. Once people are comfortable with the technology and their ability to use it, your virtual meeting productivity will be greatly enhanced if you follow these basic guidelines for effective virtual meetings:

1. Plan the agenda.
2. Distribute agenda and information in advance; confirm receipt.
3. Clarify responsibilities.
4. Arrange for required equipment, information, and people.
5. Maintain the schedule.

VIRTUAL MEETING PLANNING WORKSHEET

Situation/Scenario:

Meeting Participants/Roles:

Meeting Objectives/Desired Outcomes:

VIRTUAL MEETING OBSERVER WORKSHEET

Objectives achieved?

Best things done:

Improvement opportunities:

Notes:

VIRTUAL MEETING CHECKLIST

Before the Meeting

☐ Plan the **agenda**.

☐ **Distribute** the agenda and information in advance; confirm receipt.

☐ Clarify **responsibilities** (for note-taking, timekeeping, meeting leadership, technical support).

☐ **Identify** the appropriate/desired **technology** to be used. Confirm the availability/accessibility of the selected technology for all participants.

☐ Arrange for **required equipment, information, and people** to be involved.

☐ **Test** the technology. Make sure that things work ahead of time so you can minimize wasting people's time with techno-glitches.

During the Meeting

☐ Encourage everyone to **introduce** themselves (or verbally "sign in") at the beginning of the meeting and **identify** themselves whenever they speak (except for video/net conferencing or in well-established teams whose members' voices are recognized by everyone).

☐ Establish **expectations for involvement** by all participants (periodically pause to summarize and ask for questions, discussion, clarification).

☐ Ensure that **visual or graphic resources** can be distributed "real-time" or in advance to everyone (via email, fax, Internet).

- ☐ Remind everyone to **speak slowly, clearly, and in the direction of microphones** or speakerphones, and to request that something be repeated if not heard clearly.

- ☐ Suggest that participants use the **"Mute" button** on their phones to eliminate background noise that might be disruptive to a virtual meeting.

- ☐ Keep to the **schedule**.

After the Meeting

- ☐ Distribute **meeting summary** in a timely manner, with details regarding agreements and follow-up actions.

- ☐ Schedule any **follow-up meetings** needed.

- ☐ Implement any **action steps** that were agreed to during the meeting.

- ☐ Solicit **feedback** from participants on how similar "meetings" in the future can be enhanced/improved.

MEASURE YOUR NETWORKING QUOTIENT

Submitted by Michael Dulworth

Objectives

- To measure the quality of one's current networking capability.
- To provide useful tools for improving networking capabilities.

Audience

Ten to twenty people.

Time Required

30 to 45 minutes.

Materials and Equipment

- One Networking Quotient Survey for each person.
- One Your Networking Quotient handout for each person.
- Pencils or pens.

Area Setup

Place to sit to complete the survey.

Process

1. Provide the Your Networking Quotient handout to each person. Give participants 10 minutes to read it. Ask for questions and lead a short discussion.

2. State that they are going to measure their Networking Quotient (NQ), but first ask them to take some time to list all the people in their network universe. Say, "Your networking universe

consists of three primary types: (1) personal network, (2) professional network, and (3) virtual network. Each plays a role in determining your NQ. Your personal network is made up of your family, extended family, school friends and contacts, lifelong friends, and so on. It is also made up of your active friends (people you see face-to-face at least once a month) and people from your church, clubs, activities, neighborhood, and community."

Continue by stating, "Your professional network includes contacts from previous jobs, colleagues from other firms, and contacts in your current organization. Your virtual network is comprised of people you know only through online interactions or other non-face-to-face connections."

State that, obviously, these networks overlap. Someone may be close friends with a business associate, or a family member may help someone make a professional connection. And more and more networking is being done online. But these networks can serve as useful groupings in determining your NQ.

3. Hand out the Networking Quotient Survey and ask participants to complete it. Tell them that there are two components in the NQ: **Part A** focuses on the scope and strength of their existing networks, and **Part B** focuses on how active they are in building and maintaining their networks. Allow 5 to 10 minutes for them to complete the survey.

4. Once everyone has completed the survey, state that they should take time to analyze their NQ. Tell them to add up their answers for Part A and Part B separately. Since Part A assesses the strength of their current networks and Part B assesses the time and effort they put into networking, the scores should be somewhat similar. We should expect, after all, that there is a

direct correlation between the amount of time and effort we put into networking and the results we achieve.

Tell them that if they score much higher on one part of the assessment than the other, they should take a few minutes to consider why that may be. If the score on Part A indicates they have a strong and vibrant network while the score on Part B indicates they do not put much time and effort into networking, they are in a highly unusual situation. They have received something for nothing. Perhaps they inherited their networks or interested family members are doing all the work to keep them included. Perhaps their spouses or close associates are genius networkers and they are just going along for the ride. This could be a dangerous situation and they might wake up one day and find no one bothers to return their calls. Say, "Remember, it is your responsibility to build and maintain your network, no one else's."

Continue with, "The more likely situation, if your scores for Parts A and B are significantly different, is that your Part B score is higher than your Part A score. In other words, your networking activities are not producing much in the way of actual results." Ask them to also take a moment to look at their lowest scores on each part, which can show them where they should invest the most effort. Someone may have a large network with strong relationships, for example, but lack diversity and quality. As they work to build their networks, they can directly address those issues.

5. Tell them to create mini action plans for expanding their networks. Ask them to consider:
   - What can you do tomorrow to improve your network?
   - Map your current network; what does it tell you?
   - Where are your network's strengths and weaknesses?

- What are your thirty-day, six-month, and one-year networking goals?

Michael Dulworth is the chairman and CEO of Executive Networks, Inc., a leading provider of peer-to-peer networks for HR professionals in large organizations worldwide. His most recent books are *The Connect Effect: Building Strong Personal, Professional and Virtual Networks* (Berrett-Koehler, 2008) and *Strategic Executive Development: The Five Essential Investments* (Pfeiffer, 2005). Mike has a B.A. from the University of Michigan and an M.B.A. from the University of Southern California.

Michael Dulworth
Executive Networks, Inc.
588 Sutter Street, Suite 440
San Francisco, CA 94102
   Phone: (415) 399-9797
   Email: mdulworth@executivenetworks.com
   Website: www.executivenetworks.com

YOUR NETWORKING QUOTIENT

Michael Dulworth, Executive Networks, Inc.

Strong personal, professional, and virtual networks are an increasingly essential element in development, effectiveness, and well-being. Consider the popularity of virtual networks like MySpace®, Flickr™, LinkedIn®, and Ryze. A strong network can help you navigate rapid change in a number of ways, including broadening your exposure to information and your access to expertise. Networking is something that we all do naturally every day; we may just not call it that. The people who are most successful in life do it purposefully (they Model the Way).

You will have an opportunity to assess your Networking Quotient (NQ). By having a single measure of your ability to develop strong networks—your NQ—you'll understand the strength of your network and where you can improve.

An equation for success could be:

$$IQ + EQ + NQ = Success$$

IQ is the capacity to learn and understand and can be measured by standardized tests. EQ is an acronym for Emotional Intelligence Quotient. In his best-selling book, *Emotional Intelligence*, Daniel Goleman asserts that emotional intelligence (EQ) describes an ability, capacity, or skill to perceive, assess, and manage the emotions of one's self, of others, and of groups.

IQ, as the capacity to learn and understand, is a fixed capability in all of us. You may be pretty smart, but probably don't have the IQ of Stephen Hawking, the theoretical physicist. If we can't change our IQ and want to be more successful, what can we do?

578

We have some control over our EQ, so that can be a place to spend some time. It's an excellent idea for all of us to better understand ourselves and others from this perspective. But, like IQ, this can only take us so far. We all seem to be wired in certain ways, and it's unlikely that personal understanding, psychotherapy, or self-development are going to change these innate traits or behaviors.

It probably won't surprise you, then, that I think our NQ is where we have the greatest potential for exponential change. *We have almost 100 percent control over our ability to build, nurture, and leverage our networks.* Some might argue that being an extrovert or an introvert can greatly affect, if not determine, one's NQ score, but my experience tells me that this is not the case. Some of the best networkers I've ever met are introverts – and that includes me!

So, *IQ + EQ + NQ = Success*—and the best way to improve this equation is by improving your NQ. Before you can improve it, however, you need to know what your NQ is. Before we turn to assessing your NQ, it helps to take a look at exactly what we are assessing by taking a look at what makes a strong network to begin with.

The Qualities of Strong Networks

A number of years ago, Rob Cross wrote, "What really distinguishes high performers from the rest of the pack is their ability to maintain and leverage personal networks. The most effective create and tap large, diversified networks that are rich in experience and span all organizational boundaries."

Let's review that statement, since it captures many of the qualities of strong networks.

Quantity

Size matters—you never know when an important connection will lead to a positive outcome. Virtually everyone I talked to in researching networks stressed that larger networks are better networks. John Zapolski, partner, Management Innovation Group, said, "I am constantly looking to expand my network, especially people on the periphery of my network." The more people you have in your network, the more opportunities you have open to you, the more knowledge you can access, the more talent you can tap.

Relationships

Vibrant networks are more than a collection of business cards or email addresses; they are built on relationships. When you have a strong relationship with people, they are more willing to spend time with you, share information with you, open doors for you, and the like. You have to build those relationships, and you do that by showing a genuine interest in other people. IDEO's John Foster told me that a critical success factor in building a strong network is "making sure that you're dealing in a reciprocal relationship. You must give back to the relationship in some meaningful way and there has to be a real exchange of value for a network relationship to be worthwhile."

Diversity

As Cross indicates, the best networks are diverse and span organizational boundaries. If everyone in your network looks like you, acts like you, and has your interests, how are you ever going to learn new things, discover new opportunities, or move in new directions? John Zapolski said, "I actively look for opportunities to go to new events that are really outside of the typical domain of events that

I would normally go to. For example, I met a woman recently who works in innovation, but she has a deep science background, so in talking with her I asked her a lot of questions about her background in bioengineering and genetics and I learned a lot. Inevitably, I'll find out what groups people like this belong to, or events that they go to and maybe I'll try to attend just so I can meet people outside of my core network. I look for those new events where I can get pulled into a direction of a deeper interest." Meeting diverse people with very different interests is the best way to keep expanding your horizons.

Quality

While quantity is important, quality is perhaps even more important. What does quality mean here? As Rob Cross indicated, a network should be "rich in experience." Quality refers to people who are experienced, who have strong networks of their own, who have authority, who can open doors, who command respect in their fields. Scott Saslow, executive director of The Institute of Executive Development, recently told me, "There is too much focus on the quantity of one's network right now (I have eight billion colleagues from LinkedIn), and eventually the focus will shift to quality." In today's egalitarian world, we may try to treat everyone the same. But when it comes to networking, that makes little sense.

NETWORKING QUOTIENT SURVEY

Assess your NQ by honestly answering the following questions, selecting the one best response from those provided.

Part A: Network Scope and Strength

1. How many total people are in your personal, professional, and virtual networks? Add them all together.
   - 0 = Under 10
   - 1 = 11 to 100
   - 2 = 101 to 200
   - 3 = 201 to 400
   - 4 = more than 400

2. How strong are your relationships within your network? Is someone a just *business card trader* (you traded cards but can hardly remember where or when); an *acquaintance* (he or she knows who you are and will probably return a call); a *personal contact* (he or she will do a favor if asked); or a *close friend* (you can count on the person when the chips are down)?
   - 0 = Everyone is a card trader
   - 1 = Mostly acquaintances
   - 2 = Lots of personal contacts
   - 3 = A mix of personal contacts and close friends
   - 4 = Mostly close friends with a few personal contacts and acquaintances

3. How diverse is your network? If everyone you know is the same age and gender as you, shares your cultural background, and works in the same area, your network is not diverse at all. On the

other hand, if you network with everyone from eight to eighty, of both genders and a variety of cultural backgrounds, in different kinds of jobs in different industries, you have a very diverse network.

  0 = Looking at my network is like looking in a mirror
  1 = My network is mostly people like me, but there is some diversity
  2 = There is a good amount of diversity
  3 = My network includes people from a wide variety of backgrounds and industries.
  4 = My network includes many people from a wide variety of backgrounds, interests, and industries

4. What's the overall quality of your network contacts? Are the people in your network experienced, with significant accomplishments? Do they have strong networks of their own? Are they well-known within a professional sphere? Can they open doors for you?

  0 = I like them, but they aren't movers and shakers by any means
  1 = There are a few people with some connections
  2 = Some people in my network really command attention
  3 = Many people in my network are at the top of their fields and very well connected
  4 = I can contact almost anyone on earth through the people in my network

Part B: Networking Activities

5. To what extent do you actively work on building your network relationships? Do you follow up after the first meeting? Do you

make sure to periodically connect with people? Do you return phone calls and answer emails promptly? Do you try to meet face-to-face regularly?

    0 = I don't have time for that

    1 = I try to reach out if I can find the time

    2 = I try to make time, but it's hit or miss

    3 = I consistently make time to connect with people

    4 = I make connecting with people my top priority every day

6. How actively do you recruit new members to your network?

    0 = do nothing

    1 = hardly at all

    2 = sometimes

    3 = often

    4 = all the time

7. How often do you help others in your network (both when asked for help and unsolicited)?

    0 = never

    1 = rarely

    2 = sometimes

    3 = often

    4 = all the time

8. To what extent do you leverage the Internet to build and maintain your networks?

    0 = never

    1 = rarely

    2 = sometimes

    3 = often

    4 = all the time

Score Your Results

Add your scores together for each and multiply the total by 5. You'll end up with an NQ between 0 and 160. The following chart interprets your score:

0–80	Below Average—Networking has not been on your radar screen.	You need to be much more active in establishing and maintaining connections.
81–110	Average—Nothing to brag about.	You could benefit from being much more proactive.
111–140	Above Average—A natural networker.	You are doing well, but a more systematic effort can help.
141–160	Networking Genius!	You know it takes ongoing effort to maintain your network.

The Leadership Challenge Activities Book
Copyright © 2010 by James M. Kouzes and Barry Z. Posner.
Reproduced by permission of Pfeiffer, an Imprint of Wiley. www.pfeiffer.com.

THE LEADERSHIP PERSPECTIVE MODEL

Submitted by Peter R. Garber

Objectives

- To help leaders better understand the perspective of those they lead and what is most important to them.
- To help leaders motivate others by focusing on what is really important to others rather than just thinking about their own objectives.
- To help leaders understand how focusing on what is important to employees achieves better results for reaching goals.

Audience

Any size group.

Time Required

30 to 40 minutes.

Materials and Equipment

- One copy of the Leadership Perspective Model for each participant.

Area Setup

Meeting or conference setup.

Process

1. Introduce the activity by explaining that the perspective that a leader has concerning what is of greatest importance to others can play an important role in any initiative that may

be undertaken at work. Perspective, for purposes of this activity, means how a person may perceive the relative importance of something introduced by a leader.

2. Distribute or display a copy of the Leadership Perspective Model.

3. Introduce the Leadership Perspective Model as a tool to help participants better understand the different perspectives of both the *leader* and *employee*(s) on any given initiative, program, problem, change, or other thing that may be introduced.

4. Point out that, on the vertical scale, the arrow pointing upward indicates a continuum of that which is important to the leader, from low to high.

5. Next point out that the horizontal scale, a continuum of what is important to the employee, is displayed from low to high following the direction of the arrow.

6. Explain each of the four quadrants of the model as it relates to these importance factors for both the leader and the employee. For example:
   - Quadrant A represents that which is of high importance to the leader but of low importance to the employee.
   - Quadrant B represents that which is of high importance to both the leader and the employee.
   - Quadrant C represents that which is of low importance to both the leader and the employee.
   - Quadrant D represents that which is of low importance to the leader but of high importance to the employee.

7. Explain that this model can be helpful because it allows participants to better analyze why a certain initiative, program, problem, or change may or may not be readily accepted by either leaders or employees.

587

8. To further elaborate, give examples of real-life occurrences at work as they might relate to this model, for example, *reducing costs*. Ask participants, "Which quadrant do you believe that reducing costs might fit into?" The answer is most likely that this would fit into Quadrant A. Reducing costs is typically most important to the leader who is responsible for such an initiative, particularly during difficult economic times when a leader is held accountable for achieving this objective. Employees may also be interested in reducing costs but probably don't have the same accountability or pressures on them to achieve reduced costs. In truth, reducing costs is likely something not very pleasant or desirable for employees for many reasons, including a possible lack of resources to do their jobs properly.

9. Contrast Quadrant A with Quadrant D, which is where a certain initiative, program, problem, or change is of low importance to the leader but of high importance to the employee. Ask participants to think of examples when this might be the case. One example may be vacation time. There may be any number of issues that occur in an organization that could potentially affect vacations, such as changes in the scheduling rules, the amount of vacation time that is permitted, how vacations are allotted, even reductions in the amount of vacation time that employees are permitted to take as a cost-reduction initiative. These are all matters that are typically of great importance to employees but may be less important to a leader, who sees vacation as more of a problem or challenge to schedule.

10. Continue the discussion by reviewing Quadrant B, which is of high importance to both the leader and the employee. Ask: "What might be examples of Quadrant B?" Bring out things such

as the success of the organization, the price of the company's stock (particularly if there is an employee stock plan in place), workplace safety, bonus programs, recognition programs, or new career opportunities. Discuss how Quadrant B initiatives might be received by both leaders and employees.

11. Finally, review Quadrant C, which is of low importance to both the leader and the employee. This quadrant may be a little more difficult to identify and discuss. A little humor might be interjected into the discussion of this quadrant by offering an example of a required meeting or course that everyone is required to attend but is of little perceived value.

12. Emphasize that using the Leadership Perspective Model can foretell how enthusiastically a leadership initiative may be received, depending on where it would likely fall on this matrix.
    - Obviously, those things that fall into Quadrant B are most interesting to everyone involved. This natural interest enables the initiative to be implemented more easily. Focusing on Quadrant B initiatives will potentially will yield better results.
    - Conversely, Quadrant A matters will not be received with the same level of interest by employees. Leaders will be more successful if they accept this perspective from the very beginning of an initiative.
    - Quadrant D matters probably will be enthusiastically perceived by employees. However, the importance of this quadrant is sometimes not appreciated by leaders more focused on Quadrant A issues. This can cause problems, especially relating to how a leader is perceived by employees. If the leader is overly focused on Quadrant A matters at the expense of Quadrant D ones, employees may begin to feel that the leader

is insensitive to their needs and only worried about achieving bottom-line results. This can result in low morale or other problems between a leader and those he or she supervisors.

13. Conclude the activity by explaining that, as leaders, participants should balance their time and attention in Quadrants A, B, and D, taking extra effort to appreciate and be sensitive to the importance to employees of those matters that fall into D.

14. Finally, explain that the appropriate amount of time and emphasis should be placed on Quadrant C issues. There is little value in trying to portray something that falls into this quadrant as anything other than what it really is, a low priority but still necessary activity or initiative for everyone.

15. Debrief the activity by asking participant to discuss their personal experiences dealing with these different quadrant issues and sharing best practices dealing with each one. Use these questions to initiate discussion:
    • What thoughts do you have about the model?
    • What specific leadership behaviors will be most useful in each of the four quadrants?
    • Which of The Five Practices are apparent in the four quadrants?
    • As a leader, what might you do differently as a result of this discussion?

Peter R. Garber is the author of more than forty books on a variety of business, human resources, and leadership topics, including *Leadership Lessons from Mom*; *Leadership Lessons from Dad* (HRD Press), as well as his most recent leadership book entitled

25 Legendary Leadership Activities (HRD Press, 2008). Peter has been employed by PPG Industries, Inc., as a human resource professional for the past thirty years and resides in Pittsburgh, Pennsylvania.

Peter R. Garber
610 Garden Way
Wexford, PA, 15090
  Phone: (412) 434-2009
  Email: garber@ppg.com

THE LEADERSHIP PERSPECTIVE MODEL

A High importance to leader Low importance to the employee	**B** High importance to the leader High importance to the employee
C Low importance to leader Low importance to employee	**D** Low importance to leader High importance to the employee

CROSS YOUR ARMS

Submitted by Jonas Hansson

Objective

- To become aware of how difficult it could be to change behaviors.

Audience

Two to two hundred participants in any educational situation who are interested in improving their leadership skills.

Time Required

15 minutes.

Materials and Equipment

- None.

Area Setup

Nothing special.

Process

1. Begin by saying, "Please stand and cross your arms."
2. Ask the participants to notice which arm they put on top.
3. Ask the participants to uncross their arms and then to cross their arms the opposite way, the other arm on top. It will probably not be as easy as it was the first time.
4. Have them continue to try to cross their arms in the new configurations until they are successful.

593

5. Ask, "What happened when you crossed your arms the first time?" You will probably hear that they just did it without thinking.

6. Ask, "What happened when you crossed your arms with the other arm on top?" The participants will likely laugh and say it was difficult.

7. Discuss why it is difficult to do things in another way than the ordinary. Elicit a few responses. Explain that human beings need to create maps in their mind to handle life. We cannot think of everything every time we do something. The capacity of the brain is limited when it handles sensory impressions. We have to automatize things we do often. For example, locking the door when we leave home. How many times have you asked yourself the question, "Did I lock the door?" And when you went back to check it you found that it was locked. You did it without thinking.

8. Ask participants how it felt when they crossed their arms the other way. Elicit several responses. Ask them to discuss how they felt. Ask how many gave up trying or wanted to give up. Discuss how this could influence the possibility of making changes. Ask how this feeling can influence them when practicing new knowledge and skills.

9. Comment that, if we have found a "better" way to do things, it would be good to just start practicing it the better way. Ask, "What can you do to encourage practicing a new skill or a 'better' way?" State that, as participants learn better ways to be leaders, they need to continue to practice them—even if they are uncomfortable and difficult at first. If it is "better" to put the other arm on top, hopefully they will begin to practice the "better" way. If one of The Five Practices offers a better way, hopefully they will begin to use it.

Jonas Hansson is a consultant at the Centre of Leadership in Umeå. He works at Umeå University as a teacher at the police program. Jonas became a police officer 1993 and is also currently teaching conflict management, communication and self-protection, group processes, leadership, and human rights. He has experience in practical police work as a team member and as a team leader. His vision is to obtain a university degree and conduct research.

Jonas Hansson
The Centre of Leadership in Sweden
Ledarsskapscentrum
Box 7978, 907 19 Umeå
Sweden
  Phone: 0046730234415
  Email: jonas.hansson@ledarskapscentrum.se
  Website: www.ledarskapscentrum.se

BEAT THE CLOCK: MAKE DELEGATION WORK FOR YOU!

Submitted by Deborah Spring Laurel

Objectives

- To discuss the five delegation decision categories.
- To explain how to implement each delegation decision.
- To provide real-life examples of implementation strategies.

Audience

A minimum of ten participants so the group can split into five teams. No maximum number.

Time Required

90 minutes.

Materials and Equipment

- One Delegation Decision Categories handout for each participant.
- One Beat the Clock: Make Delegation Work for You! handout for each participant.
- One different Delegation Decision Category Worksheet for each team.
- *(Optional)* Prizes for the winning team in each round and for the grand winner.

Area Setup

Five tables in a sunburst arrangement.

Process

1. Give each participant a copy of the Delegation Decision Categories handout. Introduce and discuss the five Delegation Decision Categories. Assign a different delegation decision category to each table and provide the tables with the appropriate Delegation Decision Category Worksheets.

2. Give each participant a copy of the Beat the Clock: Make Delegation Work for You! handout. Explain the format for Beat the Clock. There are two rounds of 10 minutes each. In round 1, the teams have 10 minutes to list as many items as possible for their delegation decision categories. In round 2, the teams will have 10 minutes to come up with examples of how someone on the team has successfully applied the different items on the team's list. Each round will be scored separately; the winning team will be the one with the largest combined total for both rounds.

3. Begin round 1.

4. At the end of round 1, have each team report out the number of items on its list. Give the teams 1 point for every item on their lists. Name the team with the highest number of points as the winner of round 1. (*Optional:* Reward the members of the winning team.)

5. Begin round 2.

6. At the end of round 2, have the team that focused on the first delegation decision category read each item on its list, providing an actual application example for each item.

7. As the first team provides an example for an item, poll the other teams to see whether they accept the example as valid. If so, the

team will receive 1 point for that item. If the other teams do not accept the team's examples as valid, or if the team was unable to come up with a real-life example, the team will not receive any credit for that item.

8. Repeat Steps 6 and 7 for the four remaining delegation decision category teams.

9. Name the team with the highest number of points as the winner of round 2. (*Optional:* reward the members of the winning team.) Name the team with the highest total number of points from both rounds 1 and 2 as the grand winner. (*Optional:* reward the members of the winning team.)

Deborah Spring Laurel has been a trainer and a consultant in workplace learning and performance improvement for over thirty years. She was adjunct faculty in executive management at the University of Wisconsin-Madison for thirty years. The principal of Laurel and Associates, Ltd., Deborah has her M.D. from the University of Wisconsin-Madison. She is a past president of the South Central Wisconsin Chapter of ASTD and facilitates the three-day ASTD Training Certificate Program.

Deborah Spring Laurel
Laurel and Associates, Ltd.
917 Vilas Avenue
Madison, WI 53715
   Phone: (608) 255-2010
   Email: dlaurel@laurelandassociates.com
   Website: www.laurelandassociates.com

DELEGATION DECISION CATEGORIES

Certain decisions have to be made in any delegation:

1. When to delegate.
2. What to delegate, including how well and by when the task must be accomplished.
3. Who should be given responsibility for the delegated task, and how much authority should be granted to this individual.
4. How to delegate the task and what to tell the employee.
5. How to follow up on the performance of a delegated task.

BEAT THE CLOCK: MAKE DELEGATION WORK FOR YOU!

Instructions

This is a time-challenged exercise with two rounds.

Round 1

1. Your team will be assigned one of the delegation decision categories.

2. Your team will have 10 minutes to list as many items as possible for your assigned category.

3. Points: Your team will receive 1 point for every item on your list.

4. The team with the highest number of points wins this round.

Round 2

1. Your team will have an additional 10 minutes to come up with examples of how someone on your team has actually successfully applied the items on your list.

2. When it is time for your category, your team will read each item on your list, providing the actual application example.

3. Points: If the other teams accept your example as valid, your team receives 1 point for that item. If the other teams do not accept your example as valid, or if your team cannot come up with a real-life example, your team will not receive any credit for that item.

4. The team with the highest number of points wins this second round.

Grand Winner

The team with the highest total number of points from both rounds is the grand winner.

DELEGATION DECISION CATEGORY 1

When to Delegate

What would indicate to a supervisor that delegation may be necessary?

Round 1: INDICATIONS

Round 2: EXAMPLES

DELEGATION DECISION CATEGORY 2

How should a supervisor decide what to delegate, including how well and by when the task must be accomplished?

Round 1: CONSIDERATIONS

Round 2: EXAMPLES

DELEGATION DECISION CATEGORY 3

How should a supervisor decide who should be given responsibility for a delegated task and how much authority should be granted to this individual?

Round 1: CONSIDERATIONS

Round 2: EXAMPLES

DELEGATION DECISION CATEGORY 4

What should a supervisor tell an employee when delegating a task?
Round 1: POINTS TO INCLUDE

Round 2: EXAMPLES

DELEGATION DECISION CATEGORY 5

How can a supervisor follow up on the performance of a delegated task?

Round 1: OPTIONS

Round 2: EXAMPLES

BUILDING LEADERSHIP

Submitted by Linda S. Eck Mills

Objective

- To explore leadership requirements of building a team.

Audience

Groups of three to six members each.

Time Required

20 to 30 minutes.

Materials and Equipment

- A bag for each group with the following items:
  - One roll of Scotch® tape.
  - Twelve straws.
  - Twelve bathroom-size drinking cups.
  - Twenty index cards.
- Stop watch or other timing device.
- Bell, buzzer, or other noise to signal the end of time.
- Tape measure.
- Flip chart and markers.

Area Setup

Table for each group.

Process

1. Say that, when working to build teamwork or communication skills, a great way to get individuals to experience potential trials

is to engage them in a building exercise. The goal of this particular exercise is to build the tallest free-standing object they can in 10 minutes. Define free-standing as: no participant can be physically touching any part of the structure and it cannot lean against another object when the time is up.

2. Tell them that during the first 8 minutes participants are not allowed to speak or write any communication to the rest of the team. During the last 2 minutes, participants may speak.

3. Give the teams their bags of supplies and begin to time the activity. Announce the 8-minute point.

4. At 10 minutes, call time and use a tape measure to "judge" the building projects.

5. Use the flip chart and markers to summarize the activity, using the following questions:
   - What was it like to not communicate with the rest of the team?
   - How were decisions made during that time?
   - How was leadership determined?
   - What were the dynamics of the team?
   - How did the leadership and dynamic change after you could talk with each other?
   - What creative ideas were put into play? (*Note:* Creative teams start their building on the table. Really creative teams use other available objects such as chairs or glasses on top of the table to get even more height.)
   - What role does leadership play when building a team?
   - How can you use these points and concepts to build your own teams?

Linda S. Eck Mills, M.B.A., owns Dynamic Communication Services, a firm specializing in presenting information that has immediate and relevant implications to the work and lives of individuals by linking common, everyday objects to any topic. Her work includes professional speaking, training, facilitating, and career/life coaching. Linda is the author of the self-published book *From Mundane to Ah Ha!—Effective Training Objects* and a contributor to *Trainer's Warehouse Book of Games* (Pfeiffer, 2008), *The 2009 Pfeiffer Annual: Training,* and has written over 160 articles.

Linda S. Eck Mills, M.B.A.
Dynamic Communication Services
20 Worman Lane
Bernville, PA 19506
  Phone: (610) 488-7010
  Email: AhHaBook@aol.com
  Website: www.theconsultantsforum.com/eckmills.htm

EMOTIONAL INTELLIGENCE FOR EXEMPLARY LEADERSHIP

Submitted by Dominique Parrish

Objectives

- To raise awareness of the value and relevance of emotional intelligence for exemplary leaders.
- To identify emotional intelligence practices that promote exemplary leadership.

Audience

Ten to thirty participants who are interested in enhancing their leadership skills.

Time Required

60 to 90 minutes.

Materials and Equipment

- Paper and pens.
- Whiteboard, blank flip chart, or other medium for recording information and appropriate markers.
- Prepared PowerPoint slide/chart/overhead detailing The Five Practices of Exemplary Leadership®.
- One copy of Practices of Exemplary Leadership for each participant.
- One copy of Practicing Exemplary Leadership for each participant.
- One copy of Competence View of Emotional Intelligence for each participant.

- One copy of The Role of Emotional Intelligence in Exemplary Leadership for each participant.
- One copy of Exploring Emotional Intelligence for Exemplary Leadership—Enable Others to Act for all participants on every third team.
- One copy of Exploring Emotional Intelligence for Exemplary Leadership—Model the Way for all participants on every third team.
- One copy of Exploring Emotional Intelligence for Exemplary Leadership—Encourage the Heart for all participants on every third team.

Area Setup

Workspace with tables and room for small group work.

Process

1. Begin by saying, "Let's start by examining The Five Principles of Exemplary Leadership®, espoused by Jim Kouzes and Barry Posner."

2. Show the prepared PowerPoint slide/chart/overhead. Hand participants copies of the Practices of Exemplary Leadership handout. Briefly review each of the practices.

3. Explain that "While each of these practices is highly important for leadership, today we are going to specifically focus on three of them: Enable Others to Act, Model the Way, and Encourage the Heart."

4. Give participants a copy of the Practicing Exemplary Leadership handout.

5. Ask participants to reflect on the three practices detailed on the sheet and briefly record in the respective table columns instances

they can recall or have encountered when these practices were demonstrated in the workplace.

6. Invite participants to share their experiences, recording these on a chart under the same headings as those on the handout. Allow about 15 minutes for this discussion.

7. Give participants copies of the Competence View of Emotional Intelligence handout and introduce the notion of emotional intelligence by saying, "Daniel Goleman suggests that highly effective leaders employ specific emotional competencies and skills. His view of emotional intelligence categorizes emotional competencies into four dimensions: self-awareness, self-management, social awareness, and social skills. Self-awareness and self-management competencies relate to an individual recognizing and accurately assessing his or her own emotions and the effects that these emotions can have on him or her and others; they relate to appreciating your own strengths and limitations and responsibly managing these."

8. Read through the competencies listed under the self-awareness and self-management dimensions.

9. Focus on the social competencies by saying, "The social competencies within the social awareness and social skills dimensions are predominantly concerned with understanding others and appropriately and effectively managing interpersonal relationships."

10. Read through the competencies listed under the social awareness and social skills dimensions.

11. Ask the participants, "Do you think there are any synergies or overlaps between Kouzes and Posner's Practices of Exemplary

Leadership and Goleman's competencies of emotional intelligence?"

12. Facilitate the discussion of overlaps or alignment between Kouzes and Posner's Practices of Exemplary Leadership and Goleman's competencies of emotional intelligence.

13. Present a possible alignment between Kouzes and Posner's Practices of Exemplary Leadership and Goleman's competencies of emotional intelligence as detailed in The Role of Emotional Intelligence in Exemplary Leadership handout.

14. Organize participants into small groups of three to five participants. Assign each group one of these three practices of effective leadership: Enable Others to Act, Model the Way, or Encourage the Heart.

15. Give participants copies of the Exploring Emotional Intelligence for Exemplary Leadership handout related to their assigned principle of effective leadership (Enable Others to Act, Model the Way, or Encourage the Heart).

16. Ask groups to look at the emotional intelligence competencies listed under their assigned effective leadership principles and identify some of the ways in which they could practically demonstrate the emotional intelligence competencies listed in their work environment within their teams. Have them list these on the worksheet. Allow about 15 minutes.

17. Have small groups share their practical strategies with the large group.

18. After each group has shared its practical strategies, invite the remainder of the participants to share any additional strategies they can suggest.

19. Ask participants to take a moment to think about how often their behaviors actually reflect the strategies they listed or the strategies any of the other groups mentioned.

20. Invite participants to reflect on the activities they have just completed and consider aspects of their leadership they might adapt or enhance in light of what they have learned during this session.

21. Have participants write 1-minute papers. Say "I want you to engage in a reflective journaling activity to finish up. This is an exercise in which you write without interruption for 1 minute. I want you to write down the aspects of your leadership you will develop in light of the activities you have just completed. This is not going to be shared with anyone; the only audience for this reflective writing is you, so be as candid and honest as you can."

Dominique Parrish has worked in the education, not-for-profit, and government sectors for more than twenty-three years. She specializes in training, policy and resource development, research and innovation, strategic planning, and project management. Dominique has significant expertise in the areas of emotional intelligence and leadership and is currently completing her doctoral thesis. Dominique has been extensively involved in working with organizations to enhance and promote emotionally intelligent work environments.

Dominique Parrish
Learning Achievements and Solutions
4 Hennessy Lane
Figtree, NSW 2525
Australia
Phone: +61 2 4229 2529
Email: dom@parag.com.au

PRACTICES OF EXEMPLARY LEADERSHIP

1. **Model the Way:** having integrity and acting as a role model in both actions and words.

2. **Inspire a Shared Vision:** enthusing others with a vision of how things could be and presenting strategies for attaining this vision.

3. **Challenge the Process:** engaging in ongoing examination of why and how things are done and willingly allowing others to scrutinize and challenge one's own actions.

4. **Enable Others to Act:** having confidence in the abilities of individuals and enabling them to achieve to their potential.

5. **Encourage the Heart:** being empathetic to the needs and personalities of individuals and tailoring recognition and feedback to meet these needs and temperament.

Source: J.M. Kouzes & B.Z. Posner. (1998). *Encouraging the Heart.* San Francisco: Jossey-Bass.

PRACTICING EXEMPLARY LEADERSHIP

Briefly describe any experiences you can recall or have encountered that have Enabled Others to Act; Modeled the Way; or Encouraged the Heart.

- Having integrity and acting as a role model in both actions and words.
- Having confidence in the abilities of individuals and enabling them to achieve to their potential.
- Being empathetic to the needs and personalities of individuals and tailoring recognition and feedback to meet these needs and temperament.

Source: J.M. Kouzes & B.Z. Posner. (1998). *Encouraging the Heart.* San Francisco: Jossey-Bass.

COMPETENCE VIEW OF EMOTIONAL INTELLIGENCE

Self-Awareness	Self-Management	Social Awareness	Social Skills
Emotional self-awareness— recognizing one's emotions and their effects	**Self-control**— keeping disruptive emotions and impulses under control	**Empathy**— understanding others and taking active interest in their concerns	**Developing others**— sensing others' development needs and bolstering their abilities
Accurate self-assessment—knowing one's strengths and limitations	**Trustworthiness**— honesty and integrity	**Organizational awareness**— empathizing at the organizational level	**Leadership**— inspiring and guiding groups and people
Self-confidence—a strong sense of one's self-worth and personal capabilities	**Conscientiousness**— responsibly managing oneself	**Service orientation**— recognizing and meeting customers' needs	**Influence**—wielding interpersonal influence tactics
	Adaptability— flexibility with challenges		**Communication**— sending clear, convincing messages
	Achievement—drive to improve		**Change catalyst**—initiating or managing change
	Initiative—readiness to act		**Conflict management**— resolving disagreements
			Building bonds— nurturing instrumental relationships
			Teamwork and collaboration— creating a shared vision
			Synergy in teamwork— working with others toward shared goals

Based on D. Goleman. (2000). Intelligent leadership. *Executive Excellence, 17*(4), 17.

616

THE ROLE OF EMOTIONAL INTELLIGENCE IN EXEMPLARY LEADERSHIP

Competencies of Self-Management

- **Self-control**—keeping disruptive emotions and impulses under control
- **Trustworthiness**—honest and integrity
- **Conscientiousness**—responsibly managing oneself
- **Adaptability**—flexibility with challenges
- **Achievement**—drive to improve
- **Initiative**—readiness to act

Competencies of Social Skills

- **Developing others**—sensing others' development needs and bolstering their abilities
- **Leadership**—inspiring and guiding groups and people
- **Influence**—wielding interpersonal influence tactics
- **Communication**—sending clear, convincing messages.
- **Change catalyst**—initiating or managing change
- **Conflict management**—resolving disagreements
- **Building bonds**—nurturing instrumental relationships
- **Teamwork and** collaboration—creating a shared vision
- **Synergy in teamwork**—working with others toward shared goals

Competencies of Social Awareness

- **Empathy**—understanding others and taking active interest in their concerns
- **Organizational awareness**—empathizing at the organizational level
- **Service orientation**—recognizing and meeting customers' needs

Sources: J.M. Kouzes & B.Z. Posner. (1998). *Encouraging the Heart.* San Francisco: Jossey-Bass.
D. Goleman. (2000). Intelligent leadership. *Executive Excellence, 17*(4), 17.

EXPLORING EMOTIONAL INTELLIGENCE FOR EXEMPLARY LEADERSHIP

Enable Others to Act

Competencies of Social Skills

- **Developing others**—sensing others' development needs and bolstering their abilities
- **Leadership**—inspiring and guiding groups and people
- **Influence**—wielding interpersonal influence tactics
- **Communication**—sending clear, convincing messages.
- **Change catalyst**—initiating or managing change
- **Conflict management**—resolving disagreements
- **Building bonds**—nurturing instrumental relationships
- **Teamwork and** collaboration—creating a shared vision
- **Synergy in teamwork**—working with others toward shared goals

Practical applications of these emotional intelligence competencies include:

Sources: J.M. Kouzes & B.Z. Posner. (1998). *Encouraging the Heart.* San Francisco: Jossey-Bass.
D. Goleman. (2000). Intelligent leadership. *Executive Excellence, 17*(4), 17.

EXPLORING EMOTIONAL INTELLIGENCE FOR EXEMPLARY LEADERSHIP

Model the Way

Competencies of Self-Management

- **Self-control**—keeping disruptive emotions and impulses under control
- **Trustworthiness**—honest and integrity
- **Conscientiousness**—responsibly managing oneself
- **Adaptability**—flexibility with challenges
- **Achievement**—drive to improve
- **Initiative**—readiness to act

Practical applications of these emotional intelligence competencies include:

Sources: J.M. Kouzes & B.Z. Posner. (1998). *Encouraging the Heart.* San Francisco: Jossey-Bass. D. Goleman. (2000). Intelligent leadership. *Executive Excellence, 17*(4), 17.

EXPLORING EMOTIONAL INTELLIGENCE FOR EXEMPLARY LEADERSHIP

Competencies of Social Awareness

- **Empathy**—understanding others and taking active interest in their concerns
- **Organizational awareness**—empathizing at the organizational level
- **Service orientation**—recognizing and meeting customers' needs

Practical applications of these emotional intelligence competencies include:

Sources: J.M. Kouzes & B.Z. Posner. (1998). *Encouraging the Heart.* San Francisco: Jossey-Bass. D. Goleman. (2000). Intelligent leadership. *Executive Excellence, 17*(4), 17.

USING THE MIND SCREEN TECHNIQUE FOR FOCUS*

Submitted by Carole E. Pearce

Objective

- To practice a tool to increase focus and productivity on team projects.

Audience

Suitable for one person or a small group.

Time Required

The activity lasts for a few minutes each time utilized.

Materials and Equipment

- Imagination and your mind.

Area Setup

For one person, any place will do. For a small group, a conference table or a circle with chairs.

Process

Phase 1—Preparing for a Meeting

Close your eyes. Focus on the black space that you see. Clear your head of all thoughts. Imagine seeing a blue sky with puffy white clouds on your mind screen. Just focus on that image for a bit.

---

*Mind Screen Technique (MST) was originally used to enhance performance in a stationary cycling class. The effectiveness of this process is quite surprising and exciting! Since leaders are held accountable for completion of projects, MST has great value in the workplace.

Then shift your thoughts to the leadership project. Think about the project and nothing more. Imagine what it will feel like when your project has been successfully completed. Also imagine your sense of accomplishment as you are going through the steps toward completion. Now visualize the team players, those who are designated to assist with the project. Imagine that each one of them is cooperating and completing the tasks at hand, using the most efficient and best method to get the job done. Continue on this view, seeing team members getting along with one another, complimenting each other, and celebrating small victories along the way. Visualize only positive outcomes. Negative circumstances and team members do not exist.

Phase 2—Team Meeting

Reinforce your positive calm demeanor while working with the team members. Focus only on the positive comments made and the positive suggestions offered by each team member. If a negative comment is offered, just acknowledge the contributor and move on with your meeting agenda. Remember to guide the participants in a positive manner, focusing only on the good ideas and the helpful comments made by others. Continue to emphasize positive aspects of all contributions and suggestions that are brought to the table.

Phase 3—Reporting Team Results to Your Supervisor

When providing your supervisor with a summary of your leadership project, focus only on the good portions of your meeting and the successful completion of various components of the project.

Phase 4

Continue the focus of capturing only the positive parts of the project. If it is necessary to note any challenges, frame them in a positive manner.

Phase 5—Keep a Leadership Journal

As you are flowing through the leadership project, keep a journal of your behavior and activities as well as the behavior and actions of others. This will reinforce your efforts in using the Mind Screen Technique.

Phase 6—Train Others in Mind Screen Technique (MST)

Once you are confident using the MST, share with co-workers and colleagues. Just imagine what it would be like if everyone in your organization focused solely on the positive outcomes.

Carole E. Pearce, D.Ed., is currently a faculty mentor and methodologist for doctoral students at Walden University. Previously, she worked in workforce development for six years assisting youth and adults meet their educational and career goals. She also developed a youth leadership program as well as developed and facilitated a life skills program for homeless adults.

Carole E. Pearce, D.Ed.
Faculty in The Richard W. Riley College of Education and
Leadership, Walden University
132 Panorama Drive
State College, PA 16801
    Phone: (814) 466-6662
    Email: carole.pearce@yahoo.com or carole.pearce@waldenu.edu

LISTENING DEEPLY AS A LEADER

Submitted by Mary Stelletello

Objectives

- To assist leaders in understanding the importance of listening.
- To practice facilitative listening skills.

Audience

Fifteen to twenty-five participants.

Time Required

90 minutes.

Materials and Equipment

- One Determine What You Want to Do worksheet for each participant.
- One Listening Techniques handout for each participant.
- One Observer Worksheet for each participant.
- One Keys to Becoming a Skilled Listener for each participant.

Area Setup

Large group in conference room or circle, then ability to move into trios for the exercise.

Process

1. Give participants copies of the Determine What You Want to Do worksheet and ask them to complete it. Allow about 15 minutes.

2. Give participants copies of the Listening Techniques handout and review it with them, providing and asking for examples. Ask what questions they have.

3. Ask the group to break into trios to practice and discuss listening using paraphrasing, mirroring, and drawing out techniques. Allow about 10 minutes.

4. After 10 minutes, provide instructions to the trios and give everyone a copy of the Observer Worksheet. Tell them each will have a role: speaker, listener, or observer. Further state that they will all have an opportunity to play each of the roles. Continue describing the roles as:
   • Speaker, share your vision.
   • Listener, demonstrate active listening through utilizing the skills we discussed.
   • Observer, observe the listener on utilizing the skills and make notes on the worksheet.
   Tell them they have 10 minutes. After 10 minutes, call time.

5. Have each trio discuss what happened:
   • Observer, provide feedback to listener (things done well, what can be improved).
   • Speaker, provide feedback to the listener of "When you said X, this was my experience."
   • Listener just LISTEN.
   Allow 5 to 10 minutes.

6. Instruct the trios to rotate positions: speaker to listener, listener to observer, observer to speaker. Allow 10 minutes and then have them provide feedback as described in Step 5.

7. Repeat Step 6 so that everyone has had an opportunity to be in each role.

8. Debrief as a large group.
   - What was it like to be the listener?
   - Speaker what was it like to be listened to?
   - What did you learn?
   - How will this help you be a better leader?
9. Wrap up by giving each participant a copy of Keys to Becoming a Skilled Listener.

Mary Stelletello, M.A., M.B.A., is a senior associate with La Piana Consulting. Mary brings more than fifteen years of experience in nonprofit management to the firm. She has strong skills in organization and leadership development and planning and facilitation. She is active in community service, has been the recipient of International Fellowship in Community Development sponsored by the W.K. Kellogg Foundation, and has participated in the Salzburg Seminar in Austria on the topic of Engaging Youth in Community Development. Mary holds an M.A. in Latin American studies and an M.B.A. in international management from the University of New Mexico. She is fluent in Spanish and speaks some Portuguese.

Mary Stelletello
Senior Associate, La Piana Consulting
6400 Hollis Street, Suite 15
Emeryville, CA 94608
   Phone: (510) 808-4143
   Email: Stelletello@lapiana.org
   Website: www.lapiana.org

DETERMINE WHAT YOU WANT TO DO

What I want to accomplish: Why do I want this? (List all the things you want to achieve on the job and why.)

If I could invent the future, what future would I invent for myself and my organization?

What mission in life absolutely obsesses me?

What is my dream about my work?

What's my burning passion?

What work do I find absorbing, involving, enthralling?

What will happen in ten years if I remain absorbed, involved, and enthralled in that work?

What does my ideal organization look like?

Use this information to write your ideal and unique image of the future for yourself below.

LISTENING TECHNIQUES

Empathy	Put aside your own biography long enough to understand the other person. Suspend your judgment(s) and become really curious about what this means to the other person, not what it means to you.
Mirroring/Reflecting	Gain clarity by repeating the exact words back. If the speaker says a single sentence, repeat it back verbatim. If the speaker says more than one sentence, repeat back key words. *Use the speaker's words, not your words.* Maintain the tone of your voice as warm and accepting, regardless of the speaker's voice. Key purpose of mirroring is trust. Don't be phony, be yourself.
Paraphrase	Rephrase what was said using your own words and understanding. Use roughly the same amount of words as the speaker when you paraphrase. If the speaker's statement contains many sentences, summarize. To build objectivity, occasionally preface your paraphrase with: "It sounds like you're saying. . . . "Let me see if I understand you. . . . Is this what you mean?"

Drawing Out	Support people to clarify, develop and refine their ideas. Ask open-ended nondirective questions that do not have obvious answers, or can't be answered yes or no. "Can you say more about that?" "Tell me more." "How so?" "How is that working for you?" "Can you give an example?"
Body Language	Use your body to express openness, connection, and understanding. Make eye contact, be present.
Minimal Encouragers	Simply encourage people to talk by nodding, and verbally, but subtly encourage them to continue.

KEYS TO BECOMING A SKILLED LISTENER

- *Make the intentional choice to listen.* This means that you stop talking to others, and to yourself. Put much more energy into being receptive, not productive.

- *Invest in the other person's point of view, no matter how offensive it is to you.* As an exercise, listen to a point of view that is as far away from yours as possible. Listen, take it in, and see how it makes sense, not that you believe it or agree with it, but that you simply understand it.

- *Look, act, and be interested.* Sending a message of disinterest or disbelief will stop a dialogue quicker than anything will. You want to create an atmosphere of understanding and, as Covey states, you must "seek first to understand, and then be understood."

- *Do not ever interrupt, block, or stop communication.* Sit past your tolerance level.

- *Make your comments on the interests the speaker presents, not on your position.* Give feedback to the listener that you hear what is behind the position he or she is staking out. This is the emotional as well as the cognitive interests.

- *Listen to the words and the music.* Values, emotions, and interests all are expressed in dialogue. You miss a great deal if you only tend to the thoughts.

- *Try not to judge or evaluate as long as you can.* Listen to the person, the message, and the continuity of thought. The question is never, "Why does this person want this?" but "What does this person really want?"

- *Pay attention to your own instruments.* What are your intentions and emotions? What is negotiable for you, and what is not negotiable?

- *If anger or negative emotions surface, work hard to add light, not heat to the process.* Find your center and focus on understanding.

- *Allow silences and pauses, ask open-ended questions.* Use constant feedback to make sure that you are getting the right information.

- Remember, the more you listen, the more you will be listened to.

OBSERVER WORKSHEET

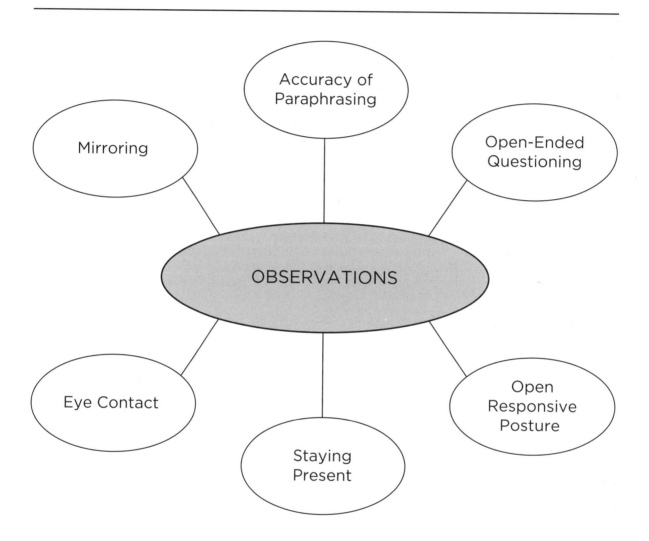

Accuracy of Paraphrasing

Mirroring

Open-Ended Questioning

OBSERVATIONS

Eye Contact

Open Responsive Posture

Staying Present

The Leadership Challenge Activities Book
Copyright © 2010 by James M. Kouzes and Barry Z. Posner.
Reproduced by permission of Pfeiffer, an Imprint of Wiley. www.pfeiffer.com.

MY WAY OR THE HIGHWAY

Submitted by Joanne G. Sujansky

Objectives

- To identify different reactions individuals have to change.
- To challenge individuals' thinking about change.

Audience

Small groups of four to six. Ideal group size is twenty-five.

Time Required

Approximately 30 to 50 minutes, depending on group size.

Materials and Equipment

- Copy and cut the provided My Way or the Highway master set cards (one card for each person). The master set contains twenty-eight cards. Extra cards are provided in case someone says, "I need a different card."

Area Setup

Round tables and movable chairs.

Facilitator Notes

In their book, *The Leadership Challenge*, Jim Kouzes and Barry Posner explore the common practices and commitments of effective leaders. They propose that the single word common to all great leaders is "we," explaining that "Exemplary leaders enlist the support and assistance of all those who must make the project work. They involve . . . those who must live with the results."

This activity gives leaders a chance to see how diverse or similar people's views of change really are. By identifying the perceptions of those involved in the change, this activity helps leaders to engage employees in planned or projected changes.

Process

1. Distribute one card to each participant.

2. Provide an example by reading a card and explaining whether or not the sentence on the card is true of you and why.

3. Instruct group members to form small groups of four to six and to select a spokesperson for the group. Have each group member read his or her card to the small group and explain why the statement is or is not true and why. Tell participants to limit comments to 1 minute.

4. Have members of each small group discuss reactions to change.

5. Reconvene the full group and ask the spokesperson from each group to briefly summarize what was discussed.

6. Ask participants what they learned or observed.

7. Debrief this activity by asking participants:
   - The cards reflect statements heard from employees during organizational change. What additional comments have you heard?
   - As adults, our many workplace experiences have influenced how we react to change. Who can share an example?
   - How different are we in the ways in which we handle change?

- It is exciting and challenging that we are all different. We can learn from one another's perspectives. When have you experienced this?
- There is no one right way to react or respond to change. How has this challenged the way you think of change?
- How does our discussion challenge your thinking as a leader about change?
- Activities are only useful if we transfer what we learn to the workplace. What will you transfer?

Joanne G. Sujansky, Ph.D., Certified Speaking Professional, Founder and CEO of KEYGroup® has worked with leaders for more than twenty-five years to make their workplaces more productive and profitable. She is a highly sought-after keynote speaker who has worked in more than thirty-five countries. Author of numerous books on leadership, change, and retention, her new book is *Keeping the Millennials: Why Companies Are Losing Billions of Dollars to This Generation and What to Do About It* (John Wiley & Sons, 2009).

Joanne G. Sujansky, Ph.D., CSP
KEYGroup®
1121 Boyce Road, 1800
Sainte Claire Plaza
Pittsburgh, PA 15241
  Phone: (724) 942-7900
  Email: jsujansky@keygroupconsulting.com
  Websites: www.joannesujansky.com and www.keygroupconsulting.com

635

MY WAY OR THE HIGHWAY

I do not like surprises.	I love surprises!
I never met a change I did not like.	I am a change junkie.
For me, change is like being boiled in oil.	For me, change is like a beautiful butterfly emerging from a cocoon.
For me, one change per year is enough.	My co-workers love change— I hate it.
The only changes I can tolerate well are changes in the weather.	Change my $5 bill, not my life.
We tried this before . . .	I embrace change.
When things stay the same for a long time, I feel secure.	The more things change, the more they stay the same.
Change makes me feel empowered.	It takes me a while, but when I finally decide to make a change . . . look out!
I cannot sit around and wait for change to happen—I have to look for it.	I know change is going to happen, but I do not search it out . . . I let it come to me.

I think that with every change there is a buried treasure waiting to be found.	I think that behind every change, there is a poisonous snake waiting to strike.
I believe that if things never changed, the world would be a more peaceful place.	I have to brace myself for change.
When a change is imposed upon me, I meet it enthusiastically.	When I cannot control a change that is happening to me, I become very frustrated and resentful of the change.
I meet change like I would meet an ocean wave.	I dive into change as if I am competing in the Olympics.
For me, change is like getting a chocolate-covered ice cream bar when I really wanted caramel.	I can always see the light at the end of the tunnel of change.

CHALLENGE LEADERSHIP THROUGH STRUCTURED REFLECTION INTERVIEWS

Submitted by Gary Wagenheim

Objectives

- To become better aware of leadership actions, feelings, and outcomes.
- To identify potential new leadership actions for increased effectiveness.
- To learn and develop a structured reflection practice.

Audience

Any size group may participate. It is best if there is an even number so members may divide into two-person teams.

Time required

30 to 45 minutes.

Materials and Equipment

- One copy of the Structured Reflection Interview Protocol for each participant.

Area Setup

A room large enough to accommodate a number of two-person conversations simultaneously so that each pair is afforded some privacy.

Process

1. Describe the learning objectives and give each participant a copy of the Structured Reflection Interview Protocol. Ask each

participant to think of a recent critical incident in his or her leadership. A critical incident is defined as a positive or negative incident deemed significant because it influenced adaptations or changes to their routine leadership actions. Provide an example from your experience. Give participants 5 to 7 minutes to think of a critical incident in their leadership.

2. Have participants pair up and take turns interviewing each other using the Structured Reflection Interview Protocol. Allow about 10 minutes for each interview so both participants receive equal opportunity to reflect. Encourage participants to use good active listening skills while interviewing, that is, appropriate eye contact and body language and asking follow-up opened-ended questions for clarification. Give a half-way signal after the first 10 minutes.

3. After both participants have been interviewed using the structured reflection interview protocol, lead a discussion about the activity by asking the following questions. You may need to point out that this discussion is actually a reflection on the structured reflection.

- What did you notice about yourself or the other person during the activity?
- What did you find most challenging or interesting about the process?
- What were you feeling during the activity?
- What did you learn from the activity?
- How will you apply what you have learned in the future?

Gary Wagenheim, Ph.D., owns Wagenheim Advisory Group, which provides training and development programs for international clients. He is an adjunct professor at Simon Fraser University and the Helsinki School of Economics and a former professor at Purdue University. He teaches courses in leadership and organizational behaviour. Gary has published in *The Journal of Management Education, The Human Resource Handbook, The Pfeiffer Annual for Developing Human Resources, 101 Great Games and Activities, The Training and Performance Sourcebook,* and the *2010 Pfeiffer Annual: Consulting.*

Gary Wagenheim, Ph.D.
Wagenheim Advisory Group
5865 Wiltshire Street
Vancouver, BC V6M 3L7
Canada
Phone: (604) 266-4866
Email: wagenhei@sfu.ca

STRUCTURED REFLECTION INTERVIEW PROTOCOL*

Could you tell me about a positive or negative critical incident you deem significant because it influenced adaptations or changes to your routine leadership actions?

Describe the critical incident: what happened and who was involved?

What was your leadership goal at the time?

What routine leadership actions were you taking?

*Source: Johns, C. (1994). Guided reflection. In A. Palmer, A. Burns, & C. Bulman (Eds.), *Reflective Practice in Nursing. The Growth of the Professional Practitioner* (pp. 110–130). Cornwall, UK: Blackwell Science Ltd.

What factors influenced adaptations or changes to your routine leadership actions?

What were the consequences of your new leadership actions?

How did you feel in the moment?

In hindsight, is there anything else you would change or do differently in your leadership?

What did you learn about your leadership from this experience?

How does this experience change your future leadership actions?

WHAT LEADERS DO TO INSPIRE (OR UNINSPIRE) FOLLOWERS*

Submitted by Michael Kroth and Martha Yopp

Objectives

- To solicit information, ideas, and opinions from followers and others about what makes work environments more inspiring.
- To listen carefully and learn real-life stories from people both outside and inside an organization.
- To reflect on themes and consistencies.
- To use the information to initiate purposeful change within the organization.

Audience

Employees, peers, and others one-on-one or in small groups. Interaction can be face-to-face or online.

Time Required

As much time as needed. It may take several hours over two or three weeks.

Materials and Equipment

- One copy Field Research: What Leaders Do to Inspire (or Uninspire) Followers for each participant.
- One copy of the Action Plan for each participant.

---

*This exercise is adapted from *Field Research: What Managers Do to Motivate or Demotivate Employees* (Kroth, 2006, p. 170).

643

- For an online version, use an online survey software package (asynchronous) or conduct an online discussion (synchronous).

Area Setup

Nothing special.

Process

1. For the next several days gather information for yourself. In various situations ask people what leaders do to inspire them at work and what they do to take their motivation for work away. Ask people how the great ones have actually involved their followers in creating a future vision for the organization. These are just casual conversations in line at the grocery story, waiting at the soccer field between periods, or sitting in a restaurant.

   During the interviews, you are not an organizational leader asking questions. You are just a neighbor or an assistant coach or a friend. You just happen to ask what they find inspiring about their work while talking about any number of other things. You are asking about other leaders in general, "What have leaders or managers you've had done to inspire you?" "What did that great boss of yours do to create a vision and a plan for the company that made you so enthusiastic?"

   You can do this either in casual conversations or ask people you know via informal email discussion or, more formally, through a short email survey.

2. Now do the same professionally, but outside your organization. Call or meet with followers you know in organizations similar to yours and ask them for some of their time. Email them if they

644

aren't located close by. Tell them you are just looking for real-life stories. Ask them the same questions as above.

3. Keep a record on the Field Research Worksheet (A through C on the sheet), and use it to reflect on how your own employees or followers would respond (D on the sheet).

4. Finally, do the same in your own organization. Realize that what you get might be somewhat biased, as people shade their feedback because you are in a position of power. The more trustworthy you are, the more concerned and truly interested in the follower's view, the more he or she will tell you the truth. Keep a record on the Field Research Worksheet and summarize what you've learned (E through H on the sheet).

5. Finally, put together an action plan to achieve an inspiring vision for your organization.

Michael Kroth, Ph.D., an assistant professor at the University of Idaho is a recipient of the university's Hoffman Award for Excellence in Teaching. He has written three books: *Transforming Work: The Five Keys to Achieving Trust, Commitment, and Passion in the Workplace,* with Dr. Patricia Boverie; *The Manager as Motivator* (Praeger, 2006); and *Career Development Basics* (ASTD Press, 2009) with McKay Christensen. He is a member of the National Speakers Association and is a member of the Theory Committee of the Academy of Human Resource Development.

Martha "Marty" Yopp, Ed.D., is a professor in adult and organizational learning at the University of Idaho Boise. Her most recent scholarship and research are in the area of developing teamwork and trust in a virtual environment. Dr. Yopp is the coordinator for the Adult and Organizational Learning program and enjoys active interaction with numerous doctoral students.

Michael Kroth, Ph.D.
University of Idaho
322 E. Front Street, Suite 440
Boise, ID 83702
  Phone: (208) 364-4042
  Email: mkroth@uidaho.edu
  Website: www.michaelkroth.com

Martha Yopp, Ed.D.
University of Idaho
322 E. Front Street, Suite 440
Boise, ID 83702
  Phone: (208) 364-9918
  Email: myopp@uidaho.edu

FIELD RESEARCH: WHAT LEADERS DO TO INSPIRE (OR UNINSPIRE) FOLLOWERS

My Record of What People Have Told Me

External Data Gathering

A. What people told me leaders have done to inspire them in their work:

B. What people told me leaders have done to make them inspired about their work, and also what made their organization uninspiring (what has taken their enthusiasm away):

C. Now ask yourself what people would say about *you*. What would your own followers tell other people in a café about *your ability* to inspire others?

D. Summarize all that you have learned so far.

Internal Data Gathering

E. What people in my own organization have told me.

F. Compare what you thought in thinking about "C" with what you are actually finding in "E." Are you surprised?

G. Summarize themes from people in your own organization.

H. What insights about your skills, style, and opportunities for inspiring others and creating an inspiring vision have you learned? What is holding you back?

ACTION PLAN

List the three most important actions you can undertake to develop an inspiring, shared vision for your organization:

1.

2.

3.

WALKING THE TALK

Submitted by Nancy Lowery

Objectives

- To experience key leadership concepts by doing through an iterative learning process.
- To recognize how the actions one uses to lead with are what others will follow.

Audience

Up to twenty, with at least two facilitators—one working with participants, the other facilitating discussion with observers.

Time Required

45 to 60 minutes with ongoing debriefings.

Materials and Equipment

- Horses on halter and lead; the more horses the more opportunity for people to participate hands-on.
- Flip chart and markers to capture learning.

Area Setup

Indoor arena or enclosed space with rails, barrels scattered around the arena.

Facilitator Note

It is imperative that facilitators have experience with horses and instructing others to work with horses.

Process

1. Introduce participants to general horse safety and participant responsibilities, such as awareness of where the horses and other participants are positioned.

2. State that leadership is the process of developing relationships through trust and respect, clear communication, and effective actions.

3. Give participants the opportunity to lead the horses. Instruction and demonstration are an important part of this progressive leading exploration. Ask participants to go for a walk, providing no additional instructions. Based on their experience and your observations, have each participant describe what happened, focusing on horse behaviors and their actions.

4. Have participants identify key elements of leadership—purpose, direction, focus, and vision. Demonstrate the impact of body language, confidence, and purpose by leading a horse in a confident manner. Have all lead again with this new learning. Ask each participant to identify what changed for him or her.

5. As awareness develops, suggest a change from a command-and-control grip on the lead to one where they are offering direction and truly suggesting an option for the horse. Ask what motivation looks like to a horse. What defines a reward?

6. Continue to build on the changes participants are noticing in their horses' behaviors. Add commands to walk, stop, back up, turn right/left. Ask the horses to trot, to the point that participants are literally dancing with their horses. Ask how a horse would define success. How did persistence show up? Where did body language impact the activity? What happened as they switched from *making* to *asking* to *offering*? *Note:* For larger

groups use key points such as dressage letters to execute patterns so horses don't simply follow the herd. Wherever possible, bring parallels from the workplace to focus changes from task to concept. Set up coaching partners if there are more participants than horses and alternate responsibilities throughout the activity.

7. Debrief with these questions:
   - What changed with the horse as you became more specific?
   - What happened when you began to focus on rewards for the horse?
   - How did your definition of success change?
   - How does what you learned impact your definition of leadership?
   - How do this learning and the related concepts apply in the workplace?

Nancy Lowery operates The Natural Leader near Calgary, Alberta, Canada. Nancy blends her lifetime passion for horses with a creative talent and energy to deliver her programs. With her over fifteen years of managing teams for clients such as Mercedes-Benz, Procter & Gamble, Nokia, Disney, and Parks Canada, Nancy's programs speak from the perspective of personal experience in both the corporate and horsemanship arenas.

Nancy Lowery
The Natural Leader
RR 2
Balzac, Alberta T0M 0E0
Canada
  Phone: (403) 669-3666
  Email: nancy@TheNaturalLeader.ca
  Website: www.TheNaturalLeader.ca

THE ROVING LUNCH

Submitted by Anntoinette "Toni" Lucia

Objectives

- To better understand the various units of the organization, including what they do and how they do it.
- To meet members of the senior leadership team(s) from across the organization.
- To build a greater appreciation for how the parts of the organization fit together to achieve a shared mission/vision.
- To increase the ability of employees to partner across the organization to improve product/service/deliverables internally and externally.

Audience

This activity is particularly useful at on off-site when you want to give members of a large, diverse, and/or dispersed organization who are coming together for the first time (or early in the history of the organization or even when the organization has been intact for a while but isn't necessarily firing on all cylinders) an introduction to the other major units and their leadership teams without doing a standard "talking head" presentation in front of the room.

This approach gives senior team members, as representatives of the various units, as well as the participants at the meeting, an opportunity for learning and asking questions on a human/personal scale. They can make connections that facilitate ongoing dialogue at an individual level as well as enhance how business is conducted and how people are managed at an organizational level.

652

Time Required

90 minutes in total. It is important that the facilitator be fairly rigid with the timekeeping. *Note:* the activity can take place at any time during the meeting as long as there is a room large enough to accommodate all the participants at round tables at one time; doing this at lunch is a way to take advantage of every minute of an agenda if time is at a premium.

Materials and Equipment

- None.

Area Setup

Table rounds in the dining area (or large room if this isn't being done over lunch) with no fewer than eight but not more than ten chairs at each table. Participants are assigned to their table groups before the activity begins. This is an opportunity to ensure cross-organizational interaction. Each table will be numbered, and all but one seat will have been pre-assigned to participants. The "roving leader" will take his or her place at the empty seat during the rounds.

Facilitator Note

Over the course of lunch, each "roving leader" will start at one table and move two more times to two different tables. (The "roving leaders" will visit three different table groups in total.) Each rover will receive his or her pre-assigned tables for each round before the activity begins. Each round will last no more than 20 minutes.

653

Process

1. Tell participants that they will have an opportunity to get to know leaders from other departments. State that each leader will remain at their tables for 20 minutes.

2. Begin the first round.
   - Quick hellos around the table (who is at the table, what is his or her role).
   - Have the rover describe his or her department in 250 words or less—what the person does, for whom, and one thing that characterizes the work of that department.
   - Go around the table giving each participant an opportunity to ask about the leader or the department, its role, its people, or other topics.

3. After 20 minutes call time. The rovers will go to their next assigned tables (where there will be a clean place setting provided by the dining room staff). Begin round 2 using the same process.

4. Repeat steps for the third round.

5. The most important part of the planning for this activity is carefully outlining the logistics for the rovers. Participants should be assigned to tables and the tables that rovers move to should be in the same general area of the room so that the amount of disruption is minimal. Rovers should have a clear understanding of the objectives of the exercise and should have the opportunity to discuss their roles and the expectations prior to the activity.

Anntoinette "Toni" Lucia is president of West End Consulting, Inc. Toni's consulting work includes facilitating strategic organizational change, team building for senior management teams, designing, conducting, and evaluating executive and management development programs, and coaching senior executives. Toni's publications include *The Art and Science of 360-Degree Feedback* (2nd ed.) (Pfeiffer, 2009) and *The Art and Science of Competency Models* (Pfeiffer, 1999). She is a member of the Instructional Systems Associations (ISA) and on the advisory board of Better Communications, Inc.

Anntoinette "Toni" Lucia
President, West End Consulting, Inc.
19 Brinckerhoff Avenue, Suite 101
New Canaan, CT 06840
　Phone: (203) 801-0733
　Email: toni@tonilucia.com
　Website: www.we-consulting.net

THIS WOULD REALLY HELP ME

Submitted by Robert Morris

Objectives

- To inspire senior leaders to express specific help they need.
- To increase communication, cooperation, and collaboration between senior leaders and enlist them in achieving a mutual goal.

Audience

Organizational leaders, such as C-level executives, directors, or others; limit size of group to ten or fewer, all of whom have direct reports.

Time Required

The activity consists of two parts: usually 20 to 30 minutes for each part.

Materials and Equipment

- Nothing special needed.

Area Setup

Setup as usual for a senior managers' meeting.

Facilitator Note

This activity assumes the company has regularly scheduled meetings of senior managers/leaders and that the CEO (or other leader) presides (acts as chair) most of the time. It further assumes that most (if not all) of those in attendance provide an update, head's up, progress report, etc.

Process

1. After all other agenda items have been covered, the chair explains that, before concluding the meeting, there will be a brief exercise in which everyone will participate.

2. She or he turns to the person on her or his left and says, "[first name], will you please go around the table and make a specific request of each person. Address that person by name and complete this sentence 'You will really make my job much easier if_____.'"

3. The members of the team take turns until each person (including the chair) has the same opportunity to make one specific request of each of the others. *Note:* What invariably happens is that many (if not most) requests generate a response to the effect "I had no idea. I can easily do that. I'm glad you mentioned it." And what invariably happens after the meeting is that many of the participants will contact an associate and say, "I've been thinking about how I could be more helpful to you and came up with [an idea or a couple of ideas]. Would it help if I _____?"

4. During the second part of this activity, preferably within a week or two after the first session, each participant provides a brief update on how fulfillment of requests has been helpful. In weeks and months to come, senior managers will not hesitate to request help or to offer it.

Variation

- The leadership team may use a brainstorming session that addresses how to make everyone's job easier.

Robert Morris has been an independent management consultant based in Dallas since 1986. He specializes in accelerated executive development and break-through organizational performance. He also reviews business books for the United States, UK, and Canadian websites of both Amazon and Borders.

Robert Morris
10438 Pagewood Drive
Dallas, TX 75230-4254
Phone: (214) 750-1465
Email: interllect@mindspring.com

CHAPTER TEN: WHERE TO GO NEXT

In This Chapter

- Describe next steps for the reader.
- Discuss other growth opportunities.

Like this book and you want to continue learning? This chapter provides a few suggestions for you.

ADDITIONAL KOUZES/POSNER READING

If you like this book and the philosophy it espouses, you may wish to read additional materials by Kouzes and Posner:

- *The Leadership Challenge* (4th ed.)
- *Credibility: How Leaders Gain It and Lose It, Why People Demand It*
- *A Leader's Legacy*
- *Encouraging the Heart: A Leader's Guide to Rewarding and Recognizing Others*
- *Christian Reflections on The Leadership Challenge*
- *The Leadership Challenge Workbook*
- *The Encouraging the Heart Workbook*
- *The Academic Administrator's Guide to Extraordinary Leadership*
- *The Student Leadership Challenge*

If you would like to receive feedback on how you are doing, check out the *Leadership Practices Inventory*, a 360-degree assessment instrument offered either online or print form. Student versions of the LPI are also available. In addition, videos and workshops are available, including the following:

- The LPI Workshop
- The Leadership Challenge® Workshop
- Leadership Is Everyone's Business Workshop
- The Student LPI Workshop
- Legacy: The Leadership Challenge 20th Anniversary DVD Collection

You can find more information about their work at www.leadershipchallenge.com.

BECOME A LIFE-LONG LEARNER

To be a true model of success and professionalism as someone who develops leaders, you will want to develop yourself as well. You will, in fact, want to become a life-long learner. Learning is paramount to achieve all you are capable of becoming. How do you become a life-long learner?

Begin by assessing where you are compared with where you want to be. Determine the gap and put a plan together to close the gap. Write the plan down or you may avoid it. Think about what you can do to improve your processes. Every time you save time by being more efficient, you have found time to learn more, to practice just a bit more, to network with someone, or to have some fun.

Be sure that you are on the cutting edge of your industry trends. What are the state-of-the-art practices? What journals should you be reading? What books are out this month that will keep you informed?

Stay on top of your customers—both internal and external. What is happening to them? Are they in pain? Celebrating? Bewildered? Whatever it is, determine whether there is anything you can do to help.

Attend learning events. Attend your professional organization's annual conference. You owe it to yourself and to your clients to invest in yourself. Attend the American Society for Training and Development (ASTD) annual International Conference and Expo (ICE). Every trainer should do this at least once in his or her training life. You will learn a great deal. Attending any conference is a great way to learn: go to a great location, meet new people, renew past acquaintances, and attend sessions in which presenters discuss new ideas and approaches.

Attend an ASTD Certificate Program; there is one on developing leadership development programs. There is another for developing your training skills. Continue to learn more about The Five Practices. Attend The Leadership Challenge® Workshop.

Attend virtual learning events: webinars, teleconferences, and webcasts. Often the event is free or a small amount of money is charged.

Go back to school, find a mentor, or join an association. Each of these will give you the proverbial kick in the pants to learn something new. If you are a trainer, consider getting your ASTD certification, your CPLP (Certified Professional Learning and Performance).

Read. Read to stay on top of what's new. Read to learn new techniques. Read to locate fresh ideas. Read business and training books, technical and professional journals, and blogs and websites online. Read. Get on the mailing lists for publishers and your association's book program.

Attend a training session of one of your colleagues. Train with a partner and provide feedback to each other. You will be surprised at how much you learn by observing another trainer.

Network with other trainers inside and outside your organization. You'll call on them when you have a question.

Enroll in a train-the-trainer, preferably one in which you are videotaped and obtain feedback on your training style.

Learn how to conduct a true experiential learning activity (ELA); check out the *Pfeiffer Annuals*.

Pay attention to what your customers (the participants) tell you on the evaluation. Make appropriate changes. Be aware of your customers' changing needs. Adapt the material and the sessions to them.

Aspire to being the best you can be. Your session participants, the leaders you train, and your internal and external customers expect you to be on the leading edge of advances in the field. You have an obligation to them and to yourself to learn and grow. Learning is an ongoing process, even if you are at the top of your profession. Often it is what you learn after you know it all that counts the most.

GIVE BACK TO THE PROFESSION

Another form of growth is to give back to your profession. Become involved. Volunteer. Share your knowledge with someone else who is just entering the field. Give back to a profession that gives so much to you and to others.

Training is a fantastic way to make a life (and a living, too). Helping to develop leaders is exciting and rewarding. It doesn't get much better than that!

ABOUT THE EDITORS

James M. Kouzes is the co-author with Barry Posner of the award-winning and best-selling book, *The Leadership Challenge*, with over 1.5 million copies sold. He's also the Dean's Executive Professor of Leadership, Leavey School of Business, Santa Clara University.

The fourth edition of *The Leadership Challenge* was released in August 2007 and is available in fifteen languages, including Chinese. *The Leadership Challenge* was number three on Amazon Editor's Pick for the Best Business Books of 2007. It was also the winner of the 1995–1996 Critics' Choice Award and the 1989 James A. Hamilton Hospital Administrators' Book Award. Another recent book of theirs, *A Leader's Legacy* (2006), was selected by Soundview Executive Book Summaries as one of the top thirty books of the year and by the *Globe and Mail* (Canada) as one of the top ten books of 2006. Jim and Barry have also co-authored over a dozen other books, including *Credibility: How Leaders Gain and Lose It, Why People Demand It*—chosen by *Industry Week* as one of the ten best management books of 1993, *Encouraging the Heart* (1999, 2003), *The Leadership Challenge Workbook* (1999, 2003), and the *Encouraging the Heart Workbook* (2006). Based on solid research involving over seventy thousand surveys, one thousand written case studies, and one hundred in-depth interviews, their books describe the leadership practices that generate high performance in individuals and organizations.

Jim and Barry developed the widely used and highly acclaimed *Leadership Practices Inventory* (LPI), a 360-degree questionnaire assessing leadership behavior. The LPI has been administered to over 500,000 leaders, and over three million observers worldwide have provided feedback using the LPI. It is the top-selling off-the-shelf leadership assessment instrument in the world. Over 350 doctoral dissertations and academic research projects have been based on their work.

The International Management Council (IMC) honored Jim and Barry as the 2001 recipients of the prestigious Wilbur M. McFeely Award for their outstanding contributions to management and leadership education. Past McFeely Award recipients include Peter Drucker, Lee Iacocca, Tom Peters, Ken Blanchard, Norman Vincent Peale, Francis Hesselbein, Stephen Covey, and Rosabeth Moss Kanter. In 2006 Jim was presented with the Golden Gavel, the highest honor awarded by Toastmasters International.

Jim is not only a highly regarded leadership scholar, but *The Wall Street Journal* has cited Jim as one of the twelve best executive educators in the United States. A popular speaker and seminar leader, Jim's clients have included Accenture, Applied Materials, AT&T, Boeing, Charles Schwab, Cisco Systems, Consumers Energy, Dell Computer, Deloitte Touche, Egon Zehnder International, Federal Express, Gap Inc., HSBC, Intel, Johnson & Johnson, Lawrence Livermore National Labs, Levi Strauss & Co., 3M, Microsoft, Motorola, Roche Palo Alto, Siemens, State of New York, Thomson Corporation, Toyota, and Wells Fargo.

Jim is also an experienced executive. He served as president, then CEO and chairman of the Tom Peters Company from 1988 until 2000. Prior to his tenure at TPC, he directed the Executive Development Center at Santa Clara University from 1981 through 1987. He also founded the Joint Center for Human Services Development at San Jose State University, which he directed from 1972 until 1980. Jim's commitment to service was nurtured during his years growing up in the Washington, D.C., area. His lifelong career in education began in 1967–1969 when he served for two years in the Peace Corps. Jim believes it was on January 20, 1961, when he was first inspired to dedicate himself to leadership. That was the day he was one of only a dozen Eagle Scouts who served in John F. Kennedy's Honor Guard at the Presidential Inauguration. Jim can be reached at jim@kouzes. com, or on the Web at www.leadershipchallenge.com.

Barry Z. Posner is Professor of Leadership at the Leavey School of Business, Santa Clara University (located in the heart of Silicon Valley), where he served for twelve years as dean of the school. Barry, along with his co-author Jim Kouzes, received the American Society for Training and Development's highest award for their Distinguished Contribution to Workplace Learning and Performance. The International Management Council named them as the nation's top management and leadership educators, and Barry was recently recognized as one of the Top 50 Leadership Coaches in America.

He is the co-author of the award-winning and best-selling leadership book, *The Leadership Challenge*. Described as a groundbreaking research study, this book combines keen insights with practical applications and captures both why and how leadership is everyone's business. With over 1.8 million copies in print, this book has been named one of The Top 100 Business Books of All Time, book-of-the-year by the American Council of Health Care Executives, received the Critic's Choice Award from book review editors, and translated into over twenty languages.

The *Leadership Practices Inventory* has been called "the most reliable, up-to-date leadership instrument available today," and the online version has been completed by over 1.1 million people around the globe. Barry has also co-authored several other award-winning, inspiring, and practical books on leadership: *Credibility: How Leaders Gain and Lose It, Why People Demand It; Encouraging the Heart: A Leaders Guide to Recognizing and Rewarding Others; The Academic Administrator's Guide to Exemplary Leadership;* and *A Leader's Legacy*.

Barry is an internationally renowned scholar who has published more than eighty-five research and practitioner-oriented articles, in such journals as the *Academy of Management Journal, Journal of Applied Psychology, Human Relations, Personnel Psychology, IEEE Transactions on Engineering Management*, and the like. He is currently on the editorial review boards of the *International Journal of Servant-Leadership, Leadership and Organizational Development,* and *Leadership Review*. Barry serves on the board of directors for the San Jose Repertory Theatre and EMQ Family First.

Barry received an undergraduate degree in political science from the University of California, Santa Barbara, a master's degree from the Ohio State University in public administration, and his Ph.D. in organizational behavior and administrative theory from the University of Massachusetts, Amherst. At Santa Clara he has received the President's Distinguished Faculty Award, the school's Extraordinary Faculty Award, and several other outstanding teaching and leadership honors. Described as a warm, engaging, and pragmatic conference speaker and dynamic workshop facilitator, Barry has worked with such organizations as Alcoa, Applied Materials, Australian Institute of Management, Charles Schwab, Conference Board of Canada, Hewlett-Packard, Kaiser Permanente Health Care, L.L. Bean, Levi Strauss, Merck, Motorola, NetApp, Trader Joe's, and the U.S. Postal Service, among others, and been involved with leadership development efforts at more than thirty-five college campuses. He has made presentations and conducted workshops across the United States, and around the globe, from Canada, Mexico, and Europe to the Far East, Australia, New Zealand, and South Africa.

Elaine Biech is president and managing principal of ebb associates inc, an organization development firm that helps organizations work through large-scale change. She has been in the training and consulting field for thirty years and works with business, government, and non-profit organizations.

Elaine specializes in helping people work as teams to maximize their effectiveness. Customizing all of her work for individual clients, she conducts strategic planning sessions and implements corporate-wide systems such as quality improvement, reengineering of business processes, and mentoring programs. She facilitates topics such as coaching today's employees, fostering creativity, customer service, time management, stress management, speaking skills, training competence, conducting productive meetings, managing change, handling difficult employees, organizational communication, conflict resolution, and effective listening.

She has developed media presentations and training materials and has presented at dozens of national and international conferences.

American Society of Training and Development has referred to Elaine as the "trainer's trainer." She custom designs training programs for managers, leaders, trainers, and consultants. To date, Elaine has designed, developed and piloted five certificate programs for ASTD. She has been featured in dozens of publications, including *The Wall Street Journal, Harvard Management Update, The Washington Post,* and *Fortune* magazine.

As a management and executive consultant, trainer, and designer, she has provided services to OSI Restaurant Partners, LLC, FAA, Land O' Lakes, McDonald's, Lands' End, General Casualty Insurance, Chrysler, Johnson Wax, PricewaterhouseCoopers, American Family Insurance, Marathon Oil, Hershey Chocolate, Federal Reserve Bank, the U.S. Navy, NASA, Newport News Shipbuilding, Kohler Company, ASTD, American Red Cross, Association of Independent Certified Public Accountants, the University of Wisconsin, The College of William and Mary, ODU, and hundreds of other public and private sector organizations to prepare them for the challenges of the new millennium.

She is the author and editor of over four dozen books and articles, including *ASTD's Ultimate Train the Trainer* (2009); *10 Steps to Successful Training* (ASTD, 2009); *The Consultant's Quick Start Guide* (2nd ed.) (2009); *ASTD Handbook for Workplace Learning Professionals* (2008); *Trainer's Warehouse Book of Games* (2008); *The Business of Consulting* (2nd ed.) (2007); *Thriving Through Change: A Leader's Practical Guide to Change Mastery* (2007); *Successful Team-Building Tools* (2nd ed.) (2007); *90 World-Class Activities by 90 World-Class Trainers* (2007) (named a Training Review Best Training Product of 2007); a nine-volume set of ASTD's *Certification Study Guides* (2006); *12 Habits of Successful Trainers* (ASTD Info-line, 2005); The ASTD Info-line *Dictionary of Basic Trainer Terms*

(2005); *Training for Dummies* (2005); *Marketing Your Consulting Services* (2003); *The Consultant's Legal Guide* (2000); *Interpersonal Skills: Understanding Your Impact on Others* (1996); *Building High Performance* (1998); and *The Pfeiffer Annual: Consulting* and *The Pfeiffer Annual: Training* (1998–2010). Her books have been translated into Chinese, German, and Dutch.

Elaine has a bachelor's degree from the University of Wisconsin-Superior in business and education consulting and a master's degree in human resource development. She is active at the national level of ASTD, is a life-time member, served on the 1990 National Conference Design Committee, was a member of the national ASTD Board of Directors and was the society's secretary from 1991 to 1994, initiated and chaired Consultant's Day for seven years, and was the international conference design chair in 2000. In addition to her work with ASTD, she has served on the Independent Consultants Association's (ICA) Advisory Committee and on the Instructional Systems Association (ISA) board of directors.

Elaine is the recipient of the 1992 National ASTD Torch Award, the 2004 ASTD Volunteer-Staff Partnership Award, and the 2006 ASTD Gordon M. Bliss Memorial Award. She was selected for the 1995 Wisconsin Women Entrepreneur's Mentor Award. In 2001 she received ISA's highest award, The ISA Spirit Award. She has been the consulting editor for the prestigious Training and Consulting *Annuals* published by Pfeiffer for the past twelve years. Visit her website at www.ebbweb.com or contact her at ebbiech@aol.com.

THE FIVE PRACTICES AND TEN
COMMITMENTS OF EXEMPLARY LEADERSHIP

Model the Way

1. Clarify values by finding your voice and affirming shared ideals.

2. Set the example by aligning actions and shared values.

Inspire a Shared Vision

3. Envision the future by imagining exciting and ennobling possibilities.

4. Enlist others in a common vision by appealing to shared aspirations.

Challenge the Process

5. Search for opportunities by seizing the initiative and by looking outward for innovative ways to improve.

6. Experiment and take risks by constantly generating small wins and learning from experience.

Enable Others to Act

7. Foster collaboration by building trust and facilitating relationships.

8. Strengthen others by increasing self-determination and developing competence.

Encourage the Heart

9. Recognize contributions by showing appreciation for individual excellence.

10. Celebrate the values and victories by creating a spirit of community.

NOTES

NOTES

NOTES

NOTES

NOTES

NOTES

NOTES

Leadership Is Everyone's Business

Enhance your workshops with Leadership Challenge tools.

Backed by over twenty years of original research, *The Leadership Challenge*® *Workshop* is an intense discovery process created by bestselling authors, Jim Kouzes and Barry Posner. The workshop demystifies the concept of leadership and leadership development and approaches it as a measurable, learnable, and teachable set of behaviors, establishing a unique underlying philosophy—leadership is everyone's business.

Leadership Challenge Workshop Facilitator's Guide Set, Fourth Edition
978-0-470-59217-5 • $749.00 US/$899.00 CAN

The all-new *Leadership Challenge Workshop Facilitator's Guide Set, Fourth Edition* includes detailed instructions, suggested experiential activities, audio/video clips including new video case studies, and a facilitator script for a complete training progam. While the ample instructions make for a turnkey solution, the program also allows for and encourages customization points that enable facilitators to tailor the program for their particular audience or situation.

The Leadership Challenge Values Cards Facilitator's Guide Set
978-0-470-58007-3 • $45.00 US/$54.00 CAN

The Leadership Challenge Activities Book
978-0-470-47713-7 • $45.00 US/$54.00 CAN

The Challenge Continues Facilitator's Guide Set
978-0-470-46237-9 • $179.00 US/$215.00 CAN

Leadership Practices Inventory (LPI) Action Cards Facilitator's Guide Set
978-0-470-46239-3 • $45.00 US/$54.00 CAN

A Coach's Guide to Developing Exemplary Leaders: Making the Most of the Leadership Challenge and the Leadership Practices Inventory (LPI)
978-0-470-37711-6 • $45.00 US/$54.00 CAN

Encouraging the Heart: A Leader's Guide to Rewarding and Recognizing Others
978-0-7879-6463-4 • $18.95 US/$20.99 CAN

We also have participant materials in the following languages:
- Spanish
- Simplified Chinese
- German
- French
- Portuguese (available Winter 2011)

Follow us on **twitter** @TLCTalk
Join The Leadership Challenge **Linked** Group
Become a Fan on **facebook**

Go to **www.leadershipchallenge.com** to learn more about these products, read case studies, and find the latest research, upcoming events and appearances, and LeaderTalk, The Leadership Challenge blog.

 www.leadershipchallenge.com

Pfeiffer™
An Imprint of ⊕WILEY
Now you know.